# IT WAS ALL

*Illustrated with photograph*

# QUITE DIFFERENT

( *The Memoirs of* )

## Vicki Baum

+

FUNK & WAGNALLS COMPANY, INC., NEW YORK

Copyright © 1964 by Vicki Baum Estate
Library of Congress Catalogue Card Number 64–13737
Printed in the United States of America by H. Wolff, New York
Designed by Adrianne Onderdonk

I

D'OÙ VENONS-NOUS?

OÙ SOMMES-NOUS?

OÙ ALLONS-NOUS?

*Tryptich by Paul Gauguin at the Boston Museum of Fine Arts*

You can live down any number of failures, but you can't live down a great success. For thirty years I've been a walking example of this truism. People are apt to forgive and forget a flop because they care little about things that aren't in the papers or on television, and a book that fails dies silently enough. But a success, moth-eaten as it may be, will pop up among old movies or as a hideous musical or in a new film version, or in a Japanese, a Hebrew, a Hindu translation—and there you are.

I sign a check in a store, or give my name and address to the man who is going to deliver the fertilizer for my garden, and I see his eyes narrow and his mind work. Gears click, bells ring faintly, little wheels begin to turn. "Vicki Baum, did you say? Now, wait a minute, I've seen that name somewhere—aren't you in the movies?"

"Nnnooo . . . ," I say. "Now about that fertilizer. . . ."

But step-by-step I'm traced down to my original sin. "I'm not an actress; never was," I admit. "I'm a writer," I confess with an embarrassed giggle.

"Sure, now I remember. You wrote that picture—what's its name? I saw it, my aunt took me, well, I was just a kid, just in junior high—now waddayaknow! Vicki Baum! Wait till I tell the wife I met the girl who wrote *Grand Hotel* . . . !"

V. B.

# ❧ KEY TO CONTENTS OF CHAPTERS

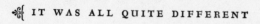 IT WAS ALL QUITE DIFFERENT

hortly after my seventieth birthday, I drove once more from my house in the Hollywood hills to New York City. And all across the vast continent, in all those three thousand miles, in all the countless little antique shops that line the highways, I couldn't find a single antique older than myself.

There again, accumulated and displayed for sale, was all the intricate, frilled, fringed, and tasseled junk that had cluttered up the rooms of my childhood—those clumsy kitchen utensils I had to keep in spit-and-polish condition as a preparation for my future as a good housewife; the oil lamps with the imitation bronze base, by whose bad light I did some needlework; the cut glass trash, candlesticks, antimacassars, and hideous beer steins. There, in some forsaken ghost town of the West, I encountered an exact replica of the monstrous flowered washbasin and pitcher out of my parents' bedroom and, to complete the set, two equally enormous chamber pots, to me the early symbols of everything unappealing and repulsive in my parents', and all parents', marital life. Now they call them period pieces.

It made me sit up and take stock of myself. So that's what you've become, my girl, a period piece. Not sufficiently old or noble to be a real antique nor so young as to fit well into the raucous, mechanized, sharp-angled present. As the witty Princess Pauline Metternich said to the people who congratulated her on her birthday: "My dear, seventy isn't old for a cathedral. But for a woman—ah, *mon Dieu. . . .*"

All right, I said to myself, if I am a period piece I had better begin by telling a little about the period: Vienna, at the turn of the century.

A gray town, beautifully gray, like Paris, like all those very old European towns that started out as colonial garrisons of the Roman Empire. Muted colors everywhere. The Danube, not blue but a lazy, muddy yellow. The velvety green patina on domes and cupolas and bulbous church towers, the highest of all in the very center—the Romanesque-Gothic church of St. Stephen, one of the oldest and most imposing of European cathedrals, around which the town had spread in concentric circles. Just as the trunks of giant redwoods widen, ring by ring, century after century, so Vienna had grown around St. Stephen's. When the steeple with its brilliant double eagle mosaic of shiny tiles was bombed away in World War II, it was the first thing the Viennese restored—with American money, I guess. Their beloved church and then, of course, their opera house. Like all paupers, they are great artists of survival, my Viennese. Not so much backbone or character, but a graceful self-irony that keeps them alive.

The sounds of my early childhood. The trap-trap of horses' hoofs on granite cobblestones—spanking pairs drawing aristocratic equipages or the smart fiacres of the rich bourgeoisie, the dragging feet of the tired nags of the one-horse cabs. The gay little fanfare of the horn of the postilion perched high on the box of the black-and-yellow mail coach. On summer evenings, ill-tuned pianos tinkling from innumerable open windows a hideous piece called "A Virgin's Prayer." But here and there also a strain of classical music—a Haydn quartet, a Beethoven sonata, a *Lied* by Hugo Wolf. The vigorous warning of the fire engine's trumpet: E-A! Every child in Vienna knows this interval and builds his sense of harmony and musical memory from it. Even today, if I get lost in a chaotic piece of new music, I find my way by this fire engine's urgent Fourth, E-A! E-A! E-A!

In the courtyards, the sound of carpets being beaten forever—Old Vienna's domestic jazz. Then there are the street vendors' multilingual calls, the market women's shrill singsong, the servant girls' harmonizing up and down the air shafts of the kitchens. Over all, and at all hours, there are the church bells.

Frequently we would see a carriage with golden wheels, a slim blue uniform in it, a white suede glove saluting continuously: The Kaiser! Our Kaiser! His Apostolic Majesty Franz Josef I. It didn't occur to us children that other kaisers might exist. We loved him dearly, this father of our country. The country's mother, regrettably, was absent, invisible, and a little later even dead.

We were in the country for our summer vacation when the frightful news of the assassination of Empress Elizabeth reached our village. Stabbed by an anarchist, said the damp, blurred extra that my uncle brought from the county seat. The villagers stood bewildered in front of their cottages, and we all cried in heart-broken, loyal grief. It was the very first extra in our innocent, sleeping-beauty world. Who could have foreseen the untold extras that were to break with their horrors into our future lives?

In panic we returned to Vienna. Flags at half-mast, black gauze everywhere in the autumnal streets, the people in mourning. The lamplighter, who on other evenings went in his white surgeonlike coat from street lamp to street lamp to turn on the lights, now made his rounds taking off the lanterns and unscrewing the gas heads. As it grew dark, the free-flowing gas ignited and huge flames shot up, flickering torches in the chill wind. The people stood bareheaded in dense black masses in the streets, and the measured drumbeats of Chopin's Funeral March throbbed in the air. I enjoyed the sad spectacle immensely. I'm sure the entire populace did.

It is strange to remember how important the Kaiser was to us, how close. We shared his sorrows, of which he usually had plenty. It was a kind of family feeling; we respected the old man, although everybody knew, and discussed without inhibition, his vast stupidity, ignorance, and obstinacy. It is remarkable that a man can be so stupid and yet so tragic. It is also remarkable how much harm the stupidity and weakness of such utterly decent, honest, and honorable old gentlemen in high places can do to the world.

Today, it is hard to imagine how closely a people will model itself after the image of its sovereign. To my personal regret, our old monarch, perhaps in protest against a population of sloppy and enthusiastic sybarites, was a slave to stiff etiquette and austerity. That's why I had to sleep in an unheated room, on the hardest, thinnest mattress available, shivering under a flimsy cotton blanket. "If it's warm enough for the Kaiser, it's warm enough for you," my father said. I got up at dawn, poured ice-cold water over my blue, undernourished body, then had a mug of pale coffee and a dry roll for breakfast— just like the Kaiser. And so on through the day; a monkish life.

In Vienna the toilet was called "where the Kaiser walks on foot." And when a well-meaning girl friend initiated me into the mystery of what men and women did to get babies, I simply refused to believe her. "Surely, the Kaiser wouldn't do such a thing," I said, and that settled it.

Vienna was a lovely town to grow up in. Closely surrounded by the wild-flower wealth of the Vienna Woods, we lived cheek-to-cheek with nature. The beautiful parks adjoining the imperial and aristocratic palaces were our playgrounds; their fountains and ponds, horse-chestnut trees and plumed lilac bushes, sweeping lawns and formal beds and hedges were our intimate friends. During the day-time Vienna was a lively city, not with today's rampant decibels, but with its own lilting rhythm. At night the streets went dark and quiet, and all life and gaiety was pulled inside the houses. Not in the least what people generally visualize at the cue of Old Vienna. Such places as bars or night clubs were still unknown, and a tourist was not some foreigner on a guided excursion but a native in leather shorts on his way to climb the Alps.

Not that those sedate times didn't have their dangers, too—oh, plenty of them! Oil lamps exploded and, for some incomprehensible reason, so did tile stoves. Especially prone to this was the beauty in our dining room—and usually when important dinner guests were expected and the table was set with the best linen and china. Houses burned down before the horse-drawn fire engine could arrive, and not a few innocent people died through mismanagement of the new-fangled gas. On the streets, horses shied and carriages ran over people and killed them. I myself saw such an accident, though unfortunately only a flash of it because Mama covered my eyes with her hands. But I had seen the run-over lady's straw hat roll down the street, with all its ribbons and bachelor's-buttons and cherries. I can still see it as clearly as I see my hands on the typewriter.

Another danger, to children and grownups alike, was personified in the Vienna *Hausmeister*—let's call him Herr Pitzelgruber. Not so gruff as the German porter, not so amenable as the French *concierge*, not so detached as the American janitor, the *Hausmeister* is an exclusive, untranslatable product of Vienna, tyrannical and obsequious, Argus-eyed, with large palms hungry for tips and bribes, filled with malicious gossip and envy. Herr Pitzelgruber knows more about you than you do yourself. He keeps himself and others informed about your antecedents, your position, your income and expenditures, your religion, your marriage, your in-laws, your children, friends, and visitors—especially late visitors whom he distrusts on general principles and suspects of all kinds of moral, political, and religious defects. At 10:00 P.M. he locks the house door to which no one but him has a key; that was what gave him his power when I was a child. If you wanted in or out after ten, you had to ring a bell and wait, ring several more times, hoping that you could awaken him and that your late homecoming wouldn't be the ruin of your reputation. Clutching the prescribed obolus in your hand, you'd hear at last the *Hausmeister*'s felt slippers *schlurp* to the door, his reproachful grumbling and chronic cough, the clank of keys, and as he opened the door a light was flashed in your eyes, making you feel as though you were facing the secret police.

The Pitzelgrubers were stout believers in the two-party system. They were members of both, a method of self-protection especially effective when they discreetly threw away Austria's red-and-white emblem and displayed the Nazi swastika providently kept in abeyance till the day of the *Anschluss*—for the genus Pitzelgruber was the backbone of Austria's Nazi movement, indeed, the prototype of Hitler himself.

Another thing I remember of that period is the third horse. Frequently, on Sundays and holidays we went by bus to visit some friends in Mauer, a small town in the suburbs. Today it is no distance at all, but then it was quite an expedition. Rumbling and rattling, the two-horse vehicle jolted over the cobblestones out of the tight old center of town. As it turned into Mariahilferstrasse, a lively shopping district, I waited excitedly for a certain ceremony to be performed. At the end of the street, where in former times the city walls had stood, there was a hardly noticeable grade. There, unfailingly, and to my childish mind inexplicably, a uniformed man appeared, leading a horse from a narrow side lane. This third horse was chained to the shaft of our bus, and with much giddy-up and cracking of whips and great activity all around, we rumbled on, horses and coachmen straining to maneuver us across those crucial fifty feet, after which the third horse was unchained, to vanish again down the lane.

Sometimes, as I look down from some skyscraper, some hilltop, I remember this little drama of old-time transportation, so far removed from the improbable web and tangle of the freeways where the traffic of our gigantic anthill, Los Angeles, spins off from an unending spool. All those loops and cloverleaves, overpasses, underpasses, the double and triple ribbons of concrete where, in opposite directions, the cars creep bumper to bumper, day and night. Overhead, helicopters watch for the inevitable accidents and jams; high up, jet planes leave their white tracings in the starless sky; in unimaginable distances man-made satellites are drawing their parabolas, revolving in orbits, sending their messages, or burning out, exploding, vanishing; and beyond them, the untold, unknown galaxies rush away toward ever wider invisible horizons.

It's too much! I say to myself, too much for me, too much progress during just one single lifetime. We've gone too fast too far. This world is no longer the same planet on which I was born.

And then I get a little dizzy, a little frightened, too, as I felt as a child when I tried to envisage infinity.

There are certain regions of fears in every one of us, balanced by certain regions of courage. We are all constructed alike, half hero, half coward. As for myself, I am, and always was, a coward about noise and speed; I am also faintly afraid of most mechanical contraptions, including the telephone and the Mixmaster. They don't like me, either. And they could explode, couldn't they?

Definitely, I'm a misfit for here and today.

On the other hand, I bear up fairly well under pain. I'm not afraid of sickness and operations—my own, that is—never was afraid of the dark, of being left alone in the house, of burglars, murderers, or monsters. Nor of death, I would say if it didn't sound so pompous. . . .

The first thing I remember having been frightened by was the wallpaper in our dining room.

It was an ugly, sickish brown with a black pattern. But I'm still a baby in the arms of my wet nurse and I can't yet comprehend a pattern. I only see innumerable little black creatures crawling all over the wall and rushing together in black masses. What are they? What will they do to me? I start screaming, nobody knows why. . . . And there are those huge faces of the two giants who belong to me. I know them by their smell as much as by their looks. I like the one that's soft and pink and sometimes licks my face, but I can't stand the other one with the curtain of bristly fringes hanging over the dark hole which is its mouth. There's a terrible uproar around me; their enormous hands pull me away from the warm little nest of my nurse's arms; they toss me this way and that, shake me, pound me, rattle me, until my last meal of grits and milk comes up, sour and bitter, and I am quickly handed back to my nurse who carries me, with much Slovakian cursing and scolding, back to my crib.

My next great fear came in summer with the boom and hiss, noise and flash of the fireworks and shouting crowds of the Kaiser's birthday celebration. I suppose that's where the fear of noise and speed lodged itself in my bones and nerves.

I was about three years old when I met once more with patterns of black dots and dashes, but these were quite different. I'm sitting on the floor, as deeply and seriously concentrated on my research as only three-year-olds can be. This time the dots and dashes are pretty—tiny people, tiny pictures, tiny friendly somethings. They don't rush together from all sides but march in neat columns straight along their own tiny streets. Some are fat, some thin, and some, no doubt, are grownups. Now I know that what I had before me were printed letters—the evening paper, or maybe the book Mama left on the blue sofa. It was forbidden to touch the book; that, naturally, added a special fascination to my studies. A few months later, after I had taught myself to read, the book turned out to have a silly and difficult title: *Problematische Naturen* by Friedrich von Spielhagen. That made no more sense than the wallpaper. It was (I found out later) a best seller of the period, harbinger of cut-rate bourgeois decadence. I still remember that it described how the wind drove dust and paper and rags across the street. These were the only lines I could understand, because this was something I had seen.

I don't know by quite what method I taught myself to read so early, but the uncluttered brain of a small child easily grasps the meaning of symbols. Today every child recognizes traffic signs, the stop and go, the X of a crossing, the S of a sharp curve. Letters are of the same stuff. In my babyhood the street signs taught me. We lived in Elisabethstrasse, a long, somewhat confusing word, but after repeated practice the sound of E fused with the letter E; true, to confound matters, there happened to be another, different, smaller "e" in Elisabeth. This, my nurse explained to me, was like herself, whom we called *die kleine* Katl, as distinguished from *die grosse* Katl who reigned in the kitchen. After such tutoring it was easy to turn at the corner into Operngasse and remember how the sound of O looked, round and sort of surprised: *O? O!* I sucked great gobs of pleasure from my growing dexterity with letters, although I had no inkling yet that the words I puzzled together from them carried any meaning. This came as a revelation to me when the rhymes of a funny picture book I knew by heart suddenly jumped up to my face, clearer and much more attractive than any of the pictures.

Later, I became absorbed in still another kind of tiny black creature, the ubiquitous ant.

In the park, or during our summers in the country, I never grew tired of watching those busy little workers and of pestering the grownups to tell me about them, tell me more, please, still more, tell me all. I thought them beautiful—they reminded me of black berries, shiny and sweet—but my early experiments at catching and eating some ended, as one would expect, in burning red patches on my skin and loud bawling for help. After the ants had thus taught me to respect them, we became great friends. Their houses, hills, holes were so well laid out, their highways so lively with little wayfarers, and they were such funny clowns when they dried to drag home some loot or hunting trophies ten times as large as themselves. Also, it was from them I learned about mutual support and the Brotherhood of Ants. Let one of them seem exhausted on the road, sick or hurt, and before it could say "Help!" an eager black huddle had arrived to drag, pull, carry, stroke the suffering companion and assist in getting it and its burden back to the home hill. . . . Or consider the trouble ants took about those whitish things we called ant eggs that actually were larvae. "Let's play earthquake," Sepp would say, the little hunchbacked goatherd who was the best, the wisest, the most beloved friend of my childhood summers. "I'll get the stick and you get an old pillowcase," he would say.

If you have never had such a wise friend, this is what you do: You spread out the white pillowcase fairly near to the anthill, and with the stick you stir up a good, strong earthquake, a catastrophe, a disaster. There are a few seconds of panic in the uprooted hill, and then the ant instinct for organization takes over. They bring out the eggs, and scurrying around for a safe place to deposit them, they discover that inviting quiet white field. Perhaps a built-in sense of mimicry leads them to put their precious white bundles down on the white pillowcase. If you need ant eggs for fishing, for instance, all you have to do then is shake the tiny things into the paper bag you brought along.

This, at least, is the theory of it; it doesn't always work. Sometimes, warned perhaps by the smell of humans, they avoid the white field and at unbelievable speed dig tiny new shelters in which to bed their progeny. Once more the future of the species, or at least of this particular tribe, is secure. Sepp laughs in reluctant respect: "Them's too bright, them critters!" he says. "Them don't make no mistake twice. Must have had an earthquake before and lost their eggs."

But what am I to think when these same neat, well-organized, and selfless ants, so eager for food and life, so careful in bringing up their offspring, march out in full panoply and make war against other anthills, ant-countries, even other ant-continents? At dusk the battlefield is covered with little corpses. "Are they crazy? Why do they make war?" I ask. Sepp shrugs. "Cause they're ants. It's just in 'em. They don't know no better. Cause ants always had wars and always will." Quite a philosopher, my Sepp.

And now I can't hide any longer that the fundamentals of my own philosophy evolved from my childish preoccupation with ants. Primitive as it is, I don't see much reason for changing it even now.

The trouble with ants is that they don't know how small they are, I meditated. They have no conception of how many anthills there are in the woods. They only know their own hill, and maybe a few others close enough to make war on. Maybe they are aware of the existence of those dozen anthills on our slope. Perhaps they have heard that other slopes exist, other woods, other clearings in the forest around our village. But this is already the stuff of myths. That there are untold forests in this one small province of Austria, untold other provinces, countries, continents, all of them inhabited by ants, must be unimaginable to them. No ant could know and live with the full knowledge of his own tribe's smallness and unimportance within such an immeasurable ant universe.

In an ant's eye, how would God look? I went on thinking. Like an ant of mythical size and power? Or like us, Sepp and me, who one day brought them the unbelievable bounty of a dead twenty-inch garter snake and the next destroyed their country and turned it into a desert? Just don't think yourselves so damned important, little ants, I said to them. I've said it to myself ten thousand times—most helpful in keeping one's equilibrium. . . .

The parallel to humanity was obvious even to me, a pig-tailed dwarf in grammar school. That's why the idea of a god watching from the sky over me, myself personally, appeared preposterous. There were other forests, other countries, other worlds. By the time I was ten I had shed the conceit of believing that God cared a fig about me; nor did I imagine that we, members of the human race, were the crown and final purpose of creation. I was beginning to form my own idea of God, my own religion if you want to call it that: a belief in an eternal law and balanced order up there, out there; and in an inner law and order implanted in each creature that lived in this and all other worlds.

As soon as I had discovered the joys of reading I began clamoring for a book of my own. There was the unforgettable moment of my fourth birthday when I woke up and through the green net of my crib, discovered The Book lying on top of my neatly folded underwear. It had pictures on the cover and inside, and its title was: *Grosse Menschen—Edle Taten* ("Great Men—Noble Deeds"). I kept reading and rereading that book for years; it played havoc with my poor small four-year-old character and, I'm afraid, ruined me in some respects for my whole life.

There was the boy who kept his finger in the dike, and the Greek youth who leaped into the crack that had rent the ground to satisfy the gods thus by his sacrifice, so that they might close the earth over his corpse. There was the Swiss hero Winkelried, who with his mighty arms grabbed all the spearheads of the enemy and pressed them into his own chest to create a breach for his friends to get through. There were Great Men and Noble Deeds spilling out from every page, illustrated. There were unattainable heights of goodness, gallantry, and self-sacrifice, inhumanly above and beyond the call of duty. Striving for equal goodness and greatness, dreaming of saving babies from burning houses or throwing myself in the path of runaway horses, I might have become an unbearable prig and dogooder. Luckily, there was enough healthy contrariness and low animal spirit in me to counterbalance the angelic martyr I was striving to become.

I remember my fourth birthday so well because until then I was a happy child. But after I was four, things happened that hung as clouds and dark shadows around me, as though the weather were never as fair as it had been before.

First of all, my mother got sick, not like I would get sick, with the measles or a sore throat and a boiling fever, but sick in some incomprehensible, intangible way.

"Be quiet, your mama is nervous," Small Katl would shush me. . . .

"Come, stay with me in the kitchen, but make no noise. Your

poor mama couldn't close an eye all night, now she's trying to rest," warned the warm and plump Large Katl, whom I liked much better than the little mouse-faced one. . . .

"Listen, you are a big girl now, you are old enough to behave and not to drive Mama crazy," scolded Father, who in my fears had superseded fireworks, explosive noises, and the dining-room wallpaper.

Loaded with the responsibility for Mama's nerves and health, I aged considerably. I aged even more when later that same year my grandfather died, the dear ugly cross-eyed little old Jew, the only person who made me feel that I was loved, my closest friend and playmate who never seemed to belong to the hostile tribe of grownups, never seemed a day older than my own four years.

I realize that it would be more becoming if I could follow the welltrodden path of autobiography and brag about the poverty and squalor from which I rose by sheer spunk and fortitude to success at last. Not so, dear reader. If I had a hard and unhappy childhood, as indeed I had, the reasons were not so simple and external. Poverty and raw hunger—although not squalor—came much later. (There was a war before the last world war, remember? And Austria lost it.) But as a child I never doubted that we were fine, wealthy people. I don't believe that any small child ever thinks of his family as poor, unless he is incessantly told so, unless parents and neighbors "rub it in" and the seed of envy and bitter competitiveness is sown early and nurtured in him.

Easygoing, happy-go-lucky Austria, although a monarchy, was as democratic as America probably will never become. There were no Joneses to compete with, no idea of strictly stratified society such as I have found over here; it was emphatically not a society graded by wealth and income. There were, to be sure, certain signs that marked us as good solid middle class. We lived in the oldest, which meant, the best, district of Vienna, in an apartment house constructed grandly, and shoddily, on the lines of the Palazzo Pitti in Florence, with enormous caryatids supporting nothing, large high-ceilinged rooms, enormous double doors, parquetry floors, whose gloss was maintained by both Katls skating around by the hour with waxed brushes strapped to their feet. There was heavy, hideously carved furniture and enough black marble to build a mausoleum. Also, our apartment had never recovered from all the huge silver wedding gifts —candelabra, bowls, and three-tiered fruit stands—and to handle the too-heavy, monogrammed silver forks and spoons at table was one of my early problems.

Each morning the *friseur* appeared to take care of Mama's coiffure, a sure sign of our elegance. His name was Herr Herring and he looked like one. Thin and slithery, with gray lines circling his round red eyes, to me it did not seem impossible that he could have escaped from a fairy tale—a prince changed into a fish by an old sorcerer? He would light his little alcohol burner and put his two curling irons to work; the room would soon smell of the singed paper strips, on which he tested the heat of his irons, and of the rose-scented hair oil that his spidery fingers tenderly smoothed over Mama's finished hair structure. He would talk with Mama in French that ran rapidly like a brook over the gravelly ground of his native Viennese. Both my parents spoke French well, and soon Small Katl was replaced by Mademoiselle as a matter of educational routine for me. I know that I liked Mademoiselle, but I don't remember at all how she looked or what she was like. I was delighted to learn French via *Ali Baba et les Quarante Voleurs,* and soon I suffered and triumphed with George Sand's *Petite Fadette.*

As Mama's nerves grew worse, Mademoiselle and her lovely French books were taken away from me. My French never recovered entirely from the grief and shock of this sudden loss, especially as a gruff watchdog of a woman took her place. She looked like a policeman in woman's clothes and was so stiffly starched that she crackled with every movement. She had enormous feet that tramped back and forth between bedroom and kitchen and made the hanging lamps tremble. Frau Spandauer was the name of this redoubtable widow with the granite chin. "Leave me in peace, I've got no time for you," she would shout at me, pressing her hands to her temples as though desperate. "Your mother is quite a case. Oh, my God, yes, quite a case!" A few times I saw her wrestle bodily with Mama, but what chance did my frail little mother have against this she-elephant? And what was I to do when poor Mama was slapped with a wet towel, pushed or carried screaming into the bedroom, forcibly undressed, and put to bed? By and by I grasped that Frau Spandauer had been hired not as my nursemaid or governess but as Mama's— sort of.

My own refuge in those years was Large Katl, my retreat the kitchen, my great good luck that Katl let me share her lover with her. August was one of the hand-picked Imperial guardsmen, frightfully handsome, tall and strong, and his lap was the warmest, pleasantest, safest place on earth.

I'm afraid August left me with a little trauma: I never overcame my pleasure in masculine good looks, while masculine intellect attracts me only in the long run.

My father was a roaring hypochondriac who never had a day's sickness in his life. He died when he was ninety-three—and he might well have lived to be a hundred if he hadn't been killed during World War II in the ill-famed massacre of a town called Novi Sad in Yugoslavia.

That, however, belongs to a later chapter.

At the first sneeze of anyone in the household, Father called for The Bag. The Bag looked like a doctor's old black satchel, worn out as though it had never been new. While Katl packed his things, Father paced the room impatiently, his lips tightly compressed, a towel held to his face as a shield against the germs. Without opening his mouth he would mumble some strict warnings to me to behave, and go off, satchel and all, to his mother.

Inevitably, he moved out as Mama grew progressively worse. "I need my sleep, I've got to work. If I don't earn the money, who will?" he would shout. "God Almighty, the expenses. Great Lord in Heaven, why do you punish me so? What have I done to deserve a sick wife? Listen, Vicki, I can't stay here, or I'll lose my mind too. You understand that, don't you? You're a big girl now. You be quiet and behave and take care of your mother, hear me?"

My bones or the inside of my head seemed to creak a little under the growing load of responsibility. Sure, I was a big girl, old, older than anyone I knew. A little old woman of five I was, dignified and serious, and filled with more worries and virtues than I have now, at seventy plus.

Yet, with all my good behavior, Mama grew steadily worse. She couldn't sleep, she couldn't eat. She lost weight, she became so thin that she hardly cast a shadow. There were crying spells, tantrums, attacks of convulsions and screaming. Her rich wheat-colored hair had become as dry as hay, and Mr. Herring didn't come any more. Poor Mama, with her tiny feet, always cold in her doll-like slippers, and her tiny hands that she couldn't hold still. Her always enormous blue eyes had grown as large as saucers, like the eyes of the dog in *Ali Baba*. Never had I loved Mama so desperately as I loved her then, when she had become torn and twisted and ugly. Never did I loathe her so much as when I felt that, with just a trifle of an effort, a bit of self-discipline, she could control herself.

If I could stop myself from bawling or screaming or misbehaving, why couldn't she?

Doctors came and went, the apartment was pervaded with the sickly ether-sweetness of paraldehyde. (Many years later I encountered the same smell in a state asylum for the insane—no, I was not an inmate, just a visitor in pursuit of research!)

From time to time Father would put in a brief appearance to learn the results of various doctors' consultations. New names flashed like blades through the air: Krafft-Ebing . . . the Professor . . . Dr. Breuer . . . Dr. Freud . . . and more and more frequently—Inzersdorf. Father would sigh and moan and make intricate calculations in his notebook. He even made me add and multiply some of those figures in my head—mental arithmetic was his hobby, and in his tight bookkeeper's mind he was convinced that there could be no better preparation for life than to confront a five-to-six-year-old with six-digit arithmetic.

Oddly enough, although I had long since begun to make up stories, I also liked playing with mathematics. Perhaps the clean, immovable lawfulness of figures was an antidote to my overheated imagination. When I was admitted into elementary school, I skipped the first grade entirely. If I hadn't been such a thin, pale, puny shrimp, they'd probably have moved me up to third or even fourth grade right away—poor precocious me.

Being by far the youngest and weakest child in my class, I should —again according to autobiographic tradition—have been bullied, hazed, and tortured by some of the overgrown girls in the last benches, those dull ones who had flunked and were as much as two and three years older than I. But nothing of the kind happened. I was well liked and well treated, almost as if the class considered me a funny little pet. Of course, we were girls—harebrained, soft-hearted, and inferior. The boys, although in the same building, were hermetically sealed off from our wing by heavy, eternally locked doors. They entered and left school by another street, and our playground, actually a forbidding yard, was separated from theirs by a prisonlike wall.

At the risk of sounding like a stupid old fuddy-duddy, I submit my impression that there is something inherently lopsided about co-educational high schools. Undeniably, girls mature earlier and faster than boys: they flaunt their sex, stick out their proud new lit- tle breasts and little round bottoms, and paint their faces. Flirts and teases, they are aggressive and fully conscious of their female- ness at a time when boys, at least two years behind in their sexual development, are still kids who by instinct only want to growl at girls and be left in peace, to play or study, maybe to dream. Sometimes, watching these nice coeducated young animals, so unequal in their respective sexual ages and drives, I think that these are the years when the American male's spine is damaged and softened so that he rarely becomes a real full-grown man but remains "just one of the boys," seeking for the rest of his life the protective company of his own sex that was taken from him too early.

I loved going to school; it was a quiet haven away from the turmoil at home. I liked my teachers and I believe that my school, the Pedagogium, had an exceptionally fine faculty. I did not have the slightest difficulty in learning, but gobbled it up as if it were ice cream (not that I knew how ice cream tasted—it was one of the things strictly forbidden by my father). I would be at school twenty minutes before anyone else, and in the delicious quiet and solitude I would ladle the requested wisdom into my head as with a large spoon through a wide funnel. This way I was always beautifully and freshly equipped with the figures, dates, succession of Roman emperors and French kings, the prickly declensions and dust-covered finesses of grammar. All of which I would forget the moment I didn't need it. But when it came to writing compositions, the stuff simply gushed out of me in my very bad handwriting and with a feverish seeding of ink blobs. When dear *Herr Direktor* Moosbauer, with the smiling, blue Santa-Claus eyes, asked us to write three pages about a given theme, I never failed to come up with at least thirty—and used any theme that inspired me.

Liking school seems to have saved me from going overboard at a time when my home was assuming more and more the character of a hell too hot and cruel to bear. Because now Mama wanted to leap out the window. Laughing and giggling, she would sneak up to the window sill whenever Frau Spandauer let her out for even a few minutes. I, trusted with guarding her, hung on to Mama's small bare feet with every ounce of my strength, begging her to come off the sill, to sit with me, I was going to tell her something funny, something real nice, a new story, very interesting.

Keeping one's mother from "killing herself" is hard schooling for a future storyteller.

I had only a hazy idea what "killing herself" meant, but I knew it was something terrible and gruesome.

Perhaps the same event that gave me an inkling of this had also planted the dark thought of suicide in my mother's head. We lived on the top, or fourth, floor (the fifth by United States reckoning), with only the servants' quarters above us. One bright afternoon a heavy shadow slid swiftly past one of our dining-room windows. Katl shrieked, dropped whatever she had in her hands, and almost simultaneously there came a strange muffled thump from the sidewalk below, like a large soft vegetable squashing on the pavement. There was a sudden silence, then voices, shouts, running steps. "She has killed herself, oh, dear Father in Heaven," whispered Katl, pushing me away as she leaned out of the window. Suddenly Mama appeared at the door and said in the high childish voice that often ushered in another attack: "Killed herself? Good for her." She laughed, the thin giggle I had learned to fear. Walking over to the window, she leaned far, far out.

That was one of the occasions on which I saw Frau Spandauer overpower my mother by brute strength.

That incident stands out very clearly in my memory, but otherwise I remember those months only as a confusion, a jumble of nightmares. I loved my mother—she was so sick, so small, so helpless —I loved her with a desperate passion, more like that of a lover than of a daughter. To stand by and watch a beloved person suffer without being able to help is the hardest thing I know. Hard for a grownup, harder still for a child—a child doesn't understand what's happening, can't express her bewilderment, is inarticulate and lost, but feels and senses with a poignancy that has not yet been blunted by experience and repetition.

If this sounds as though I were one of those wonderful suffering little angels of second-rate Victorian literature, I've painted a wrong picture. True, I was a good little girl on the whole, although certainly not by inclination. As long as everything revolved around Mama's sickness there was simply not much else I could do but be good. Child-rearing being what it was in those days, I was constantly threatened with the harm my behavior could do to Mama's nerves. Everybody—Father and Grandmother, a gaggle of aunts, Katl, and Frau Spandauer—blamed me for her attacks, convulsions, and sleepless nights. I did not have much of a skin to begin with, but what I had was chafed raw. Yet inside that skinless sensitivity I must have been blessed with a fairly robust nature or they would have broken me. Most of the time I went around with a very bad conscience, bent under the burden of my piling-up sins. I had strange feverish daydreams that left me with palpitating heart and burning cheeks. I would ask the lover I shared with Katl to take me on his lap and kiss me. I was fresh to Frau Spandauer. I had secrets, I told lies, I dawdled on the way home from school, I read the forbidden gilt-edged books by Heinrich Heine. Left alone in the apartment, I would spend long fascinated minutes studying myself in the forbidden mirror—more sin and depravity. I itched with curiosity to know how I looked. The mirror frightened me, yet I was dying to find out how I really looked, not only my face, but me, all over. Naked.

Moreover, I was a thief. I stole sugar from the larder, flowers in the park, and once I went with a bunch of kids to steal apples from a bin in front of the greengrocer's store. The greengrocer caught us at it, and the other girls ran away yelling and sneering. I dropped my apple, one of the girls stepped on it, and there it was, a beautiful stolen apple now only a squashed smear on the sidewalk. Like the servant girl whom I had heard but not seen. After this I gave up stealing. I only borrowed Mama's white satin shoes, the ones she had worn as a bride. But the high heels threw me, and I crashed into the mirror in the entrance hall, broke the glass, and cut a gash in my forehead. All very bad for poor Mama's nerves, and all my fault, my badness, my sin. The worst of it was that I began to think I was rotten and evil inside; being outwardly bad was a relief. "If you go on like this, you'll croak on a dunghill," threatened my father, "but that's what comes from reading filthy books! Listen, if I ever catch you reading those dirty things by Heine again, I'll give you such a spanking you won't be able to sit down for a week. . . ."

Suppression breeds rebellion. I wasn't sorry for reading Heine and I certainly wasn't going to stop just because my father was a brutal, ignorant moron. There were words in that red leather book with the gilt edge that cut through like a flash of lightning in a midnight sky:

*Aus meinen grossen Schmerzen*
*Mach' ich die kleinen Lieder.**

I wondered how one would go about making little songs out of great sorrows. Pale and trembling with defiance, I retorted: "I shall so read again, whatever I like. You just don't understand Heine or me or Mama. You don't understand about anything, so there!" Father took me up to the attic and gave me a methodical spanking. To top it, I was ordered not to cry, not to have red eyes, not to let

* Out of my great sorrows/I shape my little songs.

Mama know what had happened. But I was beyond crying. Before I was seven, I had held tears down in me for such a long time that I had lost the ability to cry.

I have never regained it. As in my childhood, I can only grow freezing cold in grief, trembling by the hour, a dead man's chilly fist squeezing my heart.

It was around this time, too, that I became a miniature, but full-fledged, cynic, pessimist, and agnostic. This spiritual revolt was caused by an undoubtedly expensive oil painting in my Fine Grandparents' green salon. In glistening colors and artful detail it depicted three objects. First, one saw a fat baby sitting on a velvet cushion, its naked legs, thighs, and part of its round bottom sticking out very pink and plump from under its cute, much too short baby shirt. This little garment wasn't even long enough to cover the baby's navel, and all that pink skin was painted with such obvious gusto that I had a dim sensation of looking at something indecent. But then, my grandparents would certainly not hang up anything indecent for everybody to see. Therefore, I searched for the deeper meaning of the picture, its symbolism, so to speak. This luscious creature held a goldfish bowl between its legs, just hiding the most provocative part so you didn't know whether it was a boy or a girl baby. But the most disturbing and puzzling element was the fact that the baby dangled into the bowl of water a gold chain on which was suspended a gold watch, and the goldfish seemed to be looking to see what time it was.

For almost two years I tried to find out the meaning of that painting for, obviously, it couldn't be as absurd as it seemed. I pestered my grandparents, my aunts, the servant girls, and even Frau Gross, the seamstress, for an explanation. "What is it?" I would ask. "Well, what should it be? A painting," they would answer. "Yes, but I mean, what is it, really?" "It's by a famous painter," I was told, "it's called a genre picture. Don't you like it? Look at the cute baby. Isn't it adorable?"

But why is the baby putting the watch into the goldfish bowl? What does it *mean?* There was no end to my *why's* and *where-fore's,* my preoccupation and puzzlement. The grownups grew impatient; they told me not to ask silly questions, to be quiet, to leave them in peace. This was what grownups always said when they didn't wish to tell the truth.

I shut up, brooding about all the swindles they were trying to perpetrate, the stupid lies they hoped to palm off on us children. The unexplained baby with the goldfish bowl joined the growing bunch of fraudulent mysteries: the stork, the Easter bunny, Santa Claus, the Grampus who appeared in a devil's mask but with Herr Carl's boots to punish naughty children with a birch switch; finally, even the angels and the little Child Jesus shown in countless pictures, in books, and in the museum. It's easy to tell us such stories and paint such pictures, I thought, but we don't have to believe them.

It is a terrible thing to love someone and not be able to reach the beloved, to be physically close but spiritually separated by the other's self-absorption so complete that no word, no caress, no glance can penetrate it.

Mama is sitting on the blue sofa; she has drawn into herself as a snail draws into its shell when someone tries to touch it. You talk to her but she can't hear you, for she has that small supercilious smile around her mouth, as though she knows everything. Her eyes, bluer and larger than ever, look but don't see you. You try to stroke her cheek but she doesn't seem to feel it. You kiss her hand, so pitifully scrawny and tough by now, like a bird's claw, which she rubs incessantly up and down the crystal beads of the long chain she always wears. I grab her hand and shake it; I shake her arm to wake her up, to bring her back from wherever she is, keep her from drowning, falling, from killing herself. If she would only help herself and me, only a little. If she would only not let herself drift so far away. I'm desperate, angry, furious. There is such a crushing homesickness in me for this lost mother of mine; I want her back, I want everything to be as it was before. I have an unbearable yearning for something I can't name, to be cuddled and petted, to have my hair stroked, to fall asleep on Mama's lap, to be just once more carried piggyback to my crib and kissed good night —yes, I'm still sleeping in a crib, I'm not quite seven.

It was at that time that many of my conversations began with "When I was little. . . ."

No reason for you grownups to exchange lenient "how-cute" smiles when you hear a little child talking about its past, as every child does and in the selfsame words. By the time children enter school they have lived so long, they have eaten up and digested such a huge chunk of their lives, they have seen, heard, learned, and experienced more than they will in all their future years put together. Of course they have a past, and a long and weighty one at that.

I prayed a lot during those months. Not so much to God Himself, who I knew couldn't be bothered with my small ant's troubles, but to my dead little grandfather who cared about me and whom I pictured as something of a middleman, an emissary between myself and Heaven.

I prayed to get sick.

Perhaps, if I could get sick, Mama would get well. Perhaps I could draw her sickness into me, like Winkelried had drawn all those lances into his chest. (Traces of *Great Men—Noble Deeds!*) Possibly I lived in a mythical world still primitive enough to believe that human sacrifice was needed to appease the gods. Whatever the reason, I was ready to die if that would make Mama well and happy again. In fact, I daydreamed myself a most attractive death —as every child does occasionally—and a paradise full of flowers and books, puppies and apples and little kittens. There I would take long, happy walks, holding hands with Grandfather, and he would laugh and let me grub in his pockets to find an orange, some candy, a colored crayon, as he did when he was alive.

I think there was some sound practical psychology that underlay those daydreams. Subconsciously, I probably thought that if I were to die, or just get very sick, it might shake up my mother, bring her out of herself. Perhaps if I were sick *I* would be the important one. *I* would need consideration and care. Everything had been so lovely when I was down with the measles. Mama had nursed me and cuddled me and fed me and hummed me to sleep, and whenever I opened my eyes, Mama would be sitting by my crib. There was a night light, a tiny flame swimming on oil in a ruby-red glass. How beautiful Mama's face had looked in that light! Dear God in Heaven, please . . . please, dear Grandfather, let me get sick. . . .

It seems I overprayed a trifle, because I promptly came down with scarlet fever. In those days, innocent of booster shots and antibiotics, it could be serious, and in my case it was. The danger was only heightened by the attendance of a bearded courtly personage in a black alpaca coat with cigar ashes on the lapels, that grossly ignorant oracle with the avuncular bedside manners—Dr. Pollatschek, the family doctor. Worse than my scarlet fever was a furious mastoiditis that was neither treated nor operated on but simply allowed to run its course, and from which you either recovered or died in the most horrible pain. Perversely, I did neither; I'm only dragging a somewhat impaired ear through life.

I almost died, though, during a night of blazing fever and delirium in which reality and hallucinations were hopelessly mixed. People, some of whom I didn't even recognize, stood murmuring around my crib. There was my father, but ill as I was, I knew he couldn't be there: he'd never enter a room crowded with scarlet fever germs. The dark air was full of them, I could see them, small bright-red creatures threatening me with fiery glowing crawfish claws. There was Dr. Pollatschek and another doctor who counted my pulse and mournfully shook his head. And there was, for a totally unbelievable instant, Mama kneeling at my side, tightly holding my hand to keep me from being swept off into the roaring, reeling darkness. Then there were screams; I did not know it was I who was screaming until Frau Spandauer shouted at me to shut up, for Heaven's sake. Did I want to drive Mama out of her mind?

I shut up. I clenched my fists and shut up, and wandered off into still deeper circles of my own delirious inferno.

I came back to a changed world, an unfamiliar landscape of fat pillows and a wine-red silk comforter and an abominable smell. I was lying in Mama's bed. In Father's bed a strange woman as big as a mountain was snoring. She had a face like Herr Pitzelgruber's asthmatic pug dog. Was she real? Or was I still in a nightmare? I felt hot, thirsty, itchy, gritty, buried in sand up to my neck (I had read that somewhere). As for the stench, I realized with shock that it was I who stank so, and in Mama's bed! Next I discovered that my head was bandaged, but the bandage was loose, crumpled, soaked through with the pus oozing from my ears.

I plucked the sleeve of the snoring colossus in the other bed. "You—" I said, "wake up, you! Who are you?" It took the sleeping mass some time to stop snoring, yawn, sit up, sigh, get angry, and start shouting. "Can't a body get five minutes' rest in this place? But that's what I always tell 'em, even a nurse is human. A nurse is nobody's slave, needs food and sleep like anybody else. Now look at the mess you've made again! Those ears of yours, Holy Mother of God! Who d'you think is going to wash all those stinking bandages? Me? Not likely!"

"Go away," I said. "I want Katl."

Pugface went out and Katl came in with a fat, false, grownup smile smeared all over her face. "Well, little chick, seems we are over the hump now, thank Jesus Christ and all His Saints. That night you passed your crisis—that's what they call it, the crisis—the doctors said if they pull you through it'll be a sheer miracle. But they did and now all you've got to do is drink a lot of milk and be a very good little girl and lie still and do everything Doctor and Nurse tell you and very soon you'll be as good as new and, oh, yes, August says to tell you he'll visit you first thing you're allowed to have visitors, and——"

"Katl," I interrupted. "Katl, what happened to Mama?"

"What do you mean, what happened? She's gone, your mama, they took her away, don't you know . . . ?"

"Yes. I know," I said. And I did. Through some gap in my delirium I had seen Mama; in a thin, torn nightgown she had stood on the window sill, laughed wildly, and leaped out into the jumbled night. Gone. Like the girl who had jumped from the attic. Good for her, Mama had said. Was it good for Mama, too?

Katl was still babbling, she talked too much and too fast; that's what one always does when one is telling lies. I knew, because I did it myself. "Go away," I told her. "I can't hear you. My ears hurt. I'm tired."

Mama was dead. She had gone away, and now she was in Heaven

and it was she who was getting oranges and rock candy from Grandfather Baum while I was left behind with the fever and the pain in my ears and the deaf, broken membranes and the thick, stinking pus running out of them. Mama was dead and I would never see her again, never. I put my hands over my face and turned to the wall.

I was an orphan, I was all the orphans I had ever met in my clandestine readings. It was not an altogether unbecoming role. It was terribly sad, of course, but in the deepest calix of every flower and every grief lies a grain of comfort—the bittersweet taste of self-pity, self-importance.

I can't explain why I was so absolutely certain that Mama had died. Perhaps I was hiding a subconscious wish, a dim feeling that a dead mother in paradise would be less trouble than a nerve-sick mother on earth. It's also possible that I couldn't bear the thought that Mama would desert me like this if she were alive.

My nurse was a character out of Dickens at his most lurid. Not a real nurse, she was a former midwife who had been barred from her profession for criminal practices. She was also a drunkard, and when she was drunk she liked to dance for me with a full glass of beer balanced precariously on her head, her two hundred pounds rattling the furniture. To watch her enormous shadow dancing on the wall made my ears hurt worse and my temperature rise. All her stories had to do with bloody births and mothers dying in childbed and stillborn babies and abortions, incomprehensible stories of which only the horror and blood came through to me. Although she was a miserable nurse, she was too jealous to let my Katl come near me.

This, too, might have been one of the reasons I never mentioned Mama. Another was, perhaps, the queer secrecy which is a child's very own domain. Whatever the explanation, my isolation during those long slow weeks of recovery was absolute, and I buried my lost mother the way a puppy buries a cherished bone.

My silent, lonely resignation and bittersweet peace was broken by a figure that stands out clearly against the muddled background of my childhood: Frau Gross, the family seamstress.

Frau Gross was bald, a fascinating achievement for any woman;

she had lost her hair, she claimed, during a bout with typhoid. She had, it seemed, caught every contagious disease possible and was now immune to them all. Scared of catching scarlet fever from me —not her! She laughed at the very idea and patted my cheeks and my fingers from which the skin was peeling—like little frankfurters, she described them. On one cheek she had a large brown wart, from which three long white hairs stuck out. Something was wrong with her left eye, so any garment she sewed invariably had a leftward slant. But her most fascinating feature was her left eyetooth, which was so long it overlapped her lower lip, and she used this remarkable tooth to bite off threads. She always smelled of the oil she would squirt from a tricky little can into the orifices of the treadle sewing machine. She looked exactly like a witch, and I loved her dearly.

Now, pulling her old worn tape measure from her bottomless pocket, she said, "I must take your measurements, maybe you've grown. Some grow a lot while they're sick in bed, oh my, yes. Just look at your cousin Olga, she's grown more than two inches with just a touch of the chicken pox. What do you think of that, huh?"

I refused to think anything at all about my cousin Olga. I couldn't stand Olga, who was always put before me as a simon-pure example of a good girl. I refused to compete in goodness with Cousin Olga, or with anyone else, for that matter.

I don't know if it's a curse or a blessing to be so completely lacking in competitive spirit as I have remained all through my life. So far, every challenge I've met I myself have flung out, and in all my races, whether won or lost, I was only trying to beat my own record.

"Your Aunt Jenny thinks you need a new school dress. Since your mama's gone, she's taking care of things, you know," Frau Gross informed me.

"A black one?" I asked hopefully. Me, the orphan, so lovely and pale in a black dress. . . .

"Of course not. How would a little runt like you look in a black dress? No, there's still a lot of gray wool left from last fall."

Visualizing myself in deep mourning had given me a slight lift, but now I was hit by a foul blow of disappointment. My eyes turned hot, and possibly red.

"Now, now," said Frau Gross. "Now, now, now! You mustn't cry, little mouse."

"I'm not crying," I said furiously. But I was.

Frau Gross grabbed awkwardly at my hands and held them tight. "Missing your mama, are you?"

"No!" I shouted desperately. "I'm not! I'm glad she's gone. *Glad!*"

Frau Gross refused to hear this. "Sure is a shame they had to take her away, and such a pretty young lady at that. But you'll see, it won't be long and she'll be back again. Now won't that be nice?" I pressed my hands to my ears that still hurt as if a worm were gnawing inside. "Oh, shut up! Shut up, shut up!" I shouted. "You know she won't ever come back, ever, and I know it, too. Why do grownups always lie!"

"My, my, what's got into you? Want to bet they'll get her well in no time at Inzersdorf? Why, they have the finest doctors there. Every day they're curing people that are off their rockers, much worse than your mother, and——"

Frau Gross stopped herself, clamping her tooth over her lip and her hands over her mouth. "Oh, my, now I've done it," she mumbled. "Didn't you know? Didn't nobody tell you? Oh, you poor little frog, where did you think your mama went?"

"You mean . . . you mean, she isn't dead?" I asked feebly.

"Holy Mother of God, the things that go on in that noodle of yours! Of course she isn't dead. Just very sick in the head. Off her rocker. But people don't die of being crazy. Believe you me, if she can be cured, they'll cure her at Inzersdorf, you bet they will. I don't ought to have told you. Now listen, promise you won't talk about it, you mustn't give me away, promise? But really, ain't it better you know what's what?"

I did not think so. It was much worse. There was a certain final order in having a dead mother in Heaven. A sick mother, although much trouble, was someone to lavish love and care and pity on. But a mother who was crazy, thrown in with a crowd of other crazies in some unimaginable place called Inzersdorf! There was something utterly disorderly about that. It was an unspeakable dark secret, full of shame and disgrace.

Life became still darker when—after I was safely and entirely recovered and my ears didn't smell any longer—Father returned. Such a turmoil of disinfecting and fumigating and scrubbing every inch of the place with green soap. When Father reentered the premises, he forthwith began my education, in earnest and with a vengeance. It was a painful process for both of us. Only in recapitulation can I dimly grasp my father's motive for throwing out all books, even the dull moralistic little booklets our school dished out as prizes; locking up the piano and throwing the key into the Danube, figuratively speaking; shutting away Erika, my dear little doll, and letting me play with her only on Sunday morning and under his supervision. I myself felt locked away in a box with the lid clamped down tight. He looked glum and worried and very old, but I had no sympathy for him at all. Probably he was deeply disturbed about me, a child so completely alien to him in all tendencies and traits. Probably he had decided to tear out with an iron hand the roots of crabgrass and the weeds of imagination, to clear my head thoroughly of cobwebs and the dangerous seeds of potential neuroses.

It is fortunate that dreams and fantasies are obstinate, enduring plants.

Among the many prohibitions, Number One was: Never ask questions about Mama. Never pester him nor anyone else with any *what? where? why?* about Inzersdorf. Only once did he consent to inform me that Inzersdorf was a *sa-na-to-ri-um,* a very nice, highly expensive place at which Mama was taking a rest. Period. Not another word, you hear me?

This, of course, I refused to believe. My picture of Inzersdorf ran more toward a Hogarthian bedlam where the insane tried incessantly to kill one another or jump out of the windows. Under threats of terrible punishment, Father made me promise not to mention Mama or Inzersdorf ever again; not to ask or to answer questions; not to talk about this with anyone, not anyone, do you hear?

As if I were able to discuss Mama, dead or alive or crazy, with anybody in the whole world! It was too deep an ignominy to have a mother too crazy to care for me or, at least, stay home as other mothers did.

I had known all along that I wasn't quite like other children, and now this unhappy secret set me more and more apart. At first, such loneliness was sad, but after a while it grew on me and made me feel strong, with a strength different from the mere muscles of those husky girls in the back benches—a better strength. They couldn't take what *I* had to take. They didn't know what *I* knew. They couldn't *think*. To me, thinking had become overwhelmingly important. Thinking was a strenuous occupation and often a dispenser of headaches, but it was a wonderful refuge. It gave me a feeling of power, a certain arrogance, too, that allowed me to feel sorry for those other children, the stupid ones, who didn't know life or suffering or longing for the irretrievably lost, or even the pains of a mastoiditis.

I don't need anybody, not even Mama, I said to myself. I've gone through the worst and I'm strong.

I can take it.

When my older son was six and entered school, he showed fine discrimination in choosing his friends. He would first of all trot with each of them to their homes, take a good look around, and, if satisfied, report to me: "They're nice people. They have a grand piano."

According to this test, my grandparents on both sides were Nice People. They had grand pianos—even Father's parents, who had no money, were not as fine as Mama's family, and, besides, had never played or even listened to a single bar of music, had one. It had probably been palmed off on Uncle Sandor, Father's younger brother, in lieu of money by one of his bankrupt business connections, and he had retained it to give himself airs. It stood in his room which, for added elegance, displayed two enormous fans of vaguely Egyptian design, their long broomstick handles nailed crosswise to the wall. These, too, had the incongruous appearance of things left over from an auction, a parade, a Shriners' convention.

Partitioned off from this room by faded portières was an alcove in which my grandparents' double bed stood. I was asleep in it at Grand-father's side when he, also asleep, died as quietly and without fuss as he had lived, a dear, gray-haired, kind, shabby little old Jew. On our fine, long walks he always held my hand securely in his, and he would lift me up and carry me even before I noticed I was tired. After dinner he would sit me on his knee, let me have a sip of sweet red wine from his glass, and sing funny little ditties to me until I fell asleep, curled up against his shiny old coat. I loved him as much as a four-year-old can ever know how to love.

Perhaps it was his soundless easy passing away that has kept me free of the fear of death—which doesn't mean that I might not be-have quite badly when it comes to the terminal agonies and indigni-ties my body may hold in store for me. In fact, the few times my life was in balance, the one thing I feared was that I might not bear up well under the final pressure—the fear of soldiers and prisoners. Each of us has his breaking point, but we don't know where it is until it is reached.

As for that evening, my grandfather said only that he had eaten too much for dinner—but who could resist Grandmother's cooking? "Let's go for a walk, Pinkerl," he said. "I need a breath of fresh air."

It was a lovely warm evening with a late sunset like a squashed orange at the edge of the world and I tripped along happily at his side. He was breathing deep and hard and loud; I thought he was doing it to make me giggle, so I giggled. When he stopped, ever so often, I accepted this also as a courtesy, a consideration for my short legs. We dived into one of the little hackdrivers' cafés below street level and I was delighted with the smell of it. Men and sweat and fried onions and beer.

Perhaps this is the place to confess the strong attraction muscular men had for me when I was little, and vice versa. Not only Large Katl's guardsman, August, but also the chimney sweep, the butcher boy, the coachmen waiting with their smart open fiacres behind the hotel in which we had spent the summer. They would lift me up, let me drink the foam of their beer and take a huge bite of their steaming hot, fat-dripping corned-beef sandwiches.

Feeling quite at home in the thick atmosphere of the café I

grinned up at the man behind the counter and he grinned back. He had thick hairy arms with blue pictures tattooed on them, such arms as I hoped to have myself by the time I was grown up.

With amazing clarity I remember the siphon he handed Grandfather across the counter. It was of blue glass and had an unearthly beauty, especially when we were out in the street again and the last rays of the sun played on it. The soda water in the bottle was blue, too, and so were the sparkling little air bubbles. By sheer magic it turned into a water-clear liquid as soon as it hissed into a glass. Grandfather drank it in the kitchen, smacking his lips and sighing. "Ah, that'll settle my stomach. Now I think I'll lie down and take a little rest."

"Yes, you do that," said Grandmother, absorbed in her housework. Grandfather went behind the portières of the alcove, undressed, and went to bed while I went to the piano and offered to play for him.

As early as I had taught myself to read I had also begun to piece together on the piano the music that was constantly going around in my head. That evening I was trying to play some of the ballet music that had lodged itself in my mind on the exciting day I had been taken to a matinee of *Die Puppenfee*. It was a highly successful creation by my father's best friend, the ballet master Joseph Hassreiter. (I was quite surprised when I rediscovered that charming trifle years later, choreographed and put to different music by Massine under the new title *La Boutique Fantasque*.)

That evening, in the slowly sinking dusk, I played it for Grandfather, with two fingers (the way I now type my scripts). I felt very inspired, and the melodies came dancing out easily. "Do you like it, Grandfather?" I asked over and over. "Is it pretty? Shall I play you some more?"

"Yes, yes, I like it, it's very pretty, keep on playing," he would answer from behind the portières. Then, after a while, when he did not answer and it had grown almost dark in the room—only the two Egyptian fans still caught a bit of light—I tiptoed into the alcove and heard him snoring with a funny little catch after each breath. I undressed and snuggled into the little groove beside him where I usually slept when I was allowed to stay overnight.

Some hours later I was pulled from my grandfather's side and into one of those loud, incomprehensible upheavals of grownups. Candles were burning, my father was there, also Uncle Sandor—in a nightshirt, of all things. On the floor Grandmother and my aunt Jenny were kneeling and howling and bawling and making a fuss they would never have permitted me to make. So naturally, I, too, broke into great big sobs and tears. They told me Grandfather had died in his—and my—sleep. He has left us, he's gone away; no, he won't come back, he's in Heaven. I did not understand what all this meant, but he had died so quietly, so easily, so peacefully, to the pretty tinkling of my two-finger ballet, that it was nice to think of him playing and flying with all the little angels above.

I didn't know then how bitterly I was going to miss him in the years to come. To this day he wanders through my dreams, gay, consoling, and gentle as ever.

Although I saw my grandmother weep that night, I never knew her to smile. She was a strong, cold, beautiful woman with pale blue eyes, a straight nose, the face and bearing of a Roman empress—though not one of those frivolous ones of late Rome. She was strict and I respected her, but I never felt really fond of her; and this was gross ingratitude because she was the one who handed me two priceless gifts—a tough constitution and the bracing, root-giving summers of my childhood. Neither did Grandmother care much for me, perhaps because she did not care for children in general, but more probably because she hated my mother with an ingrained, insurmountable mother-in-law's hatred. She never forgave my father for having married, and whatever went wrong in that marriage—where indeed much went wrong—she rubbed it in with an unforgiving: "Serves you right, I told you so."

Sons, at that time and in those circles, had no right to marry so long as there were unmarried sisters to be taken care of. Sons were duty-bound to save up respectable dowries for their sisters. The fewer charms a sister possessed the higher a dowry she needed. Unfortunately, Aunt Jenny's charms were scant. She was of the Small Katl type, thin and mousy, with Grandmother's pale naked eyes without eyebrows or eyelashes. She was restless, a bit of a busybody, one of those scurrying small creatures that live in neglected corners and crannies. Without a doubt, Aunt Jenny was full of all kinds of virtues—another quality detrimental to charm. She was always feverishly occupied and strained, doing uninvited kind things for everyone. Also, she was given to hysterical outbreaks, because poor Aunt Jenny, approaching her thirties, was still unmarried and (I should guess in retrospect) still a virgin. Understandably, she was eaten up with envy for my mother who, yet in her green teens, had hooked a husband.

Aunt Jenny's younger sister, my aunt Cora, was of a different caliber. Aunt Cora and Uncle Sandor seemed to have monopolized all of Grandfather's charm and good nature, together with Heaven-knows-what ancestors' good looks and insouciance. Aunt Cora's beauty might have emerged from a second-rate French novel of the time. She had soft white skin and an unbelievable wealth of bright copper hair that she wore in a coronet that added to her height. To show off her fashionably rich hourglass figure, she wore striking, low-cut gowns that revealed a good part of her overwhelmingly voluptuous bosom. Aunt Cora was an actress, not an actress like the great Duse or Vienna's own Charlotte Wolter, but an actress who was always on the road, on tour, in Poland, Russia, the Balkans. It is quite possible that this ravishing aunt of mine was fighting off men and keeping her virtue intact as decisively as any beautiful underpaid girl in a road show ever did. But to me, when I was growing into adolescence, she was sin and fascinating vice incarnate, and for this I loved her best of all my seven aunts (there were five more on Mama's side). Obviously, Aunt Cora was not good marriageable material for the eligible little clerks or traveling salesmen—too striking, too intimidating—and so she, too, seemed doomed to remain single.

Therefore, the family was jubilant when Aunt Cora returned from one of her tours with a fiancé in tow. True, he was a Foreigner; he came from Berlin, a Prussian in a word, a race that could not be more disliked by the Austrians. Uncle George was a dapper little gentleman, also redheaded, with a pirate's black patch over one eye and, it was respectfully whispered, very wealthy. Through lavish gifts, impeccable manners, and a much-traveled man-of-the-world's shrewd practical knowledge, he bribed himself into the favor of the family. To me he was fascinating, picturesque, like James Fenimore

Cooper's Freebooter, just the right husband for beautiful Aunt Cora.

Each year Uncle George and Aunt Cora returned for a visit, and soon they brought a doll-like, equally redheaded, baby girl with them upon whom I pounced with all my hungry heart. There was a strange rhythm about these visits, something entirely new to the family, namely, a flow of high and low tide. In my family, and I suppose in millions of Austrian bourgeois families, no noticeable fluctuations of fortune occurred, not so long as there was a father, a breadwinner. Rich people stayed rich, well-to-do people remained well-to-do, and the living standard of the not-so-well-to-do ones— such as my grandparents—though simpler, was stable. Poor people were and remained poor. They belonged to a different world and were no concern of ours.

But now this new uncle, this Foreigner, brought into our lives something unknown, slightly scandalous, and quite frightening: *he speculated*. He played the stock market, Father said with cold contempt. Some years the redheads arrived in full regalia, took rooms in an elegant hotel, and unpacked a wealth of gifts for everybody. Aunt Cora was adorned with feathers, furs, and jewels, the primitive tribute men pay to voluptuous beauty whether in New Guinea or Paris.

In other years, Aunt and Child minus Uncle arrived, so stone-poor they looked like the people in a heartbreaking photograph, captioned "The Emigrants," I had once seen in a magazine. There were tears, embraces, accusations, arguments, and explanations. Father and Uncle Sandor were summoned and pressed into shelling out some money to help their shipwrecked brother-in-law. As soon as Uncle George was rescued by long-distance aid, Aunt Cora and Child returned to that Prussian, that irresponsible speculator, that species unknown in sedate Vienna—a go-getter.

But whatever talents Aunt Cora had as an actress must certainly have been inherited from Grandmother. Probably the ability to stage uninhibited scenes was the best weapon women possessed until they became emancipated. Take, for instance, Grandmother's shining black hair; it was neatly parted in the middle, braided, and pinned up. I remember this so well because I was often permitted to watch her brushing, pomading, and braiding it, one of the absorbing pleasures of staying there overnight.

Grandmother walks up and down, she wears several white petti-coats and a white scalloped bed jacket, she has thin white hair on her head and thick black hair in her hand into which she brushes pomade until it shines like the black marble on our console table. But at Grandfather's funeral, Grandmother, in deep mourning, emerged with a silver gray wig, just as neat and sleek as the black one had been. The bereaved family whispered in awe that she had turned gray overnight—which indeed she had.

Her sons Grandmother held fastened to her not by a silver cord but by something more like a steel cable. And whenever she felt that her hold might be slackening (when, for instance, there was some urgent need of money, as the time Aunt Jenny's dowry had to be raised in a panic to secure a marriage for her), Grandmother would stage one of her great tragic acts. As in classic tragedy, a messenger carrying ill-tidings would arrive at our home in the middle of the night. In my childhood, messengers were a necessity, since tele-phones in the average household were not common. So there stood Herr Karl, the old family retainer, cap in hand, unwashed as always, his face creased with deep black lines in which the dust from his work as a machinist had settled for good. Herr Karl reported that Grandmother was dying. "Looks bad," he said lugubriously, "this time she won't make it." I was pulled from sleep and hurried into my clothes; the candles flickered; Father, unshaved, unkempt, look-ing awful, was pulling on pants, vest, and coat over his long-sleeved woolen underwear. I was trembling quietly, irresistibly caught in the chilly excitement.

Herr Karl had a cab waiting, but both driver and horse had fallen asleep. I was terribly sorry for the horse, I could feel in my own bones how tired it was. It could hardly get its head up and had to be whipped all the way through the empty sleeping streets of the old Inner City. It was a great adventure to ride like this in the middle of the night, the only drawback being the bad smell under the leaky leather hood of the cab, a mixture of oilcloth, cold cigars, and horse manure. Father sat moving his lips and shaking his head, a sign that he was arguing with himself about the tip he would have to give to Herr Karl.

Everybody said that Father was mean-stingy, a real miser. It was whispered in the family that he was a rich man, that he had hoarded a fortune but was simply too stingy to spend a red penny of it. It was one of the family myths, like Grandmother's turning gray overnight.

Whenever she was dying, however, which happened once every few months, she wore no wig. With her own thin white hair she looked, of course, many years older; shrunken and pitiful, she would be lying back in the deep pillows. Her mouth gaped wide and black, and she managed to produce a fine imitation of the death rattle. Candles were burning and the room was full of kneeling people— aunts and uncles, sobbing and praying, the sloppy barefooted maid mumbling Hail Marys. And here also, inexplicably, was Frau Gross with her eyetooth—how had she got here in the middle of the night? Father bent over Grandmother and asked loudly: "How do you feel, Ma'am?"—he always used the respectful son's formal *you*, never the intimate *thou*.

"Bad, my child. I am dying," she breathed. He knelt down, kissed the hand that appropriately hung limply over the edge of the bed, and joined in the prayers. To protect and console me, Frau Gross pulled me close into her oil-smelling aura.

But I needed neither protection nor consolation. I had been through exactly the same scene several times before—and Grandmother hadn't died. Children have fine antennae for detecting the phony carryings-on of grownups, probably because they themselves are so proficient at posing, pretending, and acting. Far from moving me, the performance made me feel like snickering. Curious I was, yes, and interested, but faintly disgusted, too. Why, I would wonder, did all those grownups go along time after time with Grandmother's swindle? I felt cold and I could not stop trembling (I still tremble with chills whenever I attend a great performance), but I think I already had something of the sense of standing aside, the detached observation of the future writer. Why else would Grandmother's little dramatic performances have etched such deep, lasting grooves into my memory?

She had a good sense of timing and drama, the old tyrant. She would clutch her heart; she would produce spasms, delirious mutterings; she would even manage to stop breathing and to die—almost. Summoning her last bit of strength, she would blindly grope for the heads of her sons and daughters to bless them. And after this catharsis she would whisper her last words, her last wishes. Using the most infamous blackmail, she would get her two sons to swear sacred oaths to do this or that: to take care of their sisters, to pay her sons-in-law's debts; to give, pay, help, support. Amen. Aunt Jenny wiped the sweat off Grandmother's pale brow, whereupon Grandmother stopped the death rattle, closed her eyes, and went to sleep.

Once more the danger had passed.

Everything was entirely different at the other home, that of my Fine Grandparents, the Donats. There, all was rich and opulent. The street, the house in which they lived, the marble sweep of the staircase, and even that sensational newfangled thing—an elevator! My maternal grandparents had rooms and rooms—a salon in wine-red plush, another in moss green that also housed Grandpapa's bookcases and the grand piano. There were two well-trained maids: an excellent blue-uniformed cook in the kitchen, and a thin girl, who wore, when she served at table, a black uniform with a starched white apron and cap. There was always too much, too rich, food that Grandmama stuffed into me. Still today, my friends and my children tease me about the largesse with which I, too, cook and prepare and serve up food enough for a dozen guests when I have invited two. And in one of my recurring dreams I am desperately trying to prepare dinner for a multitude of unexpected visitors and there's no food in the empty larder (it's always the old Before Refrigeration larder), not a morsel in the house, no time to search through empty markets. I suspect a psychoanalyst would interpret this dream as revealing deep-seated feelings of inadequacy; but to me it looks more like a combination of the memories of the stomach-aches induced by Grandmama's hospitality and of the very real and frightening hungry years of World War I.

I often regret that in our wanderings I lost a photograph of my grandmama and grandpapa as newlyweds, a delightful mid-nineteenth-century vignette. What romantics those stodgy Victorians were! Grandmama, so small, so frail, such a featherweight in her crinoline-skirted silk gown, stiff and heavy, with her incredibly tiny eighteen-inch waist, her large dreamy eyes, her dark corkscrew curls; more child than woman. In fact, Grandpapa had to wait for her sixteenth birthday before her parents permitted the marriage.

This marriage, too, had a family legend. Grandpapa, it seems, arrived at my great-grandparents' home to ask for the hand of their older daughter (it had been arranged beforehand between the two families). He arrived on horseback because both families lived on their country estates. (Estates, mind you, nothing like the burnt-out little farm in deepest Hungary my other grandfather had.) He dismounted, handed the reins of his horse to a stableboy, and remained in the courtyard to change his riding gauntlets to pearl-gray kid gloves. (Whenever Grandmama told me this story, which I could never hear often enough, she made quite a point of those *pearl-gray gloves*.) As he was standing there, he saw a curtain move on the second floor and caught a glimpse of a face, a little face . . . Grandmama's face! It was the *coup de foudre*—apparently as fashionable then as going to bed with someone you just met at a cocktail party is today. "Who, in the name of Heaven, is that angel?" he inquired of the stableboy. "The one who took a peek at you? That's the little one, the younger of the young ladies. Still goes to school," he was informed. In the meantime, Grandmama had been jostled away from the window by her older sister who was demurely waiting to be spoken for by the young man whom she had met so far only at neighborhood dances.

Grandmama, too, had been hit by lightning. I could understand this, because when I was little my grandpapa was still a strikingly handsome, very elegant man, every inch of what in Vienna was called *ein Kavalier*. Smartly he presented himself to Grandmama's parents, riding coat and stock, pearl-gray gloves and all, bowed, kissed Great-grandmother's hand, and said: "Madame, Sir, may I take the liberty of asking you for the honor of giving me your younger daughter in marriage?"

This, naturally, was the climax of Grandmama's story. What followed seems less interesting: turmoil and scandalized confusion, a falling-out of the families, quarreling between the sisters, threats of suicide on all sides, and, at last, the capitulation. Then the long wait until another suitor was found for the older daughter. More waiting until Grandmama reached her sixteenth birthday. It was a bit too pat, too similar to the pattern of the sentimental novels in the family magazines (Grandmama had crates full of them in her sewing room). Even then I could sense faintly the triteness of the happy ending to her tale. Yet I had only to look at that picture of the newlyweds to believe it. She was a child when she married and she remained one all her life. In that photograph she looks like a petal being wafted about, clinging to Grandpapa's arms, and he so tall, so handsome, such a manly man with his wild eyebrows and his gipsy mustache.

Grandpapa also had a legend of his very own. He was a genius, it seems. He had passionately wanted to become a great pianist; as a child he had played for the world-famous Moscheles, who had offered to take him as a pupil, promised to make another Liszt of him. But the family refused—people of their class didn't play the pianoforte in public—and so this handsome Grandpapa of mine remained a dilettante in music and a failure in practical life.

I think he wanted to be a failure. It was a demonstration, a protest. He bungled every one of the jobs the family, his or Grandmama's, handed him on a silver platter. He lost untold amounts in several impractical enterprises of his own, and yet more money for the family company into which Grandmama's brothers had taken him as a partner. At last he was complimented out of that company, which owned a timber empire in the newly acquired protectorates of Bosnia and Herzegovina, and forthwith given an "appanage." (An appanage was a yearly income that the monarchy paid to its archdukes.) Thus Grandpapa became a gentleman of too much leisure.

There were actually two of him. In the forenoon he would make a round of calls on his six daughters. During his visit it was almost impossible to be on any but the best behavior, his elegance was too imposing: shiny top hat, black Prince Albert coat, embroidered vest, tight checkered trousers, a pearl stickpin in his starched cravat, watch fob, narrow patent leather shoes, not to mention spats and gloves, both—of course—pearl gray. Smelling of expensive cigars, he would deposit hat, gloves, and the cane with the silver handle on a chair, just as I had seen Germont *Père* do in *La Traviata*, pat Mama's cheeks, and pinch mine. After politely asking Mama's permission to smoke, he would make a *Kavalier's* small talk; then, after ten minutes, he would pull out the fob with the flat golden watch and depart with the mien of a man greatly preoccupied by important business affairs. I would wipe the well-mannered grin from my face, while Mama sniffed and opened a window to air the cigar smoke from the room.

Although Grandpapa all but ignored me during his formal morning visits, the different man he was in the afternoon treated me as an intimate friend and equal, almost as though we were fellow conspirators. Riding up in the elevator, I could hear the thunder of his piano, and when I sneaked into the moss green salon, I always found him disheveled and in a state of wild transport.

Not a shred of the morning's elegance and *savoir-faire* was left, and I found only a grunting, swearing, perspiring gipsy in baggy pants, his hair falling in wild locks onto his forehead, sprays of glittering sweat emanating from him as he threw his head back to sing in an atrocious voice some phrase that particularly excited him. Off came the velvet vest, the hampering suspenders; off the necktie, collar, and cuffs, flung away with one hand while the other kept hammering out octave runs. He unbuttoned his shirt and the dark brown hair on his chest sprang to liberty—a sight that always fascinated me, that gave me a little girl's first shivering inkling of the exciting difference between women and men, even grandpapas. He pumped the pedals, breathed fire from flaring nostrils, pounced like a lion upon the themes, the melodies, his hands ferocious animals wrestling with the music. Grandpapa playing Chopin, let's say the *Octave Étude,* or Mendelssohn's *Variations in D Minor,* was such a spectacle that I would forget to listen to the music.

The only pianist in whom I found—many years later—similar thunderstorms of emotion and careless virtuosity, the same aggressive style of attack combined with the dreamy tenderness of the born romantic, was Eugène d'Albert. And only then did it dawn on me that my Fine Grandpapa had indeed been something of a genius, stunted and frustrated by the prejudices of a "good" family.

His fiercest passions, however, he poured into incessant tirades against Richard Wagner, the man and his music. It was as though he wanted to save me from Satan and the sensual seductions of his musical pit of the damned. To keep my mouth shut during those burning sermons I would let my mind wander off into the searing sweetness of, say, *Tristan*. Like my whole generation, I grew up completely drunk with Wagner and Nietzsche. I had nothing but hidden scorn for my grandpapa's silly perorations.

Now that we've come full circle, notwithstanding the beauty of much of Wagner's music—and a beauty personally reinforced for me by the nostalgic associations of my youth—I can listen to it only with difficulty and faint distaste. This whole process—the swing back to Mozart, Haydn, Bach, and even farther in the past, and the push forward into regions less sharply defined but toward, let's hope, clarity rather than chaos—is only another example of my belief that life moves in cycles, that we progress in a slow, slow spiral, if at all.

When I was about eleven, Grandpapa took to his bed. He even gave up his beloved cigars. He had always been slender, but now he lost weight so rapidly that within a few weeks he had shrunk to a mere skeleton. He died soon after of what Dr. Pollatschek pronounced galloping phthisis but what most probably was cancer of the lung.

Grandmama survived him by a few years. A diabetic long before the discovery of insulin, constantly stealing sugar and starchy cakes from her lady companion's hoard, she had grown dumpy and old, but she continued to smile her sweet, almond-eyed, long-lashed smile that easily broke into full-sized laughter, and she always wore a flower in her long girlish curls. I liked Grandmama very much, though my liking never quite grew into love. She often induced me to take her to the *Konditorei* around the corner, where she stuffed herself with hot chocolate and the strictly forbidden custard-filled pastries and fruit tarts topped lavishly with whipped cream.

It was embarrassing, though, to be seen with Grandmama. People would stop on the street, turn around to look after her, shake their heads, snicker. Because, let's face it, Grandmama was *peculiar*. On her glorious wedding day, when she became the wife of handsome Leopold Donat, she left what is called reality and never returned to its harsh, unpleasant truths. She still dressed as she had as a bride, though she had become a dumpy middle-aged woman. Floating along in the bonnets, pantalets, fichus, lace berthas, and flowing shawls of her youth, she had about her the atmosphere of an antebellum *Gone-with-the-Wind* plantation. Like Austria itself, she seemed in many respects more akin to the American South than to North Germany. Maybe that's why all those pixilated belles of Southern literature bore me. They are all my Grandmama's sisters under the skin, and I say to their authors, thanks, but I've had it.

For their stabilizing effect, I think the most important periods in my early life were the ten weeks of vacation each summer from my fifth through my fourteenth year. During those summers I grew the only roots I ever had. Those carefree weeks provided a balance for my shaky, high-strung, grossly overworked big-city life.

Beginning with my fifth summer Grandmother Baum scooped us up, me and my two baby cousins, and took us to the country. Peigarten, as our village was called, can't have been more than a hundred miles from Vienna, yet our exodus resembled a perilous expedition to a distant savage continent. Towers of mattresses and bedding were sewed into burlap, and an overcomplete outfit of kitchenware went along, as well as ample stocks of groceries, crates of tea, coffee, spices, sugar loaves, and other miscellaneous necessities, including a battery of chamber pots and Dr. Pollatschek's cure-alls of bicarbonate of soda, cough syrup, and a nasty-smelling carbolic disinfectant. Lower Austria near the Bohemian border was timber country so untouched that it took us almost a whole day to get there. We would chug off on a mean little train, change at a small station, and, while Grandmother imperiously directed the unloading of our towering bales and crates, sit down for an interminable wait. After a long, long time, a still smaller and meaner train arrived out of nowhere, we children and all the baggage were loaded on to it, and off we rattled under an evil-smelling plume of black smoke.

All this was exciting enough and full of happy suspense, although mixed with a good deal of train sickness. But the real adventure began at the lopsided wooden shack that was the terminal of this branch line. There, wearing his loudly checked Sunday coat and green hat in honor of Grandmother's arrival, Binder Franzl, our man of all work, awaited us with our nondescript calash, which was not quite, but almost, a carriage. Our *own* carriage in a country and at a time when only the landed gentry commanded such splendor! The first time I met Binder, the horses Lisl and Lois, and the calash, I was overwhelmed. But from then on, year after year, everything, everybody, each curve of the highway, each tree and stone and landmark, each scent and smell, each breath of air, everything, oh, everything, became dearly familiar. This and only this in my entire life was what in the German language is called *Heimat*, a word meaning roughly *home* or *native place*, for which I've not found the exact equivalent in any other language.

Lisl and Lois, by much clacking of tongue and whip, were induced to assume a slow trot, and off we rumbled into the summer dusk, through stands of pine and fir and spruce, across clearings over which the fragrance of freshly cut wood hung thick and resinous, along pastures where cattle stood knee-deep in the tall grass, along little checkerboards of fields with modest crops in the poor soil—potatoes, rye, a little barley, some buckwheat—and here and there a patch of glowing Oriental poppies. (By no means was the poppy ever cultivated for its narcotic properties—it was grown solely for the seed that was used in all those delectable products of Bohemian baking, *Buchteln* and *Kolatschki*.) Dear Heaven, how unbelievably sharp and clear in my mind's eye the people, pebbles, flowers, trees, animals, and clouds I knew in those happy summers.

Peigarten village was one long string of poor little shacks. The people, who were neither farmers nor peasants, belonged to the poorest class: they were weavers. From each house rose the odors of poverty, together with the perpetual clattering of the hand loom that took up most of the space in the home, most of the strength of the people, and all of their time.

They all worked for my Uncle Sandor.

A little girl has no sense of social injustice; all I was conscious of was the glory of our lording it over a whole village. Part of this glory consisted of the castle, *our* castle, into which we moved with bag and baggage. The castle stood on a hilltop at the end of Peigarten. For a long time I was convinced that Uncle Sandor, the handsome, gay, and amiable younger brother of my ugly, unpleasant father, had been endowed, by some good fairy, fairy-tale fashion, with the castle, the meadows, and the endless forests. But by and by I came to realize that this wasn't the case. He had only leased the castle for ninety-nine years from some absent baronial family. The taunts and sneers of the village children, the faint hostility I met when I approached the weavers with a puppy's tail-wagging trust, made me wonder at first, but slowly I began to comprehend. Freed more than a hundred years before, they still carried in their bones the residue of centuries of serfdom and hate for the people in the castle.

At the foot of the hill, where the highway went on toward Bohemia, we stopped in front of Stepan's pub, descended from the calash, and climbed on foot up to the castle, not without Grandmother making the most of her nonexistent heart ailment. But accomplished actress as she might be, she had nothing on Lisl who could give such a convincing spectacle of total exhaustion that Binder had to coax her with carrots and sugar, and sometimes with a burning bunch of hay held under her belly, to make the steep ascent. Occasionally it even happened that Lisl, in true prima donna temper, had to be taken off and an ox would be hastily borrowed from Stepan to pull the calash, Lois, Binder, and Grandmother up to the heavy wooden gate of the castle, over the slippery irregular cobbles of the entranceway, and into the inner courtyard, the nerve center of the old building.

There I am now, back in my paradise. Two huge black locust trees standing guard at the gate fling their showers of butterfly blossoms and their honeyed scent into the air. The swallows in their slender tailcoats flit to and fro below the high vaulted ceiling of the gateway, and my "namesake," Vicki, stands ready to welcome us. Vicki is a strong handsome woman with thick dark braids wound around her head and thick black eyebrows above bright blue eyes.

Vicki is clean and efficient, she takes care of the castle and also of Uncle Sandor during his weekly visits of inspection; she has two little boys, said to be my uncle's offspring, and a husband who is away in prison for assault with a deadly weapon aimed at Uncle. About half of the male population is usually away from home, doing time either in the army or in prison. Both institutions are mentioned with equal pride as places that impart to everyone the education they could never acquire in this edge of the woods.

A less castlelike castle than this run-down, patched-up ruin of a building can hardly be imagined, yet I came to love it with a tenacious nostalgia, clinging and tough as a weed. Some sections must have broken away with the centuries, for I discovered secret places where pieces of walls still stood, so thickly overgrown with grass and nettle it took all of my child's archeological determination to dig down to the rough blocks of granite in whose cracks toads and salamanders lived. The whole castle was sort of lopsidedly built into the rocks, four stories high in front but only one in back. The craggy stone hill beyond teemed with poisonous snakes and was inaccessible to anyone but my friend Sepp. He was a hunchback, a goatherd, a foundling of no definite age but limitless wisdom. The back of the castle, on a level with the uppermost story of the front, opened out onto a small wilderness of a garden, overrun with thistles, reeds, and vermin. There I would spend hours in deep, elaborate, and extremely fuzzy thoughts. Looking out over the rolling land, the blue forests, the toy landscape of distant pastures and willow-lined streams, I would melt and dissolve and hazily become one with my small empire.

Access to this enchanted place was gained by climbing up the rickety winding stairs of a round tower, unthinkably old and about to fall to pieces. There were other leftovers of former glory in the old stone heap. There was a chapel whose happy pagan rococo ceiling of stucco grapevines and cherubs, together with an indelible scent of old cold incense, filled me with dizzy delight. It was now used to store bales of undyed yarn. In another room, one as large as our school gym, that Grandmother called the knights' banquet hall, they stacked recently dyed yarn; the room stank like a glue factory.

Even as a little girl I felt that the physical combination of the old castle and Uncle Sandor's little textile enterprise was not quite right. At the bottom of the round ancient tower, for instance, a dungeon had been dug deep into the black rock. Smelly hot steam rose from this nether world, but, instead of skeletons of starved prisoners, it now harbored in its ghastly depths a monster called The Press. There the finished product of Uncle's factory was flattened into shape between big sheets of I-don't-know-what; a compound of rubber and cardboard, to judge by the smell. In the upper stories the wool was dyed, dried, and spun on wheels; immediately under the shoddy tar-paper roof clattered the looms on which the oldest, most skillful weavers experimented with new designs.

Today, when hand-loomed fabrics are much too expensive for the average household, it would be nice if I could brag about those designs and the high art of our old weavers, Binder, Boehm, and Eggenhofer. But the truth is that Uncle Sandor manufactured an atrociously ugly and cheap product. His bedspreads and table covers in flamboyant greens or reds with fat flowers of an unspeakably drab color insulted my eyes even then.

I always was, and still am, a creature of the senses rather than of the brain. I live strongly by tasting, touching, catching the sounds, the smells, the looks and atmosphere of places, things, people. I have forever hungry eyes. An unbalanced room pulls on my nerves; a conglomeration of bad architecture depresses me; and I reject— perhaps unjustly—all females with shrill or whining voices. Conversely, and probably just as unfairly, I stand defenseless before beautiful people, especially if they keep their mouths shut.

I remember my first wild disappointment with beauty. The puddles in the gutters had covered themselves overnight with a hard crust of ice. It glittered in the sun, it was full of rainbows and crystals and jewels more beautiful than Grandmama's diamonds. I broke off a few pieces of that precious ice and carried them home and hid them in a drawer with another treasure, my first attempts at writing with ink. I wanted to surprise Mama with them when she came home. Unnecessary to tell what melted ice will do to a little girl's first copybook painstakingly filled with French exercises in blue ink. I cried for hours. My first lesson in the painful process of learning that sheer beauty is not always reliable. Unfortunately the lesson didn't stick.

I haven't seen my village for sixty years except in a recurring dream in which I follow its advance into progress and ugliness. The dusty old road has become a slick four-lane highway jammed with traffic; no meadows seam it any longer; there is no meandering brook. It has become the concrete, glass, and steel complex of any industrialized place. Sometimes the castle is in my dream. It has been turned into a museum, but the gates are closed on Monday— in this dream it's always Monday—and I wrestle in vain with the authorities for permission to enter. Just for a few minutes, please, oh, please; don't you see? I lived here when I was a child. Ask Binder, ask Eggenhofer, ask Boehm, they will remember me. But I am sent away from the Wagnerian entrance gate that—in this dream —Hitler ordered built into the rocks in back of the castle. No more tower, no secret little garden up there, no return to my childhood. And so I drop in at Stepan's pub, where I am certain to find my friends, the old men who taught me spinning and weaving. Sure enough, they're there, but they don't recognize me and Stepan's pub now is not the one I knew with the rickety bowling alley in the shade of the old pear tree and the chipped blue bowl of milk put out for the house snake that lived below. It is a bare high-ceilinged room with cold efficient fluorescent lights instead of the dim smelly old oil lamp with a tin reflector. Stepan's, in my dream, has simply become a union hall where fists are shaken and curses called down on Uncle Sandor's head. Across the street are the neon lights of a night club. I hear the jazz rhythm of the drums and I wake up.

Mind you, this is only a night-time dream. Awake, my dreams of Peigarten were quite different. For many, many years I fancied that I might go back there to spend my old age at the dear forsaken place. Surely I should someday be able to afford to buy that neglected old pile of stone or lease it for another ninety-nine years. I, too, would take my grandchildren there. What fun to show them where the wild strawberries grew the juciest and the wild raspberries hung in unbelievable profusion, to lead them down to my own most secret and mysterious boulder in the midst of the cascading brook—my throne when I was a make-believe queen reigning over a kingdom without boundaries. In Peigarten I would teach my grandchildren everything I had learned from the village witch, Mother Schweik-hardt: which herbs to collect and dry for the kitchen, which would cure all kinds of sickness. And about a few that could be used for killing your enemies, or at least giving them a good bellyache. I would hand on my infallible knowledge of fifty kinds of the forest's finest edible mushrooms and a hundred poisonous ones, and my skill at tickling and catching fish with my hands, gipsy fashion. I would show them the small eye of black water in the midst of the bog where, I swear, one hot noon I had surprised the snake queen with the tiny golden crown on her flat head, a sight every bit as extraordinary as a flying saucer. I would teach them to steal the sweetest turnips from the fields, roast freshly dug potatoes over the fire when the sun began to set early and a hazy chill crept over the yellowing grasses and everything had the unbearable sweetness of vacation coming to an end, that last day's sweetness of a happiness or a love that you know is over.

So many last hours in a lifetime, so many departures and farewells; one had better go in training early.

The thing that put a stop to those fantasies about a return to my village was a little map and a few pictures I found in a magazine after World War II. A thick red line ran through the entire area: No man's land between Austria and Czechoslovakia. The magnificent woods had been cut down, leaving a wide barren strip before a barrier of barbed wire where any fugitive from beyond the Iron Curtain would be an easy target for the armed guards.

In those sleepy quiet summers, snuggling up to nature as closely as I could, I lived like a grain of wheat deep down in the dark warm earth. Whatever I became in later years grew from that seed.

Then and there my grandmother gave me the greatest gift of all—liberty, independence. She let me run free, do what I wanted. She didn't care whether I washed, ate, or slept with any regularity. I could roam all over the woods and hills, disappear for days, feed on berries and stolen fruit, stroll home in the dark, and saunter into The Presence with an air of innocent nonchalance. Grandmother would be unperturbed, although for formality's sake she might ask, "Where have you been all day long?"

"Taking care of the Peindl children. Frau Peindl is having another one and Herr Peindl is celebrating at Stepan's," I might answer. It was only a half-lie. Peindl was the village cobbler and they had a new baby each summer, as regularly as my cat had her litter. Some were twins, some died, but for some reason I had made the surviving brood my responsibility. Perhaps I was attracted by Frau Peindl's uncomplaining hardwood toughness in contrast to Grandmother's heart, Mama's nerves, Father's hypochondriac fussing.

By the time of my second summer in Peigarten I had overcome the initial hostility of the village. I had won friends and influenced people, especially among the children and particularly among the unspeakably wild and filthy kids of the gipsy field hands at the foot of our hill. Perhaps my affiliation with the Peindl brood had taken me over the first hurdles of inborn distrust and derision, and from there on I conquered by harsh, indiscriminate, and entirely unconscious methods. I caught lice from them, a runny nose, and untold infections; with them I acquired skinned knees, cuts, scratches and bruises everywhere, and an enormous and constant hunger unknown among good middle-class city children. In exchange, I learned all the useful lore of soil, plants, horses, dogs, ghosts, and snakes—harmless as well as dangerous. I learned to steal pears and apples from Stepan's trees, drive cattle to pasture and herd them home, find warm eggs hidden in the straw, cut flutes from reeds and play little Pan's melodies on them, and, to the vast amusement of Uncle Sandor on his lordly weekly visits, sing the herdboys' obscene little ditties (not understanding what they were about). My uncle seemed to have staked his pride on fattening me up during these vacations. Each week he would put me on the big scale where the wool was weighed. I grew stronger and sassier from week to week; my hair—aside from smelling of kerosene and yet attracting sticky clusters of lice—grew sleek and pretty, shining with golden glints from all the sun it soaked up, and my skin became brown as toast. I ate enormous amounts of any food I could grab, and I filled myself with so much zest and joy of life I sometimes felt I'd explode.

By the end of the summer I might have grown a puny third of an inch taller, but I definitely would have lost several pounds. Father, who usually arrived for the last two weeks of our vacation, grumbled and scolded as if being thin were my fault, a punishable shortcoming just like my frequent attacks of sore throat or catching every single children's disease rampant in my school.

On the whole, this reaction of my father's was a very effective part of my education. Henceforth, I was ashamed and afraid to let my parents know when I had a fever or pains of any sort. Thus, I learned by experience that you usually get better if you let well enough alone. It's a rule that has served me well in both my career as a musician on concert tours and in my daily duties as an orchestra member, and my career as a writer in meeting deadlines, on lecture platforms, or in my far-flung travels. I think all people in show business, down to the frailest young dancer, chorus girl, and trained seal, stay well because they can't afford not to. And so I am grateful to my father for having been so unjust and unreasonable as to make it almost sinful for me to get sick during my childhood.

My childhood came to an end on March 4, 1896. I was eight years old. I remember the date so well because in the gardens of the Inzersdorf sanatorium the darling little hepatica flowers were peeping out from under moldering leaves and the Countess helped me to find the very first violet. Each year after that I reckoned the seasons by it: March 4, beginning of spring, not by the calendar but in the woods around Vienna and the gardens of Inzersdorf. For many, many years this date was the fixed point around which my private seasons pivoted. I gave it up only when I settled in California where there are no seasons and no hepatica flowers; where the violets in my garden start blooming in January some years and other years not at all. Of such infinitesimal touches, that dry-throated feeling of exile is patched together.

Father and I had journeyed out to Inzersdorf—and a journey it was in those days—to bring Mama home. I didn't know exactly how long she had been away, but the motherless years can't have been as endless as they seemed for I had only passed my eighth birthday. Now, Papa said morosely, she was well enough to return; still, he added, clouding up some more, she will need a lot of care—"you hear me?"

I can hardly tell without getting maudlin with what expectations, jubilant excitement, not unmixed with subterranean doubts and fears, I prepared myself for that day.

At great danger I had stolen pussy willows in the park and deployed them all over our apartment; had clumsily embroidered doilies and laid them out everywhere; embroidered also very red roses on very green felt; opened my piggy bank and ordered our family shoemaker, Herr Adler, to make fur-lined mules for Mama's tiny feet. With Katl, I had laboriously dusted and waxed our furniture and gimcracks, polished the silver, brass, and copper to blinding brilliance, and I had poured gallons of sweat and oceans of love into painting a welcome sign. I myself was scrubbed, bathed, and slicked up as never before, my unruly hair tamed with Grandmother's thick rose-scented pomade, my nails clipped on hand and foot and the cuticles pushed down to show the little half moons—a painful process as every child knows. I had also secretly experimented with a cosmetic of my own invention. I had found that by chewing the pink tissue paper that the laundry put into Father's stiff white shirts, I could get a little pill of spit and paper with which I could paint my cheeks rosy red. This I did only partly for beauty's sake; mainly, it was to keep Mama from worrying about my much-commented-on sickly color. Green, my seven aunts called it!

I'll skip the warnings, admonitions, and threats Father muttered during the train trip to Inzersdorf, but at last we were there in what I dimly remember as a faintly rustic suburb like many others. Trotting after Father, I entered the grounds of the sanatorium, which did not have the slightest resemblance to the sinister visions that the unmentionable word Inzersdorf had conjured up in my mind.

My memories of that decisive day are fragments. I remember the hedges, lawns, and shrubbery, but not the building; a budding forsythia and cool wet air, the sky a blue wash with very white torn clouds that were in a great hurry to get somewhere. Then nothing, until the moment when Father coughed, knocked at a brown door, and shoved me into Mama's room. My throat was so choked, the noise in my ears so loud that I was honestly afraid I might die. I wore new solemn white kid gloves. I can still see my hands in those little gloves, timidly yet proudly held out before me, groping as if I were blind.

It was a large pleasant room, bright with sunlight. At the window a broad elderly woman in a blue uniform looked up from whatever work she was doing with rolls and rolls of colored crepe paper.

"Is my—isn't she here? But she knows that we were coming, doesn't she?" asked Papa.

"Yes, of course. She'll be somewhere in the garden with her doctor. He's giving her a last preaching before she gets dismissed, I guess. Want me to look for her?"

No, Father said, he wanted to look for her himself. "You stay here with Frau Anna. Help her with the packing maybe——"

"Never mind, we are all packed and ready to leave. So you're the little girl I've heard so much about? What's your name again? Missed your mummy, I bet."

"Not at all," I said, cold down to the marrow in my bones. But Frau Anna took me in a firm warm hug that felt good after those hugless years since Grandfather had died and Mama had left me and I'd become too big a girl, August said, to climb on a guardsman's lap.

"Now that's better, isn't it?" Frau Anna said as I struggled away from her embrace, from the dimly felt danger of thawing and melting the hard core that kept me from crying. "Look, little chick, you've got to get used to Frau Anna," she said sternly. "You'll see she's really not as bad as she looks, the old dragon. But as I'm going to live with you people and will be responsible for everything, we'd better put down a few rules right now so we'll have no arguments later. Like about regular hours when your mother needs absolute quiet and rest. And there's her diet. I'll supervise the cooking and all that—you got a pretty good maid, your father tells me—well, anyway, can I count on you? I mean, in case that kitchen dragon kicks, will you stand by me?"

Dear Lord, are they going to put me in chains again? Like Richard the Lion-hearted?

"You mean you are going to stay with Mama? All the time?" I asked feebly.

"Not all the time. Indeedy, let's hope not all the time. But for the first few months, just in case, you know."

"But where are you going to sleep? There's no bed. Or is Father moving to my grandmother's again?"

"What do you mean, where will I sleep? Where your mama sleeps, naturally. She was very sick, don't you know? It's at night that these cases need attention the most."

Housewifely worries descended upon me, tons of them, heavy, depressing. Dear Lord, dear Grandfather in Heaven, not another Frau Spandauer, I prayed ardently. In my mind I was already pushing furniture about, carved walnut, black marble. Large Katl will be furious, and all my dainty doilies, all our cleaning and polishing. . . . I had begun to sweat what felt like icicles down my back, and at the nape of my neck I was growing bristles like a porcupine.

Frau Anna, although not blessed with sensitivity, must have grasped at least some of my disappointment, for she took me to her window seat and showed me how to make roses from pink and green crepe paper. (I can still make them.) But if this was used as a form of occupational therapy, with me it missed its purpose. Sitting around and making paper roses instead of taking Mama home! Crazy, that's what it was. Mama must still be out of her mind or she would be waiting for me when she knew I was coming. Everybody was crazy in Inzersdorf, I'd known it, I'd only forgotten it in the excitement and happy expectation of this morning. Suddenly I was engulfed by fear, a heart-tightening awareness of being in a house filled from top to bottom with insane people. I was surrounded by goblins and gremlins, and what were they going to do to me, those crazies who simply didn't know what they were doing . . . ?

Then the door was banged open as by a strong wind—Mama at last? I choked and died another time. But the strange creature that rushed in was not Mama; a wondrous, a magnificently beautiful creature though, even if crazy—the Countess.

To this day I've remained grateful to the Countess for giving of her heart and light and joy and loud husky laughter to this, one of my darkest days.

The Countess was as tall as, and more handsome than, Katl's August. She was dressed in a man's riding clothes, but clothes only a circus rider might wear. A tight tunic of black velvet, tight black breeches, high riding boots of shiny patent leather. Under her arm she carried a riding crop and on her head was some sort of a hussar's shako. She had a wild, beautiful face, a deep strong voice, and at first I thought she was a man. Only a flowing mane of long black hair streaming out from under the shako showed me that she was, if not a lady, if not even precisely a woman, partly like a woman, anyway.

Poor beautiful magnificent Countess. Did good families stick their Lesbians away in sanatoriums in those days as they now do with their alcoholic grandmothers?

The Countess swept me up in her arms, kissed me and patted me, precious food for my love-starved skin, mouth, hands, thin arms. She made me forget my craving for Mama during that torturous hour of waiting, and she healed me of my fear of the insane. "Come, we'll find your mother somewhere in the garden," she told me. "We won't let her play hide-and-seek, her and her doctor friend. What fools, oh, what damned fools one meets here, my little one."

As we crossed one of the lounges downstairs, I saw Father for a moment. He was playing cards with three middle-aged gentlemen and as usual squinting cross-eyed through his spectacles at the fan of cards in his hand. This familiar scene was so normal, so routine, that I began to doubt the craziness of Inzersdorf.

"We are going to catch your wife—*in flagrante!*" the Countess called out. Father mumbled that he'd be along in a minute, just finish this one game. That's what he always said when he didn't want to stop playing cards. The Countess took me out into the garden, talking and laughing incessantly. She knew the name of each tree and plant and told me which flowers were going to grow in the neat round beds in summer. At last we got involved with the little hepatica stars.

We were both kneeling in the wet old leaves, uttering happy little cries over the hidden flower nests we uncovered, when suddenly she looked up and grew silent. "There they are now," she said quietly, rising and pulling me to my feet. I was so deep in my flower hunt I didn't grasp immediately what she meant. "Your mother and her doctor," she said. I had wet knees, wet shoes, and old leaves clinging to my skirt, I was sure my hair was a mess, and I had left my white kid gloves upstairs with Frau Anna. Suddenly my knees were not only wet but weak. "Where?" I whispered, strangled, dying for the third time.

"Over there. They're coming across the lawn. Go, run along, my little love." She pushed me away, but the next moment pulled me to her again. "Come, wait, let me hold you for just one more second. . . . Good-by, my little love, go to your mother now."

But that's not Mama, I thought. "That's—that's not my mother . . . ," I said aloud. But the Countess had disappeared behind the hedge with a wild rush, like a great black fairy-tale bird.

My mother—Mama—when she left me had been frail, fragile as the finest glass, thin, translucent. I had been in love with her, with her small hands and feet, her enormous eyes, her face, her pitiful being so weak, so sick, so crazy.

The woman now leisurely walking across the lawn was heavy, flabby, with round cheeks and a budding double chin. Her fat cheeks made her eyes seem smaller; they were still large, but not enormous as of old and no longer begging for pity. Her skin was pink and fluffy; it made me think of the piglets I had seen last summer.

No twilight, I thought as I tried to find my mama behind all that coarse flesh. No twilight. Mama used to play the piano in the late afternoons until the dusk would blot out the keys, but this woman, a stranger remotely resembling my mother, looked at me with bright alert eyes.

I don't know how many million times I had daydreamed the moment when I would meet Mama again. I would rush into her arms as lovers did in all the books I'd read. I would kiss her little hands, put my head into the hollow near her shoulder, feel her warm and soft everywhere in and around me. I would be dizzy with happiness. Maybe I would faint in that first moment of getting my mama back. Possibly I might even die in the too muchness of bliss. . . .

But now I stood stiffly, paralyzed, unable to comprehend the change Inzersdorf had worked in her.

She, too, had stopped, and was staring at me as if I were one of the less popular animals in the zoo whose names were always forgotten. The doctor had tactfully fallen behind a few steps. He was younger than Father but not really young. I took his appearance in at one glance: he looked like the picture of Felix Mendelssohn-Bartholdy in Grandfather's music room, protruding eyes, funny side whiskers, and all. A bit to the left of Mama, the forsythia sparkled with its bright golden-green buds. They stand there, sharply outlined in my memory, a color film stopped at that second, a moment frozen in time. My mother, yet not Mama any longer, the doctor who cured and changed her, the bold little forsythia still gleaming with the forenoon's raindrops.

When the film was moving on again, I made my curtsy and Mama came toward me. She didn't know quite what to say. Neither did I. "I didn't recognize you right away . . . you've grown, haven't you?" she said at last.

"Yes, Mama."

"And I'm a bit nearsighted, you know."

"Yes, Mama."

"Where is your father?"

"In there. He is playing cards," I said. My mother turned her head toward the doctor with a funny little smile which he returned. "He's playing cards," she repeated.

"Why not? He's killing time. What else do you want him to do while we keep him waiting?" the doctor asked reasonably. I disliked him a trifle less than half a minute before. Mama was trying to dig up another morsel of small talk. "How's school?" she asked finally, the same stupid unanswerable question of all grownups.

"Thanks, fine. School's fine." Before another silence could spread out of control I thrust my fistful of wet hepaticas at Mama. "There—" I said. "They are for you. I found them. Myself."

"Oh, really? Thank you, darling. Cute, isn't she?" Mama asked the doctor. Cute! Cute was the last thing in the world I was or ever wanted to be. Not even my doll Erika was cute, which was one reason I loved her. But then, Mama neither loved nor knew me. Sniffing politely at the blue flowers which smelled of moldering leaves, she turned to me. "But your hands are dirty, your skirt, too. Anyway, children are not permitted to run around here by themselves."

I hid my muddy hands in the pleats of my gray woolen skirt. Being another creation of Frau Gross it had a thick bunch of pleats on the left side and hardly any on the right. "I have new white kid gloves," I announced desperately. "And I didn't go by myself into the garden. The Countess took me."

"The Countess? Well! That's something, isn't it, doctor? Weren't you scared of her?"

"No, why should I be? She's nice. I like her."

"Really? Well, run along now and pick some flowers. Doctor and I, we have to talk over a few things."

It is a marrow-chilling experience to meet someone you once loved and don't love any more, and to me this experience came early. But it is also an experience that sets you free, releases you from the hurtful strings of bondage and teaches you irony and several kinds of humor and laughter.

And so the day Mama came back from the insane asylum was the day I stopped being a child—March 4, 1896.

I had my eyes wide open for the people around me. There was, much too early, a sardonic detachment in the way I observed and judged them. This was my family; so what? I hadn't chosen them. Why should I like these people who simply had been dumped on me? They didn't like one another either, judging by the way they talked behind their backs. "Vickerl, go look at the album," they would say, and as soon as they saw me planted in the kneehole of Father's desk, apparently engrossed in the album, they would happily come out with their juicy new bits of family gossip. I loved the album with all those funny old-fashioned photographs and daguerreotypes, but I kept my ears pricked up.

Very sharply, as if it were an absurd comedy scene I had seen on the stage, I remember the day the Family Portrait was taken. It was a solemn and festive occasion, the taking of a Family Portrait. This one was to be the wonderful gift to fulfill Grandmother's greatest wish for her seventieth birthday. The preparations were complicated and exciting. The four redheads arrived in full force; they had undertaken the long journey from Berlin only because they were indispensable to the Family Portrait. Aunt Jenny's husband, Leo, morose and coughing in a queer way as if he were ashamed of it, had for once risen from the divan where he spent the days of a man undermined by incipient but still unrecognized T.B. Uncle Leo was a tall, broad-shouldered man with a large nose and high, shiny cheekbones; he looked much stronger than anyone in our family, in which, I think, he was never really accepted as a bona fide member. Mama was afraid of him, and through the entire proceedings clung to Uncle Sandor, from whom emanated rich smiles and heavy gusts of superelegant eau d'Espagne perfume.

Yes, Mama was back with us, and this was her first precarious stepping out into the normal world again, a world not too felicitously represented by in-laws only. But today everybody was at his or her best except, naturally, my baby cousin Jack, Aunt Cora's second child, whom I was supposed to keep from wrecking the photographer's studio. Mama and the aunts were dressed in heavy black silk; what else? The gentlemen wore their long-tailed, self-respecting black coats and their dignity, and everyone smiled and joked and acted as if they were onstage. Only the photographer and his assistant appeared worried, preoccupied, and mournful, like undertakers.

"Well, let's get it over with," Father said. "Stop blocking everybody, please!" He was freshly shaved, on a Wednesday of all things. The photographer began to line us up, placing the children in the foreground, but as he started to screw us into position with the customary iron neckpiece, my little cousins understandably jerked away with frightened screams and tears of protest. At which my father—conditioned reflex—slapped them.

That started it.

He had put a match to the fuse, and all the dynamite, stored up in Father's family, as in most families, exploded. Aunt Cora, whom the photographer had placed in the center as the most photogenic, pulled the howling children to her ample bosom (like Medea in one of my hidden books) and let loose a voice trained to reach the galleries of theaters in Moravska-Ostrava, Lemberg, and Kaliningrad. Slightly, but only slightly, taken aback, Father boxed my ears, too, for good measure. Instinctively I ran to my mother, but Mama shoved me aside; she was trembling and her eyes flickered dangerously, and my need to be protected changed at once into the old tired need to protect her. It was one of the rare occasions on which I cried. But they were tears of rage, part of the rage that gripped them all. Uncle George had taken a stance like a fighter, ready to defend his wife. Aunt Jenny, shrill as a policeman's whistle, hung on to Uncle Leo's coattails to hold him back. Everybody screamed random insults. Uncle Leo, always rude and vulgar, broke out into an unknown tongue—Yiddish! There could be no more disgraceful act among the refined and thoroughly assimilated Austrian and German Jews.

Everything wrong and disgraceful the family had ever done was spit out in the raging fracas. The time that Father had to save Uncle George from bankruptcy, if not worse; and, conversely, the many times Father had been too stingy, too mean to help him. All the sins of Uncle Sandor's youth were dug up, his shameless love affairs, the grief he was causing his saintly mother, and the two children he had made with a certain woman (Could you just go and *make* children? How did you make them? And what was wrong with that?), and the no-good bum Aunt Jenny had married just for spite. And no use for Aunt Cora to act so hoity-toity, either! She wasn't any better than she ought to be: just remember what happened in Kecskemét!

At this point Uncle George hit Father with his fist; and while Father caught his breath Uncle Leo gave Uncle George two resounding blows—slap! slap! The women screamed and the last I saw before I buried my face between my knees was Uncle Sandor freeing himself from Mama's grip and stepping between the combatants.

The photographer had tactfully withdrawn; perhaps as a specialist in family portraits he was hardened to such small-time drama. Years later when I discovered Ibsen, I recognized the stuff from which he chiseled his plays.

As soon as the heavy artillery had run out of ammunition, the photographer and his lead-colored assistant reappeared, persuaded everybody back into the group, and screwed us down tight. A dignified, respectable family, doing their best to honor and cherish their old mother.

Now you know why we children and our mothers have red noses and swimming eyes and the assembled ten smiles look a bit cramped in that Family Portrait.

It was too bad that by the time Grandmother was presented with it she had lost the last remnants of her eyesight.

Whenever a physician takes my history, there are the same questions and answers: What about diseases in your family? Cancer? Mental illness? T.B.? Heart trouble?

Yes, Doctor. On my mother's side, all of this and then some. My father's family is of more durable stuff. My grandmother died at eighty-six, my great-grandmother at ninety-six, and her father saw a doctor for the first time when he was a hundred and four and didn't feel so well.

Your parents?

My mother died of cancer at forty-one; my father was killed by the Nazis at the age of ninety-three.

I, the accidental result of such haphazard crossbreeding, turned out a rather hardy hybrid.

Well, that sums up and answers for me the first of Gauguin's questions:

"From where do we come?"

he only real enemy I ever had was my father, or if there were others, I didn't notice.

He was the only person I deeply feared and hated, emotions for which I have little talent and that poisoned much of my youth. I don't know whether daughters, too, may suffer from an incipient Oedipus complex, but there were years when I wished, if not precisely to kill my father, at least to have him die before I should kill myself. Perhaps these are quite normal reactions. Perhaps every young person passes through them and forgets them, dumps them down into the tar pits of the subconscious. Perhaps most people are so constituted but are used to telling lies to themselves, or even in the confessional of the church or on the couch of the psychoanalyst; or they run so smoothly on the rails of convention that they shy away from acknowledging such uncomfortable truths. However this may be, I'm trying to put down candidly what I know and remember, at the risk of losing your sympathy, dear reader.

I often thought I would write a book about my father, but now my candle is burning down and I don't think I'll have time for it. And so I'd like to sketch here some of the things I remember about that unlovable yet original and funny man, Herman Baum.

There he is then, at first only a pair of spectacles I am trying to grab. His grasslike mustache and stubbly whiskers scratch and prickle when he jokingly rubs his cheek against mine, making me cry instead of laugh. He was an uncouth, clumsy man. He never learned to shave himself and could not be persuaded to go to the barber more than once a week. He had bad teeth but absolutely refused to see a dentist. At each refusal he gave himself an important and mysterious air as if there were some deep unmentionable danger involved, something like the Romanoffs' haemophilia rather than his plain funk. His being cross-eyed was similarly surrounded by legend and mystery; it had come from being in a draft, just like that, from one minute to the next.

I found my father ugly even when I was still a toddler. A man under middle-size, lumpy, bowlegged, stoop-shouldered. Well, so had my little grandfather been and yet I loved him with all my heart, and long after his death. But Grandfather was a warm, tender, giving man full of silly songs and jokes and merriment and games. Not so Father. I looked him over with the merciless animosity of my three years: he was a bad dirty man. I refused to believe altogether that he was my father; I disowned him. This may be a common passing experience of most children, but with me it stuck. I accepted Mama with all her uselessness, her nerves, her neurotic preoccupation with herself, and with all the grief she caused me. I never accepted Father.

The funny part was that this ugly little man was inordinately vain. Our apartment was plastered with portraits of him, some life-size. Hideous charcoal enlargements of stiff, gross photographs in elaborate gilt frames hung everywhere, over his desk, his bed, over the blue velvet sofa in the living-dining room: monuments to Caesar, the large N on Napoleon's chamber pot.

Father was a megalomaniac of high grade. He saw himself through the lens of a 200-inch telescope, a better, brighter, kindlier man more beloved and adored than anyone, somebody very special to whom special treatment was due. This resulted in countless collisions in a world that occasionally was blind to his greatness. Five minutes after entering a store, a bus, a train, a restaurant, Father invariably had started a row with the salesmen, conductors, porters, waiters, and managers, all the miserable pigmies who failed to recognize that this unprepossessing, unshaved person with the stained lapels—a bookkeeper at the local flour mill—was a king of men incognito.

I had to grow older before I could see the comical side of such a character; learn detachment instead of loathing, pity for a horizon as narrow as a minnow's mud-buried eye-view; understand that he must have been deeply frustrated and disappointed to need such outsized overcompensation, and that he had meant well all along.

There couldn't have been two more opposite people than my father and I. Whatever I liked he detested. Flowers to him were "Cow fodder! Throw them away at once! Do you hear me?" If I ever tried to mention any of the things that interested, fascinated, or delighted me, he would say with the full contempt of his ignorance: "Of what does the goose dream? Of *Kukuruz*." (*Kukuruz* is the Hungarian-Austrian word for corn.) He had never in his life read a book; to him they were all just filth and garbage. He would have been the first to join Hitler's book-burning brigades if he hadn't been a Jew. Music to him was an unpleasant noise that hurt one's ears. If he, in spite of this, permitted me to study it, it was only to learn to play the harp and earn some money. The only time he came to a concert where I played a solo he made a horrid scene afterward because he had caught me with my thick long hair down and, sin of all sins, tied back with a pink ribbon! "Like a dirty slut, a tramp, a whore!" he had yelled at me.

"What's a whore, Father?"

"Don't ask stupid questions. And don't use dirty language, hear me? What's a whore! A streetwalker, a sick piece of filth that'll croak on straw. Just as you will if you go on showing yourself in public with your hair down and pink ribbons fore and aft."

That I would croak on straw was the conclusion with which all our disagreements ended. In the meantime, I was hedged in by innumerable forbidden things.

I daresay, to make my passion for reading a secret vice was one of the best things that ever happened to me. I would borrow, steal, buy, and hide books as an alcoholic would hide bottles. Another thing Father strictly rejected was the theater. He had never seen a play in his life. "Me? Look at a play? What for?" he would ask. "Am I crazy? I've got enough to cry about at home."

Perhaps this was true. He had made a bad bargain when he had married my mother, Mathilde Donat. He had caught himself a wife who was no fun, who refused to burn incense to his exalted person —a neurotic, sick, and, later, quarrelsome wife on whom he must spend most of the dowry for which he had married her. He felt cheated. Perhaps he worried lest I had inherited some of Mama's craziness; possibly this was the reason he was so strict with me, so determined to block any path that might lead me away from drab reality. Off, then, with books, poetry, daydreams, with flowers and color, with play and friendship, anything that might soften and embellish my life. No candy for me, ever, no sweets or desserts, not even fruit, no toys, no gifts, no joys to spoil me. Later, not even friends were permitted, and I was strictly ordered to refuse other children's company on the way to and from school. This made me still more of a lone small she-wolf than the shameful secret of having a crazy mother.

Perhaps it was this Spartan upbringing, the unbending hardness of my father's Puritan mind that saved mine from flipping. . . .

Strangely, in spite of Father's contempt for art per se, he was passionately interested in dancing and ballet. Sometimes I think that he was, in all the innocence of his times, a nonpracticing, unconscious latent homosexual. Very often he referred to a blissful epoch of his life called "When I was married to Hassreiter. . . ." His lifelong friendship with the ballet master of the Opera was the axis around which my father's existence revolved.

I do not know how those two unlike fellows met in their youth. Probably Father hung around the stage door to express his admiration to Hassreiter, who, at that time, was still the *premier danseur* and mime of the Imperial Opera, and Hassreiter accepted the little services Father offered. A *premier danseur* needs fans, an unpaid claque, large loud hands in the gallery, loud voices to trump his rival's curtain calls. To Father, a free pass to an evening of ballet was reward enough.

I remember Hassreiter as a coarse, ribald, gay fellow, well-built, agile and flexible even when he was no longer young or a dancer, but had been kicked upstairs to the position of ballet master. He had a handsome Tirolean mountaineer's face, a neat round head with cropped blond hair, and very blue, very lively eyes.

When Father first met Hassreiter, the young dancer was passionately in love with a beautiful woman, a ballerina, I believe. Father never referred to her by name, just called her that slut, that bitch, *die Kanaille*—one of Vienna's inspired expressions of bastard French. Against all of Father's dire warnings Hassreiter married "that bitch," and, understandably disgusted with Father's insulting protests, dropped him with a thud. Father, heartbroken, but bent on revenge, went on the warpath. He began to spy on Madame, and in this respect Sherlock Holmes had nothing on Father. With his uncanny talent for uncovering sins and secrets, a talent with which I became familiar by sad experience, he spied on Madame, and soon he was perfectly sure that she, whom he had always known was a bitch, cheated her young husband with a still younger lover. In Father's tale, said lover was *"Black,* one of those *Brazilians."* Bravely he marched up to Herr Hassreiter and informed him of his wife's adultery, bringing with him a written report of the times and places of repeated fornication. Herr von Hassreiter responded with a good slap in Father's face—a *Watschen,* it is called in Vienna.

Then began an interlude of bitter silence and hurt, a pitch-dark time, until the news filtered through to Father: Madame was pregnant. When the child was born, he was—indeed, Father stormed, what else could one expect—*black.* Not as black as the Senegalese doorman of the Hotel Bristol, but black enough to vindicate Father completely. Whenever he came to this triumphant part of his tale, you had an impression that the baby was delivered black-and-brown-striped, like a zebra.

In any case, Hassreiter kicked out Madame and returned heartbroken to cry on Father's ready shoulder. This was the beginning of those shining months, the crest of his life to which he referred as "When I was married to Hassreiter." Speaking of it, Father sounded like a man drunkenly remembering his honeymoon.

Never in their fifty-odd years of friendship did the two men call each other by first names. Father retained the respectful "Herr Hassreiter" (or even with Austrian courtesy, "Herr von Hassreiter") and was in return addressed as *"You!* Baum!" No honorary "von" there.

In fact, they never realized that they were friends. In Hassreiter's absence Father referred to him wrathfully as "that scoundrel." In turn, Hassreiter spoke of Father contemptuously as "that dirty old Jew." This was another curious side of their friendship. Father was stubbornly Jewish and Hassreiter a convinced anti-Semite, although both the Jewishness and the anti-Semitism were of the mellow, passive, partly corrupt, partly good-natured Austrian brand, too tolerant, as well as too lazy, to fight. Despite the low esteem in which they held each other, there was not a day that they were not together.

After Hassreiter's marriage had been dissolved, there was an awful mess left, an Augean stable that Father set about cleaning with Herculean energy. Taking stock of the situation, adding up the debts Madame had left behind in the neat figures so dear to Father's accountant's soul; computing a budget, finding a less expensive apartment for the two of them; making menus, fighting their maid over the household money, going to market himself to search for bargains —what thrills, what joys, what high satisfactions. Better yet, now Father felt it his duty to hang around the Opera House every free minute. He had passes for every performance in which Hassreiter appeared. He met most of the ballet girls, he was introduced to the inner circle of balletomanes and dancers. Hypochondriac that he was, Father worried his head off about "that rascal's" health. He would wait in the dressing room for the sweating dancer, rub him dry, bundle him up, wrap scarves around his strong neck, stuff cotton wool in his fine ears, and try by hook or by crook to get him home sober, safe, and celibate.

All this went against Hassreiter's grain. Perhaps he accepted the puritan regime for the first few weeks as a sick man, after a painful operation, will tolerate the ministrations of an awkward nurse. He, such a ladies' man, such a favorite of the women, must have been stunned by the knockout blow Madame had given his masculine pride. But coming up at the count of nine, he slugged it out and recovered by the usual therapy of a healthy, virile, and spiteful male.

He drank and gambled, he slummed, he wenched, sleeping indiscriminately with every female he could grab. His new debts, new scandals, hangovers, were followed by artistic decline. "His knees got so soft he could hardly stand straight, lost his elevation; his *entrechats* were a spectacle to make you sick," Father would say, and even the remembrance of those long past times drove the angry blood to his forehead. Hassreiter slid down from *premier danseur* to first mime, a position usually reserved for aging, broken-down dancers. Father resolved that something drastic had to be done.

Hassreiter must get married again. To give up their idyl was a heroic decision on Father's part, but dimly he felt that a woman might have the ability to keep that scoundrel straight that he himself, unfortunately, lacked. Like St. Paul, of whom he had never heard, he seemed to conclude that for a man who apparently couldn't live without a woman in his bed every night, it was better to marry than to burn. Without discussing this with his friend, Father went into action.

I should like to have seen him sweat out that tactful, not too expensive, newspaper ad. It probably read something like: GENTLEMAN, 45, ELEG. APPRCE, SECURE POS., WISHES HONORABLE ACQUAINTANCE WITH DECENT LADY IN HER 30'S, GOOD-LOOKING, DOWRY DESIRABLE, WIDOW PREF.—this last a proud foray into sex psychology. Even Father sensed that a widow's experience would be necessary to handle his friend at this point.

For days avalanches of letters arrived at the general delivery window of the post office, not all bona fide offers of marriage. Father sorted them out methodically; it must have been a shattering glimpse of life for him who had never lived. At last he made his choice, a good-looking young widow with dowry. What followed next she told me herself.

Deliberately she arrived earlier than agreed at the rendezvous, a pleasant sidewalk café in a quiet residential suburb. She sat down at a table behind a small ivy screen from which she could observe the aspirant without being seen herself. As chaperon she had brought along the customary ugly girl friend every pretty woman uses as a foil. This Aunt Slavek, whom I remember as the very soul of kindness however red-nosed, flat-chested, and bad-complexioned, was placed at another table, staked out, so to speak, like the goat at a lion hunt. As agreed, she wore a white carnation pinned to her deficient front.

Father, too, had a white carnation in his buttonhole. He was alone, cross-eyes, bowlegs, dandruff, stained lapels, and all. He

peered around through his spectacles. The widow looked him over
from her vantage point and thought, Oh, my God! What an ugly
toad! "You go talk to him," she signaled to her friend. "Send him
away." Girl friend approached Father just as he pulled out his watch
and reproachfully held it in his hand. As he looked up, he noticed
the white carnation on Aunt Slavek and said to himself: "What?
Oh, no! This female in the shape of an ironing board will never do
for Hassreiter!" And there the negotiations would have terminated
had not the young and indeed very pretty widow risen impatiently,
whispered to her friend not to waste time, and moved toward the
exit.

In a panic about the obvious double-misunderstanding, Father
chased after her crying: "No, no, it's not me—it's *him!*" thrusting
some of Hassreiter's photographs under her eyes. Hassreiter in mufti,
debonair, dazzling; Hassreiter in costume, the tights irresistibly displaying his strong long leg muscles; Hassreiter as Harlequin in a
capricious *commedia dell'arte* pose, holding out a large broken papier-
mâché heart; and again as a romantic lover kneeling inconsolably below a painted moon at Giselle's grave.

Greatly impressed, the pretty widow and her ugly friend sat down
once more, and Father developed his plan of strategy. He demanded
her holy word of honor never, never, in all her life, to give away the
prosaic fact of having responded to a marriage advertisement. She
must meet Hassreiter by chance. Father would arrange it, and——

"And from there on I'll take over," the widow said firmly. "Leave it
to me or we'll spoil it all." She said "we," one of the great moments
in Father's life. What she meant was "you," you'll spoil it all, you
poor clumsy little schlemiel.

Since Father saw himself as a man who knew and did everything
incomparably better than anyone else, one who simply knew he was
superior to all philosophers and scientists and professors, who could
have governed the monarchy with his little finger by simply abolish-
ing all taxes, he naturally also thought himself a diplomat of the
highest order. For once, however, he deferred to another's wishes and
handed the reins to the energetic and pretty young widow. And so, in
due time and quite by accident, ballet-master Hassreiter met Frau

Cilli, fell inevitably in love, got married, and begat in quick succession three daughters, each prettier than the last.

The impact of Frau Cilli's healthy beauty, her sense of humor, her generous, warm, and decent character hit my father so hard that he never entirely recovered. Until her death he remained deeply devoted to her.

I think that Father eventually married more or less to do Frau Cilli a favor. Feeling himself to be the *deus ex machina* of their happy marriage, he seems to have expected to become a most welcome part of it. In the gay, happy, rich atmosphere of their home he installed himself snug as a little gray worm in a sweet juicy apple. Completely lacking imagination, incapable of ever noticing anybody else's reactions, his constant presence must have driven the young, though not too young, couple frantic. Until Frau Cilli, bless her, found a painless way of dislocating Father, as you dislocate a tick without breaking its head off: Father, too, must get married. He, too, ought to experience the fulfillment and joy they had found. Urged on, shoved and pressed, Father went out to look around among the daughters of the land. By the time his choice was made he was forty years old. Family legend has it that he had never touched a woman until then. Mother was eighteen, small, soft, and very pretty, the third of six daughters. The parents of six girls couldn't be very choosy and it was her turn to be married off.

After Frau Cilli had successfully persuaded Father out of his cozy berth in her marital life and into getting engaged to be married himself, she and her husband, and maybe even Father, began to worry. Would he be capable of performing his marital duty? Doubts, grave doubts on all sides. However, Hassreiter resolutely tackled the problem. In the ballet corps there existed what he called the Old Brigade, trained specialists in the art of breaking in the inexperienced sons of high aristocracy or giving the thin-blooded, overexperienced elderly members of the Jockey Club an illusion of virility.

To one of these good-natured, jolly ladies the ballet master delivered Father with discreet orders to see if he could function. The nice old girl thought it a great lark and went to work. Everything in style, the grand style of the corseted and bustled 1880's—*chambre particulière,* champagne, seduction. "It wasn't much fun, but it's all right," she reported. "He functions." And so my parents' wedding took place with the prescribed bourgeois trimmings.

I believe my mother had been playing with dolls until that day. And as her mother, too, had remained a child, she let her daughter stumble into her wedding night with no better instructions than that a bride had to endure whatever unpleasant and indecent activities to which the groom might expose her. To my mother it sounded quite similar to the lecture given before her first visit to the dentist. In her colossal ignorance the little bride probably hoped to be let off easily. The dentist had never found any cavity in her strong white teeth and had never hurt her. . . .

There she is now—and this I have from my mother herself—for the first time alone with her husband. All innocence, stupidity, obedience, with the finest hand-knitted white silk stockings, white satin shoes size 4-A, white veil, and a bride's white myrtle wreath. Father, too, is probably shaking in his patent leather shoes, because how, for God's sake, do you make a start with a *virgin?* He asks her a few clumsy questions, discovers her abysmal ignorance. He is touched by it, but this makes a difficult situation, oh, so much more difficult. The hired coach rattles over the cobblestones, it is getting dark, it's raining. Father tells the coachman to take a ride around the Ring. That's expensive but he needs time to explain the facts of life to his little wife. I'm sure he did it methodically, in good certified accountant style and in the coarse and direct expressions of a middle-aged bachelor.

Mama shivered, shuddered, sighed with fright, swallowed tears. How did Father know all those dirty things? Honest to the bone as he was, he proceeded to confess what he had done to that ballet girl and what she, tutor in the *ars amandi,* had done to him. Perhaps if he had lent a glimmer of passion or a spark of pleasure to the report about his pitiful affair, Mama might have understood, felt maybe a bit of warmth for the poor fish she had married. But he pointed out over and over, indeed he couldn't emphasize it enough, that he had done *it* only as his duty, however unpleasant, only as a favor to his friends the Hassreiters, only to make sure that he was fit to become a husband. By the time they arrived at their home (no honeymoon trip, too expensive), Mama had turned to stone.

In the middle of this utterly Victorian wedding night she ran away. Back to her parents, like many a shocked and shattered bride before. Early in the morning her father once more delivered her into the hands of her husband. Perhaps Grandfather, the man of the world, the stormy romantic, gave him a few hints about handling a very young and sensitive bride. And she submitted as she was ordered, as thousands of girls have submitted to unwanted, unloved men.

So, in due course, I was born, as fat a baby as the ambitions of those times demanded and, with our Dr. Pollatschek's assistance, it turned out to be a very difficult birth.

Extremely difficult and dangerous for my father. First, there was the disappointment of my emerging as a girl. So certain had he been of a son, that he hadn't even provided a name except Victor (although I was actually christened Hedwig and always called Vicki), and for years he addressed me as "my son" whenever he was in one of his rare good moods. No sooner had Dr. Pollatschek left when Mama suffered a heavy hemorrhage that might easily have taken her life. "Great Heavens, what a terrible day I had! Simply terrible!" was Father's comment. "It took me weeks before I could sleep well again —terrible."

As for Mama, she never recovered completely from the combined shock of sex and childbirth. I, the innocent cause and result of all the trouble, was handed to a wet nurse or rather to a succession of wet nurses, all of them rebelling against Father's suspicions and tyranny. By their very nature, as professional mothers to illegitimate babies, wet nurses were a full-blooded, full-bodied, highly emotional lot. They drank, they had lovers, they caught fleas, bedbugs, and gonorrhea. They were chronically upset, which made their milk turn sour and gave the baby colic.

In the meantime, something incomparably more important than the mere birth of a child had entered Father's life. Herr Hassreiter had opened a Dance Institute, the finest, most fashionable in all Vienna. There the children of the best families received their first instruction in the social graces and deportment. Of course, not by the ballet master in person, but at the hands of slick teachers, Herr Kopetzki and Herr Dubois; Hassreiter only put in some supervisory appearances, with Father faithfully tagging after him.

It is funny and somewhat touching to remember the extent to which that ugly, ill-groomed little man was possessed by his passion for dancing. I suppose that at first he wormed his way into the institute by keeping an eye on the teachers and the always mildly tipsy red-nosed piano player; looking after the money that came in; helping Fräulein Irma, a praying mantis sort of female, with the management. By and by he began to take an active part in the teaching of the advanced classes, showing off his inspired waltzing, bowlegged, stoop-shouldered, cross-eyed, and unshaven as he was. But his greatest joy and glory came on Sunday evenings in the two hours of what was called the "Perfection."

In the Vienna of those days there were no night clubs or dance halls. Society had their brilliant balls and *redoutes*. At the other end of the social scale, servant girls on their days off danced cheek-to-cheek with their soldiers in the low-class coffeehouses of the Prater. And the young boys and girls of good families met at modest dances arranged in dancing schools or private homes. The Perfection served a different purpose. There the gilded youth could dance to their hearts' content with Vienna's *süsse Madln,* all those pretty, gay, and sentimental young salesgirls and fashion models who wanted to get a boy friend, fall in love, and have a good time without restrictions or scruples. Looking like an old toad among grasshoppers and butterflies, Father moved sternly, without a glint of humor, insisting with his particular blindness on the utmost in chaste behavior and morals. He would separate couples whose waltzing seemed too enraptured, introduce timid fellows to forward girls and vice versa, and, sacrificing himself, he would dance with the rare wallflowers. But his most glorious moments arrived each Sunday when he chose the best dancer among the girls and in the cleared center of the hall showed her and himself off in a masterful waltz. What an exhibitionist he was, my funny father, what a demon-ridden guy when he danced! Strangely, during those crowning waltzes he shed his ugliness; whirling, floating, flying, he became the embodiment of the slightly old-fashioned elegance that was the essence of Vienna.

I believe the Dance Institute, and especially the Perfection, presented the only real fulfillment my father ever knew. Yet at home he insisted on acting the martyr. Not a free evening, no Sunday, no holiday, no rest! He was exhausted, his feet hurt, his throat was sore. He developed a nervous throat-clearing; it signaled his arrival the moment he stepped onto the wide, overacoustical staircase. A sort of panic would grip our whole ménage. Confusion and haste in the kitchen; Mama shouting contradictory orders, anxiously closing all windows against a possible draft. I would get the inhalator ready, the slippers, the greasy red fez Father wore at meals. The basin of warm water was brought in for me to bathe Father's knobby feet. Hating every second of this Biblical ceremony, I would curse all hospitable women of the Old and New Testaments for putting on an act that they probably found as repulsive as I did. Since Father had taken over the high command at the Dance Institute, his megalomania went out of all bounds. He considered himself a master, a star, and behaved accordingly. To save his voice, he spoke only in whispers, except when he forgot and shouted insults at Mama, maid, and me. He was never seen without an upturned collar plus several mufflers. Before he went to bed we had to soak old socks in lard and tie them around his throat while he coughed falsely, like a child greedy for syrup. "My God, can't you do it yourself?" Mama would ask disgustedly, spreading her greasy fingers. No, Father could not. Except on the dance floor, he was the clumsiest person on earth. Daily we had to put him into his socks and shirt, button him up like a baby; he never learned the kindergarten tricks of tying a shoelace, handling a safety pin, and at his place the white tablecloth was always a multicolored palette with the stains of soups and sauces and vegetables.

Grandmother was still alive when Father began, in unconscious imitation of her, to breathe hard, close his eyes, grope for his heart; to feel his pulse, earnestly study his tongue in the mirror, pluck at the veins on the backs of his hands. I don't know whether those demonstrations worried Mama; I think she was too occupied with herself. By and by she established her manic-depressive cycle. For hours, days, weeks she would be entirely turned inward, sitting on the blue sofa, endlessly rubbing the crystal beads of her long chain, staring at nothingness with flickering eyes. There were other days, sometimes weeks, when she was normal, only a little too much so. She would talk too much, laugh too long or too loudly, busy herself with many beginnings but finish nothing. Euphoria and melancholia took turns. Where before she could not sleep, now she didn't want to get up; where formerly she had been unable to eat, she now was gorging herself at all hours, getting fat and heavy and a bit vulgar, contaminated, perhaps, by the tone and manners of the company she met at the card games in the Hassreiters' home, mostly former ballet girls and their husbands.

To me, though, it was life-saving to be able to spend weekends and holidays with the three gay, carefree Hassreiter girls.

There everything was day-bright, easygoing, generous, a happy contrast to the dark, cramped narrowness of life under my father's dominance. And such marvelous food, such strictly forbidden delights for palate and shrunken stomach. The girls fed me, stuffed me, shielded me from my father's angry scoldings, protected me, hid me, saw to it that I, too, found a pile of gifts at their incredibly lavish Christmas celebrations. I still remember the shape and texture of every one of the old tree ornaments—they were old even then, in 1905—and to this day I insist stubbornly, and against all city ordinances, on having real candles and the fragrance of melting wax on my tree.

The three girls—Pini, Mitzi, and Bertha—were truly beauties, tall, slender, blond, and blue-eyed like their father, enriched with the laughter, earthiness, and good nature of Frau Cilli. There was a difference of six years between me and the youngest one; the oldest was out of my reach, but to the two younger ones, Pini and Mitzi, I clung tenaciously as to an older sister surrogate. I like to think that they were fond of me in their lighthearted way, amused, at times baffled, as by the antics of a somewhat exotic pet. "That child is getting too bright!" Mitzi would say, with a mixture of admiration and reprimand. . . . "Leave her alone. She can't help being a precocious brat," Pini would defend me. . . . "Yes, she is, but it isn't healthy,"

Mitzi would conclude, and then they would be off to play tennis, flirt, or dance with a flock of elegant young men who were all madly in love with them.

I realized very early that I could never be like those best friends of mine, I would always remain the child who presses her nose to the window, outside, looking in. A few years later, when Thomas Mann's first novels found their way into my hands, as in a mirror I recognized myself and them, those gay, harmless ones, unburdened, unknowing of the depths and darknesses that are the writer's province. . . .

Meanwhile, card playing took an ever larger place in my father's life; a day or an evening without it seemed as unbearable to him as the tortures of an addict bereft of his dope. In this respect, the Hassreiter ménage was his refuge. There a card table was always ready, often two, sometimes three, as at the court of Louis XIV. Mostly they played tarock, a game still played in Austria. In an emergency, Hassreiter and Father would even play a two-handed version of it— *Strohmandel* ("Little Strawman")—in the course of which they cursed and insulted each other incessantly; a healthy outlet for their aggressions, I'd say. But from time to time they would break out in a rash of games of chance at high stakes, which Father could ill afford. The odd part of those games was that Father was a schlemiel in them as in everything else. Other gamblers can count on a certain law of averages by which losses and gains will eventually come out fairly even. Not so Father. He lost, inevitably and always. He, the stingy, miserly, overcautious man, took crazy chances, threw all rules and warnings to the wind—and lost.

Late into the night the post-mortems would go on in my parents' bedroom, growing louder and louder, as Mama in crescendo reproached, scolded, cried, screamed, and Father swore and barked back. I stuffed handkerchiefs into my ears, clenched my fists, pulled my flat horsehair pillow over my head, getting greener and thinner from too much work and too little sleep.

Still, I wouldn't think of Father as having been a gambler if it were not for one surprising revelation he later made that rounded out this queer characteristic.

In a drawer of his writing desk he kept a large ledger locked away.

At times he would take it out, demanding absolute quiet: "Can't you see I'm working, it's something terribly difficult, I need concentration, you don't realize how difficult and important this is!" Under no circumstances would he disclose the nature of this work to my mother. "You couldn't understand it, not in a thousand years, a stupid goose like you. Can't even keep the household book in order, dumb cow, you!" The household book was another subject of the daily and nightly fights. True, Mama couldn't handle money, couldn't keep track of the daily expenses; she simply lumped them all together under MISCELLANEOUS.

From time to time I stole a glance over Father's shoulder and shuddered at the endless columns of digits and fractions, calculations of the sort that nowadays are made by mammoth machines. Having filled another page or two with his secrets, Father would clear his throat, slam the ledger closed, and push it into the drawer, turning the key twice for safety before he secured it on his person.

Only when he was a very old man did he disclose his secret to me: all his life he had been working on a watertight system for breaking the bank of Monte Carlo! Poor Father, poor little Sisyphus. All his life he had almost found it. Almost. Always he was just an infinitesimal fraction away from the absolute, the last, pure, unquestionable perfection.

Thus the years of my father's life went by, monotonously; he, who had never been young, did not grow old either. Shabby and careworn from the beginning, he couldn't grow shabbier, gloomier, or grayer, inside or out.

Until it came to the great, dramatic crisis in which he risked a complete break with his lifelong friend, "that scoundrel," rather than let dear Frau Cilli get hurt.

At that time he must have been in his middle fifties and Hassreiter about sixty, the somewhat unbalanced change-of-life period for both. Hassreiter, still handsome, gay, elastic, but shoved aside by Gustav Mahler's reforms, might have grown a little bitter, restless; his and Father's nervous duets at throat-clearing sounded alarming, and both gentlemen were independently warned by their physicians to cut down on drinking wine with meals and cognac during card games.

But the pleasure of a glass of wine or champagne was harmless compared to another interest entering Hassreiter's orbit just then, in the person of a not strikingly pretty nor outstandingly talented ballerina. A somewhat washed-out blond, she found a new, ingenious way to his steel-plated heart. Clearly, the ballet master had a professional's rhinoceros-thick skin as far as the beauty and seductiveness of his ballet girls were concerned. To him they were *in toto* a useless baggage.

I can still hear his nervous throat-clearing and his ever repeated clarion call: "An innocent girl! A decent, innocent girl! Would you believe it? A virgin, so help me God!"

"A virgin, oh, my ass!" Father would shout, outraged by his friend's blindness. "Now he has the nerve to bring her to his home! Frau Cilli has to shake the hand of that foul little rat! My God, that girl is no older than his daughters; has he lost his mind completely? Betraying my Frau Cilli! She is much too good for that old idiot! But just leave it to me! Just leave it to old Baum! I'm still there to stop him, the swine. He won't get away with this! Just wait and see!"

There ensued then a complete repetition of the tragedy that had ended Hassreiter's first marriage; except this time Father went into action, not to protect his friend against harm and deceit, but his friend's wife, his adored Frau Cilli. He spied upon the young dancer whom the errant ballet master promoted again and again, far beyond her actual merits. Suspecting that the girl was carrying on with one of the solo dancers, the master sleuth decided to play the debasing role of friend to both. That summer we did not spend our vacation in my beloved village but in a little old Bohemian town across the border where the Moldau burbled as young and bubbling as in Smetana's symphonic poem. There, during the week, the girl, accompanied by a sister, pursued her innocent and virginal existence; on weekends, though, the sister retreated and the suspected dancer came for a visit.

Like a desperate lover, Father would spend the nights outside her window in the hope of catching the two *in flagrante*. I don't know whether he ever did, but on our return from our four weeks' vacation he marched straight into the ballet master's office and informed him that the girl was neither innocent nor faithful and most certainly not a virgin. This, he claimed, he had directly from the horse's mouth, that is, from her young man, who had been bragging over a few glasses of beer.

Perhaps my father, poor schlemiel, expected a great triumph for himself, the undying gratitude of both Frau Cilli and friend Hassreiter. He ought to have known better. Hassreiter, in the senseless infatuation of middle age, kicked him out, forcibly and for good—out of the Dance Institute, the daily card game, his snug second home in the Hassreiter establishment.

After this catastrophe, as though Father had broken through the thin ice of a deep, black lake, the dark waters of impenetrable gloom closed over him. Once, I remember, he bought himself a ticket to the Sunday Perfection, where now the hated Herr Kopetzki reigned, slick, well-dressed, and demonstrating a waltz every bit as dazzling as Father's had been.

Next, suddenly, both our middle-aged men began to ail and get old. Father complained of spells of vertigo, loss of appetite, of sleeplessness; his hand went to his heart whenever you looked at him, and the whole man shrank and sagged, grew less belligerent but still more morose. His spirit was broken to such an extent that at last he saw a dentist and acquired a complete set of false teeth hoping to prevent his gastric troubles by chewing his food well. Now we had a new ritual: he would wear the denture all day long to get accustomed to it. Only when he sat down for meals he would take it out and dump it into a glass of water. And there it sat, between the boiled beef and the spinach, grinning malevolently at Mama and me while Father masticated painfully with his toothless gums and his stomach got worse.

Hassreiter suffered from sciatica and nosebleeds. If I remember rightly, it was Frau Cilli who, after some worrisome months, threw a precarious bridge over the abyss that separated the two aging, unhappy men. In the meantime, the scheming young ballet girl had achieved her purpose; she had advanced to the post of prima ballerina, and without much sentimental embroidery sent Hassreiter back to his connubial bed. "Best prima ballerina we ever had," the ballet master insisted, stubbornly covering his retreat. Father, for once less tactless than usual, or else sufficiently chastened, only shrugged his skeptical, round shoulders.

"Come on, let's get going, let's play cards"—Frau Cilli sounded the old call to arms, and the games resumed as though no sinister menace and deadly battle had ever interrupted them.

At home, though, Life with Father grew ever more difficult as I entered my years of adolescence and open rebellion. It's ever the same, this problem and crisis between parents and offspring. The young ones change while their elders remain static; they're stuck with themselves, sacks of cement forgotten in the rain and irrevocably hardened.

Not even when Mama was found to have an inoperable and lethal cancer did Father change. He muttered that he couldn't stand it, packed his old black satchel, and moved to Grandmother's. Once or twice a week he would put in an appearance, sit at Mama's bedside— but not too near—his face expressing his thought that cancer was a contagious disease. "And who tells you it isn't contagious? . . . The doctors? . . . Oh, leave me alone with your doctors. Idiots, all of them!" he would shout. I don't think he was ever present during the worst hours, never heard her piercing screams of pain, never at night when she was convulsed by chills, fears, doped nightmares. He was not even there when the men with the coffin came to carry her off.

But at the funeral he broke into tears. I saw him crying bitterly, heard him sobbing loudly. It's a shattering experience to see a man, a father, an enemy, cry like that. It somewhat changed my attitude toward him.

Only once more did I ever see him cry, and it surprised me beyond words because this time he was crying for me.

After the strain of being Mama's full-time nurse, I suppose my reservoir of resistance was at a low point. I felt sick for almost a year without ever missing a rehearsal or a concert; this time, I was too sick to hide the fever that for weeks later kept me unconscious, delirious, burning down like a candle. Dr. Pollatschek, after bungling the older members of the family into their graves one by one, had at last been replaced by young Dr. Popper. But neither he, nor the various consultants he called in, could come to a definite diagnosis, let alone a treatment, except packing me in ice. When I bobbed up from the blurred darkness of a streptococcus sepsis, that might at first have been a typhoid brain fever, the raging and roaring in my head gave way to a strange lucidity. I saw my father silhouetted against the window on which he was leaning, his forehead buried in his fists, his shoulders shaking. With a shock I realized: Father was sobbing!

"What's the matter, Father?" I whispered. I suppose I hadn't spoken a single reasonable word in weeks and I was helplessly weak, but the feeling of weakness and chilly clarity was quite agreeable.

"They say you're dying. The doctors. Those idiots! You're *not* dying; you hear me? You're all that's left to me! You can't leave me!" he said. It was an order.

Then the nurse bustled in, packed me tightly into a freezing wet sheet, and placed me on a layer of ice . . . like a salmon in aspic, I thought, and then I slipped once more down the dizzy chute into unconsciousness. . . .

Still, that father, that enemy of mine, had cried for me. . . .

I survived after all, my recuperation a painful snail crawl that ushered in a time of comparative peace, call it an armed truce or a cold war. As everybody knows now from bitter experience, any small border incident may be blown up into an enormity, an insuperable provocation, a precarious status quo.

It happened between Father and me when some busybody discovered that a little story I had written had won first prize in an obscure magazine in Munich. Father, hating and fearing the printed word as if it were written by Satan, couldn't have been more outraged if he had learned that I was a well-known prostitute, spreading venereal disease and unconscionable filth among my customers.

We had a row to end all rows. I ran pell-mell into the thick concrete wall of Father's incomprehension. With my harmless little piece of fantasy I had irremediably dishonored myself, his good home, him, the whole family. The names he called me on that occasion transcended anything I had been called before. The first article of my unconditional surrender demanded my sacred word of honor never in my life to write another word.

This I refused to do.

I was far from thinking of myself as a writer; to tell the truth, I never really did. I was a musician, a good, reliable professional. Music was my vocation and my life, or so I was convinced. But how could I promise to give up the delights of dreaming up fanciful little tales, threading words to please myself, choosing the dark ones to make others by contrast glitter the more? Ever since I could talk I had made up stories and told them to myself, and had written them down from the time I could write. I might as well have sworn that I'd never bite into an apple again, or try to change the color of my eyes.

This row gave me the deciding little push. I left Father and got married. I found a good middle-aged housekeeper for Father, and his life went on smoothly. I really think he was happier as a widower, without the encumbrances of wife and child. For a few months he took a sardonic pleasure in reading the responses to a poisonous advertisement he had run: WIDOWER IN SECURE POSITION, SIXTY-TWO YEARS OLD, WISHES ACQUAINTANCE WITH PRETTY YOUNG GIRL NOT OLDER THAN SIXTEEN; MARRIAGE NOT EXCLUDED. This was his idea of a good joke. Did he get offers? Of course he did. In batches, fathers and mothers, aunts and guardians, eagerly offered young girl flesh to the widower. "You see?" Father would say contentedly, reinforced in his crushing contempt for all human beings except himself. "They're filthy pigs, all of them."

That was in 1908.

It is Christmas, 1916. I have been married and divorced. I have moved to Germany, I have remarried, and now I expect my first baby. We live in Kiel, in the North, an uninviting town at any time, but in 1917, with the war almost lost and famine and general need at their height, a truly infernal place. Small, unkempt, and cold, swept by the never-ceasing North Sea winds, the town is bursting at the seams with the entire German Navy bottled up there, plus the thousands of workers building more submarines in endless day and night shifts. (Since the bloody stalemate in the trenches of the Western front, submarines are almost the last offensive weapon left to Germany.) The water in the pipes has frozen and the pipes have burst. The gas mains are turned off, except for two half-hour spells a day. There is no food for civilians, no fuel, nothing. My husband is a civilian, a musical director of the civic opera, who holds his job on a day-to-day basis. At His Majesty's decree the theaters must remain open to keep up the morale of the desperately restless men. In front of the town hall, machine guns are planted to warn the populace against revolting. Even so, a year later the revolution started in Kiel.

As a pregnant woman I had applied for my rations of baby clothes and linens. The authorities said no to such luxuries . . . I was to give birth on paper sheets, and bed the baby on paper. I was entitled to three baby shirts, three diapers, three cotton squares to wrap the newborn in. I had cut up the last of my worsted dresses and made it into little warm jackets. They were too scratchy for a baby, but there was not an inch of wool to be had anywhere. As for food, all I could procure for our Christmas dinner were a few small gritty mussels. During World War I, Father and I had exchanged occasional coldly polite letters. In one of them I had mentioned casually that I was pregnant, but had not said a word about our miserable needs. But the day before Christmas, a parcel arrived that proved to contain a gift straight from Heaven, a wealth I hadn't known still existed—my own baby layette. I touched the soft wools and batistes, the little knitted jackets and booties. Even the thick padded clothes and bands with which I'd been swaddled—now outmoded, obsolete, and long since declared unhygienic—were there. Who had kept all this through the years? Who had preserved it, found it, had it washed and ironed? Who, in Heaven's name, had thought of it and sensed my need?

What a funny, unpredictable guy he was, this father of mine.

Six years pass, it is 1922, and we face another grim winter. We have almost reached the peak of that insane, out-of-control German inflation. We count our marks in millions and billions. Promptly each noon the quotation changes. It does not gradually rise; it leaps ahead by astronomical figures. Every worker in the whole country is paid each morning his wages for the preceding day, and the millions he cannot spend before twelve o'clock noon he may as well throw away; they have no value at all. Early in the morning, lines form in front of bakeries and butcher shops, breathless old women or young boys arrive, like messengers in high drama, to deliver the worker's wages while there is still food to be bought. But frequently it is too late. The shops and markets are usually sold out long before noon, when a sign goes up in the window announcing the new, impossible rate of exchange for the day. Moaning and cursing, we, the women, disperse after another lost battle. The children cry, they are hungry. . . .

I know, I know . . . what the home front suffered during the First World War is pale and puny compared with the disasters of the Second. But it isn't much consolation to know that each war is more cruel and merciless than the one before. If the victorious world had been more magnanimous after World War I; if it had saved the beaten and chastised Germany from utter misery, hunger, and despair; if there had been a Marshall Plan then, Hitler and his mass murderers and the graves and ruins of World War II could have been avoided. This, at least, was one lesson the United States learned. Will she have learned it well enough to prevent the roller coaster of war propaganda from getting out of control again?

Our miseries now were so much harder to bear since there had been a short reprieve immediately after the war, harder also because we knew that food was there, somewhere, in the hands of black marketeers, those who could pay and swap.

I didn't belong to them. In fact, I was a bit worse off than the majority. My husband had become the General Music Director of Mannheim, one of the most cherished positions an ambitious young conductor could hope for. Meanwhile, I was left in Hanover with our little boys, five and two years old, until such time as the housing authorities would allot us an apartment at our new destination. Like everybody else, my husband was paid daily in each day's new currency, but before the mail could deliver it to me, the money was absolutely worthless. We were living, to express it plainly, on the crumbs friends would occasionally drop us. But now even these last resources had run out.

That week the desperate populace had plundered and looted most of the food stores, after which the butcher, the baker, the candlestick maker rolled down their iron shutters over the splintered windows, and sheer naked hunger stalked the silent streets. At the same time it had turned very cold, so cold that once again the water not only froze in the pipes but burst them in the bargain, making an awful mess of bathrooms and kitchens, mixing sewer water and drinking water in frozen, polluted clumps of ice. Naturally, the heating system, too, had given out, and to fill the measure, I was again pregnant —a blatant case of unplanned parenthood.

The little boys cried with cold and hunger. I bundled them up in their cribs and divided a crust of bread between them. I scraped the last bit of condensed milk from a can and was in the midst of changing an old bottle of mineral water, with the help of salt and caraway seed, into a sort of warm soup, when something went very wrong inside of me.

Losing a baby is not much fun even under comfortable conditions, and I don't propose to fish the memories of those days from the dark waters of my subconscious where I have managed to drown them. Enough to mention that no bed was free in any of the town's hospitals and it seemed an eternity before my doctor could be found. But I had given birth to both my sons without a doctor and in my own bed (partly on account of the war and partly out of an obstinate curiosity to know how it felt to give birth). My experience now was somewhat easier but it seemed less healthy, less natural, and the external circumstances were not exactly encouraging. Nor did the doctor seem to have done a good job. Toward evening I started a fast rising temperature, had chills, spasms, something like violent labor pains, and an equally violent and frightening hemorrhage.

At that time I had a ratty little teen-age maid, the sorry product of reform school and prison, out on parole; she was one of my quixotic experiments in trying to do the Right Thing (shadows of *Grosse Menschen—Edle Taten!*), all of them unbelievably unsuccessful. So far, she had outdone herself in goodness that day; had coaxed the hungry small boys into sleep, phoned for the doctor once more, even procured for me a cup of soothing camomile tea. But now, as I called her in a small panic, there was no answer. Tilly had disappeared.

This was, no doubt, what the meteorologists call a Low. I'd never felt so helpless, so angry with myself and the world as I did then. I couldn't do a thing but shake with chills while the blood fought itself painfully out of my stupid womb. I was weak, drowsy, and in this weakness I heard a familiar and always aggravating noise: Father's nervous throat-clearing. Steady, steady, I told myself, now don't let's hallucinate, no fuss, if you please, no delirium.

Then the doorbell rang.

At last! the doctor! Somehow I got myself out of bed and waded through pain and dizziness to open the door. "Oh——" I said, "it's you!"

There stood Father, with the same old black satchel in his hand. It was heavy and he put it down on the door mat. "Yes, it's me," he said. "It's a surprise, isn't it?"

"Yes. It certainly is. Why didn't you write me you were coming? It's such a long trip from Vienna."

"Seventeen hours. I like to travel but I can't afford express trains."

"Why did you come?"

"You're ill, aren't you?" said Father. "I knew something was the matter. I had such a funny foreboding. . . ."

He picked up the satchel and helped me back into the room. What a relief to be no longer all alone there. "I have a cold, a little touch of the flu," I said. "The doctor is coming——"

"I see. I knew you would not tell me the truth. You were always a liar. Now get into bed. Why don't you have the heat on, this place is like an iceberg. . . . What do you mean the heating system is out of order? Who's responsible for it? . . . The porter? Well, just let me talk to him, I'll make such a stink he'll have it fixed one, two, three! I know all about heating systems. Why, I was the director of the biggest, finest hotel in Vöslau, and then my chief made me the manager of his three apartment houses—on Kolowratring. Where are my grandsons? I brought something for them."

He had never seen his grandsons. We lived too far apart, geographically as well as in spirit. He gripped the black satchel and hurriedly trotted down the corridor to the children's room. He was as impatient to make their acquaintance as to get away from me who was sick and, most probably, a source of untold germs. Miserable as I was, I had to laugh once more about my father, afraid to catch the germs of pregnancy and miscarriage from me. Still the same old man, hard, miserly, full of conceits and such delusions of grandeur that he was leaving the unyielding ground of reality behind and taking wild flights into imagined splendors: a hotel director, a manager of real estate, the best after-dinner speaker, the most brilliant ballroom dancer of Vienna, the toast of the town, the man who was going to break the bank at Monte Carlo. . . . What next? And how, for Heaven's sake, was one to explain the tremor in some sensitive antenna of his that had sent him pell-mell on a long, tough journey to bring us food just when we needed it as never before?

Sometimes I get an inkling of the possibility that I did not inherit whatever gifts of imagination I possess from the decadent, thin-nerved, cultured forebears on my maternal side, but that my opaque, primitive, callous father slipped me a few seeds of storytelling with his chromosomes.

It was also quite in character that I did not see him again on this precipitate visit, except that he woke me at dawn the next morning, just to put his head in the door and say: "I'm leaving, got to catch the six o'clock train. Doctor Brandt says you'll be all right now, but what does he know? Bungling morons, all of 'em. A nice mess you've made of yourself; not enough that you get pregnant, as if you didn't know you can't feed a third child! Then you lose it! What did you do? Run, climb a ladder, drag the baby carriage around? But you were always stupid and negligent. I always told you, someday you'll croak on straw. If I hadn't come to save you . . . well, I'm leaving, got to catch the six o'clock train. Let this be a lesson and be more careful the next time, you hear?"

Drugged as I was with the doctor's sedatives, I had to giggle. Father had once more treated me, the proud wedded wife of a live General Music Director, like a fallen daughter, and was gone before I could fight back or thank him. When I woke up the next time I might have thought it was all a fever vision, had it not been for the perfectly real, palpable treasures he had brought us in the black satchel. Rice, flour, sugar, coffee, cocoa, tea, and a tin of the bitterly yearned-for, unavailable, nourishing lard. As a sideline, he had managed to make more rows in one evening than I could in all my life . . . insulted the doctor—who possibly deserved it—awakened my neighbors to borrow a blanket, searched the servants' quarters and kicked out Tilly's lover, and frightened my five-year-old with a toy he brought him, a paper snake purchased at the Oriental Bazaar, identical to the snake that had given me nightmares when I was five.

The next time I saw Father was about ten years later, I think it was late in 1931. I had returned to Europe after a prolonged stay in New York and Hollywood, where my play *Grand Hotel* had been produced with amazing success. Now I was invited to its première in Vienna. I had roamed far and wide, while in Vienna, Father's tarock game was going on day by day, changeless, "like a roll of toilet paper," to borrow one of Agnes de Mille's incisive remarks. Frau Cilli and her women friends had aged very little, but the men had all been sent into retirement, a condition that's apt to add years to any man's age and shrink his self-esteem like an un-Sanforized shirt. On his old-age pension, Father seemed to be considerably better off than the others. Which, of course, did not prevent him from lamenting about being a pauper, a beggar, a man who had been cheated out of his just reward for the sixty years of faithful service to the flour company and its late president.

He still lived in our old apartment, greatly henpecked though well taken care of by a housekeeper as big as a moving van. I don't know if she possessed the energy poor Mama had lacked to keep him clean, his hair trimmed, and his cheeks unstubbled, or if he had used all his spit and polish for the unique occasion of the première.

Past eighty, he still had hardly any gray in his thick shock of hair. When he presented himself in boiled shirt, with the funny old tail coat and patent leather shoes with elastic sides, it took me back to the very first years of my life when he and Mama in all their splendor would come to say good night to me before they went forth to an opera, *redoute,* or ball.

Although his wrath and his curses were as pungent as ever, he had transferred part of his malevolence from his old friend and enemy, the scoundrel Hassreiter, onto the powers that now owned the flour mills. He would clear his throat and sound the old battle cry: "Those swindlers! Those blackjacks! Sixty years of my life I've given them, and what do I get? Inflation money! What am I supposed to do with it? Use it for toilet paper? It's too dirty even for that. But the Lord will punish them, he has punished them already —you ought to hear how their children talk to them, no obedience, no respect. You see now how good it was that I was always thrifty. Your mother—God bless her memory—and you, too, didn't have enough brains to understand. Well, at least I saved a pittance of money that should see me through the few months I may still live, if it pleases the Lord——"

"Don't worry, Father," I said quickly, "you look as if you'd live well past a hundred, like your grandfather; and as for money, you know, I'm pretty well off now, and anything you may want or need. . . ."

But there I hit hard rock; he looked at me very cross-eyed through his spectacles (it had always disconcerted me not to be sure whether he really had me in focus) and answered angrily: "Who do you think you are to offer me money? Me! I'm your father and don't you forget it! Why, if I hadn't traveled all the way to Hanover in 1922—seventeen hours on a hard bench, third class—you'd have croaked. I saved your life. I don't need anything from you. Just see you won't need me someday to pull you out of some mess!"

And with this Father went to the theater where, in utter bafflement, he saw a play for the first time in his life. It was a good performance and a most gratifying success, but Father only shrugged his stooped, skeptical shoulders. Obviously he hadn't understood a word, and I wouldn't have needed to wonder if he was going to recognize some of himself, his naïveté, the smallness of his horizon, in the figure of Kringelein. "You didn't like it, Father?" I asked. "Well, it could have been worse, I guess," he answered with mere politeness.

My friend Sam Raphaelson once told me that after the sensational success at the opening of his *Jazz Singer* he met his old Jewish grandmother at the stage door. "Well, Grandma, how did you like it?" he asked, bursting with pride.

"Could've been better, could've been worse. But when the rabbi pleaded with him not to go away but stay with his family and his people, he should have stayed."

"But, Grandma," Raphaelson said, "there would have been no third act. There would have been no play at all."

"So what?" said Grandma.

I remembered that, when I left the theater at Father's side. To console me, he muttered into his handkerchief, held to his mouth as always, "Jakobi said he didn't think you had it in you." Jakobi was one of the clerks at the office; it appeared the entire office personnel had been dispersed in the galleries, tickets by courtesy of Father. He had been taught by Hassreiter that a première without a claque was an impossibility.

Herr Josef Hassreiter, ballet master in retirement, had not come to my opening. First, because to him, too, a play without a ballet in it would have been a senseless and boring enterprise. But I think there was a little jealousy involved, too, His three daughters, those beautiful belles of many balls, my dear, gay, carefree childhood friends, hadn't, in a manner of speaking, gotten anywhere while Baum, that old Jew with spinach eternally on his lapel, had managed to spawn a daughter who made money and a name for herself all over Europe and America. I think whatever satisfaction Father derived from my success was concentrated in his going Hassreiter one better. "That poor old beggar," Father would say, moved by his own generosity, "I usually let him win at *Strohmandel*. He needs the few shillings. I mean, I can't outright offer to support him, can I? After all, he was somebody. Once. Still, his *Puppenfee* is a very good ballet; I'm not saying your play is bad, but. . . ."

However, he collected every scrap the papers printed about me—luckily they were all friendly as papers will be when the local talent makes good—and he carried these clippings around with him and pestered his friends with them; and, to my amused surprise, he sent me an interview in which an eager reporter had caught him. And there Father emerged, wonderfully idealized like an allegoric figure on a monument, holding a laurel wreath aloft. He, my father, had recognized my talent very early in life; he had fostered it and nursed it by any and all means at his command. He had strictly trained me to read all the great literature, had fertilized my imagination, had tenderly but severely forced me to write down impressions, poems, stories. He indicated, even if he did not say so outright, that he, to an important part, was the actual author of my books, stories, novels, and particularly of that successful play, *Grand Hotel*. "You must make a play from this novel," he had insisted, and as I knew him to be the best, most sensitive arbiter of my work, I had written it. A world success.

It worried me slightly to see Father wander so far from reality. Did he practice levitation like some bodhisattvas? Did he think he could walk on water? Or was it simply a form of senility? And how long, indeed, did he yet have to live?

As to that. . . . When he was eighty-four he spent a few months in Abbazzia, a resort on the Adriatic coast he liked very much. "I notice that the men here wear pajamas," he wrote me. "Next year when I come back I'll likewise have pajamas."

Next year! Just like that; not even his customary "if God grants me life." In 1932, soon after I had moved to the United States, Father broke camp, to get away from under the growing shadow of Hitler. Not to America, though, which seemed too far away, too strange— why, a country where they didn't play tarock! Like the old Chinese who would leave Chinatown and travel back to China to die, Father was drawn back to the people of his own clan, roughly to the place where he was born; not Hungary any longer but part of Yugoslavia. I never found out how he maneuvered to be taken in as a highly honored paying guest by a grandniece whose family had fallen on hard times. She was an angel of patience and kindness, this woman, whom I called Cousin in a sense only a Southerner could understand. The conditions Father demanded seemed an improvement for the whole family: a larger apartment in a good house with bathroom and central heating in the new, modern quarter of the middle-sized town; an efficient maid, and excellent meals suitable to an old man's delicate stomach. The only fly in the ointment was the incurable miserly streak in Father's character. My poor dear cousin wrote me desperate letters; she couldn't let the lonesome old man down, could she? Neither was it possible by any stretch of budget or imagination to provide what he wanted for the pitiful amount he was ready to pay for it. I knew better than to insult his pride by offering him cash. Instead I secretly paid for all those comforts he commandeered, and this little intrigue between my cousin and me worked beautifully. I could sense Father's glee in having haggled down Cousin Elsa, and squeezing from her all this good food, service, and daily luxuries for so little money. What a bargain! Soon he was tyrannizing the household in great high spirits and, luckily, they all seemed to accept it in good humor and with a generosity of heart that I, guiltily, felt lacking in myself. I also sent the money with which Father contributed a "subsidy" to his friend Hassreiter—"the poor beggar"—until he died. It was another triumph for Father to have outlived this beloved and hated only friend of his.

By the time Father spent another season in Abbazzia, properly equipped with new pajamas, he was almost blind. A cataract. He didn't take this lying down, but found a first-class specialist who would operate on him free of charge. (How well my intrigue worked!) The idea of getting free of charge something for which other people had to pay dearly made the operation a pleasure for him. No sooner had he regained his sight, however cross-eyed and limited, than he wrote me a letter, full of what amounted to sentiment in a man like Father. "I'm not getting any younger but I'm feeling well. When will you visit me? Do it soon, will you? There's one thing I'd like to do—dance a tango with you once more."

Oh, my God! I thought. In Berlin I had had to take Father to all the big, gaudy, popular night clubs and dance every waltz and tango with him; he had made a foolish exhibition of it, as in the Perfection of yore, pushing and shoving me around the floor and expecting applause at the end. When nothing of the sort occurred, he scolded me, invited the star of the floor show to dance with him and when she embarrassedly refused, he started a row of the first order, that he carried up through all the echelons to the hastily summoned manager.

Even so, what could I do now but grant Father's request? I had spent many months in the perfect peace of a remote village in the mountains of Bali, and the return to the confused noises of Europe was not easy. I had my first taste of it when I left the boat in Genoa and tried to find out how to get to Belgrade. Novi Sad, where Father lived, was only a short train ride, but in 1936, Mussolini's Italy was not on speaking terms with Yugoslavia (then still a kingdom). Nationalistic pride was high on both sides. The best I could do was to take a train as far as the border and find my way from there. In Italy people strictly refused to speak or understand anything but Italian, but I could stumble my way through in a traveler's smattering of their language. Not so in Serbian, which was spoken exclusively from the moment I arrived late at night at the border station. I got hungrier and hungrier, since only Yugoslavian money was accepted and, unlike other border stations, there was no place to change even a good, valid, American traveler's check. Altogether, I got the impression that tomorrow war between those two countries might break out, so belligerently guarded were the trains on both sides by heavily armed soldiers who, with sinister faces and characteristic swagger, patrolled each car in each of the countless stations. This, I suppose, was the realm of the Irredentists who had constantly made trouble when I was still a child in Vienna, who seemed to have been connected with the assassination of Archduke Franz Ferdinand and thus had dropped the spark into the powder keg that exploded into World War I. I hoped they wouldn't explode another war while I was joggling interminably toward Belgrade; I did not know that the fight about the old trouble spot around Trieste would drag on beyond World War II and take up a lot of the U.N.'s time and effort. But it was in the air, it definitely was in the air. . . .

I still can't understand how my train managed to take three days and nights to cover the insignificant distance from Milan to Belgrade. There was no first class, no sleeping car, no dining car, no washroom. I had various traveling companions, of whom I remember two. One was a Yugoslavian officer who spoke French, of a sort, that is. *"Parlez français?"* he asked, giving me a winning smile. I smiled back and poured out my troubles. I was hungry, nobody would change my money for me. Was I on the right train at all? When were we getting to Belgrade? And how, *nom de Dieu,* was I getting from Belgrade to Novi Sad? My officer smiled, kissed my hand, got up, took off his tunic. *"Coucher avec moi?"* he said. This was all the French he had. I thanked him for the obviously well-meant offer, refused with polite regrets. I was tired, not quite well, and married. He locked the door to the compartment and tried to kiss me. *"Coucher avec moi?"* he repeated in various keys of expression. I struggled, laughed, because this really was too ridiculous a situation, but just as I contemplated pulling the emergency cord, he suddenly drew himself up and put his tunic on again. My nervous laughing must have hurt his male pride because he muttered something that I took for a Serbian curse, made a short bow, opened the door and left.

I turned the little switch at the door and stretched out to sleep. A few minutes later the conductor opened the door with his master key and told me with unmistakable gestures that I was not allowed to lock myself in. Behind him stood two grim guards with bayonets on their rifles. It was pure Hitchcock. What now? Would they arrest me for insulting an officer? Hand me to the secret police as a spy? Things like that invariably make me laugh. When they saw me laughing, they, too, laughed, which did not prevent them from popping into my compartment every half hour throughout the night. I cursed myself for not knowing a word of their language, not having any Yugoslavian money to give them a tip, if that was what they expected. Two or three times during that night, my friend, the officer, also woke me up. Each time, when I opened my eyes, he was standing there, grinning sheepishly, expectantly, a naughty child: *"Maintenant, coucher avec moi?"*

The next morning new guards and another officer took over, but they were of sterner stuff and inspected me and my passport without any attempt at fraternization. The third day, when I thought we could surely be not far from Greece, if not Turkey, another fellow traveler came to share the compartment with me. Although not in silver armor like Lohengrin, but in a gray business suit, to me he appeared to arrive with the same Wagnerian chords of a Heaven-sent savior. He was a civilized man, he spoke much better French than I, although with a slight German accent. In fact, he was a German who introduced himself with a very German clicking of heels as he handed me his card. "And you, *gnädige Frau,* are the well-known author, Vicki Baum," he remarked—not a question but a statement. How did he know me? Simple—the tag with my name was dangling from my suitcase in the overhead baggage rack. He knew some of my books and discussed them with German thoroughness. "And you are visiting your father in Novi Sad," he informed me. "Did you read this, too, on my tag?" I asked, surprised. "No, in the papers," he answered. He, too, lived in Novi Sad; naturally it was interesting to meet on the train. No, he didn't know Father personally, only by seeing him in the street, the old gentleman was such a well-known type, everybody knew him. Shyly he confessed that he wrote occasionally for some local papers, and would I permit him to ask me a few questions, such a feather in his cap, an interview. . . .

Of course I would. I had learned to handle reporters with loving care and so I chatted along, willingly and frankly telling him whatever he wished to know.

When I showed my relatives in Novi Sad his card, they gasped. He was the head of the local Nazis, feared in the entire district, their local Führer, high commander of the dangerous gang in the Brown House in which Nazi headquarters had been established. Obviously the Party had been watching me from the moment I had set foot on European soil. I laughed when they warned me tremblingly of the danger hanging over me and, by association, over them also. To me, an American citizen, just emerged from the deep tranquillity of my East Indian island, this seemed too silly for words. I did not understand then, nor for a long time, the thick fog of fear enveloping all countries and peoples, particularly the people over there.

Father had aged a little, that is, his thick hair had grayed a bit, but his skin was without a wrinkle and he dazzled me with a set of new white teeth and a field hand's appetite. His digestion had given him so much trouble before, but look, no trouble at all since he got his new dentures. It was miraculous, because he took them out whenever he sat down to eat and placed them neatly on a little saucer next to his plate. The family watched me sidewise to see if I was disgusted with this, but, Heavens, I remembered when Father's teeth had grinned at me from his water glass. I was hardened to his little peculiarities. As for the family, they seemed sincerely fond of him and there was a lot of good-natured teasing around the table. It was all so familiar, a homecoming to the cozy little Hapsburg world I'd left behind so long ago.

I was growing slightly sentimental when Father excused himself and went to his room. While he was gone I began to understand why the family felt so proud of the old man. He had entertained them with interminable tales about his important part in developing me into an internationally known author, a world success. Well, my girl, I told myself, maybe he's not so far off. If he hadn't built so many high hurdles on my course, would I have learned to jump? All the tears I had swallowed because I was forbidden to read! How precious every single word becomes when it is stolen goods. If you ask me why Johnny can't read, I'd say because it's rammed down his throat. Make reading a forbidden pleasure, for adults only, and Johnny will go after it like a shot.

They produced Father's scrapbook: all about me. I never had a scrapbook, wouldn't dream of collecting those mummified leaves of past successes. I shuddered at the anecdotes about me as a child that Father had made up of whole cloth and imbedded in interviews in German, Hungarian, even Serbian. By God, he'd managed to learn this difficult Slavic language in his eighties! Some father!

Soon he made a great entrance. Dressed in his old dinner coat, black tie, stiff shirt and collar, smelling slightly of brilliantine and mothballs, he shouted the old battle cry: "Let's go! We're not here for our pleasure, let's work!"

"Work, Father? You mean——"

"You know what I mean. How's your tango? I hope you haven't forgotten what I taught you. Go, get dressed, put a little make-up on. The ladies here use a lot of rouge and lipstick. You look green, it's disgusting."

"Isn't it a bit late for going out, Father?" I tried, but knew I didn't have a chance. It was almost midnight. I was stiff and sore from three days on a miserable train, bone-tired, sleepy, still leached out from the malaria I had caught in Bali.

"We're just right. The Maritza doesn't open till ten o'clock and now is the best time. You'll love it."

Well, consideration for others wasn't one of Father's strong points. The Maritza was all you would expect the only night club in a small Yugoslavian town to be. The usual Balkan smells of the urinal, flies, sweat, onions, of perfume, shashlik, and pilaff. Officers, officials, clerks—no Nazis, no Hungarians, either. A hangout for the Daughters of Joy whose favors the local blades had to share. Handsome young wenches they were, though. Altogether, I found the Yugoslavians a strong, healthy, attractive species with red cheeks and the kind of golden glow in hair and skin that a lucky mixture of sunshine and moisture in the air gives its favorite children. Obviously Father was well known here; the girls greeted him with squeals of *"Herr Ballettmeister! Gospodin Ballettmeister!"* and the small band struck up a waltz that I recognized with a sudden pang of nostalgia—the waltz from the old ballet *Die Puppenfee,* Hassreiter's masterpiece. On that banal little melody I sailed back, way back into the past, to the evening I had played this waltz while Grandfather was quietly dying. . . .

I might as well confess right here that I have inherited some of my father's dance craziness; there were years in my life when dancing held for me a greater joy and relief than anything else. And as I grew older, and gave up dancing for dignity's sake, it was not only a deep loss, but promptly the pent-up, unrelieved strains came out as a good case of arthritis. A bad bargain, but what can one do? The spectacle of my old father shuffling around in what he believed to be a tango taught me when it was time to stop. That night at the Maritza he made such an exhibition as if he were a mere seventy; as in the Perfection, the other couples stopped dancing, they stood in a circle around us, grinning, and when the band stopped at last, they applauded. For those little whores and their temporary companions, the old man was a good joke to which they were obviously accustomed.

That night I uncovered a new piece of fanciful thinking in my father. He had shed his identity, a worn-out snakeskin, and slipped into a more becoming one, more becoming according to his lights, at least: he was now the famous ballet master of the Vienna Opera . . . in retirement, of course. Not only had he inspired all my books, he was also the author and choreographer of *Die Puppenfee* and many other famous ballets. He had been a personal friend and collaborator of Johann Strauss and had known most of the young archdukes intimately. "Herr Baum," Archduke Otto had often said, "I would rather spend an evening with you at Sacher's than with Fräulein Schleinzer." (All of Vienna knew Fräulein Schleinzer as the most beautiful solo dancer in the whole corps de ballet and as the wild, handsome Archduke's *maîtresse en titre*.) "Baum, you lazy dog," Johann Strauss had told him, "when will you be ready to work on another ballet with me? Haven't I waited long enough?"

I hoped Father had danced to his heart's content during my visit. We had gone to Belgrade for two nights, to a larger, livelier night club where Father had had the unavoidable row with the floor show star, waiters, headwaiter, master of ceremonies, and manager. By now I almost enjoyed such episodes, for wasn't it a sign of Father's undiminished vigor? The other nights we had given an exhibition at the Maritza, except one evening when my cousin arranged something like a family day. It was a strange assembly, mostly old people, dozens of them, taken out of mothballs for this event. They were dressed in black; the ladies in dresses that had been out of fashion for decades, the men in the sort of cutaways now seen only in family albums. They came up to me one by one, dignified and polite, bowed, and introduced themselves in a formal, obsolete German dialect. "Also from Parabutch," they said, one after the other.

"What the hell does Parabutch mean?" I asked Cousin Geza in a whisper. He grinned. "You mean to say you don't know where you have your roots? They're *Schwaben*, Swabians, early settlers. Parabutch is the village where Emperor Joseph settled some Germans at the end of the eighteenth century, our great-grandfather among them, and this is what's left of our clan, yours and mine."

They gave me a daguerreotype of that great-grandfather as an elderly man—I still have it—an old farmer with a hard-bitten face, in a farmer's vest and coat, with large silver coins for buttons. I hadn't known I belonged to a clan, rootless me, alien corn everywhere.

Still, that gathering of the clan would have been of no importance except for later events. . . .

There were, of course, no tears when I took my farewell of my father. For a moment he seemed to make preparations to kiss me, but as he had never kissed me in all my life, he did not do so now. He held out his hand, I shook it, a cool, dry, high-veined old man's hand, and then I remembered my Austrian education and what was expected of me, and kissed it.

When the war began in Europe, direct communication was no longer possible, but the United States embassy, helpful above and beyond the call of duty, kept me informed of Father's continuing good health. Then, when the U.S. entered the free-for-all, these messages, too, stopped.

One morning, in 1943, I received a mysterious telephone call. A man's voice, in a hard, not unpleasant accent, demanded that I meet him, he wanted to talk to me. No, not in my house, at a certain little eating place and, as I hesitated, he said, "I have a letter. About conditions in Novi Sad. About your father."

"How is he? Do you know? Is he. . . . I've been out of touch for so long. . . . I mean, is he still alive?"

"No. I regret to tell you. I'll show you the report. Will you meet me?"

I still don't know who the young man was, probably a Communist, I thought. He muttered a Serbian name, not necessarily his real one; he was good-looking, polite, but completely detached.

The letter he showed me was written in Serbian, the Cyrillic alphabet unintelligible to me, but its content was brief: a terrible massacre had occurred in Novi Sad in the course of which every man, woman, and child in the district where Father lived had been killed.

Killed by whom? The Nazis?

"Who else would do such a thing? They are hyenas. But they will get theirs soon, if that is any consolation to you."

"Well . . ." I said, "he was a very old man." Maybe very old people die easily, I thought. I hope so.

After the war I heard more about that historic massacre at Novi Sad in which more than fifteen hundred people had been killed—strangled, stabbed, shot—and whose bodies were thrown into the Danube. Their murderers were Nazis, not German, but Hungarian Nazis. One mustn't generalize about nations and nationalities, neither glorify nor condemn them in toto, even though it's easier than trying to sort the truth from conventional lies and propaganda.

A letter I received from my cousin, Doctor Geza, started with these words: "As the only survivor of a family of the more than eighty people you met here, it is my sad duty to give you my report about your father's end. I myself lost my wife and children. I was saved because I was working in the hospital all during that horrid day. In the evening I went to Norava Ulicze. Your father was lying on the floor, unconscious, terribly beaten up, and covered with blood. At his side I found my youngest child, three years old, slain. There was still a trace of life in your father, but he died within the hour without regaining consciousness. . . ."

How each one of us secretly carries his private cemetery around with him and watches it filling up with ever new graves, the last one to be our own. . . .

mong the Hassreiters' retainers was a tall, horse-faced, widow and her equally tall, horse-faced daughter, Bertha. Both were fidgety, obsequious, smiling the too-eager smiles of poor relatives, and dressed in refurbished hand-me-downs usually too dressy for the occasion. I seem to remember that they lived on a small pension allotted officers' widows. There was some tale that they had gone to Russia, where apparently an astonishing metamorphosis had taken place, for on their return, mother and daughter were well-dressed, less fidgety, and not ingratiating at all, in fact, almost arrogant. Russia was great, they declared. Bertha had found a job there, a wonderful job, and they were returning there for good. It had been mentioned occasionally that Bertha played the harp, but no one had paid much attention to it. Now it turned out that such an utterly useless quirk as playing the harp could be lucrative. Good harp players were rare, so rare in fact that even the finest orchestras would pay well for a lady harpist, the only female admitted into opera and symphony orchestras, in those days strictly the male preserve.

I suppose my mother pricked up her ears at this news of a suitable profession for a young lady of good family; not as drab as that of teacher or governess, not as exhausting as being a nurse, not as aggravating as becoming some cranky *grande dame's* companion, and better paid.

I have sometimes tried to untangle my mother's reasons for taking the initiative this one time in her life. There was the new energy and self-assertion that the young doctor in Inzersdorf had infused into her. Perhaps he had been a little in love with her, and she was definitely in love with him. Today it would be called transference and I venture to guess that he cured her mainly by letting her talk and complain and confess, and finally made her face reality—as the saying goes, face herself.

Mama decided that I must become a harpist. In this first spurt of facing reality, she went out to do battle for me. There was a family tradition of frustrated musical talent that had done more than enough damage to her own father and to herself. Under no circumstances would she permit the same damage to be repeated if I showed such talent. She wanted to secure for me the independence she herself had never been allowed. If I could support myself I would be free—free to marry when and whom I wanted or not marry at all, because marriage was a prison, a terrible prison where innocent women served a life sentence.

But of this Mama spoke to me only many years later, when, just before she died, she broke out of a deep two-week coma into a half hour of superclarity. . . .

At the time Mama did not tell me at all what she was up to. In their bedroom she argued with Father every night, not in the loud, shrill voice she so often used since her return from Inzersdorf, but in a constant murmur, a running brook of words I could not catch through the closed door. Next I was taken to a birthday party at the Hassreiters, and there was Bertha, in flowing chiffon with sequins and a long train, if you please, and a golden harp, so dreamlike, such a fairy-tale thing it made even Bertha look almost pretty. As she let loose the silver arpeggios and golden glissandi of an obnoxious composition named *Le Sylphe*, I found myself transported into an enchanted world. I saw it all: the moonlit night, a high rock from which a waterfall rushed down in an aura of white mist and rainbows, jewels dripping from bluebells, and little elves in flowing veils and dragonfly wings dancing over the waters. I came home like a sleepwalker. This had been better than any of the ballets I had seen in the opera. Ballets were just make-believe. But this I had seen myself. It was as though I had a third eye some-where inside my head, that strange eye of imagination that does not look out but is turned inward. I can still see many things with this eye. When I write my stories I only have to put down on paper these things that I see as clearly as though my characters were acting it all out for me on a stage.

"What do you think? Would you like to learn to play the harp, like Bertha?" my mother asked me nonchalantly the following day. Perhaps she held her breath awaiting my answer, but she did not let me see what an important issue this was to her, nor did she mention the many obstacles she had overcome before she put the final decision to me. But I had been trained in self-discipline and control since I was four and I was holding myself reined in even at this moment of dizzy delirium. Maybe I trembled a little, secretly, with the ice trickling down my back and my hands clammy.

"Yes, Mama," I said quietly, "I would like it."

That is how I became a musician.

I haven't touched a harp in forty-five years, have long forgotten how to play it, and, throughout the last few years of my career as a musician, I had been bored and greatly annoyed at the limitations of that stupid instrument. Looking back, though, I can see that the serious study of music and the hard, strict professional training coming at the time it did, was the greatest stroke of luck I ever had.

I can never understand why people are full of surprised admira-tion if a child is a good musician, for in making music, as well as in dancing and drawing, children find their most natural means of expressing their dreams and emotions—joy, sadness, passion—for which they yet have no words, or which, perhaps, cannot be ex-pressed in words, ever. There is nothing except the limitations of the small body, the weak arms and fingers, to hold back the child musician, if there is talent. Of course, it takes patience to master the techniques, but patience is an integral part of talent. People who have (or believe they have) talent but no patience are and remain dilettantes. Sure, my six years of learning were strenuous, often exhausting, but full and happy at the same time, each lesson a thrilling challenge, three challenges weekly, not a minute left for mischief, or getting bored like other children. Far from boring me, the three, four, six hours of daily practice were a blissful refuge. Nobody and nothing could hurt me while I wrestled with some difficult passage. It is the same with writing. No more reliable painkiller than concentrated work.

In the earnest study of music a child finds a worthwhile goal, a purpose, an incomparable outlet for his energies and dreams. More important yet, a good teacher will take the small student as seriously as he takes himself. Again, it was my great good luck to have a wonderful teacher. In Vienna there are still dynasties of instrumentalists: cello families, French horn families, all sorts of families in which the art of playing a certain instrument in a certain style is handed down from one generation to the next. This gives Vienna orchestras their singular beauty and unity of sound.

My teacher was the head of such a family, the Zamaras. The Old Professor—so called to differentiate him from his son, the Young Professor—was an old Italian, very tall, white-haired, blue-eyed, beautiful; not just handsome, but beautiful. I was taken into a small room filled with dried laurel wreaths, sunlight, two marvelous golden harps, and an enormous dog, a Great Dane. I curtsied to the Professor and also to the dog. The dog looked me over, and sniffed me, and then put a large paw upon my shoulder. "Good. Caesar, my friend, he likes thee," said the Professor. "Now we see if I like thee, too. I tune the harp and you tell me is too high, too low, is maybe right. *Capisce?*"

Well, this was almost too easy; I guess I grimaced instinctively when an impure octave, a smudgy chord hurt my ears. Professor laughed. He sat down at one of the harps and told me to listen well to what he played. A little theme in E-flat, simple in its clarity and restrained joyfulness, no waterfalls or fairy-tale elves but it might have been Haydn. He played it twice and asked me if I could remember it. "Naturally," I said, a bit miffed. I was propped up on pillows, and for the first time I felt the weight of the harp leaning round and sleek and friendly against my right shoulder. Professor put my right forefinger on a string and told me to try and pluck out the little melody he had played. Nothing could have been easier. Eight bars of the first theme, eight of the second, then the first part repeated itself. Professor grinned with pleasure. "Now try both hands," he said. I found the lower octave; my left arm seemed a bit short but I made it, guided by the blue and red strings among the drab ones. My God, what does he think I am? I thought angrily. A baby? An idiot?

"Not so bad," said the Professor. Later I found that this was the very highest praise he would ever concede to anybody or anything. "Now," he said, "you stick to the melody, you play *da capo da capo da capo, capisce?* Not mind what I play, you stick to your melody." He sat down at the other harp and I began once more with my little two-finger plunking. I sounded awfully poor and weak and lonesome. At the first *da capo* the old man came in with some figurations; it dawned on me that these were going to be variations and I stuck to my theme. Miraculous things happened as his hands brought ever richer sounds from the strings, ever new effects, each variation in a different style and mood, mounting into a crashing crescendo, with me trying hard not to be drowned in the broad river of arpeggios but plucking along as loud and hard as I could. The dog Caesar had jumped up, his ears stuck up stiffly with an air of amazed listening, his tail wagging furiously. We ended, still together. "*Brava, brava,*" shouted the old man. He separated me from the warm vibrating weight leaning against my shoulder. I parted with it reluctantly, it was so alive, such a friend, such a beautiful body—I wish I had words to express the inexpressible bond and affection that ties an instrumentalist to his instrument. Harps are manufactured in factories, by the same method, after the same model; they look alike, they sound more or less alike. But your own instrument becomes an extension of your body. I guess this feeling of an instrument as part of oneself is what the enthusiastic driver, the racer, the hot-rodder feels for his car.

The Old Professor picked me up, swung me high into the air, and, my God! he kissed me. I fell in love with him instantaneously, hopelessly, abysmally, and incurably in love. I had been in love before, constantly, in fact, but never in love like this, so deeply, so enchantingly, so unbelievably full and happy.

It was—lucky me—not a case of unrequited love, because the Old Professor decided right then and there that in my case he would make an exception and, bloody beginner or not, he would not hand me on to his daughter but teach me personally. This decision made, he began by taking me down a notch or two. "You think you play nice, yes? I show you; my dog, he play much nicer. Caesar! *Per favore,* you give little concert for little girl?"

Caesar yawned and turned his stern toward the harp. The old man did some trick with the pedals and said, "*Eccolo!*" at which Caesar executed the most perfect glissandi with his tail, strangely enough with the same beauty of tone as the Professor himself. This tone, this technique of making a harp a singing instrument capable of playing a melody, a legato instead of the usual plink-plunk, was the Zamara family's fetish, the glory and power of which were steadily preached to us pupils. It was an absolute faith, like the Old Testament's avowal that there is no God but Our God Yaweh or the Moslem's cry of "Allah-il-Allah."

We pupils believed. Of course we believed. Any other method was an invention of the devil and plucking the strings without making them sing a deadly sin. I can still pick out the sound of the harps from the jungle of modern symphonic orchestration, and separate the noble offspring of the Zamara school from the toneless, ordinary string-pluckers taught by lesser methods.

I remember something Arthur Nikisch, the greatest conductor I ever knew—and I have known and played under many great ones— once said to my young conductor-husband: "If I cannot make the bass clarinetist feel that the whole first movement of Tchaikovsky's *Pathétique* depends on the little passage in which he substitutes for the bassoon—well, then, I am a bad conductor."

As long as I was under old Professor Zamara's influence I remained convinced that nothing in the whole wide world was as important as to play the harp well, not only well, but better than anybody else. By the time I finished my studies, after six years, I had become completely impregnated with the proud assurance that I, Vicki Baum, was the best harp player on earth.

Perhaps I was; so what?

When I told my publisher that I planned to write my memoirs he asked whether I had thought of a title.

"Not so important!" I said.

"On the contrary, my dear, the title is very, very important."

"But that *is* my title: *Not So Important!*" I tried to explain. This my publisher strictly rejected. "Too negative," he said, "it wouldn't do, wouldn't sell." I don't know what my various publishers will call these random memories by the time they're translated into the several languages in which my books are usually read. Yet not to take myself, nor the world per se, as too important has been the leitmotiv of my life. It's part of the philosophy the ants taught me.

Luckily, the years filled with the ambition and self-importance my teachers had injected into me were just a phase (to use Gesell lingo), but while they lasted they did a lot of damage to my nervous system. They left me with a greener face than ever; I was jittery, and thin as a sour herring. The responsibility of becoming, and remaining, the best harp player on earth gave me migraines (I still have them occasionally), shattering stage frights, sudden blockings of memory when I appeared as soloist, and a general feeling of being such a frail creature that I, too, might someday end up in Inzersdorf.

On the basis of this personal experience, and taking advantage of an old lady's privilege to ramble, I can assure you that facing our individual and cosmic unimportance is healthy training. To my mind, nothing is as malignant a sickness as the tendency of the present generation to endow their little egos with an importance out of all proportion. It is a road that leads to breakdowns, drug addiction, alcoholism, mental disease, and to a general softening of will power, intestinal fortitude, and brain. How much of this must be put on the debit side of the popular sport of psychoanalysis in our Western civilization can be judged only in the future, when it has become either a passing fad or, historically, the first warning crack in the tumbling structure. I am a simple, down-to-earth woman and philosophy behooves me not, nor do I please myself in the role of Cassandra. But this much I know: if you think yourself so important it follows that your toothache will be a very, very important toothache indeed, and hurt like the devil. If you break a leg, no equally important leg has ever been broken. Everything gets enlarged and twisted out of proportion—your ambitions, your successes, your failures, your children, your marriage, your vices, neuroses, aberrations, and guilt, as well as your supreme goodness and virtue, your joys, which by nature are always in a minority, and your sufferings that your self-importance makes unbearable. "Watch out!" I feel like shouting from the roof, "you're not so important, no, not important at all!"

Now, back to school.

The Vienna Konservatorium, founded in 1817, supported by the venerable Gesellschaft der Musikfreunde, did not propose to produce mediocrities, let alone dilettantes. There was such a broiling, steaming abundance of talent that the very walls seemed to give off vibrations, heat, and a never-ending stream of music. The curriculum was strict, the sights high. We, the students, were constantly tested, graded, sifted, and resifted in a nerve-racking network of examinations. Like any famous old institute, the Konservatorium was a microcosm held aloft by its own laws, taboos, traditions. In the archives in the basement, the realm of the famous musicologist and historian Professor Eusebius Mandyczewski, stood Haydn's and Mozart's clavichords; there, with the musty smell of untold yellowed manuscripts, was the proud heart of Austria's great musical heritage. Most of our teachers, those jolly high priests, had known or been pupils or friends of the recently deceased Brahms and Bruckner; Hugo Wolf was still active though mentally sick; and the chain of tradition, reaching back to Schubert, Beethoven, Mozart, and Haydn, had never been broken, style and phrasing having been handed down from master to student, generation to generation.

But during the years in which I grew up, everything in music was ferment and rebirth, centering on Gustav Mahler. "Tradition is sloth!" cried Mahler, as the latest heir to the throne of the great Austrian composers. He was the exciting, the venerated idol of us young musicians. Now it was our turn! At the first performance of a Mahler symphony, the galleries steamed with enthusiasm, we young ones sweating with the strain of comprehending this new music, the orchestra sweating to do justice to the ever-growing difficulties of sound and technique. We felt that our applause, our understanding, was part of tomorrow's music history. We, too, would someday be able to tell how Mahler looked, what he said in rehearsals, how it was when we played the very first performance of *Das Lied von der Erde*, and what happened at the tumultuous scandal of the Sixth Symphony première. In the meantime, Schönberg had cut loose from his eclectic-romantic beginnings and evolved his twelve-tone series, and there was another, still fiercer fight and scandal at the performance of his *Pierrot Lunaire*. And already the first Schönberg disciples were at work—Alban Berg, looking like a slightly damaged Greek sculpture, Anton von Webern, Béla Bartók.

There was a second hemisphere to complete our world—the Vienna Opera in the throes of Mahler's reforms. Up on "Olympus," the famous Fourth Gallery, we boiled with enthusiasm or froze a poor performance with merciless contempt. Frequently, fanatical partisanship caused fist fights, broke up friendships and love affairs. We had no eyes for the silly gesturing of those fat, barrel-chested Wagnerian heroines and/or gods; we detached ourselves from all that was second-rate in opera as a form of art, and we were nothing but ears. With closed eyes we would crouch on the floor, leaning against the back wall under the red exit light, and test each other about the orchestration, the key, the pitch, the tempi. One recognized by ear who was singing, who conducting, even which of the two concertmasters was leading the violins. Both were masters of playing flat in the high registers; the elder of the two was the most feared teacher and examiner in the Konservatorium.

I can't imagine under what pretexts I swindled or stole the money and time I spent in the Fourth Gallery. I only knew I had to be home by 10:00 P.M., before Herr Pitzelgruber locked the door. Thus I never knew what happened in the last acts, and was disappointed to find out years later that neither *Aïda* nor *Carmen* had the happy ending I had anticipated.

For me, as for most young people—young intellectuals, I would say, if the word had not since been loaded with wrong connotations—the Fourth Gallery of the Vienna Opera represented at least half our lives. The heady excitement, the transports of a *Tristan and Isolde* performance under Gustav Mahler, the fiery arguments, the shadowy faces of the habitués are as present to me today as if I had been up there last night. In the meantime, though, more than fifty years have gone by. The building has been bombed out and reconstructed, but the outer shell is still the same as it was when I passed it daily on my way to school. I wonder if the young people "on Olympus" can still burn and blaze in the white glow as we did? Do they still swindle themselves in on student passes not their own? Do they stand in freezing huddles all through a night of rain or snow and then yet a whole day, to devour five hours of *Götterdämmerung,* hear *Rosenkavalier?* Do they still observe the unwritten law by which you lose your place in line if you have no substitute to hold it while you follow a call of nature? Do they know how to win the race on the shallow steps of the stairs to the gallery, or is there a scuffle at the doors of elevators? Elevators! In the Opera? I don't know if what I was told is really true: when the Opera—the old one—was built and finished and opened with due imperial pomp, it turned out that the architects had forgotten to provide toilets. One of the builders committed suicide—a Viennese hara-kiri —and the new-fangled luxury was squeezed in as an afterthought. Does today's youngster in the Fourth still lose his place if he leaves it for a moment before the big chandelier is lit, but have a legitimate squatter's right to it from the moment the lights are up? Or is there no big chandelier at all in the modernized auditorium, no glittering brooch on the giant bosom of the domed ceiling? I really must visit Vienna soon, if only to see what's going on in the Opera. . . .

Wrapped up in music as I was in those years, the camera in my mind watched and registered. I even sketched into a copybook some of the things I felt or saw in the Opera and the Konservatorium. Many years later I put those fragments together into a book, *Eingang zur Bühne* ("Stage Entrance"), a sentimental, melodramatic, and trite first story, that was surprisingly successful because of what was described as flashes of humor and a talent for background and atmosphere. This book, I'm afraid, is the reason I have no clear recollection of those Konservatorium years. A little idiosyncrasy of mine: if I wish to remember an address, a phone number, I must not write it down. To me, once it's written down it's done with. Writing, to me, means unburdening myself of some nagging question, remembrance, or problem.

(When Bruno Walter, visiting Gustav Mahler at one of the lovely lakes near Salzburg, admired the landscape, Mahler said, laughing: "Never mind, everything you see is composed already.")

Done with.

If one was graduated from the Konservatorium at last, especially with top honors, one could be fairly sure to find a job, however obscure and poorly paid, as I did in the excellent symphony orchestra of the Vienna Konzertverein. In rarer cases a graduate went on to sensational success and became world famous. But obviously, even the best harpist on earth has little opportunity to cause a sensation.

At twelve I was put in front of an audience: my hair mercilessly pulled back, stubborn curls plastered down with Vaseline, my dress of thick pinkish cotton lace, a hideous creation of Frau Gross ("Arms and legs like matchsticks," she had said reproachfully), and my feet, in those terrible shoes of Herr Adler's making, tramping around on my harp's seven pedals. Nothing is more exposed than a harpist's arms and feet, and nothing could look worse than what I had to offer. On top of everything, I had a sore throat, a little fever, and consequently a rich, inflamed crop of blisters around lips and nose.

I played well at my debut though, and the audience liked me. Much more important, my teacher was satisfied, not my beloved old Professor Zamara (who had joined Grandfather in some Heaven), but the old man's son, the Young Professor, just as tall and beautiful and as strict a master.

Soon after, I was invited to give a solo and also to play the accompaniment to Brahms' Songs for Women's Chorus with French Horns and Harp, in a concert performed by a small, select chorus society. I was to be dressed in black.

Nowadays to be dressed in black is probably the dream of every adolescent girl, but it definitely wasn't done during my teens. There were loud arguments and bickering before Father agreed that I might play if I fitted myself into the black uniform that our maid wore when Mama had guests for tea. At that time, our maid was no longer my Katl, but Marie, a large, plump country girl. Since Mama had come back, there were constant scenes and quarrels in the kitchen and no maid stayed more than a few months. I was as thin as ever, and Marie would not permit a stitch to be changed on her precious uniform. There were more safety pins than you can find in a notions department, used to tighten the damned thing, shorten the skirt and sleeves, turn down the collar. The result was, of course, a little girl parading in Mother's discarded clothes. Depressed by this, I probably played my solo with more expression than I might have otherwise—I'm always at my best when I'm unhappy.

The big surprise came the next day: for the first time I had been heard and written up by the leading critic of Vienna. Here it was, in print: I was lovely, beautiful, interesting, I had an abundance of grace and personality. Me! in Marie's pinned-up uniform.

I wouldn't have been a normal young girl if such compliments had not pleased me. Still, something rankled. Why, anyone playing a golden harp can look pretty and graceful; even buck-toothed Bertha had. Silently I protested against being stamped, patronized, suddenly in vogue, not because I was the best harpist in the world and a very serious musician, but because people found me cute, such a sweet child (oh, my God!), a conversation piece.

I want to put down a few words about that era because it registered the Proustian colors of a society on its way out. These were the years of the *jour fixe*, the twilight of the dying salons. The circle in which I was caught did not belong to the absolutely flawless, stiff-necked highest nobility, although there were the characteristic wealth, superficiality, paucity of thought, gracious chitchat, good manners; all the characteristics of the aristocracy, plus the spice of a bit of dubious ancestry here and there. As in Proust's salon of Madame Verdurin, one had to show his loyalty regularly by making an *acte de présence* on the *jour*.

In one of my recurring unpleasant dreams I relive my arrival at the palace of the Prince and Princess Liechtenstein. I am ushered into the huge salon where the Princess is sitting on a settee, ramrod-stiff, very tall and unbelievably slender, a masterpiece of corsetry, elderly, her face not only painted but enameled, her coiffure a crown of obviously false auburn braids. The Prince, just as tall, stiff, and slender in his Prince Albert coat sharply nipped in at the waist, stands smiling behind her as if posing for a picture. Two flunkies serve the ever-same *petits fours,* which are inseparable from those served on the *jour* of any of the great ladies. There's nothing wrong with the Prince's line of ancestors, but it is said that he went into politics and became the leader of the anti-Semitic movement (and how mild and conciliatory that Austrian anti-Semitism of 1900 appears in view of later events!) because his misalliance had displeased the great, reigning Liechtenstein family. Gossip had it that the Princess, a great beauty in her youth, had been painted in the nude by Makart, the creator of huge, sumptuous, enormously overrated canvases; anybody who cares can see her in the museum, one of the three voluptuous female figures in the painting called "Emperor Karl's Entry into Antwerp."

It was difficult to reconcile the rich, nude flesh of Makart's painting with the dried-out, stiffly laced elderly lady in her salon, but I didn't care a fig about the gossip. The Princess was my main benefactress, she invited me often to play at her musical soirées and also to be her guest, not only on the *jour fixe* but at odd hours in between. She hung me with jewelry (it would have been in bad taste to remunerate a guest in cash), sent me elegant little accessories, had her own dressmaker fit evening gowns, vaguely Empire in style to go with my harp. I was infinitely grateful to her for finding an amiable and tactful way of getting me out of the imprisonment of Frau Gross's scarecrow creations.

In my unpleasant dream, though, as I am ushered into the salon and cross the familiar stretch of slithery parquetry floor to make my curtsy and kiss the long, bony hand, the Princess cuts me cold. I am acutely aware of the reason. (Did you ever notice that dreams make perfect mind readers of us?) "As you haven't come to my *jour* in sixty years," I know the Princess is thinking, "I don't wish to see you now." She still wears her emerald necklace to match her green eyes, and the worst part of that dream is still to come. Her face cracks; under the enamel there is a strange substance, something between rubber and marshmallow, that stretches, bulges, crumbles, melts; the emeralds also melt, like green candles, green streaks, green ghosts—and I wake up.

I knew another lady of nobility, an old countess who occupied a most unpretentious flat; she had neither *jour fixe* nor emeralds but her genealogy was flawless. I liked her because she answered so perfectly my idea of how a noble old lady ought to look and speak and act.

A lacy *petit rien* of a bonnet on her white hair, she used to sit in the deep, sunlit window seat; she would put a bookmark into the book she was reading and ring the bell, at which a possibly still more ancient maid brought in a lovely Old Vienna porcelain platter (rose pattern) of homemade cookies. Not the ubiquitous *petits fours* from Demel's Konditorei, but delicious cookies that I adored, the recipe for which had come down through several generations from the imperial kitchens of the great Empress Maria Theresa, the mother of Marie Antoinette. But what I liked most was the parrot. A threadbare relic of a bird, he sat on his perch clutching the little crossbeam in his steel-like claws, his feathers bleached by time, sleeping the hours away. For my benefit the old countess would wake him up, and sometimes he would condescend to take part in our conversation. The wondrous thing was that he spoke the obsolete court language of long, long ago, a mixture of garbled yet formalized French and the old Austrian dialects that the nobles had probably brought from their country estates. That parrot talked like the characters in Hofmannsthal's *Rosenkavalier*. "Because he has lived at court," the old countess would explain with a smile. She had been a lady-in-waiting in her youth and had inherited the bird from one of the ancient court charges who had claimed it had belonged to Maria Theresa herself.

I suppressed my doubts about the age a parrot could reach and enjoyed the fairy-tale quality of it all.

One of the tricks to bitching up a social rival's *jour* consisted of announcing your own *jour* for the same day and snatching away as many of the "regulars" as possible. Countess Hoyos, for instance, was a caricature of Princess Liechtenstein. She, too, had a painter in her past, Amerling, one of her husbands, perhaps a slightly better, though less spectacular, artist than Makart. She, too, was old, wrinkled, enameled, tall, thin, crowned with false red braids, her neck propped up with jewelry. But while the Princess was somewhat in the caustic style of the great English ladies Oscar Wilde and Somerset Maugham wrote about, the Countess exaggerated each copied detail till it was ridiculous. Her house, really Amerling's, was one of the showplaces of Vienna and the crowd there, intermixed with the higher *bohème,* seemed more amusing. There was a feeling of Lautrec in the air, a whiff of the brothel even to my innocent but eager nostrils. One of the rooms was sheer Orient. (Perhaps Amerling had been influenced by Ingres; or maybe he was a sensualist, plain and simple.) There were low divans around the walls, silken pillows on the floor, a fountain and tiled basin in the center. Adjoining, and always hospitably open, was the bathroom.

Like Paris, like all very old cities, Vienna was at no time famous for the excellence of its plumbing. But here was the bathroom to end all bathrooms, an ostentatious place of vice and lust, large enough to hold a good number of Ingres' fat Odalisques. Its marble floor was covered with prayer rugs and polar bear skins, as were the steps leading down to the spacious sunken pink marble bath. On the walls exotic bronze vines crept and tangled and, sensation of all sensations, they blossomed with electric bulbs in various colors. You could fill the room with hushed, seductive pink—like the Venus grotto in *Tannhäuser*—or make a moonlit night of blues, a sunny, yellow summer day, a green spring morning. It was an invitation to debauchery and orgiastic sin, that bathroom, and there never was a *jour* at which not one of the more questionable guests would, thinking it a great joke, turn off the lights, causing much squealing and giggling of outraged femininity. Now we had Anna—not Marie any more—who would accompany me there and wait in an anteroom with the other duennas, to take me home. But after she told Mama about that bathroom, my visits to the *jours* of the Countess

Hoyos were put on the list of strictly forbidden things, and my career could go hang.

There was nothing wrong with Princess Lubomirska, except that she was Polish, oldest, highest Polish nobility. She had no palace of her own in Vienna but had left her estate, somewhere in the easternmost part of the monarchy, to come to town for the winter season with her father, Count Zamoisky. The old Count was a magnificent figure of a man and I adored him; but then, I always had a grandfather fixation, and Count Zamoisky, with his white hair and mustache and fiery eyes, also reminded me of my beloved old Professor Zamara. Every Saturday night they had a party in the long sweep of reception rooms that they leased or, more probably, borrowed from some of their friends. There were the same *petits fours*, and some of the faces, I knew from other *jours*. But otherwise this was a different world. Much livelier, much less formal, more amusing, mainly because there were always droves of young people and lots of champagne. There was an almost barbaric wealth of thick-clustered antique jewelry, the ladies in formal evening gowns, with trains and deep décolleté—never mind an occasional wine or grease stain, eighteen-button gloves not quite clean, high-heeled satin shoes a bit soiled and scuffed. There was much coquetting and flirting and laughing, and the Princess and her father were most amiable hosts. It was all so lighthearted, so pleasantly sloppy. Later in the evening, we, the young ones, were invited to dance; a pianist was conjured up, the Count shepherded the older guests into another salon and he himself closed the high double doors behind the last of the brocade trains, uniforms, and tail coats.

Only years later did I learn that we, the young ones, had been used to camouflage the conspiracy behind those doors, where our elders were preparing the Polish provinces for their liberation from the Austrian yoke.

And now? Poor Poland. . . .

I don't know whether it is good or bad to be exposed so very young to High Society. There might be a certain glamour to it when seen from afar, or from a distance of fifty, sixty years, the verdigris shimmer of things long past and irrevocably gone. But when you're in the midst of them as I was then, you soon look through the sham, the silliness of it all, and you grow bored and jaded. To this day I have a shuddering aversion to parties, receptions, and similar affairs. That's a most unfriendly way for me to feel, especially in view of the rich, colorful material all the different classes and types of people I have met have brought into my ken.

One of the objections that critics, especially American critics, have to my books is that my writing is flamboyant. I daresay that's true and I humbly accept those raps over my knuckles. But, dear ladies and gentlemen of the literary supplements, kindly consider the sort of world in which I grew up, the environment that formed this objectionable, flamboyant side of a young creature belonging to a flamboyantly dying town and country.

What I learned during those years was poise and a lot of protocol, completely useless after 1914. I knew in my sleep whom to address as Your Grace and whom as Your Highness, or Your Royal, Your Imperial Highness; whether to make a curtsy or a deep reverence, when to stand up, sit down, or, occasionally, to kneel as, for instance, when kissing the ring on the papal nuncio's gloved finger. To dance with the charming Chinese ambassador without getting tangled up with his long, wig-wagging queue or stepping on his toes in the shuffling, soft-soled slippers. He danced a marvelous waltz and had obviously learned his astounding Viennese vernacular from some humorous fiacre coachman. I learned to banter with gay young aristocrats and keep them at a safe distance without hurting their feelings; to have long, fascinating conversations with the elderly Count Wilzceck with whom I shared an explorer's interest in the old—a crumbling fountain, a charming little baroque Madonna in a narrow suburban lane, a barbaric, hardly recognizable bird offered as a kind of pagan sacrifice during one of Vienna's medieval plague epidemics. It amused Wilzceck, a great connoisseur and author of archaeological books, that a kid like me would know so many of those forgotten, hidden bits and always be looking to discover others. Perhaps it amused him the more as it so happened that most of such treasures were to be found in streets and lanes now taken over by the lowest brothels of Vienna. I think this search for my town's hidden beauties was part of my do-it-yourself education. It taught me some history and a lot about the styles of art through the centuries. Fused to my fairly solid knowledge about the parallel styles in music and all the literature I'd swallowed and the information I'd siphoned out of books, it formed a nucleus of what I hesitate to call culture. *Bildung* is the regrettably untranslatable German word for it. I don't remember who said that *Bildung* is what remains after you've forgotten what you've learned in school. Like patina, it forms, shapes, builds itself; it can't be manufactured. I doubt that it can be taught in classrooms. It includes tact, taste, discrimination, good manners beyond those disseminated at the usual sorority tea. I'm often asked if I think a college education is necessary to become a writer. From my experience I'd answer with an emphatic No. I truly believe that any ragged snippet of real life a young person may grab is a better preparation for writing than the confined atmosphere of the campus or, God forbid!, the summer workshops where literature and writing techniques are rammed down the throats of the defenseless pilgrims in a sort of instant concentrate. Such conferences always remind me of turkey farms where the poor gobblers get fattened up for Thanksgiving.

I myself left regular school at the somewhat premature age of thirteen; whatever I know I have taught myself by the simple process of looking, reading, sorting out, reflecting, absorbing. In a word: living. In the normal course I would have gone on to some school of higher education, but the Konservatorium, and later my career, left me with no time for it. Even with a seven-day week and eighteen-hour days it wasn't easy to keep up with the demands. Sometimes I wonder where I found the time for my secret reading, opera-going, and the fun I did have while accumulating my growing lump of *Bildung*.

Of course I had two great advantages: the discipline I'd learned as a young musician—that becomes second nature—and the old cultural soil in which I was raised.

Whenever I drive through one of those bleak, ugly, main-street small towns plunked down in the vast flatness of American prairies and cornfields, it saddens me to think how hard and long the road must be for the young American in quest of those evasive things: beauty, art, culture. It takes the inexhaustible American energy, optimism, ambition, unceasing drive for self-improvement, to find ways and means of pulling up and out of the monotony of small-town main-drag civilization. I often quote what my friend Helen Thompson—today the manager, soul, and driving spirit of the far-flung American Symphony Orchestra League—once laughingly told me. In the small town where she grew up they had just one yearly concert, one great, exciting musical event: when the Swiss Bell Ringers put on their one-night stand and sweated out "Yankee Doodle," Brahms's Lullaby, and last season's hit song. And I think how easy I had it in comparison. I remember very clearly my first awareness of—well, call it by that obsolete romanticists' word "beauty." The object that caught my eye very early in life was a large fountain, the Donner Brunnen, so called after the baroque sculptor who created it. It stood on one of the many old squares, the Mehlmarkt, and the memory is inextricably mixed with the smell of cheese, for on that same square there was a large, famous store that sold nothing but cheeses. On certain days the leftovers, the red rind of Edam with still a bit of yellow clinging to it, Swiss gone slightly stale, the dry debris of the colossal slabs of Italian imports, were given to the poor. Long before the set hour a line would form in front of the store, women in shabby clothes, children whose toes stuck out of torn shoes, a few dirty bums. Once a week Father forced me to go with our maid to obtain some of that free cheese. I, the child, was sent along dressed in a special torn and faded beggar's outfit to make our grumbling, handkerchiefed Katl, Anna, or Marie look properly pathetic. I daresay most of the women put on old rags and borrowed some neighbor's whining children for the same purpose. But then, they were poor, and we weren't. I suffered deeply during the waiting in line. I would have been the first to storm the Bastille if there had been one. Still, while I waited for the charitable cheese, there was the Donner Brunnen for me to look at, a piece of sheer beauty in the late afternoon sun, with the water shining on the lovely long marble limbs of the nymphs.

It is amusing to ponder the influences that formed me during these so-called formative years. I remember that soon after my twelfth birthday I—like probably every normal child—was gripped by the urge to be *bad,* no more of that dull good-girl stuff for me. For the time being my depravity took the form of a crush on a middle-aged opera tenor; he was blond, getting fat, very charming on the stage, although with a regrettable inclination to flat the high notes. What made my crush depraved was the fact that he had a mistress, not just an affair, but a *maîtresse en titre* like the French kings: what's more, she was a ballet dancer and a redhead. I had heard the Hassreiter girls discuss her. "I can't think what he sees in her," Pini, the youngest, said. "She must be sexy. All redheads are sexy. . . ." "And look at her white skin," said Mitzi. "That's what excites him. Men are so sensual. . . ." *"Garde l'enfant,"* Pini said primly, "you ought not to say such things in front of the brat."

But the damage was done. The vague stirrings inside me had suddenly found a love object. I daresay this crush kept me out of mischief for the next two years, far above the fumbling of sweaty, acne-spotted boys closer to my age. Shy as any true love will make you, I never came within one hundred yards of my tenor. I did not even dare write him for his autograph. Yet my innocent crush came to a bad end when my father, the master detective, discovered a kind of shorthand diary scribbled on my calendar. "Saw S. in X. Flower aria perfect." "S. in *Traviata.* Indisposed. Sorry for him."

Then the whole of Vienna was thrown into festive convulsions when Kaiser Wilhelm of Germany came to visit our own ancient monarch; never mind what fatal alliance was cooked up on that visit. In my abbreviated diary I jotted down: "Tonight gala command performance for Kaiser Wilhelm II. S. sings Don José. Lucky Kaiser!!!"

Did you think my parents smiled when they found this scrap of childishness? The hell they did. I received one of my rare though severe spankings, and never again was I permitted to hear that adorable voice with the flat high C.

My personal situation might have formed the background for an ideal movie script. As a harpist I was that unique, glamorized orchestra member, the only female among eighty to ninety men.

Once more I was treated as a mascot. In reality, those exclusively male surroundings seem to have grown something like a tortoise's hard, thick carapace on me. All boys and men were just friends to me, no vibrations, no sex, no romance, no nonsense; we were tied together by mutual work, music, the countless hours of rehearsals and concerts. In all my years as an orchestra member I remember only a single pass a young, curly-headed fiddler made at me; promptly and spontaneously my hand flew out and landed on his cheek with a loud clap. Both were embarrassed, both apologized—a little misunderstanding—and we remained good friends.

So my childish crush on my fat opera singer simultaneously shielded and nourished me between my twelfth and fifteenth birthdays. I learned to know many operas. Over the years kids have howled and swooned at Sinatra, Presley, and their like. Let them. It answers a need in them and, anyway, it's just a passing phase. I had never spoken to my tenor. Nevertheless, from the day of my first menstruation a new *idée fixe* took possession of Mama, and another chamber was opened in our domestic hell. It concerned that priceless treasure of the Victorian age, though its source lay in far deeper strata, in much more distant times and places, way down in the bottomless shaft of myth and ritual when virgins were venerated and sacrificed: in a word, Mama now worried herself crazy over my virginity.

I was anemic, overworked, under the constant emotional stress of my musicianship, and so my cycle was not regulated like the moon's. Every time I was late, Mama went wild. I was put through the third degree, threatened, wheedled, pushed and slapped, screamed at, cried at, implored to confess that I had done it, lost my virginity, been seduced, or raped, perhaps? When, where, by whom, how?

The terrible thing was I had an inkling that Mama liked these scenes, that she wanted to give her fantasy a free run on that awful merry-go-round of sex and rape and seduction. Poor me, I still had only a very nebulous idea of how one went about losing one's virginity. The little I knew I had deduced from poetry and my aunts' whispers.

Dimly I remembered some impossible nonsense of Didi's. I

hadn't believed a word of it. "Our Kaiser wouldn't do such a thing!" I had said, indignantly. Aside from what our old Kaiser would or wouldn't do, it sounded like a very difficult, perhaps even dangerous maneuver. I had forgotten it; repressed it, according to Dr. Freud.

Explaining sex to children is not as simple as modern education assumes it to be. You can draw diagrams, you may call a spade a spade and a toddler's penis a penis, but you can never explain to a child the compulsive urgency of sex, its ecstasies, its mysteries. I suspect also that modern psychology overrates the healthy, normal child's interest in and curiosity about sex. There are so many more fascinating things to be explored in a child's own world. I remember a friend of mine who went to great pains to explain to her five-year-old daughter all the how and why of life, sex, and procreation. "And now," she concluded, hugging her little girl, "now Mommy has told you everything. But if there's anything else you want to know, trust me, ask me, and I'll always tell you the truth." At which little Ada, who had listened with rapt interest, said: "There's just one thing I really want to know, Mommy: how do pictures get into picture frames?"

That's me. I was and still am the girl who wants to know how things are done, what makes clocks tick, politicians lie, murderers kill, what makes things and people act the way they do. I am singularly uninterested in my closest friends' sex life, and I never ask or even guess how old they are, a very un-American state of mind. Facts, dates, numbers, are irrelevant to me except when I need them as background material in my writing, and then I am the most obnoxiously pedantic researcher imaginable. But, as I did in school, I painstakingly forget all the gathered information as soon as I've used it.

Any girl growing up in any Central European metropolis was, and is, exposed to men whose sexual compass is slightly off—old gentlemen hanging around girls' schools, young thugs in the park, pinchers, mashers, mumblers of dirty propositions, addicts of indecent exposure. However, Central Europe, not afflicted with those spinster neuroses and rape obsessions of the Anglo-Saxon Puritans, takes these matters in stride and with a smile, unless real harm is done. Nor were we kids haunted by traumas after such experiences. At least I wasn't, nor any of my friends. I didn't know what it was all about, only that these were things not to be discussed. Children have their own discretion. To be accosted, followed on the street by men trying to pick you up, was rather flattering proof of being pretty and desirable.

Naturally, one did not react to such overtures, but played deaf-mute and walked on with a haughty air. But I was so flattered when Felix Doermann accosted me that I answered him. Felix Doermann was a poet; I had seen his picture in the papers and even read some of his poems. He had published a slim volume, *Orchids*. He was, or wanted to be, a Viennese version of Oscar Wilde, minus the wit and the homosexuality. But there was the same pose, the same load of precious adjectives in his writing, the same slightly boastful attitude of man grazing deep in the pastures of *Fleurs du Mal*. Also, he was handsome and exceedingly well groomed.

You couldn't refuse to speak to this paragon of depravity, could you? I was on my way to my lesson in French conversation and obediently told him so. At which he immediately switched to impeccable French which I countered in my own rather peccable French. He asked me if I knew Oscar Wilde. Not personally, I said. Doermann—who, by the way, at a later stage of my life became a good friend of mine and my first husband's—soon sensed the limitless innocence of my thirteen years: he put me politely on the trolley that would take me to my French lesson.

But I was no Lolita; babbling nonsense had not prevented me from focusing acutely on the humor of the situation. That night I rounded it out, sharpened it into an impudent little story which I sent to a magazine called *Die Muskete* ("The Musket") modeled after the bitterly satirical, famous German *Simplizissimus*.

They accepted it, and asked for more. After the third story they invited me to come to the editor's office, they wished to meet me in person, discuss with me the possibility of becoming a permanent and regular contributor.

And there I was, still in short skirts and pigtails, the disgraceful badges of still being considered a child. I bought hairpins and safety pins and kid gloves; I pinned up my hair and let my skirt down, fastening it to my petticoat and hiding this ingenious arrangement under my coat. I pushed my old round schoolgirl's hat forward and marched into the lion's den with incomparable dignity and *savoir-faire*. After all, I had learned to show poise on the concert platform, why not in that smoky, unimpressive editor's office? I crossed my legs and grandly accepted a cigarette, hoping it would not make me sick. After a little while more and more men sidled in, a few sat down on the desk or on the arms of the editor's chair, some remained leaning against the wall, and others stood in the open door and grinned at me. I felt that I was doing fine; my conversation was sparkling and sophisticated and my only worry was to keep my coat tightly down over my knees where one of the damned safety pins holding down my short skirt had snapped open and was sticking me.

Baron Schönpflug, the editor in chief, told me years later how baffled he had been at first and how he had sent word to the staff to come and look at the Headless Wonder—they hadn't seen anything so funny in years.

But the really funny part of it was that one-half of myself stood outside, clear-eyed and watchful, observing with humorous detachment the ridiculous poses and antics of the childish other half. This inborn compulsion to self-irony, sharp observation, and detachment seems to me to be one of the most important ingredients of a writer's talent.

It was about this time that the Young Professor honored me by inviting me to his studio for private lessons and instruction. I am not quite sure that all his lessons were as harmless as the ones I received, the atmosphere was too erotic, as even a pollywog like me could see. Madame, the Professor's wife, was never present; in class it was whispered that he had married her for her fabulous wealth; if so, I think she got her money's worth. He was outstandingly handsome, his light brown hair falling onto a Roman forehead; his deep-set expressive gray eyes, little silk beard, long and mobile musician's hands. He smoked incessantly, and the scent of his exotic perfumed cigarettes, combined with that of an incense burner, made heavy air in the satin-draped room. Above the couch hung an intriguing painting—a naked woman, very pink against the darkish grays of a big cloud, sitting in a pose I found not only ill-mannered but graceless. If I had ever sat like that my mother would have given me what for! "It's only a copy," the Professor said. "Correggio. Jupiter and Io. You can see the original in the museum. Now listen, what Schopenhauer writes here. . . ."

I still don't know for what perverted reasons he initiated me into the misogynous philosopher's prose, if not to laugh about my angry protests. . . . The short-legged, under-sized, broad-hipped sex we were, indeed! If anything, my legs were too long and still growing longer!

I emerged from those private lessons with an outwardly improved technique for making the harp sing and an inner aversion to Schopenhauer and to philosophy in general, that to this day I have been unable to overcome. Also, I decided to find out what was the matter with Jupiter and Io. He came to her in the shape of a cloud, it said in Grandpapa's mythology. Jupiter was always up to some prank in disguise, everybody knew that.

I can see myself wandering through the Museum of Art. Still in short skirts and my round schoolgirl's hat, I stare at the paintings until I have them imprinted on my brain and can carry them with me (this was still ages before photogravure and color prints). The museum became a refuge from the endless bickering of Sunday mornings at home when Father didn't go to his office. For some of his queer reasons he permitted me to visit the Museum of Natural History but not the Museum of Art; so, naturally, to the Museum of Art I went. Soon I developed a strong personal revulsion to Hélène Fourment, to all the blue-white fat of Rubens' women, his cupids dragging garlands of improbably swollen fruit and flowers. By association, I got bored with the sumptuousness of the Venetian Renaissance painters hanging in the same hall; it was too rich for me, too beautiful, too perfect. I loved the Breughels, they were so full of simple people to make friends with, ugly yet lovable, like real people. But my own home in the museum was the first hall with the small paintings of the nameless primitives. They were not to the average

Viennese taste, so it was always quiet and empty there, like being inside a golden ringing bell or shell. It was a place where rhymes and poems began to sound in my head, all by themselves. Sonnets. Ritornels. The more complicated the meter the better.

Next I discovered Ibsen's *Ghosts*. I found the tattered pages among some junk in a discarded chest of drawers in which I was invited to rummage while Pini and Mitzi Hassreiter played tennis. I suppose I missed much fun through my professor's strict prohibition of sports, and tennis might have ruined my hands for the subtle touch of the Zamara tradition. But not for a wilderness of monkeys— or tennis partners—would I have given up that feverish afternoon of my first encounter with Ibsen.

There it was, everything rotten—*vermoulu*, young Alving called it—everything I had known and despised all along, the fake and lie and phoniness of the grownup world. Family. Teachers. School. Bourgeois complacency, bigotry, hollow patriotism, humbug, swindle —cesspools, badly camouflaged. When my friends returned I rushed at them with excited questions about this man Ibsen of whom I had never heard. Neither had they, for books had little place in their gay extrovert world of flirtation, dancing, skating, and prospecting for future husbands. How this copy of *Ghosts* ever came into their possession is still a mystery. Timidly I asked in a bookstore if they had possibly heard of a playwright by the name of Henrik Ibsen. Indeed they had. Bless the late Herr Reclam in Leipzig, he had published all of Ibsen for 12 kreuzer (three cents!) a volume in his ubiquitous ragpaper editions. I bought them all, I ate them up, including the rather indigestible historical Norse dramas. I don't know how I came to the conclusion that I was the only person to know, read, and understand Ibsen, except that none of the people with whom I tried to discuss him seemed to understand what I was talking about.

Later, when I was almost sixteen and in love with a man twice that, the first bridge between us was that he, too, was at home with Ibsen. Suddenly my ingrained loneliness vanished. There were two of us on an island, amid an ocean of people who had never heard the call of that great man from the North.

It is amusing to observe how the taste of a youngster, uninfluenced by others, will form itself, grow away from tradition, grope for something new and different and thus discover the style of his time. Suddenly there exists a whole new generation of such lonely explorers and a new art is born.

It is a curious fact that mellow Vienna always puts up an iron resistance against any reform or reformer, yet at the same time is a fertile breeding place for the new and revolutionary. Freud and the new school of psychology, Schönberg and his followers in music, the Vienna *Werkstätten*, from which stem the Bauhaus and modern architecture, to mention only a few such movements. I remember the rude laughing and jeering with which Vienna greeted her first modern building, the Secession, a place where the seceding revolutionary artists could exhibit their rebellious, antiacademic works. The Golden Cabbagehead, it was called, on account of its dome of bright bronze laurel leaves that dominated the squat monolithic, faintly Assyrian-Egyptian walls, a bastard conception if there ever was one; even I could see that it was ugly, yet I defended it heatedly. It was different, it was new, it was *us,* the young ones.

How old, how impossible that style of *art nouveau* looks today; it spread like a grass fire when I was a kid. And the great new painters of that time . . . how ridiculous, what fools! How quickly their fame faded and died—Klimt, Böcklin, Segantini, Hodler, the too-flattering portraits by Lenbach and László, the neoclassicism of Puvis de Chavannes. In the meantime, the French Impressionists were at last rising to the top and the next revolution was already in the making: Léger, Gauguin, Gris, Van Gogh. I remember the bewilderment with which I—we all—tried to make sense, find contour and meaning in their unrealistic colors, the sun-exploding spectrum, so new to our eyes. Then the pointillists! And already Picasso was at work, and Kokoschka, and Orlik with the Japanese woodcuts he had brought from the Orient. You had to learn seeing all over again.

It was all there—the seeds, the larvae of today's art.

On the backs of envelopes, young architects sketched houses in an entirely different style, housing projects right for industrial districts, with air and sun, playgrounds for the workers' children, new schools, new theaters, new museums, new everything. Not to be outdone, furniture designers created new fashions, new crafts, threw out the dust-catching gimcracks and ornaments of the nineties. Painters talked cubism and abstractions; dancers were breaking away from their petrified techniques; on the stages appeared new, stylized sets that, in turn, demanded a new style of acting; poets threw off the stiff corsets of metric rhyme and form and wallowed happily in free verse. And writers groped in all directions to express the eternal conflicts and quests of man.

Having seen so many new artists, new styles coming in and going out even before the First World War, I remain rather cool and detached when it comes to the very latest in art, music, and literature. How much or how little of it will last? Time is like a high wind during threshing; most of the day's harvest blows away like chaff. Only a very few really worthwhile grains remain for the morrow.

I was lucky to be a tiny particle in a period of churning and fermentation, luckier still that I was not conscious of it. Out of the cradle of those first ten years of the century we, the young people, nursed and nurtured all that gives the present its face—Kafka and Proust, Joyce and Rilke, Klee and Picasso and Bracque, Freud, Schönberg, and the Bauhaus. And last but not least the saintly little man who needed a haircut and who said: $E = mc^2$.

F O U R

here were two mirrors in our apartment, one above the monumental washstand of my parents' bedroom and one in the huge entrance hall. I was strictly forbidden to look into them. This, naturally, made mirrors doubly fascinating. When my parents weren't home, I would stare at my reflection in the forbidden glass for half an hour at a time, asking the highly important question: How do I look?

Green in the face? No, more blue, sort of; deep, blue circles below much too large gray-blue eyes that looked out from under a wilderness of black eyebrows and lashes. Too small for my age, skimpy, underweight, under-everything. The other kids in my class began to sprout little breasts but I, the youngest and smallest, had nothing but a rib cage.

It's not true that narcissism means to be in love with oneself; on the contrary, the true narcissist suffers from discontent, a nagging feeling of being ugly, inadequate. Innocent of today's cosmetics, I had to invent my own. Soon the pink tissue paper from Father's shirt fronts was not enough: I had to buy and chew many such sheets of paper to paint my cheeks. I rolled up my knitted camisole beneath my tight, straight school clothes, thus producing a nice, appealing bulge across my chest. I forgot that a corresponding bulge would protrude on my back. Each time Mama passed me while I was practicing on my harp she gave me a sharp slap and push. "Sit straight! You're becoming a hunchback!"

I was dressed abominably, I don't know whether it was because of a determination to suppress any trace of vanity in me or through sheer clumsy neglect. My dresses were still "created" by Frau Gross who wasn't even a dressmaker, just a seamstress. I loved the dear old witch, but she knew only one pattern: the scarecrow model. I was covered from head to toe with stiff, scratchy materials. I wore long black cotton stockings when all the other girls had lovely striped little socks. Coarse high shoes with hooks and eyes instead of smart buttons, a debasing mark of inferiority when some of the girls wore charming patent leather slippers for everyday. Oh yes, we, too, had our status symbols. There was a chasm between the privileged kids with the pinafores and such as I, in shapeless smocks.

To console myself, I invented a counterpoint to Andersen's fairy tale: Once upon a time there was a beautiful young swanlet; her mother was very proud of her—it was, of course, a little girl swan— and everybody came to the lake to admire her. But as she grew up her lovely swan's neck shrank and got thick, her snow-white fluffy feathers turned a dirty brown, her body became short and fat and waddly, and her spoonlike beak looked stupid and greedy, good for nothing except to gobble up slimy mud and refuse. In short, the beautiful swan ended up an ugly duck.

So far, so good. Making up defiant stories was a consolation, but still, what I saw in the forbidden mirror was an ugly duckling. The youngest, the smallest, the thinnest in class; still worse: the brightest. All our teachers were men, good objects for hero worship or to fall in love with, which I did promptly. Our principal, *Direktor* Moosbauer, was my special favorite and, I believe, vice versa. Gray-haired, smiling, pink-cheeked and extremely blue-eyed, *Direktor* Moosbauer would have made an ideal Santa Claus. He would put the batch of copybooks on his desk, push his eyeglasses up on his turnip nose and twinkle from under them at the class. "As usual, our Bäumchen delivered the best composition. But, also as usual, it is much too long. Much, much too long. How many pages was it to be at the most? Six pages, Bäumchen, just six! And what did you write? Thirty-two and a half!" He would open my copybook and lift it high for the whole class to see, the red ink slashed across page after page.

"Bäumchen, Bäumchen, when will you learn to hold your horses? And to stick to the given theme? Well, in spite of it I'm afraid I'll have to give the Bäumchen an A-plus."

All through school, in my professional life, and until I was a grandmother, I remained Bäumchen to colleagues and subordinates alike—a diminutive, a neuter, a little Baum or tree.

I remember one of the many times when I not only drifted away from the given theme but revolted against it. The theme was the *Nibelungenlied,* a eulogy of Teutonic virtues, German valor, and armed loyalty, personified in their highest glory by the blond hero Siegfried. Well, I had taken apart those wonderful Teutons and their virtues and found them all, including their damned hero Siegfried, a mean, corrupt, swindling lot. The only loyal character I could find in the entire heap was Hagen, the dark-haired, villainous, sinister opponent and killer of Siegfried, and not even *Direktor* Moosbauer could force me to write against my conviction. My thesis seemed to have touched him in a sensitive spot, because I was called out before the class, soundly scolded, and given a furious F. Yet, terrible as this was, I stuck to my guns.

Some forty years later, when I was trying to write for the movies, I went through clashes identical with this one; there was nothing new to me in their idea of a black-and-white simplicity of good and evil —white hats for the Good Guys, black hats for the Bad Ones. Nor did Hitler's pure Aryans surprise me after I had fought it out, once and for all, with my otherwise so dear *Direktor* Moosbauer.

Still my books run to too many pages and a surfeit of adjectives, and every so often I hear Moosbauer's admonition just when I'm going strong: "Bäumchen, Bäumchen, when will you learn to hold your horses . . . !"

The peril of being that loathsome creature, the Class Primus, the best pupil, teacher's pet, was constantly hanging over my head. Only by great efforts did I circumvent the danger; by prompting, letting anybody copy from me, doing homework for the hopeless ones, and, in an emergency, making a few intentional mistakes or letting myself be caught reading under my desk. There was greater heroism involved in this subterfuge than anybody guessed. Unlike other girls, whose delighted parents gave them five pennies for each A, I received a spanking for each B, not to mention the sermons, the punishments, the withdrawal of even the scant privileges I enjoyed—no dessert, no opera, none of those life-saving weekends at the Hassreiter villa where my girl friends coddled me, where the air was so light and gay and the food so good. Like all the educational tortures to which my father exposed me, these castigations were perfect training for practical life. They grew my rhinoceros hide, made me impermeable to pain, mental or spiritual. The worm turned early—at the age of ten I was an accomplished liar; like any normal child, a deft operator and psychologist, thoroughly masked and armed to defend my secret private life. I lived underground in a burrow of my music, my studies, my thoughts, the books I was forbidden to read but read all the same, the stories I told myself when I couldn't borrow or steal a book.

From that moment until this I don't think there was a single day in my life without some reading; on second thought, I will except a few weeks when, as happened a few times, I was out and under with delirious fevers of various kinds, doped after one or another operation, or strictly forbidden to read by some ill-advised doctor.

But although books mean so much to me, I refuse to believe that illiteracy is detrimental to culture. I found that many people, and peoples with very old and subtle cultures, cannot read or write but know more about their history, their nations or tribes, their laws and legends, their gods, philosophies, and religion than the average reader of newspapers, magazines, and best-selling books. The storyteller in the market place, the wandering players rigging up their stage on the village square, the endless, countless depictions of gods and heroes on the walls of temples and churches, all keep alive the accumulated knowledge and wisdom of a people, and hand it on from generation to generation. I would almost say: where the printed, the readable word begins, there begins the lie; from the outrageous, bootlicking, flattering texts on Sumerian and Egyptian walls to today's angled political pronouncements. If, as it often seems to me, we are at the threshold of an age when only a small group of specialists will be able to read, it might be all to the good.

When my Fine Grandfather died, he willed his books to be divided between those of his grandchildren who were old enough to read and had shown traces of intelligence. The distribution of these books, however, was handled in my family's usual peculiar way. You would have thought that one child would have been given Goethe, another Schiller, and so on down the line. Not so. Each child received the same *number* of books, which meant that all those beautiful complete editions were taken apart. I still haven't quite recovered from these ragged beginnings of my acquaintance with the classics. I received not one play of the great dramatists Lessing and Schiller, just a load of their prose—magnificent prose in Schiller's case, cut and dried, highly professorial prose by Lessing; the endless and confusing novels of Goethe and his delightful autobiography. Of Hauff I didn't get the dearly beloved fairy tales but this strange thing: *Der Mann im Monde* ("The Man in the Moon"). I did not understand that it was a witty and poisonous travesty, a parody of an author of best sellers of that time. It was trash of the highest potency, full of sly, coy smuttiness mixed with melodrama and sentiment thick as axle grease. I read it in breathless excitement, secretly, under my blanket, under my desk in school, during prolonged sessions in the toilet. And there, there was the prototype and ancestor of all the lovers in all my books. Herr von Martinetz was his name, he was pale, dark-haired, and a stranger in town, mysterious and unhappy. Every midnight the sexton would unlock the church for him, and for an hour he would kneel in the light of a flickering candle (flickering candle, for God's sake!) at the feet of the Madonna, beating his chest, moaning and sighing as if he wanted to die. Until a young girl, her innocence and skin as white as snow, makes him confess to her his deep guilt (he killed his friend in a duel, I believe) and saves him through the power of her love and her described-in-detail high marble (marble!) bosom.

If meeting this cursed Martinetz was a traumatic experience, I can't help it; perhaps a psychoanalyst could have freed me of it, at a high cost, and from there on I might have filled my books and my life with unattractive intellectuals.

The chances for doing this were great, whether you believe in either inherited, or otherwise conditioned, traits. According to all findings of psychology, my childhood was of the kind usually blamed for every later aberration, addiction, crime, and self-destruction. Humbly begging pardon for contradicting the sages and prophets, I submit that one can learn to swim against the current instead of drifting with it. One can live and act not "because" but "in spite of." It may take a bit stronger moral fiber in the beginning, but it is no harder to develop that than it is to train your muscles to play baseball or your brain to work out mathematical problems.

At twelve years you are a tadpole. You still have gills and a little tail but you also have legs and arms. Part of you is still a child and yet other parts are quite grown up. It's a tumultuous age, what with all the goings-on in your glands and your mind, so much to shed, so much to ingest, digest, so many things still blurred and yet others so unbearably sharp and bright. With surrealistic clarity you see foremost the grownups, their injustice, bigotry; who do they think they are to act so overbearing? . . . stuffed shirts, phonies, fakes, and humbugs. So you build your barricades and set up a revolution, each child his own, all alone; which adds up to a whole generation of rebels.

Children can't understand the absurd extravagance with which grownups bolster their swindles. What kind of a supercolossal conspiracy is this? Just to make a fool of you, the child? Ridiculous, incomprehensible! Those silly stories about the stork bringing babies. The hell he did! When I was a tadpole I got my instruction piecemeal. The drunk monster that nursed me during my scarlet fever had told me how women bled and screamed when they gave birth to a baby. But this I remembered more as part of feverish dreams and nightmares. Then there was a girl, somewhat older, who lived in the same house. I sincerely disliked her, but she had nice dolls and came to play with me; what we played was always the birth of a baby. She would put her big doll in her doll bed and, screeching at the top of our lungs, we made the big doll give birth to my tiny doll Erika. Early masters of Technicolor, we even sneaked tomato paste into the confinement to make it a good, bloody event.

The next step in my education was taken care of exceedingly tactfully by our laundress, a heavy-set, freckled, redheaded woman, whom I loved dearly. "My, you're getting fat; do you eat so much?" I asked her. I had vaguely noticed that ladies grew fat and thin in cycles, like the moon. My seven aunts, for instance. "Just watch me, little one," my laundress friend told me, "soon I'll be thin again."

Sure enough, two weeks later she wasn't fat any longer. "Remember what I told you, little one?" she said. "You know why I'm thin again? I've had another baby. See?"

I saw. I understood. I daresay, you couldn't be told in a more direct way where babies came from. How they got there was another question, which didn't interest me then, nor for years to come. There was, in the fourth grade, a small committee of three or four girls who would pull you into a corner and ask you—with feverish giggles and whispers—the eternal question of the budding female: "Do you know where babies come from?"

"Of course. From the belly," I said, bored and utterly blasé.

"Nya, nya, but I bet you don't know how they get *into* the belly, do you?"

"Maybe not. But I know what love is," I said grandly. Well, that floored them.

"What do you mean, love? How do *you* know what love is?"

"From *Cavalleria Rusticana*," I said and walked away proudly. What did these dumb little girls know about the Opera House where I was quite at home? Sometimes I was taken along by the Hassreiter girls, sitting proudly in a box, with burning cheeks, ice-cold hands in little white kid gloves that smelled of cleaning fluid. More often I was seated high on "Olympus" as part of Herr von Hassreiter's claque for a new ballet. Having been subjected to ballets since I was knee-high, they bored me to death; I only endured them on account of the opera that followed. Later, under Mahler's regime, the pre-opera ballets disappeared almost entirely, and who, if you please, could have digested a ballet on the same menu with the interminable operas by Wagner?

I was too young when I left school, just thirteen. But my days had been crowded to bursting: six hours in school, six hours practicing the harp and two hours of piano, plus the time spent in the classes for these two instruments, and homework in theory, instrumentation, music history; far more hours yet for chorus rehearsals, orchestra rehearsals, and a growing schedule as a concert soloist. How I managed to squeeze it all in, I don't know, but I did and still found time for myself.

t was a great time to grow up in, that last era of European peace, there was so much beginning in its daybreak air, such a good, fertile dawn. It was for us, my generation, to bring about the liberation of women, of love, of sex; we were the first to experiment with new concepts of psychology, with social ideas that long since have become self-evident and commonplace. We were not satisfied to tear down the obsolete, we did our best to create something better. And we did it against such high odds and under such heavy pressure that I can only chuckle about the war cries of today's Angry Young Men and overpublicized beatniks, especially since Vienna has had her coffeehouse culture and her beatniks since the second siege of the Turks, and her young men have been angry for a hundred years, and with good reason, although they have too much Lao-tzu passivity and too little taste for publicity to rant on so noisily. In Vienna, to be beat is a natural condition.

Clearly, I had neither time nor thought for such stupid enterprises as the "dates" of American adolescents. I had no puppy love, and my childish crush on my tenor, who was getting older and fatter before my disillusioned eyes, was petering out. I graduated from the Konservatorium with honors in the shape of the much coveted Silver Medal, that was dangled in front of our noses like the carrot designed to lure the recalcitrant horse Lisl up the hill.

Soon after, and simultaneously, two important things happened. I became the harpist of the excellent Vienna Konzertverein, the symphonic backbone of Vienna's musical life; and the conductor of a chorus society in whose concert I had played a solo asked me, softly, as if it were a dangerous secret: "Tell me, dear, would you, how old you are?"

It is the prerogative of youth to be in a mess all the time. No sooner do you scramble out of one than you find yourself up to your neck in another. You fall in love with the wrong person; you marry another man in furious despair, equally wrong. You burn your ships and dynamite your bridges. You get divorced, fall in love again and again. You make every one of the mistakes youth makes. You want to kill somebody, your parents, your love, yourself, and you fail even in this. Your glands work overtime, your metabolism is high; simple and ordinary biochemical processes, but they blur your vision, stupefy your faculties. "I am so confused," youth says, writes, sings, rhymes. "I'm bewildered, what am I to do now? What happens to me, to us? Where are we going from here? Is there no way out of all this heartbreak or no holding on to this unbearable hot sweet happiness?"

Everything happens to you for the first time. Consequently and logically, it can never have happened before, not to anyone. "But you don't see," you say in contradiction to every moderate voice, "this is different. I am different, my love is different, no one can understand what I am going through. Such pains, such ecstasies, such deadly, tumultuous bliss."

Oh youth, oh for those cursed, blessed first times. . . .

In retrospect it seems to me that the inevitable messes young people of my generation got into by way of love cut deeper, were not spread so wide and shallow. We did not analyze each word, movement, subconscious thought and emotion like characters by Sartre, we went at love naïvely, wholeheartedly. We were simply not so afraid of getting hurt by loving as youth appears to be today, hedging each emotional risk they take like seasoned manipulators of the stock market and the race track.

I can understand why the newer writers are trying to circumvent this boredom and repetitiousness by pulling out all the stops on sex. Writing, like reading, is a sensual occupation full of vicarious pleasures. "Make mine rare" is the insistent cry of readers so immature or so senile as to need being titillated. But after a while mere fornication gets boring, duller than old-fashioned love, even if described with every clinical detail. I, for one, am getting awfully tired of getting pushed into unmade beds or onto uncomfortable back seats, being forced to watch sweating bodies in their more or less successful copulations, and getting full information on the number of their orgasms and the unreliability of their contraceptives.

It is true that we, the girls of my class and my generation, were thrown into the deep waters of sex without having learned to swim. Blunder and thrash though we did, we somehow managed to stay afloat. If I can go by the letters addressed to the women who give advice to the lovelorn in the daily papers, the ignorance of today's youngsters has a different face. Hardly a day without the anguished cry of a fourteen- or fifteen-year-old: "There's this boy I'm going steady with . . . I think I'm in love with him but I'm not sure since I met this other boy. . . . Please tell me, how can you know if it's the real thing?"

No such doubts for me when I fell in love, or rather when I loved, for the first time. I arrived on this new planet untouched, inexperienced, my feelings unimpaired yet astoundingly mature. Still, it was a wonderful thing to happen to me, at the right time, with the right man, right for my kind of love.

Lucky, first of all, that I had not frittered my emotions away in silly dates with adolescent boys tortured by acne, pipe dreams, and fumbling doubts. I had not spoiled my appetite by eating green apples, had never been kissed or pawed or sweatingly panted at in a car, either front, back, or rumble seat. There were few cars yet anyway, and a girl riding in a hack or a fiacre with a man alone, unchaperoned, was considered a fallen woman.

There is nothing easier than to ridicule a love when it is past. It would save us a lot of despair if one could apply the same humorous detachment to a love that's still present and alive. For more than fifty years I've treated my first love, my Great Love, as a huge joke. "Tell again about your First Love!" my children and grandchildren prompt me, getting ready for a good laugh. "He was so beautiful, so romantic, come on, tell, he had a Flying Dutchman beard——"

"Yes, a silky little beard, black, with a bit of gray in it——"

"Eeek! How icky! Vicki's Great First Love was a beatnik!" (Come to think of it, beards at this moment aren't quite as funny as they were ten years ago.) At last there are cascades of laughter at the idea of Grandmother having been young and in love at some prehistoric time.

He was the materialization of my wildest dreams and he did look like the Flying Dutchman—dark, pale, with a Vandyke beard, romantic to beat the band; he also looked a little like the Black Knight in the abridged version of *Ivanhoe* I had devoured as a child. He, too, was always dressed in black, either in his conductor's slim tail coat or a black velvet jacket and flowing necktie, the prescribed fashion for artists and musicians.

And he opened new gates to music for me. So far, I had accumulated a fair knowledge of opera and the symphonic repertory. Now I was introduced to the severe, serene, and pure world of chamber music and the wealth of *Lieder* literature. I learned not only to read and listen, but to do so with a new understanding, to analyze why I liked this or that, to discriminate, not to be lured by the easily understood, the trivially expressed; by what a new, young, and very promising writer by the name of Thomas Mann was calling "the Tristan optimism."

I, being used to Mahler, Bruno Walter, and the enormously efficient and experienced keepers of the daily repertory, found this lack of routine touching. He reminded me somewhat of Debussy, who had recently been our guest conductor and had waved a rather bewildering baton. My Flying Dutchman, too, was of French descent, with a French name, French features, French spirit, and elasticity.

Following the first part of a concert in which I had played a harp solo at his invitation, we found ourselves alone in the Green Room of the Opera House, while somewhere in the distance, a contralto dipped into the honey-sweetness of Delilah's aria. Having been amply warned of the perils of being with a man unchaperoned, I went to the door. He blocked me. "Wait, stay a minute. I want to talk with you. About a concert—my chorus society has a concert next month, I'd like you as soloist."

"Yes?" I said.

"Yes. Tell me, are you as sensitive as you look?"

A silly question to which I knew no answer. The next moment he had his arms around me and kissed me. I had never been kissed before, and in 1903 a first kiss meant incomparably more than rape means today. In spite of the unspeakable things that some heretofore unknown, complicated machinery in my body responded with, he must have sensed my innocence because he let go of me at once, took a step backward, and said huskily: "Aaaah . . . how old are you, child?"

"Almost sixteen," I said. (I'd just passed my fifteenth birthday.)

"Oh, my God. But the way you play! You're a woman . . . a wild, passionate full-grown woman when you play!"

There was a hot weight in my groin, a tense hot wire pulling at the inside of my thighs. I wanted . . . I didn't know what. I needed to be kissed again, and again. But he went to the other end of the room and sat down, his long musician's hands hanging between his knees. His face, usually carved ivory, had turned white and a little snake of a blue vein had sprung up on his forehead.

"I am warning you, Mignonne," he said, "I am warning you. I am a sensualist, I was born with an erotic nature, and, so help me God, I'm afraid I'm in love with you. Come here . . . kiss me once more. . . ."

I guess today's girl, confronted with such a situation, would say: "How corny can you get? Dry up, pal." But I could only tremble, wade across the room with heavy legs, close my eyes in a trance, and, with a swan dive, land in my lover's arms.

He was engaged to marry, had been engaged for years, was, in fact, honor-bound to marry his patient and understanding fiancée as soon as his opera would be finished, accepted, and, no doubt, successful. In retrospect I can see that he used this drawn-out engagement as a shield against the many girls with whom he fell in love successively and who, naturally, all wanted to marry him. For me the situation was just right; it was, to my fifteen-year-old mind, tragic. Such beautiful heartbreak, such silent storms of jealous sufferings, such a romantic sense of loving the unattainable, knowing the fierce sweetness of a love that was eternal but could not be realized. It was just up my alley! I, the rebel, had nothing but contempt for marriage. Me? Rather dead than to love, yet never possess.

As this man was a musician, and a very fine one—conductor, composer, and teacher—our official meetings were in the disguise of lessons and rehearsals, under either the eagle eyes of my mother or the very lenient ones of his old-maidish sister who probably got vicarious kicks out of her brother's peccadilloes. But as we both knew we would perish if we couldn't see each other every day, life became a hectic round of secret meetings, good-night kisses in dark corners, telepathic messages, long ecstatic love letters, that I would pick up at the general delivery window and keep where prostitutes were said to carry their wages of sin—under my garters, inside my scratchy black cotton stockings (lisle when I played in concerts). No wonder I was simply dripping with poems.

Promptly, too, I began to write a play. The first line was: "Thank you, but I carry my violin alone." Sheer, crystalline symbolism! Then came the heartbreaking story of a young girl virtuoso who, during the evening of her first recital and sensational success, discovers that the man she loves, a conductor, is betraying her with a married, sophisticated old woman of twenty-two. But gallantly she goes through the program until the end, and the last line is the same as the first: "Thank you, but I carry my violin alone." It all takes place in the Green Room before, during, and after the concert. I sure had learned from Ibsen the Aristotelian principle of the three unities. I still believe in it, up to a point. Meandering through biographical years on the stage or the screen can be fairly entertaining, but to my mind it lacks the compression necessary for real drama.

I have a good idea of what made me see myself as the adorable heroine of a remotely autobiographical play. My kind of love, I have been informed since, dates back to the times of King Arthur and the Minnesingers, the fatal, all-engulfing Tristan and Isolde passion that could only end in death. It had all the prescribed trimmings: It was forbidden, sinful, and secret; in revolt against my background, family, everything conventional, at best it was hopeless. Untainted by any trace of the bourgeois or the practical, it was in direct opposition to anything as prosaic as the thought of marriage.

This kind of undiluted romantic love is now extinct. Post-

Freudian psychology, biochemistry, and a more or less clinical approach to sex have killed it, or at least chased it away for the time being. I would say good riddance—the current version is healthier—if I did not feel that youth is being deprived of something important, the shimmering down, the bloom on the peach, not to mention what this very healthy and lenient attitude is doing to writers and writing. I have only to read the papers with their crop of *crimes passionels* to notice that sex, whether raw or well analyzed, plays worse havoc with people than our obsolete romantic love did.

If my lover had wanted me, I wouldn't have given a fig for that confounded virginity of mine. I was constantly in a swooning "take-me-I-am-yours" state. I've often thought since that it would have been better for my libido not to have been kept steaming in an emotional pressure cooker. We, lucky pre-Freudians, didn't know we had a libido; all we knew was passion, love. But he refrained carefully from seducing me. Instead, we sublimated like crazy.

Whatever I became later, this first man in my life shaped and developed it in me. With a born teacher's or gardener's care he raised every sleeping seed in me to bud and flower. He brought order and sense into my haphazard reading, guided me through all kinds of literature, from Andersen's fairy tales up to and including Huysmans, whose Satanism was the latest cry, or Otto Weininger and Karl Kraus whose pessimism put them into the dark niche more or less inhabited today by Sartre and his school. He took me to the great Russian and French authors, and, not only had he read Ibsen's plays, but he knew them almost by heart. No longer was I alone and lonely, happily I gave up my hard, proud solitude. We shared our treasures as children swap colored marbles, searched and found more, holding hands on secret strolls.

Not quite so secret, though. It could not fail that somebody saw us or that we were caught in Father's espionage nets. Earth-shaking scenes were the consequence, strictest prohibition to see that scoundrel again, Mama's tears and screams, once more the house smelled of paraldehyde, it got so bad that I fainted once or twice. I was submitted to some awful, debasing examinations by young Dr. Popper and declared intact but gravely undernourished. If I had not had my job with the symphony and my career as a soloist, Father would have put me under house arrest. He did not realize, the poor boob, that all this necessarily only strengthened my resistance. I reared up on my hind legs, I broke out, I kicked; to myself I had become the tragic heroine in a great drama, battling against a world filled with dust and ashes, the blind stupid world of old people. Not grownups any longer, for by now I was grown up myself, just old, old and stinking with convention and corruption, the corruption of their minds.

One Sunday morning Father put on his top hat and went forth to have a serious man-to-man discussion with the alleged scoundrel. He was going to ask him point-blank either to marry me or keep his hands off. The scoundrel, I was informed, squirmed and stalled. I can picture him; confronted with Father's dry and stern common sense, he must have tried to sound equally reasonable. He gave his word of honor that he never had, and never would have, anything but the purest friendship for me and interest in my talent. He talked about my career that came first, and about his obligations—two sisters to support on a musician's limited earnings, one a spinster, the other a widow in poor health and with several children. He wisely refrained from mentioning the fiancée in the background. He wished nothing but to help me in my career; he had some influence, hadn't he? After all, he had placed me as soloist in several concerts; how could he do that if he was told "hands off," he concluded, with a neat excursion into polite blackmail.

The outcome was a short reprieve, a kind of armistice, a short-term truce. Father muttered that perhaps the man wasn't quite such a fool as my rantings made him out to be; maybe not an absolute scoundrel either, taking care of his sisters, working hard. Now what about that opera he was talking about?

Yes, what about that opera? Never had an unfinished *oeuvre* been celebrated with greater importance and higher admiration and hopes than this one. Every small piece of inspiration was brought to me. Soon I knew every tone, every word of it by heart. How did I like this modulation? Had I noticed the finesse of voice leading into the sixth bar of the quintet? What did I think about letting the big duet fade away in the wholly unexpected G-minor, or would that be too

new, too daring? Oh, the holy innocence of those last adherents to
that last thin trickling music of the romantic school.

But as the opera progressed, it took up more and more of my genius' time and thoughts. As a harp player I knew only too well what
happened to a string drawn too tight. It must break at last, with a report like a shot. Something like this happened to our high-strung
platonic affair in its second year. After my father's clumsy *démarche*
it petered out, and no wonder. But of all this star-crossed love, one
small practical thing remained strongly in my memory. It had seemed
strange to me that my friend, my beloved, had mentioned his obligations, his limited earnings, to my father, it was just not in keeping
with my image of him. To me, he appeared the apex of elegance in
his slim black tail coat, with his perfect manners, his flawless French
and Italian, the easy hospitality, the tasteful chamber music evenings
in his patrician home where ancestors' portraits looked down on fine
antique furniture and some of the finest minds of Vienna. I hated to
talk or think of money; I still do, perhaps because there was so much
noise about it at home. With all the flowers and books he brought me,
the secret trips in hacks and fiacres, the many concerts he invited me
to, it had somehow never occurred to me that he spent money on
me, even less that he had to count it. Like Grandpapa, he must be
rich because he wore a silk top hat and gleaming patent leather
shoes; even when it was raining.

Came the day when, during the armistice between Father and
him, I went with his small chamber music group on a concert tour to
Prague and a few other towns. At the last moment his sister, supposed to chaperon me and a young singer, came down with a cold
and stayed home. Naturally, I did not inform my parents of this
change in the program.

Also at the last moment, his sister, hastily unpacking and repack-
ing, asked me to take along a pair of his shoes in my suitcase. As I un-
wrapped these high patent leather shoes in the hotel in Prague something seemed queer about them: a deep indentation in each heel.
"Show me," said the young singer who shared my hotel room. "Oh,
my God," she said, "don't you know what it means? These are a cav-
alry officer's shoes, don't you know? That's where the spurs are at-

tached—I know it from my brother. Oh, the poor guy! Has to wear secondhand shoes to keep up appearances. Poor silly beggar, carrying those sisters and their brood on his back, and his feet in somebody's sweaty old shoes! Well, let's hope his opera will make enough for him to buy himself new ones. . . ."

It was at that moment that my glorified image of the man toppled and something entirely different, entirely new took its place. For the first time I was touched by compassion for the man I had until then blindly adored. Suddenly I knew that I had forced him into playing a role, hiding behind a mask as we all do in life and in love. I think it was one of the decisive moments in which we grow up or grow old. Heat changed to warmth, admiration to sympathy. For the first time I felt not with a girl's stormy emotions but a woman's maturity.

The opera, by the way, was a crushing flop soon after this, and our great love, like an untended oil lamp, sputtered out with an occasional rendezvous, a cramped letter. I was left behind, alone after two years of high dreams of twosomeness, more lonely than before. I remember that I borrowed or stole a pistol from a young sculptor who was just then making a portrait of me and in whose studio I did a bit of target practice to limber up from the sittings.

But before I got around to practicing on myself something happened that made it my duty to stay alive.

or a few days Mama had complained about lumbago, rheumatism, a vague discomfort and stiffness in her back. Father was out of town with the regular tarock crowd, I think on a wine-tasting tour in the hills south of Vienna, and I remained at home with Mama who had taken to her bed.

I was in the kitchen preparing a hot-water bottle for her when suddenly the Sunday afternoon drowsiness was torn by screams from the bedroom, so terrible that I didn't recognize Mama's voice; slaughterhouse screams they were, not quite human. I dropped the hot-water bottle, felt the scalding water splash over my hands, and rushed into the bedroom. I remember (and to my lasting shame) saying aloud, impatiently: "Good Heavens, what's she up to now? New tricks? New scenes? If that's her idea of a joke. . . ."

But even these first few minutes of the onset of pains had changed my mother into a helpless, almost unconscious bundle of destruction, pulling me down with her into the nightmare of that shrieking, burning, Indian summer day. She was screaming, shrieking incessantly: "A doctor! Morphine! Morphine! A doctor! Get me morphine!" And her screams, becoming hoarser and still more piercing, followed me down the stairs as I ran for the doctor who lived on the first floor. But when no one answered the bell, I remembered that he and his family were still in the country on their summer vacation. I raced back upstairs, trying to calm Mama, begging her to stop screaming. "Please, please, pull yourself together. I'll get Dr. Popper, yes, yes, he'll give you something, morphine, sure, sure," as if I didn't know that Mama couldn't and never would pull herself together. Oh God, stop her from screaming so, let her faint or something, I prayed. Yes, of course, in spite of all my arrogant agnosticism, I prayed under the pressure of those hours. "Grandfather, do something, help me if you can," I begged the memory of the kind shabby little old Jew who had been dead these thirteen years.

Not that it helped. The few people who had remained in the large apartment house that Sunday, alarmed by those screams, peeked out through a chink in their doors, and the *Hausmeister's* unfriendly wife shouted across the courtyard, "What is the matter, has anything happened? Somebody stop that racket!" "It's nothing," I said, "Mama wrenched her back. I must phone for a doctor." Yet I couldn't leave Mama alone; to tell the truth, I thought her screams indicated only a violent recurrence of her former mental sickness. But phones in private homes were still not common. "The *Herr Justizrat* has a phone; ring his bell, if they're home maybe they'll let you use it," someone suggested.

The *Herr Justizrat,* two floors beneath us, was an old bachelor who lived with his sister, a spinster deep in widow's weeds and somewhat pixilated. As a child I had often seen her on the stairs, faintly scared by her antics, muttering to herself and always walking three steps forward and two back; whenever she realized that she was being observed, she would make a tremendous effort to walk normally, but she couldn't, the compulsion was stronger (except that we didn't *know* yet about compulsions; we only had them). Having to ring their bell, explain Mama's screams, beg to use their phone, and then enter the dusky apartment with its sandalwood atmosphere, added to the nightmare quality of that afternoon, evening, night.

It was as though a curse had taken all doctors out of Vienna for that last warm September weekend. Neither the ones I knew nor those I fished out of the telephone book were available. The Hassreiters weren't home either, but the elderly lady, stone-deaf now, who had chaperoned Frau Cilli on that historic date with Father, promised to give them my message when they returned. I wouldn't have known what to do if the fey, compulsion-driven Fräulein had not quietly, politely, and with perfect understanding helped me with the telephoning while I raced back and forth up the stairs to look after Mama, whose inhuman screams continued without letup.

It was 2:00 A.M. by the time a strange young doctor appeared at last, seemingly just as bewildered as I was, shrugging, not knowing what to do until it dawned on him what he had before him: obviously, this shrieking, convulsed creature was a hophead, a dope fiend deprived of her dope. "All right, all right, I'll fix you up for the night," he said morosely, filling his syringe and giving Mama an injection. After a few minutes her insane screams subsided into a pitiful moaning, like that of a little dog I had once seen run over by a coal wagon. "She'll sleep now," he said, looking me over. "And you need a rest, too. Take this, a harmless sedative, dissolve it in a cup of hot tea, it'll stop you from shaking. First thing in the morning you talk to her doctor; what's his name? . . . Ah, yes, I know Dr. Popper. I'll make a report to him. I'll send you my bill. Good night, or rather, good morning."

I put the kettle on the little alcohol burner for the desperately needed cup of tea, but before the water had come to a boil, Mama cried out again. She was retching, compulsively throwing up because, contrary to the young doctor's diagnosis, she had never before been given morphine and her body was rejecting it violently. Throughout the endless hours of night and daybreak she kept on throwing up, crying out, and sobbing. And when I tried to change her nightgown and bedding I discovered that she couldn't move from the waist down, her limbs as heavy as if this part of her had already died.

But although cancer of the breast—till then undetected—had spread throughout her body and, in that horrid night eaten its way into her spine, Mama was young and her heart was strong and it was to be almost a year before she was allowed to die.

Almost a year, and each day filled with the pains and agonies and screams of which that first night was the beginning.

Naturally, Father and black satchel moved away, back to Grandmother, by then a very beautiful but completely blind old lady. My Flying Dutchman quietly bowed out of my life at the first sign of sadness and sickness at my home. I locked the loss away in my heart, as a child will store away the silly playthings of last year. What those months gave me was rigorous training in mute heartbreak, a not unimportant requisite for a budding writer, an indispensable lesson in developing into a full-sized human being.

At the danger of sounding like the proverbial nurse complaining to the visiting physician—"My, what a terrible night I had, Doctor!" —I simply cannot skim over those darkest months in my life, when my mother pulled me down with her into deepest purgatory. Poor Mama, who never had any self-control, nothing to hold her up, none of the imponderable strength called morale; no interests, no love, no religion—poor Mama gave in entirely to the torturing pains of cancer. She was a bad patient. Like most neurotics and psychopaths—all criminals, too—Mama was completely self-centered, introspective, with no thought or consideration for others. I often wonder which comes first: Does such total absorption in oneself cause the neurosis? Or does the neurosis draw those pitiable border cases into the added sickness of egotism?

With morphine the only shield between her and the pains, she soon became addicted. With severe chills and convulsions—all the grim exhibitionism of addiction—she would scream, shriek for the needle for hours. Medical ethics, I think, have grown more merciful since then, but as it was, I and I alone was Mama's nurse, and the doctor with steely insistence kept both of us to the prescribed doses and schedule—day and night, one shot every four hours, although its effect lasted for only two of them.

I still dream of those small capsules for which I had to account. I still get nauseated by the smell of ether in which I had to clean and keep the syringe. I still recall, although muffled by time, the fights against the temptation to give myself "a fix," as today's rough jargon has it, to get some rest myself. I still suffer nightmares from the feeling of slack skin pinched between my fingers for the subcutaneous prick, and from the weight of Mama's paralyzed body choking me. But the worst dream is the one of my dead mother having returned, not knowing what I know: that she and I must live once more and again and again through those endless hours of her dying.

This, too, played its part in molding me. I became a good, though unregistered, nurse. For six months I never slept in a bed, but sat up in an easy chair like any night nurse, the small reading lamp shaded toward my patient. I would read, doze off exhaustedly, take a brief nap from which Mama's moaning soon called me awake. Old Frau Gross made me a padded robe to keep me from shivering through those nights.

I dearly loved this robe. It is in times like these that small comforts blaze with joy, like bonfires—the cup of tea, the pine-needle fragrance of a warm bath to ease the stiffness in the body; the very chair in which I spent the nights became a friend; the books that were strong enough to distract me or insipid enough to make me doze; the first deep breath of fresh air on leaving the house—how precious these are when nothing else is left. One of my best friends in those months was our maid, Vefi, a Tirolean peasant girl, strong, clean, and beautiful like a wood-carved peasant Madonna in a Tirolean village chapel; just to look at her would brace me up for the day. Another friend who did much to keep me going was a seal pup in the Schönbrunn Zoo. I visited him whenever I could steal an hour from the symphony rehearsals. Usually, there was just enough time for me to get back home for Mama's next shot. But, bless the classic symphonies, from Haydn to Brahms to Bruckner, in which no harp is used; in those harpless hours I often escaped to my sleek little friend in the round, open seals' basin. He knew me, he would wait for me, give me sly winks, clown for me; he would come out of the water and flop down at my side, and barking and trumpeting with joy, show me every little trick he knew. I loved him dearly and, as there was no one to love me, I made myself believe that he, too, liked me in his funny seal's way. Maybe he did.

Sometimes I would spend a free hour just walking, just breathing; all my life I could walk off loads of grief and trouble. Here, in Los Angeles, you cannot walk; that's part of my feeling of being an exile. Try to take a walk and you are among three million cars that honk furiously for you to get out of their way. Or all too often one politely stops and offers you a ride; and when you say "No, thank you," he asks if you're really okay, *really*? Or a cop stops you because the sheer, simple act of walking makes you suspect, especially if you are taking a walk in the much too rare rains.

Sometimes, while the orchestra rehearsed an inviting Brahms or Mozart, I would creep down into the narrow dark corridor below the huge concert platform and dance the kind of dance nobody had ever danced—until, many years later, Mary Wigman appeared, and Martha Graham, and gave it a name and a form. But, Lord, what a release it was to free myself in those impossible dances of all my pent-up passions, uncried tears, unlived emotions! Shed all weight and grow light, graceful, and happy with Brahms and Mozart. And Haydn and Schubert, of course. Voice of experience: you can't dance Beethoven, not really dance. And you can't dance Wagner or, God forbid, Bruckner, who was then our daily bread. But Brahms's third movement of the Second—oh, yes, I still would like to float away on it. And I would have dearly loved to dance Mahler's Second.

When it came to performing Wagner, Gustav Mahler, Richard Strauss, or Debussy, we poor harp players needed all the arms of Shiva and the feet of a centipede to be adequate to the demands of the composers who were my contemporaries. Much of this new music we rehearsed and played under the baton of a young conductor with beautiful dark eyes and a small dark beard that he grew as a mask of authority, for the obvious purpose of making himself appear older than he was. We all loved him because he made every one of us play better than we had known we could. Against the dreariness of the daily orchestral routine, these rehearsals, these first performances, were life-saving. I don't know how I could have carried my load through those years without the counterbalance of music, the new, exciting music of my time.

I think I had quite an impersonal, but grateful and profound, crush on that young conductor; in fact, I still have. His name is Bruno Walter.

But then, I have been lucky all my life. Troubled as my childhood and youth may have been, it never lacked enough joy to sustain me. In the worst crises, something would always happen to restore the balance, to light a candle when it got too dark.

So it happened that at the lowest point of my strength, when the old war cry "I can take it!" was growing faint, I met a man, still young although ten years my senior, who became a dear friend, an amusing companion, and later, temporarily, a husband.

In our loosely knit group a young poet, one of Vienna's white hopes, was introduced to me; his name was Max Prels.

Immediately, stormily, he fell in love with me the way only a poet could wish to or be able to love: hopelessly, beseechingly, devotedly, and tenaciously. I was still bruised and sore from the infamous petering out of my first Great Love, from the painful discovery that even a Great Love can shrink and become a Small Love, and then die, at last, from undernourishment. Yet I was still miles and years away from knowing that you can and will fall in love again, that in the gipsy's crystal ball yet another love will always show.

It was to his advantage that he looked, and was, the opposite of my beautiful restless Flying Dutchman. No chaos, no bitter surrogate there. Barely middle-sized, he seemed slightly out of proportion, having the too-large head, too-short shuffling legs of a pale, rickety child. Small, washed-out eyes sat flat in a too-long face, dominated by the silly, oversized, blunt nose of a clown. He was a clown, or maybe he was playing in self-defense the not unbecoming role of the self-deprecating, melancholy clown. I was sorry for him, sorry that I could give him no more than gratitude and an amused affection, and I told him so. No more lies, please! I wanted one corner, one person with whom I could be honest and candid.

I don't know why Max insisted on marrying me under these not very complimentary conditions; perhaps he was wise enough to know that to love unhappily is better than not to love at all.

The evening I met him he saw me home. In front of my house, in the shade of those enormous, nonfunctional caryatids, he took off his top hat—the badge of the gentleman—and kissed the air half an inch above my hand, as one does with royalty. "I shall see you soon," he said. He did not say *Auf Wiedersehen,* and he did not ask, "May I, will I, see you again?" He simply made a statement that I forgot a minute later. I hastened upstairs, it was time for Mama's injection.

Next morning, as I left for rehearsal, he was standing beside the giant calves of the caryatids as if he had remained there all night. It took me a few moments to recognize him. I remember it was a cold foggy morning, silver ice in the gutters, a pale red sun beyond the green dome and the high gray columns of the Karlskirche. A military balloon hung aloft, the fine black spiderwork of its gondola next to that thick sun-orange. I had seen this sight on a thousand mornings when I left for school or for the Konservatorium. I suddenly realized that during the last months I had lived without eyes; now I saw again. This morning I felt as though I had been through the meat grinder; Mama had had a very bad night which meant that I hadn't slept at all. I yawned as wide as the hippo in the zoo, gulped down the cold air, so cold it hurt high up in my nostrils, and stared with watery eyes at the young man, trying to remember who he was. He took off his hat (a silk top hat at nine in the morning!), he had a baby's silky blond hair, and his radish of a nose was frozen brick-red.

"My God, Dr. Prels, where do you come from?" I asked, surprised. He pointed vaguely across the street: "Had breakfast at the Café Museum," he said. "Best view of your house from there. I wrote a little poem for you while I waited. It's positively *b'schissen*. First commandment: 'Thou shalt never try to write when thou art in love.' But what else can a man do to keep from exploding?" He pulled a slip of paper from his coat pocket but tore it to bits and blew it away before I could snatch it from him.

"You're bright, aren't you? Make me curious, yes?"

"And are you?"

"No," I said. "It's a pretty act, though. You probably threw away your laundry bill. Unpaid? Or, if it was a poem, I bet you copied it!"

"How do you know?" he asked, laughing.

"Clairvoyant," I answered. I had never told anyone that I, too, wrote poems in moments of internal spontaneous combustion. "Well, *adieu*, I must run to my rehearsal."

"Look at that gutter. Beautiful! Pure crystal! Don't you like sliding on the ice?"

"Of course. What child wouldn't?"

"Fine. Let's slide, then," he said, and clapping his silk hat upon his head, he took both my hands, crossed arms with me, and pulled me away with him on the narrow band of morning silver. The weight of the shrieking, sleepless night was lifted from my eyelids, my shoulders.

"You looked so tired before. Someday you'll tell me what is the matter with you," he said, suddenly quite serious and gentle as he deposited me at the entrance to the Musikverein building.

"Nothing's the matter," I said. I don't quite know why, but I had never mentioned to anyone that I took care of a sick and dying mother. I think I slipped into a shell of silence as into a protective armor. I still do when things get really bad. Once you begin to talk and complain you are lost to self-pity, and nothing causes people to withdraw their sympathy so promptly as when you show that you need it.

"Don't prevaricate. Everybody carries some load on his back."

"Do you?"

"Do I? Heavens, do I! Do you know what it means to be a hysterical widowed mother's only son?"

"I'm an only daughter. And my mother is sick." The moment I said it I was sorry. First chink in the armor. "Well, good-by!" Angry at myself, I trotted off to my rehearsal.

When I left the Musikverein three hours later he stood in the drafty entrance to the stately building. I gasped when I saw him. It had begun to snow, his face was wet, his light coat drenched.

"*Herrgott,* you weren't waiting for me?" I said angrily.

"Why not? I brought you *maroni.*" (That's what roasted chestnuts are called in Austria and Italy.) He grabbed my hand, pushed it into the pocket of his soaked, too-thin coat, and closed it around the warm little paper bag. The chestnuts smelled and tasted wonderful. I had not found *maroni* in a pocket since . . . yes, since my little grandfather had died. I hope they're still there, the street vendors with their small iron braziers.

"You see? I know what you need," he said contentedly. "You have the lips of a frustrated *maroni* gobbler, the eyes of a baby gazelle, the voice and the hands of Andersen's Little Mermaid. Hey, don't be so greedy, leave some for me!"

That was the man with whom I stumbled into the brief, silly improvisation you could hardly call a marriage.

Although Mama was sinking now, the poisons distilled by her sickness, together with increasing doses of morphine, kept her bolstered up with that queer kind of optimism that frequently accompanies a deadly disease. I still told her each day and each night that she was getting better, that the inflammation in her spine would be gone by spring, or summer at the latest. (That was the merciful fiction her doctor and I had decided upon and that she believed, or possibly feigned belief to make it easier for us.)

It was life-saving to know that Max was there for me, gladly, unselfishly, unfailingly, always. Apparently he liked nothing better than to be useful to me; following me around like a devoted dog, he was happy. There was not an ounce of meanness in him. His clowning, laughing, weightless presence, his Bohemian happy-go-lucky ways were a soothing, healing medicine against the cramped, restricting discipline I thought my duty. I carried the responsibility of my puritanic upbringing, and I don't think I wasted any thought on the question of how a grown-up man could spend so much time on being in love. Gratefully, I soon took it for granted that he was there for me. Always.

I had not yet learned that mature males, real men, can give only a small part of themselves, their time and thought, to women and love. Believe me, ladies, the great lover is no bargain in the long run!

Spring came, and the death smell filled the sickroom. The doctor called in a nurse and at last instructed that we give Mama all the morphine she asked for. To be there at the end that was expected any hour even Father came home. But Mama was young and her heart still would not give in. For seventeen days she lay in a deep coma, an unconscious, decaying body, dead except for that small clockwork that had not yet run out.

One afternoon I had closed my eyes for a brief rest when I heard a sound that frightened me as no nightmare ever had. I heard Mama laughing—the high, malicious, insane giggling of that long ago time before she had been sent to Inzersdorf. It did not seem possible; for a shocked second I thought I had dozed off and was dreaming. I rushed to her bed: Mama was brightly awake, fully conscious, laughing. She even propped herself up on her elbows, while the nurse quickly pushed some pillows behind her back. Nurse was a broad, callous, efficient woman, but she, too, seemed frightened by her patient's breaking through the walls of her long coma. "Who's she?" Mama said loudly to me. "Send her away. I must talk to you. Alone."

I am not sure why I want to tell about that hour when my mother turned back from death to talk to me—perhaps I am trying to get rid of, for once and all, that frightening experience that still echoes through some of my more unpleasant dreams, those in which Mama has returned from Inzersdorf and, once more, from death's threshold.

In old reports, letters, memoirs we often read about such moments of clarity, euphoria, when the dying assemble their family around their bed and in great dignity give them their blessings and advice, make their last wishes known, the reality of scenes such as my own grandmother had artfully performed. Perhaps it was such a bugle call, urgent enough to wake up Mama to do her last duty toward me, her only daughter. It must have been a superhuman effort that brought her back after seventeen days of unconsciousness. But instead of blessings, she brought forth obscenities straight out of the inferno of insanity: not the artfully formed inferno of Dante, nor the romantic visions of Doré, but the abstruse, monster-filled hell of Hieronymus Bosch. Giggling, laughing, cursing with her last breath, Mama warned me of men—somewhat too late if the truth be told—of the hideous, unspeakable things men did to women, and she did it in a flood of the filthiest, lowest gutter talk. Psychiatry is familiar with such outbursts of obscenity in which repressed sex explodes; the more refined and innocent the patient, the worse the wildly pornographic fantasies, the dirtier the words that inexplicably find their way into the demented mind, the ladylike vocabulary.

But, naturally, I was far from such psychiatric insight. I was shocked, frightened, revolted, and filled with an overwhelming pity for my mother whose mind had dwelt in this slimy hell and who, by superhuman effort, had risen from the dead for the special purpose of saving me from it. In spite of this pity, I wanted to laugh, hysterically maybe, at the shattering incongruity of the situation. At last I calmed Mama down with another shot of morphine and remained kneeling at her side, holding her slackening hands until she seemed to sleep. Shaken and in furious haste I dressed and rushed off; there was a symphony concert and I was on duty. Max was awaiting me downstairs, as always. He studied my face. "Is it over?" he asked, cautiously.

"No. Not yet. She is still terribly strong," I said.

But when I came home after the concert—a pompous, all-Wagner program—Mama was dead. The nurse had tied her chin with a napkin. It made her look in death as though she had a toothache. Her face still bore that horrible smirk. Father put his hand on my shoulder, a rare but inappropriate gesture, and moved back to Grandmother's immediately. I did not see him again until the funeral. The nurse, too, had already packed her grip and left. Only Vefi, sobbing in the kitchen, stayed with me, with Mama's still body and the unbearable smell of the mute sickroom.

The next noon two jolly men from the mortuary came, bringing with them a squat black box into which they loaded my mother's remains and carried them down the four flights with various bumpings and calls of: "Watch your step!" "Steady there!" I was half-dead myself, after almost a year of no sleep, except brief naps at her bedside as I tried to see her through another night and yet another one.

I traipsed down the steps after the men. Max, of course, was waiting for me. He slipped his arm into mine. "I saw the hearse," he said, nodding toward the two men loading the black box into the black vehicle. "Now it's all over, my girl," he said. "Aren't you glad?"

I stared at him, benumbed, surprised. Suddenly I was flooded with relief. "Yes, of course, I'm glad, I'm very glad. And I'm very, very glad you're here. You won't leave me alone, promise?"

"So, now we'll sit in the Café Museum for a few minutes. You need a cup of coffee and a cigarette. That's what you need," he said. "Then I'll take you for a walk in the park. It's such a lovely day. I pushed the clouds out of the way all morning to make good weather for you."

Thank you, I thought, thank you for the weather, thank you for being here.

The terror and pity that Mama had funneled into me in that ghastly bequest might well have made me frigid for the rest of my life. Fortunately, her words had come too late: I had got rid of that cumbersome, cursed virginity weeks before. It had been the least I could do to show Max my affection and gratitude. Being fond of him but not in love, I had not by any means found in his timid, queerly humble love-making the passionate heavens and hells the poets sang about, but I had accepted it casually as a not unpleasant, rather unimportant experience.

But then, I told you I'm a lucky girl, didn't I?

I suppose I had used up my last reserves, because soon after my mother's death I fell gravely ill. It started, harmlessly enough I thought, with the kind of sore throat that I was used to not mentioning. For one thing, Father had moved back, and I did not want to disturb his contented widower's existence by telling him I felt miserable, alternately chilled and feverish. But one Sunday afternoon, returning with him from one of his protracted tarock games at the Hassreiters', I lost consciousness halfway up the four flights to our apartment. The grainy stone of the stairs bucking up and hitting me on the forehead was the last thing I remembered for several weeks.

I was lying unconscious, burning away in such an impossible high fever that the headshaking doctors, consultants, and specialists could not agree on a diagnosis, let alone an effective treatment, and gave me up for lost day after day. During this period in which I had no contact with present reality, I remembered, relived with an almost unbearable clarity, every smallest detail of my long since buried and forsaken childhood.

Every sight I had seen, from the brown, black-dotted frightening wallpaper to the thickened, coarsened mother who returned to me from Inzersdorf, I saw again. Every word spoken or screamed at me in all those years, I heard spoken and screamed once more. All the voices, the joys, the fears came back. All the books I had read against

Father's prohibition stood up around me: I knew them by heart. The small sounds, the smells of the apartment from which we had moved ten years ago, were there. The smoking kerosene lamps, the solfeggi sung in the neighbors' flat, the steel girders being loaded on a lorry downstairs, the carpets being beaten in the courtyard, I heard them all. I smelled the fine fragrance of a wild rosebush in the castle's rocky garden, I tasted the steamy, warm air of the kitchen on wash-day, felt the stiff silk of Grandmother's skirt between my fingers; sat on my little grandfather's lap sipping a bit of red wine into which he had stirred water and a lump of sugar.

During those weeks in which I moved mainly in the company of my dead, content to have died myself, a teeming river of remembrance streamed through my head. The past came out of a corner of the wall that I saw although I never opened my eyes, too weak for the effort. It was a weird condition, known probably only to people in trances and visions, a state of total recall impossible to express in words. My pulse was racing, each beat roared and thundered through my head with the sound of a tidal wave, a hissing, pounding surf surging up the cliff of a wild coast. And while my brain produced these spectacles, my past rushed toward me with the speed and impact of many express trains; not one train at a time, as in normal thoughts and memories, but many trains, on many rails, simultaneously. I can only guess that my organism must have manufactured both its own poisons and my own individual antitoxin.

By this method I underwent something like a psychoanalysis in depth, with the difference that my psyche spit out and cleansed me within a few weeks of all the buried and suppressed debris; a result that would have taken psychoanalysis years, and me a fortune, to achieve.

In all those weeks I could not keep down as much as a teaspoon of water. I simply burned away, ate myself up, what little there was of me. Afterward I had to be fed like a baby for weeks before I had enough strength to lift even a spoon to my mouth. It was months before I could stand on my legs, learn to walk all over again, learn to live. At last, finally, learn to play the harp once more, beginning way back with a beginner's first exercises.

But I was happy and life tasted sweet. I felt proud and strong because I had survived. I had pushed the shadows of my grim childhood away. I was free at last. I took an old school copybook and a pencil and wrote down much of what had been so vividly resurrected in my fever.

It was a terribly maudlin and saccharin story, full of phony naïveté because I tried to tell it from a child's point of view (aren't most first stories so told?) but had neither the technique nor detachment. I thought it atrociously bad, but I did not throw it away when I sorted my belongings, left Father, and went off and got married.

I sometimes wonder, in these days of supercommunication, how a certain word or expression suddenly comes into vogue. Perhaps it first pops up in some intellectual context where it belongs, accidentally catches the eye of a not-so-intellectual reader, who, impressed by it himself, adorns his own vocabulary to impress others. From then on that poor expression filters down, flung indiscriminately all over the place, gets blurred and smudged, and is at last dropped into the ash can. A few years ago, magazine and copy writers had a spree with being "nostalgic." For a while this ran neck and neck with "man's inhumanity to man," which won the race. Lately, you can hardly read a newspaper or listen to a speech without encountering "the human condition." It is taken for granted that to be human is, under all circumstances, an inherently incurable, tragic condition. It may be so, but I personally doubt such general statements. I have found that the human condition can be rather pleasurable at times. Nor do I believe that all the scribblers who mention this *"condition humaine"* remember Malraux's exciting book of this title.

True, the French Encyclopedists of the eighteenth century, who actually coined the expression, were skeptical debunkers. But the human condition of their time has hardly any relation to the freedom and materialistic luxury of the present. If we agree, though, with D'Alembert's remark *"La condition humaine est déplorable,"* we must also note that humans of all races and nations are at all times inventive enough to find means to ameliorate their deplorable condition. Stimulants and tranquilizers are by no means new. The Oriental smokes opium and chews betel; the Arab has his hashish—the same mildly intoxicating weed called marijuana in Central and South America; in Brazil, swaying in the hammock is called "the poor man's narcotic"; and in the rocking chairs and swings of our own American porches our teetotalers and rheumatic oldsters may lull themselves into a similar slight stupor. The Indians can get wildly drunk on almost anything besides their very own mescalin and peyote. Of course, alcohol and nicotine are used from the North to the South Pole, when the human condition gets unbearable.

In Austria, especially in Vienna, our dope and narcotic was the *Kaffeehaus.*

In 1683, when Vienna broke the siege and advance of the barbaric Eastern hordes for the second time, the Turks left behind in their retreat some sacks of coffee and subsequently there arose the first *Kaffeehaus.* Since then, the *Kaffeehaus* has been a second home for the Austrian, an institution with a firm tradition, though flexible enough to adapt itself to all kinds of people, classes, and places.

The *Kaffeehaus* is more subtle and much quieter than the Anglo-Saxon equivalents of bar, saloon, pub; widely more democratic than a club, though it has some features in common with all of these. Mainly, it is a home to its regular guests who take roots there.

In the *Kaffeehaus* you write your letters or, as the case may be, your poems, essays, Ph.D thesis, the first chapter of a novel that may never get beyond its third. There exists, or existed, something called *Kaffeehaus-Literatur,* weightless things, graceful, polished fragments eminently suited to the Viennese style and character. In the *Kaffeehaus* you met your friends, your sweetheart, your mistress, your best friend's wife; occasionally even your own. Here in the smoky air maybe you got ideas for your next *feuilleton,* you honed your wit and sharpened it in the swift talk and pointed arguments at the round table reserved for your little clique. Here you learned the latest news, the latest gossip, and from here were launched the bon mots and jokes which tomorrow would be retold and savored all over town. Here the coming successes or flops were prophesied; here young and not-so-young firebrands would fight heatedly over girls or politics. There were quiet corners reserved for the chess players,

back rooms for loud, late card games. Money was discreetly borrowed and reluctantly lent, five o'clock stubbles were quickly shaved
in the privacy of the men's room. I don't remember a ladies' room in
the *Kaffeehaus,* although as girls grew more and more emancipated,
we broke into these sacred realms of clubs, bars, coffeehouses, and
universities. Poor men, how relentlessly they were driven from their
reservations by what is still called the weaker sex!

Only in Vienna was it possible to spend the greater part of your
life in *your Kaffeehaus.* The cup of coffee you paid less than a nickel
for (and what incomparably strong aromatic coffee it was!) entitled
you to take root, enjoy the compassionate attention of the waiter,
his knowledge of, and tender catering to, your individual taste. You
did not have to order among the ten or more varieties of coffee; the
waiter automatically brought you the one you preferred, tirelessly
wiping the marble top of your little table, refilling your water glass,
fetching the newspapers you read regularly; and forever after remembered your habits and preferences.

It is told that Trotsky, on his first escape from Russia, became a
regular guest of the Café Central, until 1917, when he went back to
his destiny. Years later, a fugitive once more, he stopped over in
Vienna and visited the Central. "My, my, Herr von Trotsky, *Kaffee
verkehrt, Neue Freie Presse,*" said Heinrich, the famous old headwaiter, "and why don't we have the pleasure of seeing Herr von
Trotsky for quite a while? May one ask where Herr von Trotsky has
been all this time?"

Viennese courtesy had a handle for proper address: each green
student was *"Herr Doktor,"* each member of the professions *"Herr
Professor,"* and the commoner, unadorned by any of the many
bureaucratic or military titles, received at least the noble and
aristocratic "von." So, the most radical of all Communists was
knighted by the headwaiter of the old Central.

The *Kaffeehaus* was the very life element for Max Prels and his
kind, the climate in which their special style and talent flourished.
That's why I think his waiting there for me at all hours was less of
a sacrifice than an excuse. Out of the blue smoke-hazy air, full of
the good bitter aroma of mocha, he fished ideas for his charming

little *feuilletons*. Adding to the smoke with the countless cigarettes he held in nicotine-stained fingers, he would scribble on paper napkins—witty aphorisms, observations, fragments—polish them, and, giving himself an important air, send them to the evening paper for which he occasionally wrote reviews of books and plays.

Max had come along at the right moment. I don't know if I could have kept myself and Mama going without him. Now he was always there for me, like a sentinel standing guard at a queen's palace. He made his headquarters in two coffeehouses, the Café Museum across the street from, and the Kremser nearby, the Musikverein building where I would pass on my way to and from concerts and rehearsals. Both of these coffeehouses were frequented by young artists, musicians, critics, writers, while the older generation had long since settled in the venerable Café Central.

How tightly the eggshells of our bourgeois upbringing still clung to us in spite of our Bohemian posturing! Having shared Max's studio couch, it was a foregone conclusion that we would get married. Father, of course, had refused at first to give his consent, without which I, still under age, could not be wedded.

But during the days of my undiagnosed illness, when I hovered between life and death, Father softened, or was softened by the unswerving devotion and tenacity of this strange bird Max Prels, who lacked all the solid qualities that Father demanded in an acceptable husband for me. Also, I think he was impressed by the fact that Max contemptuously waved aside the question of a dowry. He was relieved that Max nursed me and fed me and taught me to walk again and altogether took care of me during the long months of my recovery, leaving Father free to return to his daily card games and his friends, the Hassreiters, and the invigorating waltzing with Fräulein Steffi in the Sunday Perfection.

And, of course, I had some money of my own, at least I hoped so. Ever since I had begun to earn my musician's wages I had had to hand them to Father, who put them in a savings account for me. This I confessed rather shamefacedly to Max because of my incurable aversion to discussing money, probably the result of listening to my parents' endless squabbles over it. Besides, anything as humdrum as a savings account was unsuited to the airy creature Max saw in me. "Like having big, flat feet," I said with an angry laugh.

"Never mind, I'd love you even if you had a million," said Max, magnanimously. "How much is it, anyway?"

"I don't know. Maybe Father used it during Mama's illness. Or mine. Maybe there's nothing left at all."

"Why don't you ask your Old Man?"

"Because I don't care."

"Well, if you don't care to ask him, I do," said Max. "You earned it, after all, and it's yours, isn't it?"

He did ask and Father produced some money, together with a small ledger with a floridly written "With God" on the flyleaf and on its pages in his neat bookkeeping a record of my earnings on one side, the expenses for my room and board and doctors' bills on the other. "Anyway, there's a little nest egg," Max said, exhaling, "for us little birds *sur la branche*. . . ."

Oddly enough, Father was highly pleased with my fiancé's interest in my savings; it was the first sign of practical responsibility he had discovered in his future son-in-law.

An apartment we had, the same one where I had given up my virginity. It was in a quiet house in a quiet street of the Fourth District. One of Max's many friends had, so to speak, made him a present of it when he went to Italy.

Surging ahead with full sails, Liberty written on our banner, proud to be free souls and Bohemians, it seems incongruous that I established our little household in my bourgeois, orderly, and organized way, but it was the only way I knew. There were well-cooked meals and a nicely set table, no dirt swept under the carpet, no spots on linen, silverware, or china, never an unwashed dish in the sink—all this thanks to Mali, a sparkling jewel of a maid, round as a dumpling, appetizing as a polished apple. Mali's shiny face and perfect *Gugelhupf* (and where in the world but in Vienna could a coffee cake get such a name?) are the things I remember best of my married life. And the ridiculously small Dachshund puppy Max brought on the day of the great dénouement. . . .

I made Lumpi a house from an old hatbox, cut a door into it, padded it well. I placed the edifice on an old rubber sheet (I hadn't been a nurse for nothing) and crowned my work of love by presenting one of my slippers to my baby dog. It was one of a pair, richly embroidered with gold and simulated jewels; an old lady who claimed to have been Tchaikovsky's housekeeper had brought them to me from Russia. Lumpi instantly accepted his gift, made a big act of growling and yelping and threatening, chasing and catching, wrestling and conquering it, and at last dragged it into his house, never again to be seen for a single moment without it. Slipper had to be dipped into Lumpi's food in a make-believe of sharing it, and on our little outings slipper had to come along to partake of the pleasures of every lamppost and fire hydrant. I was overflowing with a particular happiness that evening, in a glow of a new inner warmth; I did not know yet that it was the first stirring of maternal instinct. Indeed, I had no idea that I possessed such an instinct; for the time being anything that smelled of family, of a settled life, of babies, ties of any sort, was disgusting and far beneath me and my featherweight poet-husband.

his was the Twentieth Century at last. It was called the Children's Century; and observing today the results of sixty years of progressive, permissive, and pragmatic education I often want to shout: And look at the mess you made of it! But, leaving the Freudians to one side and the pragmatists to the other, we, the young people of this young century, felt a brisk breeze blowing around our noses. We kicked out the cluttered bourgeois tastes and musty, cumbersome precepts and the untenable political ideas of the nineteenth-century class society. We looked around. We coagulated in small lumps of similar goals and tastes. By an almost automatic reflex I landed in a little group that called itself no less than The Young People's Society for Music, Literature, and the Fine Arts, the same circle where I had, a few years before, made a mild sensation in our maid's black uniform.

We discovered that we were not so alone as we had believed, not outsiders, each individual involved in his or her own private revolution—we were a generation.

Life was easy, we had a good time, much fun, plenty to entertain and interest us. The key to our apartment door was always under the mat, friends would drop in at all hours, the entire Young People's Society for Music, Literature, and the Fine Arts wandered in and out. There was laughter and wit and serious discussions deep into the night, much unveiling of sensitive souls and coarse ribbing of same. Fiestas were held over mountains of bread and butter and sardines at financial high tide or, when the money ran out, margarine and cottage cheese.

But after a while our crowd trooped back to its native habitat, the *Kaffeehaus.* There the young intellectuals would heatedly proclaim new theories about art, sex, politics, and the world in general, exactly as similar young people were doing on the Left Bank and in Bloomsbury—except that Vienna was too provincial and self-contained to make herself heard beyond the borders of the monarchy. Austria, the old glamour girl, did not quite realize how feeble and creaky she had become with age. She was still the heartland of Europe, still beautiful, still the fairest of them all in her own enchanted mirror. In the meantime, the parliament was almost paralyzed with the fights and brawls between the too many parties, too many nationalities pulling away from the government, the center personified by a very obstinate, very pious old gentlemen, a tragic and ridiculous figure in his complete lack of understanding and his perfect integrity.

Of course, there were political cliques in the *Kaffeehaus,* just as there were chess players; in our crowd, though, the surge toward socialism played no important part. By natural inclination we were on the side of the underdog: for the Boers in their war against the British, for the poor little Japanese against the gross, strong Russians, for the underpaid workingman against the bourgeois moneybags with their full, fat bellies. But this was only incidental. Politics were beneath the artist. So was the thought of money or success. ART was the all-important thing, the new image of the world we carried in us, the dreams we spun out across the chipped, stained marble tables. In a word, we believed and thought and did precisely what a certain percentage of every young generation ever did, does, and will do, bless 'em. Naturally, all this is much simpler and funnier and clearer in memory than it was in the thick of it.

I don't know why I remember so little about the two years my socalled marriage lasted. Not for the psychologist's usual reason, that we push unpleasant memories down into our subconscious. On the contrary, those years were pleasant, a great relief, liberation; not a marriage, for sure, but rather a romp of children, youngsters playing hooky from school.

There is no reason to mention those years at all, except that it was then, quite unexpectedly, that I was forced to learn my future craft, my métier, from the ground up. This, too, was fun, much more fun than the daily discipline of practicing scales and five-finger exercises on the harp.

Max Prels had convinced my father, my innumerable aunts and uncles and also my grandmother—by then a most impressive, white-haired, totally blind old lady—that he was a full-fledged and well-paid editor of a respectable evening paper. Perhaps he had even convinced himself of it. The bleak truth emerged after our first month together: he was no editor, had neither a fixed job nor a salary, but had been limping along on the pittance the paper paid him for an occasional theater or book review, a little *feuilleton,* an aphorism, a freely invented anecdote. These earnings he habitually rounded out by skillful juggled loans among his bunch of carefree friends, and by carrying anything not nailed down or locked away to "Tante Dorothea," Vienna's nickname for the dignified gray building in the Dorotheenstrasse that housed the municipal pawn-shop. To me, a miserly bookkeeper's daughter after all, this was a bewildering dénouement. My young man's flat blue eyes were washed in tears when he confessed the financial mess we were in, but I laughed him out of his melancholy. This was the other side of liberty, freedom from bourgeois pedantry, the glorious *vie de bohème.* I recited La Fontaine's fable of *La Fourmi et la Cigale* with all the rhetoric tricks Mademoiselle had pounded into me. No doubt, between the two of us, mine was the less attractive part of the thrifty, industrious ant. As a matter of overcompensation, I went out and recklessly spent almost all of my small savings on thin net lisle hose, taffeta petticoats that whispered frou-frou, and more ostrich feathers than were becoming to a shrimp like me.

By and by, though, I learned that Prels was not entirely and hopelessly broke. He had, it turned out, an agreement to write six stories for Velhagen and Klasing's *Monatshefte,* a well-liked and well-paying German monthly magazine. The trouble was that the first deadline was staring at him and he hadn't produced a single usable line. To tell the truth, neither did he have a halfway usable idea for a story in his head.

I find him writhing in the throes of fruitless labor pains. The floor is covered with crumpled and discarded sheets through which he is wading up and down the study that swims in bitter, gray smoke. His eyes are red-rimmed, he smokes incessantly, the cheapest cigarettes available in the K. & K. Tabak Trafik (tobacco was an Austro-Hungarian state monopoly, one of the sources of the monarchy's meager revenues); and he is snapping his fingers like castanets as was his habit when he was thinking, or trying to think. He snapped them so hard and so often that he had grown callouses on both his middle fingers, those long, thin fingers, always stained with nicotine. The odor of cold cigarettes surrounded him like an aura, his skin was soaked in it, his nice blond hair, his clothes and underwear; the apartment, too, and everything in it—the book I opened, the sofa pillow against which I leaned, the bed in which I slept. I didn't mind this, not in the beginning; but in my memory it seems to me that I actually noticed many such details for the first time that evening, imponderabilia that by and by, termitelike, make sawdust of many a marriage.

At that time we hadn't yet heard of a writer's block, but the symptoms existed, the painful staring at the deadline, the total void in the brain. I tried to tease and laugh him out of his frustration, unfamiliar as I was with the disaster of such mental droughts. I reminded him of little stories and entertaining observations he had sketched for me into the hazy coffeehouse air, "enough to write ten stories," I said. I was an old hand at inspiring the creative mind, wasn't I? He took a deep breath and glumly sat down at his typewriter. The puppy had fallen asleep on my lap and my heart was awash with love for the small lump. His warmth, the sheen of his loose black skin, the brown marks around his muzzle lovely like peeled horse chestnuts. I left Max to his work the next hour. "When do they expect your story?" I asked. "Yesterday"—the journalist's accepted answer— "and I haven't a single lousy idea. What am I going to do? Goddamn them with their deadline on the 'ninth inst. at the latest'! And the widow Prels screeching for money, and if I don't spit out thirty-five kronen the pledge for my gold watch at Tante Dorothea's is forfeited . . . the only thing I inherited from my father . . . and . . . and——"

"Wait a moment," I said. "Maybe, maybe you could find some idea you could use among my things . . . I mean . . . just a moment, let me think where I put the trash." But Max hardly heard me, he was pacing the room, stomping through the rustling, no-good pages.

It was a remarkable evening, the consequences of which I had not the faintest inkling. In our entrance hall stood the large wardrobes I had inherited from my maternal grandparents. Closets being unknown in central Europe, such wardrobes stood in all entrance halls —anterooms they were called—and held as many objects as Fibber McGee's subsequent closet. Somewhere among them I had tucked away a large cardboard box of manuscripts. I rooted out a couple of stories, not good enough to please me, not bad enough to be thrown away. Hesitant and embarrassed, I carried them in to Max who, in the meantime, had poisoned himself with another gallon of pitch-black coffee. I didn't quite know how to begin. "I'm sorry," I said timidly, "I'm so terribly sorry, my poor darling, if I . . . but you see . . . I mean. . . ."

A good friend told me yesterday that it is characteristic of me to be so sorry for anybody who did me in that I feel I must apologize and console him for the situation he got himself into by swindling me. Well, maybe there's a grain of truth in this. I wasn't aware of it till yesterday. But my deep embarrassment in trying to extricate Max from his doldrums may serve as a sample.

"Well, what is it?" he asked in annoyance. "Did the pup piddle a puddle on my bed?"

"No, I thought . . . I mean, I sometimes write a little—it's all nonsense, of course—but I mean . . . maybe you could find a little flea of an idea in this . . . if you wouldn't mind . . . just to get you started, you know. . . ."

I felt as though I were a very small tugboat trying to pull afloat a huge liner that had run aground. I put my stories on the desk and fled into the bedroom, to Lumpi.

Max changed two commas to semicolons, put a title on the head of an untitled manuscript, signed it with a surprisingly unashamed "by Max Prels," and carried it personally to the nearest mailbox. "I didn't know I married a little witch," he said. "If you have more such conjurer's tricks up your sleeve you better warn me beforehand.

You know what? I think I couldn't have written a much better story myself. Let's keep our fingers crossed and pray it won't be a homing pigeon."

It wasn't, and from there on it was smooth sailing. I wrote Max Prels's short stories and they were published under his name. It never occurred to me to be proud of the stories or to resent my anonymity. I just wondered how anyone as bright as Max Prels could be unable to do anything as simple as writing such stories. I don't remember a single line of them, but I guess they were the corny, sentimental kind that family magazines preferred then and, with some sex and violence thrown in, prefer today.

Meeting those deadlines, working up a new plot each month and learning to communicate with my readers was the most valuable training a young author could wish for. And if you were to ask me what is the strongest inspiration, I would have to answer: the need for money. I don't mean Big Money, and I am not speaking about best sellers or plain commercial writing or the fortunes gained by sales to the movie industry; I am talking about the dire need of buying bread and milk and new shoes for the children, a bit of warmth in the stove, or of calling the doctor when someone is sick. I have no patience with people who, at the sight of palm trees or a South Sea island or a lovely spring landscape, sigh, "Oh, what an inspiration that must be to you!" In my experience, such lush things only make you lazy. As for myself, I do my best staring at the white-washed wall of a monkish cell. But if you lack the money to buy the barest necessities for your family—my, what juices and ideas the glands produce and how all the tiny brain wheels begin to turn and create!

Thus, the curtain closes on the first act of the tightrope walkers' marriage as the man diligently types out his wife's penciled manuscripts and blithely signs them as his own.

The second act takes place, for the most part, in the café where we meet our friends daily at a sort of floating round table, an earlier and definitely Viennese version of New York's Algonquin group, only without any wish or talent for publicity.

Here my husband was at home; this was his world, an amusing, stimulating world in whose crisscross net I was quickly caught. I am a homemaker at heart; not a coral that is tightly cemented to the ground, but rather a snail that carries its house with it, quick and mobile, though, as snails go. I had started us in his nice apartment with a well-organized household run on a small but orderly budget. The *Kaffeehaus* attracted me, though, because I soon discovered that if I wished to share my husband's life I, too, must move to the *Kaffeehaus*. I didn't mind; I was fascinated by it. All my life my curiosity has driven me to gobble up all the different people and backgrounds I can lay my eyes and hands on. In the *Kaffeehaus* I learned more than any college might have taught me: how to look behind the façade, to size up a person, a book, a play, sort the fake from the true. I had always been ahead of my age, precocious, old. Now I began to grow up a little, grow younger. In the stories I was writing for Max the descriptive parts, the background and atmosphere, created themselves, but the dialogue was stiff and troublesome. In the swift conversations of the *Kaffeehaus* I learned to listen, then to handle the material, first in talking myself, then in writing. Of course, we were clever, bristling like porcupines with irony and cynicism.

Spending hours and hours in the *Kaffeehaus* was at first a stimulating pleasure, then a daily habit, and, as is the way with habits, at last an addiction. I resented my becoming dependent on this daily dose of Café Kremser. I began to be bored by the continual merry-go-round of intimate gossip, the hidden envy at one's small progress, the charming witticisms, the amiable backbiting. I grew sensitive to the subtle cannibalism with which we were feeding on each other, and to a certain stagnation within our repetitive exhibition of mental vivacity. Yet, when I tried to stay away, give up the dope, I couldn't.

How right my instinct was I saw when, in 1932, I returned to Vienna for three days after an absence of twenty years, for the opening of *Grand Hotel*. In the meantime, Austria had fought and lost the Great War, the old monarchy had been cut up and made goulash of, governments of various shadings had come and gone,

Hitler and those who had worked for *Anschluss* with Germany were in the ascendance. But Vienna herself appeared not much changed. Accidentally and hardly aware of it, I walked past my old haunt, the Café Kremser; with a slight stab of recognition I looked up and in through the plate-glass window: and there they were, still!—a bit older, a bit faded like everything in the town of my birth, yet not much changed: Joseph Reitler, Max Graf, Dr. Konta, Theodor Csokor, Soyka; and even my first Great Love, my Flying Dutchman, only slightly moth-eaten. With a cool shudder down my spine I thought, here, but for the grace of God, am I.

I am afraid I shall never belong to the charming-all-too-charming town of my birth. My scant virtues, much as I try to disguise them, are without charm: I am a hard worker, reliable, conscientious, disciplined; a cursed Spartan, a stoic. I would have almost said, a Prussian full of Kant's nasty Categorical Imperative. God knows what strict genes those early German settlers and pioneers of Parabutch have planted in me. My ample shortcomings, though, are all Viennese, Austrian. The sloppiness in daily life, the contempt for money and business, the tendency to compromise, appease rather than fight; the touchiness in matters of taste, the obsolete and unspoken attachment to nature, the need to remain near it. Even the facility of whatever talents I was born with—they're all Austrian.

I think it is Aldous Huxley who complains in one of his essays about the futility of influencing or changing a reader's preconceived ideas through the printed word. I have written, lectured, shouted from the rooftops that Vienna never was a gay town, that the populace did *not* spend its time waltzing and carousing, that the people, if anything, were all tinged with a congenital, bittersweet, melancholy resignation. We Viennese, living in the capital of a dying empire, balanced forever precariously on the edge of suicide. Making jokes about it was and is our only weapon. I put this down here once more, knowing at the same time that it is absolutely to no avail. Ah, those gay Viennese, those laughing and crying and loving girls! Life is just one swirling, happy waltz! Forgive me if I say: "Bull!"

:

On our stage, then, we have one of Vienna's two or three cafés specializing in intellectuals, a cross section of the town's and the time's spiritual life and taste. While there are political round tables, in our crowd there is only a mandarin's contempt for politics and politicians, for wealth or power or influence; and success is outrightly suspect. Art, literature, the new ideas, the new style—these are the important topics. Much good and fast dialogue flies across the marble-topped tables, along with the witty and bitchy gossip, the nonchalant interest in other people's lives. As horses are discussed in England or baseball players in America, women are discussed point by point. A large portion of the dissection revolves around one young woman: married almost two years to Max Prels and as far as one can see, she hasn't taken a lover yet. Why not? It's not quite natural, the table agrees. "She is cold, no temperament," claims one or the other who tried and was rebuffed; not even rebuffed, but, worse, whose sizzling advances remained unnoticed, were drowned in the girl's good-humored equanimity. ("Cold," they say; what they mean is frigid, a word used at that time only in clinical parlance.) "Cold? Girls with such heavy eyebrows, such velvet eyes, are dynamite once they are awakened," protests a voice. A strong belief, shared by both sexes, is contained in the magic of the discreet word and indiscreet act of "awakening a female." "All right, just try and awaken her, Casanova!" someone says irritably, a minor composer and music critic, an elderly person who recently joined the regulars; among the fashionable toothbrush mustaches he looks outlandish and romantic with his dark little Flying Dutchman's beard. (Now that the girl is married and he still is alone, there is nothing to keep him from seducing her.) "Perhaps she is in love with her husband," the youngest and most talented of the circle ventures; he is the husband's friend and the girl's favorite, a frequent guest at their apartment, where he shares their salami. When the girl plays in a late concert he is even trusted and honored with taking Lumperl out for his evening promenade. The others study him with faint suspicion and a whiff of jealousy.

"How can she be in love with a zero like Max Prels? Ridiculous!" says a fellow whose mind is so negative and analytical that he is unable to produce three continuous lines and therefore hates everybody, most of all, himself. The others speak up for Prels. He is a nice guy, they all like him, so amusing, no zero, he. "Look at his stuff in Velhagen and Klasing's. He's got something, that guy."

"What's he got? That *Kitsch*? The trash he writes?"

"Sure, but there's talent in the *Kitsch*. And he's working on a serious novel. Just you wait and see. There's more behind that little clown than we know——"

They change the subject as the young woman enters the café and comes up to the table. She seems thinner still than in the first act, pale under the white balloons of the gas lamps, but bright-eyed with gaiety. Without the least fuss she fits herself into the company. There is no gallantry, no getting up to greet her, nobody lights her cigarette or brings her a chair; as in the orchestra, the men treat her as an equal and that's exactly how she wants to be treated. What men may think or fancy, that's another matter. Obviously by now she, too, is quite at home in the *Kaffeehaus* and, with its intellectual regulars, she soaks up the atmosphere, listens to the clever talk, throws in some amusing remarks of her own. She has learned a lot from these knowing and knowledgeable people, and she is still learning. Not by intention but by osmosis, she says. The waiter brings her tea with a double portion of sugar, a slice of lemon, a small jigger of rum, the same barbaric mixture that her father and her grandfather drank. The waiter brings her an evening paper that contains her husband's nicely worded review of the famous Berlin troupe which comes for a short stay each spring to show Vienna how to play Ibsen. After a solicitous glance at her the waiter also brings her a glass of Seltzer. The wise old man is the only one who senses that she has a headache and is bone-tired. That's why she acts doubly gay. To her it seems that she has been overworked and tired, with never enough sleep, since her fifth year. But as the talk grows more absorbing she gets her second wind. This is too fascinating to be missed.

It would be nice if I could report that most of the members of our round table became great and famous. Alas, nothing so brilliant as the last chapter of Murger's *Scènes de la Vie de Bohème* happened in our circle. Although most of those early friends later made a respectable name for themselves, their fame for the most part was limited to the boundaries of Austria. We lacked the go-getter spirit, the mutual admiration and publicizing of, for instance, the Algonquin crowd or the Bloomsbury coterie; we were not market-minded in the least, although I can say, in retrospect, that Karl Kraus and Polgar, Franz Werfel, Stefan Zweig, Kafka, Musil, and various others were there too. But, like most artistic movements that started in Europe, it took thirty years on the average before they really arrived in America and I often find myself confronted here and now with names and styles that were part of my youth.

In the second year of our marriage, or companionship, the charms of *la vie de bohème*, the decadent coffeehouse atmosphere, the skeptical wit of our friends, began to pall. Also, I suppose I was a little overworked again. I was holding on to my job in the symphony orchestra, and (somewhat below my standard) playing the harp in churches and synagogues and behind the scenes at Monday afternoon performances of classical dramas for high school students. This kept me busy enough, but what with also writing Max's stories and pinch-hitting for him with *feuilletons* and reviews and sitting up till all hours in the coffeehouse, my face was green again and I had to buy many sheets of pink tissue paper to keep the bloom on my cheeks up to par. Max, noticing a slight falling off in my barometer, bought me silly gifts, a muff (right out of *La Bohème!*), some perfume I detested, baskets of flowers, silk petticoats.

Needless to say, every one of Max's friends had tried in the beginning to establish the traditional triangle, with me in one corner. It was a matter of simple courtesy, I suppose. But as I met them, one and all, with the bland camaraderie that had become my second nature among the ninety men of my orchestra, they had now dropped all such efforts, just when I was ready for a radical change. I had been good long enough; now I made up my mind to be bad. I had only a nebulous idea of how to go about it. Once before I had passed through what is known today as a phase: at the age of twelve, after shaking off God and religion, I had likewise resolved

to be bad. Not much had come of it, except my childish crush on
my fat, aging tenor. But now. . . .

As I said before, it is youth's privilege to get into one mess
after another and this was the psychological moment for me. The
mess I chose though, in the long run, turned out to be just as fruitful for my apprenticeship as a writer as being forced to write short
stories for Max had been.

One nice day my husband, unwisely for him, as it turned out,
introduced me to a young man who had been his friend at the
university, of whom he had lost track but now presented as a long-
lost prodigal son. Against the pale-faced, somewhat seedy-looking
coffeehouse crowd Godfrey looked like an emissary from foreign
shores. He was tall, good-looking, impeccably dressed, well-mannered,
with the marks of good pedigree, the easy movements of a well-balanced sportsman. "Be nice to him," Max whispered to me. It was not
difficult, it was as simple as opening a window to let fresh air into a
musty room.

One of my husband's pleasant traits was his complete lack of
possessiveness and jealousy. Although Godfrey was a hunter, Max
had brought him in like a trophy, to be stuffed and hung on the
wall. In the case of Godfrey and me, he went too far out of his way
to let our friendship ripen undisturbed. The reason for this, though,
was not entirely noble: Godfrey came from a well-to-do family and
had recently come into some money. As far as I could make out he
had never done a stitch of serious work but dabbled in the esoteric:
heraldry, the writings of old German mystics—Angelus Silesius,
Jakob Böhme—the history of the Carolingians. Like any well-bred
Austrian, he was a passable pianist. He had traveled much, read
widely, reaching out in all directions without finding a purpose or
goal.

Max Prels, though, had imported his friend Godfrey for another
purpose: Godfrey's function was to finance a Little Magazine to be
founded, created, edited by Max Prels. That was his dream, the
same dream that's still prevalent among young intellectuals, and was
probably just the same in Plato's time.

No child can ever be so beautiful as the yet unborn, no book so great as the one to be written tomorrow, or the next year; no Little Magazine was so unique and wonderful as the magazine Max carried in his head and for the publication of which he lacked nothing but money. The further the mirage receded, the thirstier he grew; the surer, too, that only in his own Little Magazine could his genius fulfill itself. The lesser lights of our round table were all for it; they all needed a medium in which to air their ideas. They considered this a gift from Heaven: with Godfrey's money and Max's talent, the Little Magazine was to be founded. It would give purpose and direction to the lives of both of them. It would be the voice of Austria's Young Generation, our generation. It couldn't fail to flourish, make for both of them a name and, as a sideline, money. In other words, it was to do what every Little Magazine hopes for but seldom does.

Godfrey took to the project eagerly.

Then came the various stages of my husband's rather difficult pregnancy: morning and evening sickness, false alarms, neurotic behavior, strange appetites in the matter of layout and content, steady demands for utter consideration, encouragement, moral and financial support.

At last the baby was born. As magazines go, it was a *very* Little Magazine, and, like most newborn, rather ugly to look at, a bit underweight and pale, its upkeep extremely expensive. Anyone who had ever tried to publish a highbrow magazine on a limited budget could have warned us what would happen. And soon it was obvious that Max Prels was as much of a dud as an editor in chief as he had been as a short-story writer. By the time we had used up the last of Godfrey's money in bringing out the fifth issue, I, under an interesting motley of pseudonyms, was writing the whole damn thing singlehanded: editorial, *feuilleton*, a short story, two poems, and all the book, theater, and concert reviews. It was a priceless exercise in editorial experience and versatility, and it was huge fun. In the natural course of events it kept the three of us working closely together; in the natural course of events, also, things came to a pitch between Godfrey and me, to nobody's surprise, least of all my husband's. Max was not jealous; I should almost say he pushed

Here is Vicki Baum at 46—a poised, elegant, successful editor and writer. The bitter childhood years seem far behind her.

When Vicki was still a teen-ager, she was a competent professional musician, playing her harp at Vienna's musical affairs.

The dancer Joseph Hassreiter, creator of the ballet *Die Puppenfee,* was probably the only person the vain, mingy Herman Baum ever loved.

Vicki's husband, Dr. Richard Lert, the eminent musician, poses with their boys.

In Berlin, at the gymnasium of Sabri Mahir—with whom prize fighters trained—Vicki, along with Marlene Dietrich, endured grueling physical workouts that kept her superbly vigorous. In her office at Ullstein House (*below*), Vicki wrote for *Die Berliner Illustrirte*. The magazine's brilliant editor, Kurt Korff (*below, right*), came to America to start *Life* magazine just before he died.

Vicki Baum poses here (*above*) after American beauty salons had transformed her from a well-groomed European woman to an American glamour girl. The unbelievable Vicki at 65 (*below*) looked as chic as the stars she wrote movie scenarios for.

Vicki poses here with one of her dearest friends and colleagues, Oscar Straus, the composer of *Ein Walzertraum*, which Hollywood filmed as *The Smiling Lieutenant*.

In her Hollywood home (*below*), Vicki recalled the years in which "it was all quite different"—and wrote her memoirs. This photograph was taken just before her death in 1960.

us together and then stood aside, amused, like a tactful elder brother.

In the meantime, our little affair progressed in the approved style of an Arthur Schnitzler novel—with long hikes into the soft hills of the Vienna Woods; lying side by side in the meadows that are carpets of violets and primroses in spring, daisies and pink lupines in summer, rich with blackberries and red foliage in fall. We would chew blades of grass, peel off willow twigs, and in low voices talk to Godfrey's handsome setter, who was our steady chaperon; and we did not dare more, as if at the lightest touch of our little fingers the whole hill and forest would flare up in fire. We would swim in a dead tributary of the Danube and afterward stretch out on the sand of a beach, which was completely empty and unknown then, though a few years later it was developed into the Gänsehäufel, an overcrowded, loud, vulgar Viennese version of Coney Island. Toward evening, sunburned and with wet hair, we would wander to one of the old fishing villages along the shore of the Danube, eat cheese and salami and black bread in the candlelight, and grow mellow and a bit tipsy on young, gold-green wine. It was only an infatuation, a little affair, but in Vienna at that time such things were handled with patience and taste; given some poetry, music, some of the *Rosenkavalier* gracefulness to heighten the suspense, a little affair seemed like a great love.

For a while, with all the strolling, hiking, swimming, and my discovering that I was a female, I looked much better. I filled out, grew sleek and shiny, my hair bronze with blond highlights from the sun. There is no finer cosmetic than an affair with a convincing lover; it you happen to be married to one, so much the better. But I wasn't the only one to discover I was a woman. All the men I knew, and some I didn't know, suddenly made the same discovery. They knew that I was having an affair months before it was true. Suddenly every man and his grandfather was after me, which was flattering and very good for me, but it was a mess all the same. I was growing tired of all the fussing and prevaricating, of the stolen hours and the secret rendezvous; of the small indignities and broad discomforts that are part and parcel of adultery. Of trying for convention's sake to hide our all-too-transparent state of sin which everybody had known, tolerantly accepted, and even applauded long before we ourselves knew where we were heading.

Each month it became more hopeless to scrape up the money and material for another issue of the magazine. One time we had a windfall. I sent one of my short stories to a contest run by another moribund magazine in Munich, *Licht und Schatten*. It was the first thing published under my real name, and the thousand marks I received as first prize paid some of our debts to the printer.

After that brief lift we were on the skids, and once you begin to slide you go downhill faster and faster. Godfrey, with a lover's stubborn pride, or perhaps from a sense of obligation, continued to support the Little Magazine. He borrowed money at outrageous interest from professional usurers, he sold his jewelry, he talked his sister out of hers, I think he stole and pawned his mother's diamonds. He even began to work, selling advertisements, books, patent medicines, and God-knows-what other questionable products of fly-by-night industries. Our personal finances had also become an impenetrable tangle, as Max, on his part, had piled up more debts and told me more lies than he himself knew. "The three of us," he wailed, "are worse than the Laocoön group."

And a few days later he said: "I had a talk with Godfrey. Did he tell you?"

"No. Does he want us to give up the magazine?"

"Oh no, he wants to go on as before. Only . . . Listen . . . he asked me, would I mind divorcing you."

"Well, would you?"

"Would I what?"

"Mind giving me a divorce?"

"Darling, if I say I don't mind, well, that's not very gallant, is it? And if I say I do mind, it only makes it difficult. I guess I'm not a husband, whatever you say."

"We had a nice gentleman's agreement, though, remember?"

"Yes. Let's remain friends and all that. Like one of those plays for the Deutsches Volkstheater matinée. Second curtain. I don't mind my wife having a lover, they all have; but, darling, I don't like my wife to parade a fiancé. Agreed?"

"Right."

It was as simple as that, and we did indeed remain friends until Max Prels's early death.

When we were finally completely and hopelessly stuck and gave up the magazine, we were deep in the expenses and grotesque complications of the divorce.

At the time Max and I were married, it had seemed the simplest thing in the world to make our gentleman's agreement: let's try it, see if it works; if it doesn't, we'll part as friends, no fuss, no hard feelings. But marriage and divorce weren't handled like that, not in Catholic Austria, not in 1910. Although Max had formally and deliberately renounced his church and I had never belonged to it, the proceedings of untying that loose little knot were a wildly absurd farce. Some of the obstacles were inherent in Godfrey's insistence upon our getting married as soon as possible. I suspect this was as much a matter of expediency as a proof of our undying love. Under the malicious tyranny of the *Hausmeister,* whom the law armed with a thing called the *Meldezettel,* living in sin was, if not impossible, at least infernally uncomfortable. The *Meldezettel,* which had to be filled out and handed to the *Hausmeister,* was a document of such snooping indiscretion it left not the smallest shred of privacy to the tenant; especially if the tenant was not sufficiently affluent to bribe the tyrant. The furious master of the house made it hell for the tenant, particularly if the tenant happened to be a woman in the disgraceful process of getting divorced and, moreover, a young woman receiving daily visits from a young man obviously her lover. Morals, at that time and place (and, I suspect, at any place and any time), had a double bottom. Love affairs of married ladies had a playful sort of rococo flavor about them and were a well-sanctioned institution. The lover was expected to hand royal tips around and, in return, was then addressed as *Herr Baron.* But there was an absurd law that flatly forbade a divorcee to marry the man on whose account she had been divorced. Furthermore, the law forbade said divorcee to enter into any marriage before the expiration of one year after the divorce became legal—apparently to allow a cooling-off period during which she would be cleansed of her illicit love. It seemed a cruel and senseless law so long as the three of us were dancing circles around each other, around the attorney appointed as Defender of the Marriage Tie, and the three leering, lip-smacking relentless judges. Later, I found that law a blessing, because the cooling-off did not even take a year. By the time we had our divorce, the shine and sparkle had rubbed off my emotions.

I felt trapped. Serves you right, you infatuated goose! I told myself grimly. Why can't you, in your choice of men, use a bit of the discrimination and good taste you show in music or books? And Godfrey was a disappointment all down the line. He belonged to that class of men whose attractiveness depends on the background of money acquired without toil and elegantly spent. Such men wear badly, like clothes of some synthetic materials. When I had first met him he made my *Kaffeehaus* friends, all those literati and cognoscenti, seem like pale wispy ghosts. He is a Man, my man, I felt, overwhelmed by my first encounter with straight, handsome, uncomplicated masculinity. But Godfrey, in debt up to his eyebrows, worried, whining, having swapped his nice tan for the stooping shoulders of an unsuccessful job hunter, was something else entirely. The starch had gone out of him together with his last twenty kronen. (These, the three of us, characteristically, had spent on celebrating the divorce by taking a fiacre and riding up and down the Prater Hauptallee where the haut monde of Vienna each afternoon paraded its horses, carriages, and clothes.)

Three years ago I sat in a performance of *My Fair Lady* and suddenly, unaccountably, my eyes were awash with tears. What a thing to happen to me who can never cry! But there was this sudden grip and wrench of nostalgia: Look, oh look, how elegant they are! How elegant the world of my youth was! How much effort men put into being attractive, boastful like male birds growing bright tailfeathers, strutting their plumage to seduce and conquer. Lost, all lost, I snuffled and sobbed; damn the new, the predatory female of my species that has killed male grace, effort, and elegance!

Later, after Godfrey had lost all his money in our foolish enterprise, he claimed he had walked into the partnership with open eyes; his only reason, he loved me madly, wanted to be near me, tie me to him. Of course he had lost everything, was in debt over his head, but it was worth it.

"Don't you see? I loved you so . . . !"

Well, this sounded like Maupassant, a gallant and flattering lie, a melodramatic fabrication in the dated French style, burdening me with an obligation.

I felt sorry for Godfrey, but if I wanted to be stuck with an inefficient fellow to be sorry for I might as well have stayed with Max Prels. Now I had a new responsibility. What the hell was the matter with me that I had to carry to the utmost the consequences of each of my mistakes? Was it my upbringing, or was I born that way? Would I always attract the chipped, the slightly cracked porcelain, what the trade calls the Seconds? (Yes, probably always, a small voice in me answered; you always loved the broken dolls best, remember?) I had a desperate sensation of being walled in (*Aïda*, last act), claustrophobia of the soul. I was in for it.

Once, on a hiking trip through the Tirol, I was almost killed in a landslide. There had been a flood and the wild white waters of the mountain streams had washed out parts of the narrow trail. I was clambering up a scrubby slope toward the shade of the high spruce on the steep mountainside. As I reached it I stopped for a moment to look up into the soughing treetops. There was a strange nervous movement in the tips of the branches, a fluttering like trembling fingers.

I was still staring when the entire mountainside came creaking, rumbling, thundering down, with bursting trunks and leaping boulders shaking and sliding with such noises, in such unbelievable rapidity that I hardly understood what had happened. I think I leaped back, astonished rather than panicked, was thrown to the ground, bumped around, torn and scratched. Almost unconscious, I rolled with the punches. And then it was all over. The landslide had come to rest at the bottom, in the stream, and where the high spruce had stood a minute ago there were now only naked rocks sticking out from the mountain's flank like fractured bones.

That is how almost unnoticeable are the first signs of decline and danger, of skidding down to disaster.

First, Lumpi got sick, my beloved little clown of a miniature

Dachshund. His eyes lost their shine and his nose was warm. Trembling, he rolled up into himself in his little hatbox house. T.B., said the veterinary. Not much to be done, too finely bred. Lumpi had come from the famous imperial breed of the Emperor's hunting castle in Mürzsteg and heaven knows what strings Max had pulled to get him for me. I loved Lumpi dearly, and he died like a little gentleman.

Then there was that pathetic *malheur* of Mali. Mali was our maid, an apple-cheeked girl fresh from the country, a wonderful cook, the proverbial jewel, thrifty, reliable, and gay, the backbone of the household I had set up at the beginning of my marriage. Mali was very religious; her free Sundays were spent with confession, high Mass, and the activities of a Catholic *Jungfernbund,* a society of sworn virgins. Twice a year their Bund invited a Bund of equally virginal Catholic men to a church supper and dance.

We had been away over a weekend, and when we came home there was no Mali. "She must be somewhere," said the omniscient *Hausmeister's* wife, "or we would have seen her go out."

We found her, at last, in her room in the attic. She was unconscious, swimming in blood, literally bled white, hanging on to life with a frightening thin, slow thread of pulse. "Tried to abort herself, the damn nitwit," Dr. Popper said. "First they whore around like bitches in heat and then they make a pigsty of it. I ought to call in the police; anyway, that's what they will do if I take her to the General Hospital." He didn't though; we persuaded him to take the poor silly creature to a private clinic, that charged us so much for its discreet handling that our finances went from the chaotic to the catastrophic. While Mali was being patched up I discovered angrily how useless I was in doing a housewife's job. I still had a sworn Bohemian's contempt for such menial tasks—besides, at that time, no household was so poor as to have no help or servant—but it would have been nice if I had known how to scramble eggs or boil potatoes. Both my men pitched in the best they knew how, but we were soon camped in a swarm of unmade beds, soiled towels, rumpled clothes, dust, and dirt, letting things drift for Mali's return.

But the girl that finally slunk back to us was no longer our apple-cheeked Mali. Pale, listless, haggard. "That one has had it," commented our *Hausmeister*'s wife, Frau Pitzelgruber.

"For Heaven's sake, Mali, why did you do it? Why didn't you talk with me?" I asked her.

"Talk with you? What for?" she asked. Her expression told me clearly that I, the Free Soul, the sophisticate, couldn't have helped her; that I was a little goose who didn't know the first thing about real life. That I was childish, immature, just playing at being grown up. It was a sudden, painful revelation, but how truly right she was I understood only much later.

"But how did it happen? Who got you in trouble? Why didn't you get married and have your baby?"

Mali's answer perplexed me. "He was one of the Catholic Young Men's Bund," she said. "He said he wanted to marry me, but first he had to make sure that I really was a virgin. Such a fine young man. Very pious, he is. Naturally, since I committed this terrible sin he wants nothing to do with me." "Oh, Mali," I sighed, trying not to laugh at the adroit ways of primitive man.

"I guess I'll go home to my aunt. As weak as I am, I can't work. If the *Herrschaften* will just pay me last month's wages. . . ."

Exit Mali and with her all semblance of order. In the meantime, Max had secretly sold the only piece of jewelry I ever cared for in my whole life: the string of beautiful pearls I had inherited from Grandmama, a fashionable length of precious moonlight to hang down to my knees or be wound four times around my neck.

To me the loss of those exquisite pearls at my husband's irresponsible hands seemed the final symptom of our being on the skids. The next stage was bedbugs in the apartment. Bedbugs are not precisely a rarity in such an ancient town as Vienna, but it was a last filthy indignity. At such a time any small disturbance can bring down a mountainside. This was the landslide that almost buried me.

On a miserable November day I trudged along the interminable thoroughfare leading from the First District, where I had been in a rehearsal, way out to the Eighteenth District where I was to give a lesson. A vicious wind was driving a hard, cold rain against me. The clouds low overhead were dark, slow. A bus lumbered by, splashing me up to my face with dirty slush. A thickish gray river was sweeping empty matchboxes, old pieces of paper, dogs' excrement along the gutter where a used condom, caught in the sewer grill at the corner, completed the still life. Crossing the Gersthoferstrasse, with infallible vaudeville humor I landed with one foot in that miniature river. I felt like crying, but I set my teeth and took a firmer grip on my dripping, insulted, long skirt. I had reached the outskirts of Gersthof; another twenty minutes and I'd be safe and warm under Frau Libussa's wings.

I veered from cussing myself to cussing the goddamned Little Magazine that was at the root of all our trouble and debts. We, the three of us, had been feeding that monster as the Aztecs had fed their bloodthirsty gods, far beyond our power. In the end, all the borrowing, the signing of I.O.U.'s, the haggling with unpaid printers and professional usurers had made me feel dirty and debased. With a burning sense of shame, I remembered my pilgrimage to my mother's wealthy uncles who, understandably, had received me with marked coolness. With the volubility born of desperation I managed to extract a loan from them, to be repaid within the year at normal interest, but on condition that I make my husband stop fooling with that magazine. That was one of the reasons for living on cauliflower and Frau Libussa's disguised charity, for of course my two men went on with the magazine against all sense or reason.

Also, since my divorce I was no longer anybody's mascot. Society cut me cold, not that I cared. I had trouble finding an apartment, few invitations to appear as soloist. I was a tainted woman, and old, terribly old. I have never again been as old as I was at twenty-four. For a while, I thought seriously of a career as a *femme fatale*, a *grande cocotte*, a fallen woman, really bad.

Since I had become that contemptible being, a divorcée, men flocked around me, hot on the trail. I felt soiled by their glances, their touching me as if by accident, their hinting and prancing. Why not go the whole way and live in a kept woman's luxury? I asked myself, and set to work. My plans for achieving this new status were simple enough. I would drape myself seductively, scantily, and appear in one of Vienna's two *Varieté* shows. The rest would follow automatically.

I had myself photographed in some drapery, and some no-account actor recommended me to some no-account agent. The agent looked at me, looked at the photos, burst out laughing, gave me a fatherly pinch on the behind, and told me to go home to Mama.

My children still roar with laughter when I bring out—at their request—these old photographs. I look every inch like Rautendelein, the innocent nauseating sprite in Gerhart Hauptmann's whimsical, gagging *The Sunken Bell*—long wavy hair, enormous frightened eyes, a creature to make anybody but the most perverted sex criminal take flight.

I doubt, though, that I ever was quite as innocent as I looked; long thick eyelashes are deceptive in that respect. Even though the straw fire of my affair had quickly burned out, while it lasted I had made amazing discoveries about myself. My body had passed its eager apprenticeship, been taught the pleasures of sex, yet found them a bit overrated, a highly perishable goods on the whole.

I can see now that Godfrey's only function in my life was to make me aware that I was a woman, make me aware of sex—mine, his, ours. Till then I had known starry-eyed romance in my cloudlike relations with the Flying Dutchman; friendship, companionship in my bantamweight marriage; comfortable "let's-be-pals" relations with my colleagues in the orchestra and men in general. Suddenly I found myself up to my neck in a burning and irrevocable lava stream.

Perhaps I was, in my sex life, a case of arrested development, a kind of female time bomb. I ought to have passed that senseless and wonderful explosion and eruption when I was sixteen, as kids do today and always did in all sane and sound civilizations. Do I hear some growls of protest? Well, Dante's Beatrice was nine when he fell in love with her, Romeo's Juliet was fourteen. Marie Antoinette was married off at the ripe age of fifteen and given delicate advice by her imperial mother and her pater confessor on how to titillate her royal spouse's jaded desires. Not to mention all the primitive societies who know and celebrate their girls' maturity around the age of twelve and train them for love and marriage right then and there.

To be infatuated is a most agreeable condition to be in, but it's a mess, too. Infatuation doesn't look for superior qualities in its object, or else detects such qualities in the silliest irrelevancies, but, God! what those silly details do to your metabolism. What upheaval in your body chemistry, what happy tumult in your glands, and, oh, what delight to shut off your higher intellect and let the animal have its way!

f there is one thing in which I really believe, it is that in the final summing up every one of us re- ceives the same amount of happiness. And by happi- ness I don't mean good luck or success, not joy or pleasure, or even contentment or satisfaction of one sort or another. What I mean is that clear, sharp, floating, singing, overwhelming feeling that is so rare and lasts so short a while. If it would last it wouldn't be happiness any more; if it were our daily bread we wouldn't appreciate it. But of these ecstatic moments of happiness every one of us gets the same amount, I am sure.

It is my experience that we don't feel this sort of happiness in those moments when, according to convention, we are supposed to feel it. Not on the day we marry the person we love; not when we win the sweepstakes. The boy who makes the deciding touchdown doesn't feel it at that moment, nor the winner in a race or tourna- ment, nor the scientist who gets the Nobel Prize, nor the business- man who succeeds in clinching the most important deal of his life. There is too much strain in all this, too much anticipation. It seems to me that every fulfillment carries with it a drop of disappointment. The lovely thing about real happiness is that it is there all of a sudden, unexpected, weightless as a summer cloud and just as radiant and intangible. And so, if I were to tell only about the happiest moments of my life I should have no story, no plot, no substance or continuity. But while I have forgotten many important happenings in my life, those brief, floating moments of real hap- piness stay on in me, unforgettable, ineradicable.

:

When I was a little child I loved picking and arranging wild-flowers. (I still do.) And the earliest enchanted moment I remember has to do with flowers. We were in the country, where I had a habit of losing myself in the woods and coming home late for dinner. It is a summer evening; the late sunset has left rosy mother-of-pearl clouds, and the road that winds through the woods is pink with the reflection. I am marching along, singing to myself and trying to imitate the little cries of the birds in the birches. Suddenly I am stopped by a lovely fragrance; I follow it and as I step out into a clearing it seems as though the glowing sunset sky had fallen down into the grass. I tiptoe closer and there it is: a carpet of flowers the likes of which I had never seen before. Carnations, millions of them, with the faces of fairies, with a loveliness beyond all loveliness. I stood there and didn't dare to move and I knew at once that these flowers were not to be picked, and I was so happy I felt like crying.

Yes, just a patch of wildflowers, but I'll never forget them.

Then there was a time when I was very young and very poor and very lonely. I lived in a shabby little boardinghouse and my land-lady was a widow, as embittered and unfriendly as only widows renting furnished rooms can be. She had a child, a little boy who was paralyzed and half-witted. A mean little creature, locked inside the walls of his defectiveness, soiled and dirty, unable to speak, snarl-ing like an animal at everyone who approached him. But I found out that when I played the harp, something like a human expression would come into his face. From then on I took great trouble about the boy and slowly, very slowly, he learned to know me. Came the day when the child smiled for the first time in his life; he recognized me, cuddled up to me, and tried to say something. That moment, for me, was filled with a hot, peculiar, almost painful happiness that I have never experienced since. It was like in the fairy tales, when you suddenly understand the language of the animals and no bar-riers exist between creature and creature.

There was the New Year's morning when I had decided not to celebrate the night before but had gone to bed early. That morning a certain young man whom I loved—and who is now my husband

—came to pick me up for a sleigh ride. The world was white with snow, the bells tinkled, the horses steamed, and everything was gay and brisk and fresh and wonderful. We watched the last bedraggled, straggling people stumble home while we drove toward the rising sun, and it was such an exuberantly fine feeling to know that everybody else had a hangover. There was an almost biological happiness about that morning; the happiness of being young and strong and healthy, with every gland working well and every hormone in its right place and every bone and muscle as it should be. I laughed so much during that ride that I cried, and I remember that the tears froze on my eyelids and this, too, seemed very wonderful. I also remember the date. It was January 1, 1914. After that year, happiness took on a different color, because it had to be picked up from among the shambles of the war.

In the third year of that war we were living in Kiel and I was awaiting the birth of our first baby; in that year of privation and austerity, buying a baby's layette was impossible. There were no cloth diapers (we used paper), no blankets, no linen. I had refused to take chloroform because I am a curious person and I wanted to know exactly how it feels to give birth to a child, every minute of it. And besides, we were short of anesthetics in 1917. It may be a commonplace to say that giving birth to a child is the greatest happiness there is. But I am not speaking of generalities. I am speaking of the exact moment of birth that relatively few women experience consciously. There is nothing in life to compare with it. That moment, when the pain stops as abruptly as if cut with a knife, and the labor is done, the tiny new being is lifted up for you to see and to touch—so miraculously perfect and complete and all your own —well, take all the riches of the world, all the ecstasies of love, all the dreams fulfilled, and let me keep that happiest moment of my life.

But again I say, happiness is not in proportion to the importance of the moment. I remember that a cup of hot cocoa that someone gave me in the midst of famine filled me with a great and serious happiness that lasted until my stomach started gnawing again. I remember the happiness of dancing the most perfect waltz of my life with a man whose name I didn't catch when he was introduced to me, and whom I had never seen before nor ever saw again. There are short cuts to happiness, and for me dancing is one of them. I suppose drinking is another, but I am no expert at that because all that drinking does to me is make me sleepy and dull. Of course, love takes you through a veritable fireworks of flashing, dizzy moments of happiness. But then, any love that can make you deliriously happy also seems to have the power to make you twice as unhappy, and the final balance may be unfavorable.

But there are less spectacular things that make for happiness. Listening to the gurgling of a stream, climbing a mountain, picking wild strawberries in the grass, the smells and noises of a stable full of well-kept horses, the sound of ripe fruit dropping from a tree, the moment in a theater before the curtain rises, or working at the writing desk through the night and watching the dawn come up when one is almost drunk with fatigue—these are some of the fleeting little things that make me happy.

Come to think of it, most of the happy moments of my later years have to do with travel. The minute I step on the planks of a boat I seem to live in an elated world. I feel the vibration of the ship, hear the ocean swish past the porthole, and I am happy. Strolling through native markets, mingling with the people always makes me happy, whether in Mexico, China, or the Indies.

In my travels it often seems to me that some peoples are more gifted for happiness than others. If you want to know real happiness, watch a Chinese coolie eat his rice and joke with his friends. The Mexicans, too, seem to have the gift. I am not so sure that a talent for happiness is among the many talents the Americans possess. We are, maybe, too ambitious, too restless, too busy, too tense. We have a lot of fun, but fun is not happiness.

Happiness cannot be forced or coaxed or commanded. It comes all by itself and every one of us has a share. But our share may be a little bigger if we are ready to be happy: ready and relaxed and willing to recognize the rare bird when it alights in our hearts.

ut I've strayed afield. Back to the Gersthoferstrasse where I trudged ahead becoming more miserable and hopeless with each step. I dreaded the lesson I'd have to give to my unpromising pupil. My coat was drenched, my hair an unmanageable burden of tangle and weight, and my hat acted as a rainspout, steadily spilling water down my back and inside of my collar. Water was squishing in my high button shoes and pulling at my long skirt, which was slathering cold and wet around my knees.

I was fed up to the gills with everything; the stagnation all around —the town, the people, with the situation I had maneuvered myself into, even with my harp. That day it seemed as if all the exits were blocked. As a musician I had gone as far as one could with as stupid, as utterly diatonic an instrument as a harp. I was beginning to hate the moody thing that went out of tune when it was cold and whose strings broke in the midst of a solo when it got warm. I loathed the inanities of which compositions for the harp consisted, and the composers, from Mozart to Mahler, who insisted on writing for five fingers when harpists could use only four. I was tired of my insignificant part in the ever-repeated symphonic repertory and of our conductor's solid but stale leadership.

I hated the weather, the street, the town. I hated myself, and for several good reasons. Only an idiot would stubbornly refuse to wear galoshes or carry an umbrella (an idiosyncrasy I haven't overcome to this day). Only an idiot would start on an hour's march in such swinish weather. There was, to be sure, the electric trolley line; there was a bus drawn by broad-beamed horses; there were one-horse hacks to be found, and elegant two-horse fiacres. But such luxuries were not for idiotic me. If I paid the trolley fare I might just as well have canceled the lesson and stayed home in bed, so little did they pay me. Nitwit that I was to have let my pupil's mother talk me into teaching her child for such a disgraceful pittance. If that child would at least show less laziness and some talent; or if I had not taken such an instant liking to the brat's mother. . . .

It seems, though, that there exists a silent understanding whereby certain professions, under certain conditions, are expected to give their services for free: physicians, clergymen, attorneys, sometimes. Actors, singers, stars, quite often. Teachers, particularly music teachers, especially in Old Vienna, regularly.

Frau Libussa Lert (and who else but my future mother-in-law could have carried the unique and somewhat overbearing name Libussa with such natural poise?) was a short, plump, middle-aged woman with such a handsome face and proud expression that you thought of her as tall and slender and young. With her zest for life, her humor, generosity, and sweep, she made a satellite of every-one who came into her orbit. She was the sort of person around whom legends and fairy tales grow, the born matriarch, the Great Earth Mother of mythical cultures. From the first moment, she reminded me of the statue of the wise, kind, and gay Empress Maria Theresa, sitting just as broad-beamed and self-assured upon her marble throne, except that Frau Lert was an inveterate chain-smoker. With her shining dark hair and eyes, strongly corseted and impeccably, however simply, dressed, she gave an impression of vivacious agility, although I have seldom seen her other than rooted to her chair at the center of the table upon which mountainous, exceedingly good meals were served to the family and sundry dropper-inners.

These meals played a not unimportant part in my attachment to Frau Libussa. She sized me up, underweight, overworked, and troubled as I was at that time, compared me with her three plump rambunctious daughters, and decided at once to take me into her brood hen's warmth and care. Care and affection, with Frau Libussa, automatically transformed itself into food. She promised to pack some twenty healthy pounds of fat on me soon if only I'd share their meals as often as possible, at least the three times weekly I came to give her child a lesson. She apologized profusely for being unable to spend a decent honorarium for those lessons, and wrapped the question of paying me off in victuals into so much tact and hospitality that she made it not only easy for me to accept, but almost impossible to refuse, her offer.

Now, trudging through the whipping downpour, I still had to grin at Frau Libussa's little maneuver, and at her being much too intelligent to think that I hadn't seen through it. The rain seemed to let up for a minute as I thought of the warm room, the rich table, the aroma of roast meat and the mounds of cakes and cookies that awaited me.

I was hungry, plain and simple, or, to express it with greater precision: I hungered. I had had to put myself on a strict budget and an even stricter diet—a cup of tea and a slice of dry bread for breakfast; a cup of tea, a slice of dry bread and ten hellers' worth of cauliflower or two eggs, for dinner, was all I could afford. No lunch, no snack, no expensive indulging in, for instance, an apple or a couple of frankfurters. Under these circumstances Frau Libussa's food was indeed saving me, if not from out-and-out starvation, at least from fainting during a concert.

You dumb fool, you silly ass, I told myself, trudging through the rain, you brought it upon yourself. Can't you read the signs? Road closed. Bridge out. No through street. But no, you must run your head against the wall, just to see what'll give, the wall or that soft-brained noodle of yours. Oh, shut up, I said, only two more months and I'll have paid off all the debts left behind in the debris of my silly marriage. All right, and what then? After the debts are paid? Don't you see how absurd you are? Afterward there's plain nothing in store for you. A mess worse than the mess you're in now. Polonius was right, speaking of befuddled, disappointed, skeptical youth: "But, Sir, such wanton, wild and usual slips as are companions noted and most known to youth and liberty."

Looking and feeling as if barely saved from a shipwreck, I arrived at the Lerts' apartment. Like most Viennese middle-class apartments, it was too small for the large family and Frau Libussa was singularly indifferent to the way it looked. Her demands were few: first, an apartment had to be kept clean, spotlessly so; next, there must be a space for the piano, a concert grand, because all her children were students of music. The two oldest sons had already left her and made a fine start in their careers, Ernst Lert as a stage director and Richard as an opera conductor. The four others still at home, three girls and one boy, would no doubt follow. Often Frau Libussa referred to the beginnings of her own mythical opera career that she had sacrificed to marry the subsequent father of her brood, geniuses one and all; and then she might break out into a Verdi aria or a soliloquy from the classics. There was enough zest, dramatic talent, and ambition in her to protect all six of them and still leave a little for me and a few other such thin and defenseless creatures. Aside from the dominating piano, the apartment contained only enough beds—mostly the pull-out or trundle type—as were necessary for six people and an occasional guest; and a table on which to feed them. For this large table—the other center of the Lertish Way of Life—there was not enough space in the jumbled three and a half rooms. It stood in a bright oasis, a glassed-in veranda, looking out onto a small garden, green and fresh in summer, but on this dripping, bleak November day, as bedraggled as myself.

As usual, Frau Libussa was anchored to her chair at the table, upon which was piled the afternoon snack, the fourth of the five daily meals, the Viennese *Jausen*. I was happy to see her again after two weeks; she had been away to visit her sons in Germany, the *Herr Oberregisseur* in Leipzig, and the *Herr Hofkapellmeister* in Darmstadt. At once she took command of me. My wet shoes were taken away by force (I remonstrated because I was ashamed of them; they needed resoling and I didn't want to be pitied). My stockings, my coat, even my soaked skirt were taken to the kitchen to be dried and pressed. Luckily, my two petticoats, though damp, were decent enough although somewhat too froufrou, the props of a well-dressed divorced young woman. I dried my hands on my handkerchief and warmed them on the teapot that Frau Libussa, knowing my aversion to coffee, conjured up for me by an imperious wink to my pupil. After a few minutes in her broad presence I felt warmed inside and out, and the hell with Polonius. "Now tell me all about your trip and your sons and everything. I missed you very much," I said.

I had no idea that this merely polite small talk was to become the foundation on which the structure of my life still rests. "Tell me all about your sons," I had said, and she told me.

There was less enchantment about her first-born, Ernst, and his truly brilliant position in the important Leipzig Opera. I sensed the reason. Ernst had married a young actress of his own choice, he was growing away from Mother and the silver cord, although not cut, was stretched. But, oh, how marvelous it had been to watch the younger one (Hansl, the family called him, and Hansl he still is to his friends), how he had developed, what a glorious future lay ahead of him. "And Darmstadt," Frau Libussa said, building with her hands and words an entire little cosmos for me, "you can't imagine anything as lovely as Darmstadt! It's so clean, so clean you want to eat off the cobblestones. It's light and warm there, the sun shines every day, and there are woods all around, the plums and grapes were just harvested, such nice friendly people everywhere. Hansl says it's the apple cider that does it, hard cider, you know. And, of course, their wine is world famous and the best vineyards belong to the Grand Duke. He is crazy about the theater, the Grand Duke is, rarely misses a performance, naturally that keeps them constantly on their toes. It's absolutely incredible how well their operas are performed and how the people enjoy it and how proud they are of it.

"Right behind the theater is the Schlossgarten, that's a beautiful park, old trees, a little lake, swans, black ones, too, with blood-red beaks, beautiful. My Hansl says the Grand Duke is a true artist at heart, he's very devoted to him, and the Grand Duke believes in my Hansl, he sits in at rehearsals and watches everything like a lynx. A real Maecenas, that Grand Duke, I didn't know that species still existed. He supports the theater out of his own private income, that's the sort of man he is. Not like our rascals of archdukes who spend the appanages the taxpayer shovels out for them on sluts and whores and gambling and getting drunk. No wonder the Hessians love their Grand Duke, and there's no socialism and no *Arbeiterzeitung*, no obstruction and fighting. It's so restful in Darmstadt! And so clean! There's the New Palais, quite close to the Hoftheater, and you know what? All around that *palais* the sidewalk is laid out in mosaic! Imagine, not just pavement, but the nicest mosaic, I don't quite know how they did it, of dark and bright pebbles, I guess. Mosaic for a sidewalk, prettiest thing I ever saw! Can you imagine how filthy such a thing would be in Vienna within a week? Take a dirty day like today. . . ."

I had a sudden vision of that sidewalk of mosaic. So nice, clean, bright in the sun. My petticoats were steaming, my nose was running, I had a blinding headache, chills were running down my back. "I'd sure like to be in Darmstadt," I said. Or the It within me said.

"You would?" asked Frau Libussa. "Well, I could write my son. I seem to remember he said something about the orchestra looking for a new harpist. You know, they're all young people, the *Intendant* and the *Kapellmeister*, and the Grand Duke, too; they want to pension off the old war horses and bring in new blood."

Perhaps Hansl's mother was not quite so innocuous in her enthusiasm for Darmstadt because she dropped the barely asked question and asked the girls to bring her "that box." "Now I'll show you something very sweet. I hope you'll like it, too. My Hansl gave it to me," said Frau Libussa, smiling in anticipation.

Out of the box tumbled a tiny Hessian village—half-timbered houses, stables and barns, a steepled church, a small castle with a round tower like the ruined one in Heidelberg, like my childhood tower in Peigarten; fences and yards, pigs and piglets, cows to be taken to pasture, a hay wagon with a pair of Percherons—all in miniature, finely shaped by the ancient craft of German toymaking.

Mother Lert cleared a space for it between the coffee cake and cookies of the *Jausen* and began to set up her village. "May I?" I asked timidly, equally entranced, and soon was happily lost in playing along with her.

In the night, somewhat drowsy with fever and a superdose of aspirin, I awakened smiling at the thought: what sort of man would this *Herr Hofkapellmeister* be, this Hansl who was trusted to stage Wagner's *Ring* in an all new, all different style, and who bought his regal mother a little toy village to play with?

I have learned that foresight and long-range planning are not for me. Any methodical, well-thought-out *démarche* will unfailingly land me deep in quagmire or up against a wall, whereas my spontaneous decisions, in which some impractical, illogical, unthinking instincts take command, usually turn out for the best. Four months after I said—and immediately forgot that I ever had said—"I'd sure like to be in Darmstadt," I was there. The *Herr Hofkapellmeister* had come home at Christmas, a nice young fellow with thinning blond hair and the high cheekbones and green-flecked cat's eyes five of the six young Lerts had inherited from their father. I was amused to see that, for all of Frau Libussa's dominance, this taciturn, perhaps inarticulate, hardly noticeable father had proved himself the stronger in the matter of genes. My own sons, nephews, grandsons are steel poured from the same mold; we, the women in the family, are mere catalysts, refining the heavy Lert bones a bit, maybe shaping their eyes a little larger, and, in my case, delivering them rather over-articulate. Father Lert was an ugly man, but the *Hofkapellmeister*, in spite of a strong resemblance, was quite good-looking (going on seventy-five by now, he still is!).

He was polite and reserved as befitted his superior position combined with self-conscious youth. Besides, I was not at all his type, his taste being conditioned to Wagner's Valkyries. "What a poor shrimp you have caught there, Mother," his look summed up his first impression of me and he went off to join a gaggle of loud, high-bosomed cousins and girl friends. But before doing so he had put a contract under my nose and showed me where to sign it, which I did in a state of complete bewilderment. The possibility of leaving Vienna, my orchestra, my pupils, had never occurred to me. But there it was, the red light showing an emergency exit unnoticed before, the prison door someone forgot to lock. Pay off the last debts, cut the strings of a moribund love affair, start life from scratch. Be free at last. . . .

In March I went to Darmstadt and through the formality of an audition before the heads of the opera department and, of course, for the Grand Duke's approval. For my audition I was invited to play solo at one of the rare receptions in the so-called Old Palais. Not the modern one with the mosaic sidewalk where the ducal family lived, but the castlelike building with the large reception hall and the Blue Room where the throne stood under its canopy of ornate velvet and ostrich feathers, used for highly official events only. Sensitive stickler that the Grand Duke was in matters of taste and style, he permitted only candlelight in the Old Palais, untold numbers of candles burning in chandeliers and sconces, and their soft shimmer, broken in rainbow cascades of crystals, reflected dazzlingly in the small mirrors covering the walls.

From the first moment I hit if off well with the Grand Duke, through no merit of my own. I suppose he had cooked up the idea that a harp played by a young woman would fit better into this setting than, let's say, a string quartet of the old war horses, the Court and Chamber Musicians in their shiny old, sweated-through tail coats. But what absolutely delighted him was the dress I had by chance brought along. Forever dreaming up stage settings, the Grand Duke had asked me to the Old Palais in the afternoon for some sort of rehearsal; where to place me and my harp, how to light us, and, if I wouldn't mind and would forgive the imposition, could I perhaps show him what gown I was planning to wear that night so he could seat me against a harmonizing background, a screen, if necessary, you know. . . .

I produced my maternal grandmother's ball gown—that dress which I had by sheer accident brought along—genuine Biedermeier, the kind one sees only in museums, striped silk with rose garlands in impertinent pinks and greens. The Grand Duke went into a transport, not about me, the artist, less about me, the girl, but about this gown. All afternoon he was carrying my harp, arranging the scenery, shirt-sleeved and easygoing, with laughter and pleasantries, the least formal royalty I ever knew.

I don't know how well or how badly I played that night; I have never failed to meet important occasions in my life—like weddings, childbirths, premières—without a sore throat, fever, blistered lips, runny nose, and lame brains. Psychosomatic, I suppose, but in 1912 medical science did not yet know or had long since forgotten about the unity of soma and psyche.

Thanks to that heirloom of a gown I was immediately given the coveted title of "Grossherzogliche Hof-und Kammermusikerin." And in August I left Vienna, without tears.

I once wrote a novel, *Marion Alive,* by no means autobiographical although my only subjective book; in it I tried to give a picture of the various epochs and some of the worlds I have lived in. (And, oh, how it bores me to see such simple things pompously called "Orientation in Time and Space," and "Spatial Man" being dragged into every run-of-the-mill story about the timid adultery of some exurban public relations hero!) In one episode of that novel I sketched the peaceful, warm atmosphere of those lost, small German courts like Darmstadt, and I will not do it again here. At the danger of being thought a reactionary—and nothing could be further from the truth—I still think that Germany, predominantly a tribal conglomeration, is ill-served by Bismarck's or Hitler's efforts at forging her into unity, into a Reich. History shows that she grows her finest blossoms and fruit in the peaceful cultural competition and simultaneous economic interdependence of such provincial cystallization around a capital, governed and inhabited by people of its own breed, dialect, habits.

I remember an amusing incident in connection with *Marion.* *Time* magazine, seemingly sensing material for some piquant gossip, sent a very nice young man to interview me. "Now tell me frankly, Miss Baum," he said, "it is autobiographical, isn't it?"

I was a little appalled, as the basic theme of that novel is the problem of, at a guess, millions of women; namely, how may a woman, having intercourse with her husband as well as, occasionally, with a lover, know which of the two is the father of her child? Gasping a little, I cried, "But no! How could it be autobiographical? I know the father of my boys!" At which *Time* printed the most impossible photo of me they could dig up in God-knows-what morgue, with the waspish caption: "Vicki Baum. She knows the father of her children."

Said father, conducting some concerts in Paris at the time, sent me a cable: "Thanks for giving me credit stop grateful for small favors."

Darmstadt, then, had a definite, most pleasing atmosphere, a feeling of a cultural obligation, of being avant-garde. Behind this stood the Grand Duke who eagerly drew to this small town as many leading artists as he could grab. The small-townishness of Darmstadt was not its least charm. The Grand Duke, son of an English mother, still young and strikingly handsome, was the ideal amateur. The theater that he generously supported as a matter of self-evident duty was his darling; he would sneak into many rehearsals, pop up in his box most evenings, and, indeed, what other entertainment did Darmstadt have to offer at night? Naturally, the populace, from the court's noblemen and gentry down to butcher, baker, and candlestickmaker, were eager to share Serenissimo's pleasures, and the theater was always sold out. The Grand Duke had the young Bauhaus crowd build an artists' colony in what was then, in this progressive corner of South Germany, and is today in the United States, modern architecture. Publishers published, writers wrote, painters painted, poets wrote poems, composers composed, and the Grand Duke, watched by the experts with a mixture of irony and gratitude, dabbled in all of it.

He made to the State of Hesse a present of his outstanding art collection. (I wonder if its pride, Lochner's "Madonna im Rosenhag," is still there?) From time to time he would happily come prancing up with some new acquisition, not all of them worthy of his enthusiasm. In such cases, the diplomatic formula for us was to assume the connoisseur's thoughtful stance and assure him, "Why, Your Royal Highness, this painting is *very* . . . really, very . . . very. . . ," thus saving our integrity and his sensitive ego.

It may be hard to understand today how a people could be so

fond of a ruler they had not elected but inherited. Yet, there being no fanfare, no image-builders, no busy public relations peddlers, the Man-at-the-Top had to stand or fall by his real worth. The Grand Duke was liked because he was a likable person; he was of his people's blood and bone, he understood them and vice versa. He was simply a country gentleman to whom the weather, the crops, health of the cattle, quality of the year's vintage, were as important as to them. What endeared him particularly to his sturdy, square-faced, easygoing subjects was a certain stubborn, nonconformist streak in him. He had, it was said, fallen passionately in love with, and been married to, "a Russian," a Romanoff princess. It had been a stormy courtship and marriage; the Grand Duchess was given to throwing glasses at her husband, smashing plates, and turning on some fierce Mongolian tantrums. When the Grand Duke had had enough of it, he got himself divorced from the otherwise brilliant beauty—not a small scandal for a reigning Royal Highness—and married a quiet, shy, greatly beloved Cinderella of a country princess from "an older, much better family than those upstarts, the Hohenzollerns," the people said with pride. South Germans, of Franco-Allemanic stock, abhorred the Prussians. One of their jokes claimed that all you had to do was to stick your fingers into the Rhine: wherever its water smelled bad, the Prussians reigned.

I often think that cutting Germany into West and East was one of the most fateful mistakes after the last war; the natural cleavage is, and always was, between North and South. Unfortunately, the unlimited idealism, generosity, and good will of Americans is regularly hampered by their incomprehension of other countries' complex geography and history, and by a naïve, if not willful, inability to grasp any but the vaunted American Way of Life.

I have jotted down so much about that small grand duchy and its sovereign because it was characteristic of the intrinsically healthy, happy, fertile patchwork that was Germany up to the First World War. Life blossomed in Darmstadt; it did, also, around the corner in Karlsruhe, Stuttgart, in Kassel, Weimar, in many more of those much ridiculed little kingdoms from whose modest soil did not come today's utterly materialistic and vulgar *Wirtschaftswunder,* but an old nation's wealth of culture, great music, poetry, philosophy.

When I consider the happiest periods of my life I always remember Darmstadt. I had left the awful mess and muddle of my Viennese youth, cut off all ties, and, even if I may have left behind a bit of skin, it was worth it. True, the orchestra was not half so good or large as the one I was used to; but to get away from the old symphony routines and to be broken into the completely new and different technique and repertory of the opera was invigorating. I had to be on my toes all the time; once more I became a kind of mascot to a circle of friends. It was a nice group, bright and young, gifted, witty, but not as cynical, callous, and tired of life as my coffeehouse crowd had been. Erich Kleiber, a curly-headed, mercurial youngster, and Hans Oppenheim, who later became important in establishing the Glyndebourne Opera, were our babies. There was a worldly-wise young dramatist from Prague with Kafka overtones. And the local pharmacist, a shy, tubercular fellow with a long, deeply cleft face, was a bottomless well of kindness, eager to do everybody endless favors in return for the honor of being tolerated by us, the artists. Another of the regulars was a young actor of intellectual and literary bent, the brother of the then very widely read Jakob Wassermann.

One day he said to me: "Listen, you ought to try and write down some of the things you talk about. Might be amusing."

"Oh, I've written oodles," I said. "Once I even got a first prize for a story. The magazine died right after they printed it! You can see what a writer I am."

Wassermann remarked that he'd like to see some of my writings, but I was not sure that I had kept any of the stuff when I broke camp. I rummaged through my luggage, however, much to the distress of the widow who owned the house where I had taken two (Two! What luxury!) furnished rooms, with a view of the *Schlossgarten* and its population of black swans, their faces villainous masks of Renaissance Venice. I found, among other odds and ends, the story of my early childhood that I had jotted down after the crazy fever of my streptococcus sepsis had pushed me through a concentrated self-analysis. "It's all stuff and nonsense," I said, handing it to young Wassermann, and I meant it. A week later he said, with much hemming and hawing and suddenly growing very formal, that he hoped I would excuse him but he had taken the liberty and sent my manuscript to a friend of his, the esteemed publisher Erich Reiss. And there was Reiss's answer, and he hoped I didn't mind. . . .

Reiss wrote that, yes, he, too, thought I was a gifted young writer, and he would like to publish this story of my childhood under the title of *Frühe Schatten* ("Early Shadows") if I or somebody else— perhaps Wassermann?—would translate it into German.

"What does he mean, translate it into German?" asked I, who had reared myself on the flawless prose of Goethe, Lessing, Heine. Slowly it dawned on me that the curse of the many German dialects was on me, too. They vary so greatly that a man from Hamburg will be pressed to grasp the basic facts of what a man from Munich tells him, and often he cannot understand even that much. Patiently, slowly, Wassermann persuaded me that *die Jausen* was a typically Austrian meal, that nobody beyond the borders would know that a *Pauxerl* was a baby, and that the *-erl* ending of all diminutives was a unique Viennese idiosyncrasy. (Even today I am Vickerl to my Viennese friends, and anyone I like gets that little tail of an *-erl* stuck on.) Of course, we all learned to speak and write *Hochdeutsch*, but it came out stiff and funny. It took Hitler to spread a sort of *Reichssprache* which, I notice with chagrin, prevails today in Germany's moving pictures and radio speeches and is exactly the strained yet vulgar way in which the *Hausmeister* Pitzelgruber expressed himself when he tried to speak *Hochdeutsch*.

Anyway, with Wassermann's help I cleaned my story of all the *Pauxerls,* and the Reiss publishers sent me a contract; there was no mention of any remuneration nor did I expect any. I felt rich and secure with my one hundred twenty marks monthly salary, more than *Second Hofkapellmeister* Erich Kleiber or *First Hofkapellmeister* Richard Lert received. In fact, within a week I had forgotten about the entire business of getting a book published. I was still a musician, one hundred per cent. By then also, I had something more absorbing to think about.

Obviously there was a wide difference between the girl I was and the girl Darmstadt saw. What the provincial town saw were the clothes, the looks, the behavior of a woman coming from a metropolis famous for its elegance and frivolity: a *mondaine,* divorced and consequently seductive, dangerous, experienced, and approachable. I, on the other hand, at twenty-four, felt unspeakably old, serene, disillusioned. I had left the unrest of the world behind me and was ready to live out the years of my senility in peace.

Among our little community of inseparables, Lert was the senior by two or three years, also a few steps ahead in the strict hierarchy of the theater; we all appreciated him greatly as a conductor, but were careful not to show him the respect we felt. Those young pups of our group would leap around him, tease him, like yapping, impertinent little terriers playing with a large, quiet St. Bernard. Lert, the private person, was eminently good-natured, simple, a proficient eater, sleeper, perspirer; "the steaming clod of soil," the more sophisticated youngsters called him. Lert with baton in hand, though, was—still is, for that matter—an entirely different creature, a man possessed. Sometimes, in the turmoil of emotions evoked by a great score, the effort to transmit it, yet keep it controlled, would leave him pale and shaken. At other times, he would seem to be breathing fire, *furioso,* whipped by the special demons that ride on every great musician's back and set him apart.

As Hans's landlady cooked for our gang—an arrangement of great advantage to our finances as well as hers—we were quite at home in his quarters. They were in a poor district on the wrong side of the tracks, barely furnished, completely impersonal except for the rented, indispensable grand piano where he, indefatigable and at unbelievable speed, hammered the entire opera repertory into the typical musician's hollows and bulges of his long skull.

I was somewhat closer to him than to the others, at meals, on our daily communal trip to the Oberwaldhaus, a nice place in the Odenwald that closely embraced the town, where Hans performed great feats of capacity as a plum cake eater, and at the pranks and practical jokes that we would play if we emerged keyed up from a performance. During the previous summer Hans had been home for a while, and as I had become almost one of Mother Lert's many foster children it was natural, and very comforting, to look upon him as a kind of older brother, a comfort of which my single-child's loneliness had never dreamed. I was proud of him when he did well, ambitious for him, although never as painfully ambitious as his mother and himself, hurting for him over every real or imaginary little setback. In a word, from the cool retreat of my senility I was fond of the fellow.

It came as a shock, then a rude surprise, when it turned out that Hansl's feelings, if brotherly, were definitely on the incestuous side.

Once I had chewed and digested this, I left my peaceful old age behind and grew young at great speed. It is funny to contemplate of what tiny pieces the mosaic of love—as we silly romantics understood love then—puts itself together. Hans's room with the tasteless lower middle-class furnishings, contained one single thing that belonged to him—a coarse eathenware bowl, peasant ceramic, always filled with apples from the ample harvest of the Hessian hillsides. Once you were past the cabbage, onion, and cauliflower smells of the staircase and entered this room, the clean, tangy apple fragrance leaped out at you, a pleasant contrast to the inevitable odors of glue, paint, sweat, and dust that cling to every stage. As my fellow, to this day, is unable to express himself other than in music, I never received an answer to my first question: What sort of a man is this, ridden by the particularly vicious demons of grand opera, yet buying his mother a childish toy village?

As I live mostly by curiosity, everything in my life starts with a question. Every relation, adventure, friendship begins by my need to know: what? why? when? how? Every story I ever wrote started off with a large, urgent question mark. If such and such a person would undergo such and such an experience, get into such and such a situation, how would he react? What would he think, say, do? How would he pass life's ordeal by fire and water? Needless to say, I never use models from real life; nothing would bore me more than writing of people I know, if not personally then through reports, gossip, biographies. What sets me off is the infinitesimal flicker of an impression: the thin, veined hands of an old woman on a bus, the way they are crossed over the bulky parcel on her lap. A dirty little boy sitting at the curb with his feet in the muddy water of the gutter. A young girl, a beautiful girl, studying herself with profound unhappiness in the mirror of a department store window full of flowered Easter bonnets. People, millions of them, in markets, parking lots, elevators, doctors' waiting rooms, airlines, on benches waiting for the bus, in parks, drugstores, under the dryer, everywhere people. Each of them a question upon which I feel obliged to brood for an answer. Like any writer worth his salt I know ten times, oh, a hundred times, more about the characters in my books than I put down on paper.

Therefore a ride on the subway, a stroll through a large market, a line at the post office or in front of the bank teller's window is a small gold mine for me; so many people to guess, puzzle, and invent about, such nourishing food for my curiosity. When I was younger my curiosity made me restless, I suffered a strange sense of bad conscience because there were so many cities, countries, continents, I had not visited. At the end, I think I shall be extremely curious to learn how it feels to die.

In the meantime I wonder forever how the tiny wheels in my watch work, or the electrons of those superhumanly clever computing machines. With tense curiosity I listen to the words people don't say, search for the unwritten thoughts between the lines; and don't care a fig for the jabber and show on the surface.

At certain moments I have turned my curiosity on myself, as at the birth of my children. How that feels, nobody can tell you, and so I had both of them at home, in my own bed, and didn't let a physician come near me because I was afraid he would muffle and blur with his sedation the great moment about which I wanted to gain clear, undiluted information. For the same reason I have always refused the cheerful "little hypo" customary after operations. I was curious to know how much pain I could stand.

But generally, in contrast to most post-Proustian writers, I never looked for, or found, any golden nuggets by digging into myself. I'm not curious about what's there, thanks, I know too much about myself as it is. Introspection is a dreary business. I, for one, am not interested in pursuing it, to diagnose whatever psychological and neurotic ulcers, scars, lacerations, or growth, life has embroidered me with.

Even my first stories, written in my early teens, had nothing to do with myself, except *Early Shadows* conceived while I was semi-conscious and experiencing a complete self-analysis. No treatment, electric shocks, or truth drugs could have done a better job. Once I was rid of my childhood—no, I refuse to write the jargon and call it traumatic experience—I was free to turn my full attention upon the world around me. There's one thing I may have in common with writers much better than I am: I can only write about characters that are created with a feeling of pity mixed with a sense of the comical. Self-pity goes against my grain and I had shed it early, as a polliwog on maturity sheds tail and fins. As for the comical side of me, yes, I'm quite aware of that. The few times I slipped a little self-portrait into one of my novels they were near-caricatures, completely irrelevant to plot and action; like Hitchcock when he pops up in Hitchcock films, as a waiter, a cop, a taxi driver—a walk-on, a five-second part.

But that's shop talk, of no concern to anybody, and more than enough of it.

I won't claim that I fell in love with Hans Lert just because his room smelled of apples, or because of the inner and outer cleanliness of him. In fact, we did not mention that perishable, vulnerable thing called Love. I think ours was the first generation to distrust the overblown kind of love that had been circulating for, roundly, a century. Ours was by no means the all-excluding passion advertised in books and plays, but rather a feeling of belonging together, of sharing or exchanging part of ourselves. Neither of us thought of marriage; in the theater, ties like ours are figured by careers, length of contract, season—from the beginning of September to the end of June. Next season, a brilliant and ambitious boy like Lert might wander off to greener pastures. So, for that matter, might I. As for marriage, I had had a noseful of it, as the Germans say. Hans, on his part, constantly warned by his possessive mother against the cohorts of females who all pursued him with the evil purpose of getting him to marry and support them henceforth, was perfectly conditioned against any thought of being tied down. Although according to the provincial mores of the town, love affairs were not to be tolerated, the theater teemed with them. But unless you were formally engaged, you had to keep it a deep, dark secret. Such secrecy, although a bit uncomfortable, added an imponderable charm. We continued to move with our crowd, but now there was a tactfully mute understanding that there was "something between us." It was a merry time, our lives well-balanced between work and pleasure, much fun and laughter as a group, and quiet enjoyment of each other. By the end of the season, the underside of this easy arrangement caught us short: as pleasant as it was to be together, to the same degree it was sad, almost unbearable, to think of parting, even if it were only for the summer vacation.

As it turned out, it was the last summer of Europe's and the world's peace, the tranquil sunset of an age that by now seems as deeply buried in history as the Thirty Years' War.

In the year 1913, Wagner's operas came into public domain. This meant that the theaters—of which there were hundreds in Wagner-hungry Germany—no longer had to pay royalties. Better yet, Bayreuth lost its monopoly of performing *Parsifal*. All the opera leaders swore they would respect the Master's will and not produce *Parsifal*; all produced it. The Grand Duke, of course, had a busy and happy time designing sets and costumes, in silver, aquamarine, and amethyst—a nauseating color scheme, we thought. "Your Royal Highness, that's very . . . ," we said, "indeed, very . . . very. . . ." The orchestra pit and music stands were painted a dark battleship gray and equipped with strangely hooded lamps to prevent any glare from reaching the stage. We sat for endless rehearsals, filling the depressing gloom with the sacred turgidity of the music. The only bright spot was young Lert's prematurely bald shiny pate. I almost succeeded in convincing him that his Royal Highness had ordered that this disturbing object should be painted, too; battleship gray, of course. We watched Hans worrying over this; he was very funny in his inner fight between fury and resigned compromise. Afterward, we all laughed a lot about it. Laughter was dearly needed during those weeks of flat-footed Wagnerian solemnity.

One of the best things we have between us is that he thinks *me* quite funny while I know that *he* is funny. We smile, grin, and laugh a lot about each other's foibles, where more irritable couples would probably bicker and fight. Not that we don't occasionally trample on each other's toes and sensibilities, as what married people do not? Both of us being musicians from Schubertland, we were taught that one of the fundamentals was not to leave dissonances hanging undissolved in mid-air.

In the summer of 1914 we had no vacation but something far better. Berlin's Imperial Theater des Westens, usually reserved for drawing-room comedy, was muscling in on the year's Wagner craze. The *Ring des Nibelungen* was to be produced and shown all summer long at lower prices than in the Royal Opera House. The short, shallow stage was unfit for the great old magician's spectacle; there was no machinery, no orchestra pit. There was, though, this young fellow, Richard Lert, known to have staged Wagner in Darmstadt on entirely stylized lines and new ideas. He wouldn't object to anything, but probably be happy to meet the problems and the challenge head-on. Besides, one would save a full salary by appointing that youngster as all-around director; let him stage *and* conduct it, find young singers at lowest pay, get an orchestra together, coach everybody . . . too much work? . . . Why, the fellow's young, he sizzles with ideas, you'll see, he'll simply lap it up. . . .

For once the voice of the agency had spoken the plain truth. Lert was on top of the world. A superhuman load of work, such unbelievable difficulties, such high hurdles to be taken, all those marvelous granite walls to run his head into—he was in his element! And somehow out of the chaotic, low-budget muddle, thrown-together beginners' cast, impossible stage, inexperienced technical personnel, he managed to shape a miraculously felicitous whole. This boy and man of mine just thrives on difficulties; if there weren't any, I suspect he would create them.

As for me, I took the place of six harpists, besides being the will-

ing receptacle of a steady stream of complaints. He is a master com-
plainer, my husband is, although he never complains where it might
do any good, only to helpless me. Which is good for my self-respect;
gives me the feeling of being needed, even in my decrepit old age.

It is almost impossible to recall the total innocence, the harmless
sleepwalking insecurity of that happy, busy July, 1914. War, to us,
was a winged, meaningless word in schoolbooks. Not anything real,
certainly not something that could happen to us.

The second *Extra* I saw in my life (the first one had shrieked
of Empress Elizabeth's assassination) I bought in front of the
theater from an excited, shouting old man with bad teeth. I remember a fleck of spittle in his gray Nietzsche mustache, and that
one of the pockets on his shabby jacket was torn. The paper was
damp, the print blurred, the sidewalk soon littered with such sheets,
read and thrown away. Another assassination in the hapless
Hapsburg dynasty: ARCHDUKE FRANZ FERDINAND AND HIS WIFE AS-
SASSINATED IN SARAJEVO. And so what? I thought.

Nobody in Austria had cared much for the two; they were cold,
without charm, unpopular. Not worthy of such a dramatic end, I
thought. "Her beauty got us in trouble," one of the bass fiddlers
said, reading over my shoulder. At the stage door a small clump of
stagehands discussed the news, their faces serious. "Those Haps-
burgs, there's always *something* the matter," said our Wotan (he
was De Garmo, a young American with a glorious voice) as he
passed me. "You're Austrian, aren't you? What do you think is going
to happen now?"

"Happen? Nothing. Some other archduke will take over; we have
plenty of them."

I wonder what Hans will have to say, I thought. But Hans,
Director Richard Lert, had more important worries that night:
Sieglinde was so indisposed she had to be replaced by a green under-
study, and there was trouble in the brass section. Besides, a theater
is such a hermetically sealed-off microcosm the voices of the world
outside are heard only as a dim, far-off, insignificant murmur.

Perhaps that is the reason my recollection of the following weeks
can't be trusted. In my memory the war started the next day. History,

however, tells me that a whole month went by, with business and pleasure as usual, until the Austrian ultimatum to Serbia, and whatever tensions and apprehensions there existed were kept shut away in secret conferences of chancelleries. And then, of course, even the most naïve average citizen gathered that, all of a sudden, there might be war. Somewhere far off, of course, as wars used to be. As Goethe says in *Faust*, Part One:

> *I know naught better on a Sunday or a holiday*
> *Than chat of wars and warlike pother*
> *When off in Turkey, far away*
> *The people clash and fight with one another*
> *We stand beside the window, drain our glasses,*
> *And see how each gay vessel down the river passes,*
> *Then in the evening homeward wend our ways,*
> *Blessing with joy sweet peace and peaceful days.*

Far-off wars, as some still are: Manchuria, South Africa, Serbia . . . Hiroshima, Korea, Vietnam, Algeria, mythical, unreal, alien names. As if mere distance made the fighting and dying less true. As always, the operations performed in unknown hospitals on strangers are painless, and only "my operation" hurts like the devil and is of towering importance.

Berlin, as a great musical center, was filled with music students from all over the world; eager and gifted, a good number of them had found a niche in our *Ring des Nibelungen*. Singers from England, Canada, the United States. Bassos from Russia and what was then still called the Ukraine, from Galicia. Hungarian violins, French woodwinds in the orchestra. A sprinkling of Slovakians as is to be found wherever good musicians are needed. That evening they sang and played for the last time in Berlin, and never better than through the scrim of blurred fears and future tears. Everybody was keyed up; already the wild humor and absurd before-the-battle jokes masked our presentiment and anxiety, probably the same adrenalin-caused jokes made by the soldiers besieging Troy, or by Caesar's legionnaires. Friendships, new ones and those of long standing, had to be abruptly cut; young love affairs, hopeful careers, the high enthusiasm of a cast forged into unity by common work —all was at an end. The friends, lovers, disciples, colleagues of today were damned to become tomorrow's enemies. What else could we do but laugh? I remember very clearly the clowning of our two first cello players, a German and a Belgian. They were very fond of each other, they kept grinning and teasing each other, and they played their difficult soli in the first Siegmund-Sieglinde scene of *Die Walküre* like angels. Furtively they would glance at each other as if to imprint the friend's face in their minds, to be sure to recognize and not to kill him in the heat of battle. They would aim their bows at each other in desperate fun, salute each other, friends and enemies. When the performance was over and the lights went down over the empty house they busied themselves with their instruments, their pages of music, as if they couldn't dare look at each other lest their grins be shattered by sobs. They held out their hands, then suddenly they embraced, two rough men, shame-facedly pounding each other's back. I was the only witness, hidden in my corner; I was the last one in the empty pit, I had to button my harp into its padded night robe. Last performance. Abrupt end of a summer season. End of a period in history.

The following morning all subjects of the Austro-Hungarian monarchy stood in long lines before their consulate, jabbering away in at least nine languages and untold dialects. They all wanted to volunteer or, at least, not miss out on their military duties, Hans among them. Able-bodied men, they had all served in the army, most of them the prescribed three years of the common soldier. But my boy, whose parents had been able to give him the costly secondary education, had enjoyed the privilege of only one year of so-called voluntary service, at the end of which he was discharged with the modest rank of Second Lieutenant in the Reserve.

Their patriotic enthusiasm blazed high; they were angry when they were told they were not needed . . . not yet; keep your pants on, men! Leave your address, go home and wait. If the army should need you, you'll be called. Probably the war will be over long before that.

I don't know if my own warrior was angry, disappointed, or relieved. He buried himself in next season's opera scores and waited. I could do nothing but wait with him. We wished urgently to go home—to Darmstadt, not to Vienna—but there was no transportation available for civilians. From one day to the next we had become that different, slightly inferior species: civilians.

It is unbelievable with what illusions, what joyful enthusiasm, what total ignorance we, the people, our generation, entered that war. It is one of humanity's great tragedies that, again and again between wars, a generation grows up just as ignorant, just as ready to think of war as a lark; as a means of getting away from the routines of school, work, business, from the boredom or irritation of a job, of a marriage, to the liberty and adventure of camps and conquests. In spite of all the sinister warnings in the writings and preachings of our time, once more nobody, but really nobody, seems to have enough imagination to visualize how such a next war would look, and a next and yet a next one. As weapons grow more potent and deadlier, since the first stone that Cain threw at Abel, wars get less and less honorable and polite.

In my research for *Tale of Bali,* which deals partly with one of the Dutch colonial campaigns, I came across the baffled remark of a native rajah: "Why, how could we fight against an enemy who did not honor the most fundamental good manners in warfare, namely to stop fighting during the hot hours between noon and three, when each soldier needs to cool off in a pond or stream, quench his thirst and rest till the fighting would resume in the shade of the afternoon? What barbarians, those whites!"

As late as Napoleon's time, the generals would choose a suitable battlefield, draw up their forces in battle order as for a tournament of chess, and agree upon a day for the fight. In a word, war was the exclusive business of soldiers. Naturally, civilians might accidentally suffer or, just as accidentally, even profit by it, but this was only an unavoidable by-product. I believe that it was not until the First World War that generals used the civilian population as an extra weapon, killing children through starvation, pushing wives and mothers into famine, ruin, and desperation, grinding down civilian resistance.

My mind retains just a few glimpses of the beginning of that complete muddle and confusion that was to go on for four and a half years.

A late evening. There's a strange rumbling and clanking in the street. I am waiting in Lützowstrasse, Berlin, where I have a room at the widow Pachulke's. I look out my window, heads appear in all the windows of the neighborhood. Down below, small cannons are being pulled along the pavement, some by two, some by four horses. Sleepy boys, artillery, are riding in their van. Cannons and soldiers are decorated with little wilted bouquets of flowers that were fresh when their girls and wives tied them on in the morning.

"Where're you going, soldiers?" someone calls to them.

"To the front, Pop, where else?"

No secrets yet, no "security." We, the neighbors, nod knowingly. "Give it to them, but good! Those damned French swine!" a woman screams.

"Don't dirty your pants, Mother; we will!" the artillery answers gallantly. We can't imagine what it is, the front. As little as we can imagine hell. Or heaven.

I remember an afternoon when Hans and I were sitting with a few friends at a sidewalk table of the Café des Westens (sure, there were coffeehouses in Berlin, too). And Max Prels, my former husband, was one of the regulars, swept by some fluke into an obscure editor's job in Berlin. He is making cynical jokes about the war and trying to promote a small loan from me. The war is still in its first week and we haven't quite sorted out who's with us and who against. Never again will I be able to trust in allies or alliances, or the sworn, signed, and paid-for loyalty between governments. The headwaiter appears and morosely hangs up a blackboard with the latest news. "Russian forces only nineteen kilometers from Berlin" is chalked there in trembling letters, "the enemy has poisoned all wells and reservoirs along their route. Warning: beware of drinking water. Keep calm."

Pushing our water glasses away and grinning idiotically, we pretend to keep calm.

There was nothing, no rumor stupid enough not to be believed in those first days.

Another afternoon Hans and I took a trolley ride to the Grunewald. We are lying on the slick, needle-covered ground, looking up
into the swaying tops of the pine trees. Sparse, North German trees,
with pieces of forget-me-not sky and cloud-white spaces up there.
Peace. Blissful quiet and peace. Then an increasingly louder noise
comes to us from that sky, a new strange noise. We sit up, tense.
Not frightened, but tense and curious. "Flying machines? Russians?"
Hans wonders. In Darmstadt, over the sandy parade grounds beyond
the railway tracks, a few young fliers we knew had been experimenting with their flimsy, toylike double-wingers. Why not the Russians, backward as they may be? We have no idea what harm a
Russian flier could do to us, but we hold our breath until the
noise in the sky fades away, somewhere across the lake. We never
found out what or who made that noise. It was probably an early
ancestor of today's Little Green Men and their saucers.

A month later, we are on a train creeping westward. Timetables
and train schedules were the first victims of shock and confusion,
just as they usually are the first to go to pieces in any time of
crisis. We have been on the way for days, with no promise that we
would ever reach Darmstadt. We get unloaded and reloaded somewhere, somehow; pushed into another overcrowded train; it dawdles,
stops, stands at some siding for half a day, clunks on again. Nobody
knows exactly where we are, already the thick fumes of military
secrecy choke us civilians, together with the rotten-egg stink of the
locomotive's belching. I remember the advice an old lady gave to
the squatters and pushers who were squeezed into the narrow corridor of the car. "Listen, children, change all your money into gold
pieces and hide it, bury it; and store up all the dehydrated split-
pea soup you can get. Then you won't starve. All you need is some
hot water, see?"

"Plem-plem," giggles a young woman, tapping her forehead. "She's
nuts, isn't she?"

"No," the old lady replied, "just old. I know a few things. I went
through the war in 1870. In Paris we ate rats and cats, if we could
get 'em. I'm from Alsace. We were French then; soon we'll be
French again, mark my words."

Senile. Off her rocker. . . . I've often wished I had listened to her. Later, when my babies cried for bread. . . .

By and by we began to recognize certain landmarks, a church tower, a castle's contour on a hilltop. After four days, we are back in Hesse. The train comes to a spine-cracking stop outside a station. Suddenly there are hoarse shouts. *"Raus!* Everybody leave the train! Get going! Hop to it!"

A little lieutenant pops up, a mere schoolboy, with his right arm in a sling, sloppily saluting with his left. "Sorry, but we need the train. Transport of wounded. Thank you."

We are silent, shaken. Wounded. The first wounded soldiers we were to see. Somehow we had thought of war as an all-or-nothing gamble. You came home a victor or you died on the field of honor. Now there were wounded. How young they were in their large old uniforms, and how gay. We did not know yet that they were glad to be out of it for a while, the lucky guys, the walking wounded with just a bullet in an arm or a neatly bandaged gash in a skull. Heavens, how many thousands, millions, of wounded soldiers we have seen since.

Yet, nothing of what came later hit me with the terrifying impact of this first encounter.

Time has squeezed the color and juice from my memories of that war. For all the intense experiences of those years, little is left worth telling. And what, indeed, does an old woman have to tell who has lived on the periphery of two hot wars and one cold war, yet never was bombed out, never, by the grace of God, lost a son or husband.

The years went by and ground us down, slowly at first, and later with inexorable rapidity. Once we walked through the *Schlossgarten* behind a young couple, a servant girl and a soldier on leave. He was clad in the field-gray uniform that had soon replaced the light blues and sharp greens of peacetime that had made such easy targets. But the new uniforms looked worn, faded, and dirty by the time a man was wounded and on leave. "Tell me, Heiner," I heard the girl ask, "what's really going on in the war?"

"Nothing is going on," he said. "Us shoots at them and them shoots at us. That's all war is."

I can only give an approximate translation of his childishly soft Hessian dialect. But in spite of all the generals' memoirs, I've never heard a clearer summing up of warfare.

If I have learned anything from such memoirs, and from unbiased historical surveys, it is the fact that general staffs and high commands and generals in general have no higher intelligence than the average members of any other exclusive club. Military genius is as rare as Caruso's voice, and the backbiting and jealousies among the high brass, ours or anybody else's, remind me strongly of the goings-on backstage at the Grand Opera. Of course, vanity, conceit, and posing are indigenous to both professions. Except that an operatic tenor may look fat and act like a stuffed liverwurst or be as unmusical as a butcher's mutt without dire consequences to anyone but himself. But the mass murder a muddle-headed, stubborn, unimaginative general can perpetrate—well, better not to talk about it.

Nor would I, as an individual, choose to trust my person or my family and friends to the hands of leading politicians. And yet it is in the mediocre minds of politicians, high brass, chiefs of industry, and, lately, the reckless bandarlog level of propaganda and communication, that decisions are made for us while we, the citizens, sit by in growing helplessness, caught in a playpen.

I know, I know, these are sacred cows. In India, if you insult a sacred cow the mob will stone you. But I don't live in India.

In 1916 *Hofkapellmeister* Lert was offered a position as director of the opera at the municipal theater in Kiel. It was a smaller, less esteemed stage, but a higher, more independent post; a trampolin, in the lingo of the stage, that might bounce him high and far, the prescribed next step in a young conductor's career. In Darmstadt, where he had Felix Weingartner as *Generalmusikdirektor* (oh, those German titles!) over him, he had no prospect of further advancement. He accepted Kiel, not exactly enthusiastic but hopeful.

Then we made a startling discovery about ourselves. All along, we had assured each other that we were completely free, independent, unencumbered. We wouldn't let ourselves get too involved (once again that old idea of love being a gentlemen's agreement). Not a thought or word of marriage. Why, we had our careers to live for; Lert would rise fast and go far in his, and I, in a more limited way, also had a future. Bruno Walter, the new *Generalmusikdirektor* in Munich, wanted me for his orchestra; less important, in 1914 the Verlag Reiss, to my surprise, had sent me a book, nicely bound in blue linen:

*Frühe Schatten*
*Die Geschichte einer Kindheit*
VON VICKI BAUM

There it was, black on white, with my own name on it. I had forgotten all about it, and young Wassermann had enlisted and been killed on the field of honor. Poor, quiet, shy shadow, I could not even thank him. Understandably, Erich Reiss wrote me that this was not the kind of book to sell during the war, but as soon as we had won and were at peace again—it can't be long—will you have patience?

I still have that one copy; I don't know what happened to the rest of the edition. It disappeared without leaving a trace, as many things do when a war is lost.

So much about our respective careers. But when it came to parting it became glaringly obvious that it just couldn't be done. We were caught, tied, hooked. Opera Director Lert needed a home, a wife, an anchor in these anchorless times. I . . . well, I needed, with an ever-growing biological urgency, to have children. There was no question that no one but Hans must be the father of those unborn babies. I had at that time evolved an image of myself as a frail, overly sensitive creature, sophisticated, raised on *Fleurs du Mal* and Rilke, with an inherited tendency toward neuroses. Hans was simple, uncomplicated, strong, and healthy. I needed him if ever I needed a man. A born mother's son, he was born to be a father, the father of my children. I think the rising flood of divorces and unhappy marriages could be diminished if just one ordinary truth were hammered home into every hopeful bride's mind: the man you marry is not the man you are married to. Well, that's one of the facets and disguises of love.

He loved children, babies, he was not disgusted by diapers, not afraid of babies' tiny, lobster-red tantrums. The worker's family that lived below him in his rooming house had twelve children of whom five or six were always underfoot. Hans said they didn't disturb him; he liked to have children around, he said. It reminded me of my early friendship with cobbler Peindl's numerous offspring in Peigarten. When we walked to the theater across the Schlossgarten, usually a flock of urchins would follow him. They pulled at his sleeve, his trousers: Papa! they would call him, Papa, Papa! Their fathers, of course, were in the war, if they still had fathers. Hans had fun with them, he knew their names, brought them candy, a rarer and rarer luxury, pennies, silly little toys. It was a wholesome attitude that went well with the fragrance of apples in his room and with his much-washed, expressive Gothic hands. That in the course of our marriage he turned out to be the fragile one—complex, easily upset, and by no means unneurotic—that's another matter! I never found out, and it really isn't important, whether I became the tough old girl I am by a process of necessary adjustment, or if my former frailty was only a fashionable little pose. Anyway, to our own surprise we soon found ourselves in Kiel, married, and, on my part, pregnant.

Darmstadt had been a home—vineyards and apple orchards, peaches and corn, art and music, old castles, old cathedrals—the heart of South Germany, closely related to Austria. But Kiel was the utmost North, cold, rude, unfriendly, an alien land.

My first child was born in Kiel. When my labor pains started in the afternoon I did not tell my man so as not to upset him before an important performance. After I had seen him off, however, I phoned for the midwife. While I waited for her I prepared some food for the coming days—what we called food, that is, for the screw had been turned very tight during the winter of 1916-17 and there was practically nothing to eat for useless civilians like us. With the entire German Navy landlocked in that small university town and the shipyards working madly to build Germany's last hope, submarines, we struggled to keep alive. Each payday machine guns were posted at the main intersections in case of hunger riots or sailors' revolutions, such as Russia had experienced. (A year later the volcano erupted.)

My nice midwife arrived and managed to keep me out of bed until my *Kapellmeister* came home. He looked very smart, white tie, white vest, tails, patent leather pumps. He had no time to change—stayed with me all night long to get pushed and pummeled like a punching bag—and was still in full dress when his first son was born. In the cold dawn I watched the sea gulls tossing in the air outside of my own window. My girl, I said to myself, just look how far you have come. . . .

As I write this I am reminded of the melancholy joke that made the rounds among the German emigrants during the mass murders of the Hitler interlude. "Now we are in America," the one said, "where shall we go the next time?"

"To China," says the other.

"China? But China is so far."

"Far? From where?" asks the other, the uprooted, homeless, disillusioned wandering Jew. . . .

The other remarkable thing about Kiel were The Cans. The Cans played an overwhelming part in everybody's life. I don't know how things are nowadays with Kiel's sewer system, but in 1917 it was nonexistent. Nor had the magistrate ever heard of such a simple solution as cesspools. His deputies explained the institution of The Can by pointing out that they had no money to build a sewer system and they could not let the narrow harbor be polluted by the offal of the overcrowded town. Therefore: The Can.

The Can was just that. A garbage can of average size placed, or rather sunk, into an otherwise quite decent looking toilet. Two hefty unfragrant men, clad in leather from head to toe, would pick up the full Can and replace it with an empty, duly disinfected one—twice weekly for a family of five, once a week for people like us. Why The Can was designed too small from the beginning, even for chronically constipated people, nobody knew. But if the family enjoyed a normal, regular digestion, the matter (Matter!) went out of bounds, so to speak; if one or the other had a little attack of the trots—a frequent event under these not overly hygienic conditions—gloom, disaster, and infernal stench would invade the home. The Can permitted deep insight into the character of people, or what is editorially called "Man's inhumanity to man." The one Can being filled to capacity, people would drop in on friends and deposit their load, as the unconscionable cuckoo drops his eggs into strange nests. Lover did it to lover, friend to friend. Under these circumstances romances wilted, friendships grew cool, sociability and the graces of good neighborliness stopped. It was a fine study of character. Some did their evil deed shamelessly, others with embarrassed giggles and a plea for commiseration; some very sensitive ones might even bring a little gift along, in exchange, one might say. A dab of pot cheese, the precious tailend of last week's kippered herring. Great treasures at a time when getting "our" herring was as improbable as winning the Irish sweepstakes. I suppose there were people who had food, people with Black Market connections or relatives among the farmers. But we were foreigners in a foreign land; we didn't even understand the natives' language, closer to English than to German. Sad to say, too, corruption was at work not only in the intake of food but also in the disposal of it. The men in the leather aprons were bribed with foodstuffs or money to pick up The Can twice a week instead of just once. Or to leave an empty extra Can there for the inescapable state of emergency. In our own case, we corrupted these worthy men with free passes to the theater, which at least could be excused as educational. On the other hand, the very institution of The Can incited class strife, envy, and the evils of snoopers, stool pigeons (what an appropriate word!) and a secret-police spirit among the hard-pressed populace. There existed in Kiel, as everywhere, an overprivileged class: high magistrates, politicians, industrialists, admirals, the wealthy in their fine villas. A few of them got official permission to equip their homes with real plumbing: "Naturally, *their* sewage is so refined it won't pollute the harbor like ours would!" the embittered populace muttered. "Sure, if we were eating lobster and venison instead of boiled turnips day in, day out, our crap would also smell like eau de cologne." Others were rich enough to connive with plumbers and engineers to install the forbidden W.C. secretly. And so the magistrate was forced to employ a health commission, inspectors who came and turned your place upside down because there were, naturally, anonymous denunciations galore, and if they discovered the hidden grotto it depended once more on bribe and power whether they'd let it pass or tear it up, wreck the premises, and make you pay a stiff fine. Finally, socialism reared its head and the leather aprons went on strike, a catastrophe worse than the war. There was an epidemic of typhoid, officially described as intestinal catarrh, and the Can-bearers got a raise. That's how inflation starts, said archconservative Upper Kiel. Just wait and see, things can't go on as they are, swore the Lower Classes.

A nice kettle of fish, that Can of Kiel.

My husband was rather unhappy with his job at the theater in Kiel, and, Heaven knows, it was no bed of roses under the daily growing restrictions of war in a town completely given over to a paralyzed navy, martial law, and submarine warfare. The pay was pitiful, the weather and climate were harsh, and starvation is a lingering ailment that leaves even strong young people fatigued and listless. During the years, though, I found that my husband seldom was entirely happy with opera, but a man obsessed seldom is. Opera, at best, remains a compromise between the purity of music and the inanities of most librettos, between the singer's golden voice and the disillusioning reality of *embonpoint* and inability to act; and, since Wagner, between the orchestra's overblown sonority and the modest possibilities of the human voice, but, most of all, between the usually routine work of the stage director and the conductor's soaring image of what ought to be. As the years went by, I realized that opera, the stage, the theater *per se*, was not a happy place for the innocent I'm married to. Still, he was possessed by opera. It took me years to find out that the clean fragrance of apples does not mix tranquilly with stage dust and politics.

Proud of his position as chief of the opera, Hans had made only one condition when we married: his wife, *Frau Operndirektor* Lert (don't you love the way German wives share their husbands' pompous titles?) was not to play in the orchestra. "Solo, yes. But never under anyone's baton. Right?" "But gladly," I said. For a few weeks I still kept on practicing and then I was pregnant, a totally absorbing and wonderfully satisfying condition. But if you've been a professional musician you can't become a dilettante, better give it up entirely. I sold my harp; we usually say we sold it to pay for the baby carriage. If this is not absolutely precise, it more or less covers the basic facts, for we ate up the harp during the unpaid summer interim that followed the brief season in Kiel. To become the wife of an orchestra conductor means to become a nomad, as such careers are counted in stations. Darmstadt, Kiel, Hanover, Mannheim, and, at last, the Mecca of them all, Berlin. Accordingly, my main efforts at interior decorating consisted for years in making and remaking curtains and lampshades, arranging wicker furniture bought on account of its light weight and secondhand couches on account of their minimal cost. Our only claim to prestige was the inherited Biedermeier pieces we dragged with us in all our wanderings and then emigration. Yet, with the indispensable rented grand piano, a few do-it-yourself shelves filled with books and scores, a vase with a few flowers or green twigs, we always had a home pleasantly suited to our taste and style even though money became ever rarer.

ans had gone to Hanover for a test period at their first-class Royal Prussian Theater. He had been invited for a month of guest conducting and, if found satisfactory, was to get a three-year contract.

Sure to succeed, or at least acting as if he were sure, my boy went off. He conducted one performance and then the stage burned out. Tough luck. He could remain in Hanover until the stage was rebuilt, and then continue being tested. Prospects seemed quite favorable, he wrote. Okay with you?

Okay with me. I waited.

One day, suddenly I had enough of waiting for the Royal Prussian Court Theater in Hanover to make up its mind. Enough of sitting in Kiel with my baby like a deserted wife. The days were precious, every one of them. Any moment now my husband might have to go to war; they were scraping the bottom of the barrel. If I didn't hurry I might never see him again.

I packed our nomadic possessions into a van and my four-month-old into a large round wooden hatbox, and boarded one of those wartime trains whose time of departure or arrival nobody knew.

Before I went on this trip, however, something happened that was not as inconsequential as I thought at the time. I had kept up a friendly but loose correspondence with Max Prels. In his last letter he had announced that he had married again and had an editorial job at Verlag Ullstein, the enormous publishing house in Berlin; things were looking up, but could I help him out with ten marks for just a month or so? . . . Sorry, pal, broke myself, I wired back. Now there was another letter. He was deeply disturbed to know I was in financial straits, but if I couldn't help him, perhaps he could help me. Ullstein needed new novels for its paperbacks. The little Ullstein carts peddling Little Ullstein Books, a certain kind of not-too-bad escapist fiction, were a popular feature of every German railway station. "I remember you had an unfinished novel among your manuscripts, background the Vienna Konservatorium. Do you still have it? Did you ever finish it? If not, send it to me in any case, maybe I can get you a contract on the strength of what you've got, and soon a bit of advance money. Of course, the Little Ullstein Books are not Literature but they sell like hot cakes, and I'd see to it you'd get a neat handful of cash and then you can pull me out of this momentary jam and. . . ."

I dived into the mess of loose pages stored away and forgotten and from the chaotic debris sorted out and assembled the fragments of that story. To call it an unfinished manuscript was a bold understatement. Yet, I have—and had even then—an insurmountable aversion to letting anybody look at anything not finished, rewritten, and corrected to the last comma. Just as unacceptable to me is the idea of getting paid in advance, a little quirk that has caused various publishers dire worries and suspicions. But the very thought of having been paid for something that I can never be certain of bringing off makes me impotent . . . handcuffed, paralyzed, blocked, unable to write.

Left alone in Kiel with nothing to do but breast-feed that greedy, long-boned, ecstatically loved small center of my universe, I concentrated myself into a trance that took me back to the Konservatorium. The forgotten figures came to life for me, they moved, talked, sang, made love, suffered, and commited suicide, as if on stage. All I had to do was watch them and write down what happened, which is, as I have said, the only method by which I can write.

I sent the finished stuff to Max Prels, and Ullstein lapped it up. This neither surprised nor noticeably elated me. I suppose, though, that the fortune of five hundred marks duly received, and, if I remember rightly, shared with Max Prels—swept me on to Hanover and a still undecided future. The Little Ullstein Book *Stage Entrance* sold something like one hundred and sixty thousand copies which goes to show how far it was from being literature. I can't explain why the relative success of this my first book seemed so important to me. Perhaps because I had not worked on it the way I, the musician, understood work.

The journey from Kiel to Hanover was endless, what with changing trains, waiting at out-of-the-way stations, the engine rumbling and belching, the cars crowding up more and more. My baby son, gurgling merrily in his pillow nest in the round wooden hatbox, sleeping and being fed at the prescribed intervals, was an amusement center for the entire car. The feeding in particular was an event of great interest and hilarity. From an old evening gown I had made a most practical and attractive blouse, if I say so myself: soft black chiffon velvet smartly embroidered in white, close around the neck but wide as a tent at the bottom which was pulled tightly into the waist with a drawstring. Came feeding time I loosened the string and pushed my suckling inside the tent: an example of modesty, decency, foresight, and maternal perseverance.

Here I should like to comment on one of the few things about which I feel deeply, and that is how sorry I am for any woman who misses breast-feeding her babies, whether by her own choice or through the inexcusable routine usual in most United States hospitals. In my experience, nothing, and I mean nothing, can compare with the exquisite joy, the utmost fulfillment inherent in this simple act. Refusing to nurse one's young, to me, seems just another facet of frigidity. The complete circle of woman's sex life consists of maturing, conceiving, giving birth, and suckling her child. To reject any of these steps marks the frigid woman.

"But I haven't any milk!" the girls wail. "I can't be tied down to Baby's schedule." "Doctor says it would only make me nervous and that's bad for Baby." "I don't want my figure to go to hell.". . . Oh, for God's sake, girls, use some sense! Take a good look at the proud bosoms and bearing of the hard-working unneurotic peasant women of Central Europe and the Mediterranean world, all those beauties from the Latin countries over there and in South America, not to mention my little friends on Bali, and stop making those silly alibis. I am sorry for the women—so many according to the late Dr. Kinsey's research—who are frigid in bed and—whatever the reason—can't help it. But the higher percentage of those with bottle-fed babies are frigid by their own choice, and that's a *triste* state of affairs.

But enough of my preaching a useless sermon. I'm still on the train to Hanover. Hanover, in 1917-18, had an English past and a decidedly Prussian present—a cold, windy, unhealthy town, bigoted and hypocritical on the surface, a murky swamp underneath. Politically, worms and termites were gnawing in all directions, making way for future Nazis and Communists. Soon the entire structure was to come tumbling down. Starvation had become open famine, in the midst of which the Black Marketeers were growing fat and rich and impertinent. The people had given up hope that the war would ever end. More discouraging than anything else were the lies we were fed by the press, manifestoes on propaganda posters. We had stopped believing anything. We were finished—no food, no light, no gas to cook on, no hot water to take a bath, no shoes, gloves, clothes to replace our worn-out rags.

I remember the bitter physical needs of those times only as a dark background against which our life rolled past, inexplicably gay, happy, full. We were young, we were devoted to each other, we had that unique miracle, a little son crowing merrily in his laundry-basket crib. My man had all the overwork and conducted all the operas a young conductor ever dreamed of. Singers and orchestra loved him, and, astonishingly, those stiff, cold audiences thawed out, grew warm, grew what in those Northern climates could only be called enthusiastic. The very deprivations of daily existence brought along their own comedy and farce, food for laughter and crude fun.

There was the tomato plant, for instance. A green-thumbed old lady who had befriended us had managed to grow a few tomatoes in her window-box. Tomatoes!—imagine!—at a time when the country had even run out of last year's turnips. *Frau Justizrat's* secret was in fertilizing. We placed our plant in the small garden patch in back of our apartment but, of course, we had no fertilizer. There was little traffic left on the street; no automobiles, no tires, naturally no gasoline, and the few nags not requisitioned by the army were brought into town only to be slaughtered. But behind curtains and blinds we hid at the windows, ready with broom and shovel. If a horse was sighted and, with great good luck would drop a turd, a kind of gold-rush started, a race to be there first for the claim. Pregnant once more, I seldom won. (I am always the last one in a queue, on a bus, the subway.) Our precious tomato plant seemed doomed to starve and die. "Listen, child, here is what you must do. Dig a hole next to the plant and ask your husband—and perhaps some of his friends, yes?—to do like cats, you know what I mean? Do Number Two into that hole and cover it with earth. . . . What do you mean, he won't? He loves you, doesn't he? Well, then. . . ."

And so my fastidious musician, to give me proof of his love, descended into the back yard each evening "under the sable skirts of night" and did like a cat. Sorry to say, no tomato crop ensued. The climate of Hanover was against us.

Then there was the carp. I once wrote a little Christmas story about it which one of my publishers used for a greeting card. Eating carp on Christmas Eve is a German custom that probably goes back to her pagan past. Some friends of ours, a reigning industrial family, mentioned casually one day that their carp pond was to be drained before it might freeze. "And the carp? What are you doing with all the carp?" we asked in breathless unison. "Oh, the carp! We give them away to our men. Want one?"

"For Christmas? Good Lord, if that were possible——"

Well, no, they said, Christmas would be too late. By the middle of November. Maybe we could keep it alive in some fountain? Or in the bathtub?

"Sure, sure," we said, "just let us have the carp, we'll take good care of him." Mind you, this was long before the invention of refrigerators and frozen food.

We got the carp, a lovely big, fat fellow. We were walking on clouds, we felt outrageously rich and privileged. Every morning my husband and friend carp frolicked under the icy shower that replaced yesterday's water in the tub. Carp thrived on goldfish food and Tender Loving Care. Carp smiled and jumped at the sight of his friend, my husband.

The point of the tale is obvious.

When Christmas arrived nobody wanted to catch him, kill him, cook him. Somebody's hard-bitten widow, invited to the festive meal, did it for us. My husband left the table when Carp was served, to hide his emotions or perhaps to throw up. I didn't ask. The widow ate the whole platterful, and the rest she took home.

Just as unprofitable was our only Black Market Deal: The Pig.

There were two trumpet players in our orchestra, both, by some fluke, trained butchers. There was also an ailing, middle-aged friend of ours, and his devoted and most efficient housekeeper. The latter two knew of a live pig for sale, Black Market sale, in one of the outlying villages. Then ensued such long drawn-out and complicated negotiations as if we were arranging for an armistice. At last the proper conditions were arrived at: we would share pig and expenses equally. Our trumpeters went to the village, loaded the pig—Him, they always called the pig—into a large trunk and the trunk into a relic of a taxi. Unfortunately Him suffered from car sickness and diarrhea, squealed alarmingly, and the taxi driver had to be bribed into keeping the crime unreported. Trunk and pig were hastily deposited in an empty garage belonging to some friends of ours, and the two trumpeters just had time to change into white tie and tails for the night's performance, *Tristan and Isolde*. My husband, likewise in full dress, cut short his curtain calls because the trumpet players, pale and perspiring, were worried about what Him might have done in the meantime. Out of a dim sense of obligation *Herr Hofkapellmeister* accompanied his two accomplices to the dark place of the planned crime. While they did their work, Hansl prayed no one might hear the poor pig's squeals. There was a kind of Shakespearean flavor to the scene.

I spent the evening in high suspense with the friends who had instigated the whole damned thing. Late at night my husband and the two butchers, all three still in tails and white tie, arrived pale and exhausted, with the remains of dear Him. All night long and all through the following day earth-shaking activities went on in the inadequate kitchen. The housekeeper, remembering her young years on the farm, was ecstatic. The mere smell of lard and grease and flesh and blood was enough to make your empty stomach feel as if you could never swallow another bite in your life. There was great jubilation and a rustic feast of roast pork and much beer and good wine, and in some mysterious transfiguration, half of Him was at last delivered to us. Canned meat, smoked ham, and all the *Wursts* of the German cuisine: liverwurst, bloodwurst, mettwurst, braunschweiger wurst. We hung it all in our small larder and felt that now we could face famine and war, however long it might last. And never mind that the last of my Ullstein earnings and our minute bank account had gone into the great enterprise.

Him had tasted peculiar even on the night of the feast. As the weeks went by he tasted more peculiar. The larder, too, smelled peculiar, sweetish, musky. By and by something happened to our treasure of wurst. They shrank inside their skins. They kind of devoured themselves. They began to look like the crumpled silk dress of an old woman whose breasts have shrunk to nothing underneath. We cut one of the salamis, it smelled like a musk bull at mating time, and there was hardly anything left inside the skin.

I discussed the tragedy with our friends' country-bred housekeeper. "Yes, I know," she said, resignedly. "You know what happened?—the pig was *pramsh* when they slaughtered him. One must never slaughter a *pramsh* pig."

"*Pramsh?*" I asked, ignorant but eager to enlarge my North German vocabulary.

"Well, you know what I mean. Him was a Her. And Her just happened to have her days. The curse. Those trumpeters ought to have noticed. We was taken for a ride, that's all."

That ended my dealings with the Black Market. I began to write another novel. The Ullstein publishers, after the lively sale of the first one, urged me to go on. It is nice to earn money when you dearly need it—and let no one tell me differently—also flattering to be told to write another novel similar to the one before. A sequel to it, it's the easiest thing! It is also deadly. But after spending our last nickel on *pramsh* Him, I felt a bit guilty and besides I had nothing to do during the evenings when my husband conducted; after all, you can listen to *Czar and Carpenter* just so many times. That's how my habit of working at night got started. Once your nervous system is used to a certain schedule it does not function otherwise.

It is past 2:00 A.M. now, no telephone calls, no dissonant scores on the piano downstairs, no phonograph records thumping up against the floor of my cubicle. It's a good hour to conjure up the lights and shadows of the past. . . .

Within the flux of the years there had also been the small matter of a revolution. Immense relief to us, the people, the mothers, wives, families; great hopes and promises for a free, shining future in most quarters. Only a small minority of professional soldiers, diehards, and inexperienced young hotheads seemed to care about the lost war. Bitter curses followed the Kaiser, the sabre-rattling windbag who had run away and left us in the soup. Hanover cheered her greatest citizen, the wise old soldier Hindenburg, who had stopped the sense-less dying and killing, had sued for an armistice, brought home what was left of the German Army, and returned to retirement and the card games with his old friends.

I suppose the revolution was modeled after the Russian example. Red, proletarian, radical. Still, it was a thoroughly German revolu-tion, well-organized, orderly, clean, sober. The functionaries wore a red band around their sleeves—they called themselves Spartakists, after Spartacus, the leader of the rebellious slaves in ancient Greece. The theater received orders to keep up business as usual. Although the Kaiser was on the run, the imperial offices in Berlin still issued their Prussian commands. Troops of Spartakists searched the house during performances; they claimed that machine guns had been placed on the roof and fired into the crowd, and they threatened reprisals. With shaking voices and knees, singers and musicians went on with their cadenzas. Between the theater, the nearby railway station, and the residential district where we lived, the Spartakists had built barricades. The usual little red lanterns of the street maintenance department outlined those barricades in the dark so nobody should stub his toe in climbing over them. I can't think of a neater symbol for that neat German revolution. The mess and muddle only came later.

Our Brave Soldiers, after their helter-skelter retreat through the rain and mud of France, imported in their ragged uniforms the various plagues of any beaten army: lice (Communist and pubic), scabies, dysentery, an impressive variety and amplitude of venereal diseases, the coarse habits and language of trenches and brothels. Also, as after any war, homosexuality flourished. No wonder, really: all those frightened, lonely youngsters huddling together under fire; the girls and women, too, left behind, freezing, worried sick, exhausted, starved for a bit of warmth to give and to receive.

If you live long enough you see the merry-go-round turn and turn, and with each cycle, after each war whether won or lost, you pass the same landmarks, again and again. Even the much-advertised "Economic Miracle," the German *Wirtschaftswunder,* is only a repetition of what we witnessed before. So is the flaring up of anti-Semitism, the nostalgia for The Good Old Times we had under Hitler, under the Kaiser. There is also the ever-present seed of civil war, the Germans' inherent instinct for fratricide. Berlin was never the united city, Germany never the undivided nation of which she dreams, on which Americans as well as Russians count, each in its own ideology. If the streets of East Berlin are bleak and dreary, with few people, few cars, shoddy goods in the shops—well, that's nothing new. Kurfürstendamm with its luxury goods consumption, and what before the last war was called *der Norden,* the workers' district, were two sharply divided worlds, ever since the industrial revolution, I guess, the one bourgeois, the other split yet once again into Communists and the more moderate and reasonable Socialists. Take away the pressure of foreign occupation and influences and I bet the street fights, riots, and upheavals of pre-Hitler days would promptly return.

There was a short period when life seemed almost normal, although in a different key, to express it in musical terms. This was the victorious reign of the Common Man, bless him. Councils were elected, soldiers' and workers' councils—which meant that the same experts as before kept things running, only they were now called workers and stayed on top through elections. For a while there was some food, a small measure of comforts. Then things got worse again, we did not quite understand why. We were as ill-informed as ever, scapegoats were searched for and found; political assassinations, murders, *putsches,* and crimes everywhere, some under the guise of patriotism, guerrilla gallantry. A complete, insane inflation stampeded us, Black Market and starvation were worse than in the war. There was one moment when I was glad we did not have the money to buy Black Market goods. That was when the Harmann case exploded. It was the purple touch to complete the picture of postwar Germany.

Harmann, a mild, soft-spoken, ingratiating person, used to hang around the railway station at night, where vagrants and homeless unemployed would sleep on the waiting-room's hard benches. It was also the main hangout of the town's homosexuals. Harmann would approach some youngster, invite him to spend the night at his flat in the picturesque and dangerous slums of the Old Town, treat him to sandwiches and beer and kill him, probably while the lad slept. He then would cleanly dismember the body and reduce it to nicely boiled, potted meat. Said meat, labeled pork or veal and attractively packaged, reached the Black Market where it brought good prices.

When at last the crime was discovered and Harmann made a full confession, there was much silent shock, frightened inspection of hidden larders, some discreet vomiting, and a general throwing-away of expensive potted-meat jars. Harmann was executed. My friend George Fröschel, who had interviewed him in his death cell, showed me a postcard Harmann wrote to him before his execution. "Dear Dr. Fröschel," it read, "I'm sending you my final greetings before the ax falls; I've always been especially fond of you. . . ."

I happened to be in my seventh month of pregnancy at that low point.

"When may we expect the new novel?" Ullstein wired.

"Soon, I hope," I replied. "I want to finish it before the middle of January when I'm expecting my baby."

The same week Ullstein wired me two thousand marks. "A little advance," their telegram said, "we assume you might have use for some extra money for the happy event. Congratulations."

It floored me. Two thousand marks! For a novel that was not written and that might turn out to be unmitigated trash. (It did, by the way.) I don't know what's the matter with me, but not for a minute did I consider accepting this unasked-for largesse. It went back posthaste, with an apologetic letter to Paul Wiegler, the editor with whom I had been corresponding. Later I learned to know Wiegler as one of the most lovable, unworldly, almost saintly, kind characters I ever had the good fortune to meet. He belonged in the hustling, commercial ant heap of Verlag Ullstein as a Trappist monk belongs in a debating society. But the Ullsteins ran their far-flung empire on the principle that it takes all sorts of people to make a publishing house.

I think I had, in all innocence, stirred up quite a turmoil in the Ullstein book department. I had no contract with them; they had not offered me one, and indeed I might have refused to sign. There's this incurable aversion in me to forming ties about my writings. But obviously, as I deduced from what followed, the Ullstein psychology didn't include cases like me. Aha! the Ullstein men said to themselves, that girl plays hard to get, if she has not—perish the thought —been already snapped up from under our noses by the competition. This demands quick action. We can't let a natural best-seller talent slip through our fingers.

One of the things I had learned in my ghost-writing days with Max Prels was to respect deadlines. My novel was finished three days before I gave birth to my second boy; once more in my own bed and without a doctor's help. Hanover, at least at that time, had a poor crop of doctors, and the midwives were worse. The baby was too fat for narrow-hipped me, the birth was complicated. Unfailingly, the event was followed by my usual fever, strep throat, and two weeks in bed.

I was awakened one morning by the ringing of the telephone. "Sorry," I heard our maid say in her chilliest, most refined Hanoverian voice. *"Frau Hofkapellmeister* cannot be disturbed. *Frau Hofkapellmeister* must have complete rest. Doctor's orders."* Lisbeth was the proverbial gem, so refined that she would only address me in the formal third person. Loyal to a fault, unfriendly as only a true Hanoverian can be, she transmitted—in spite of her refinement—her fiancé's pubic lice to our three-year-old's silver-blond eyebrows and lashes.

"A certain Dr. Herz was calling for *Frau Hofkapellmeister*," she said with a contemptuous sniff.

Dr. Herz was one of the grand moguls at Ullstein's. As chief of the book department, he had charge of its enormous stable of contemporary writers, from young Bert Brecht all the way down to a promising heifer like me. After reading my second opus Herz had rushed to Hanover; it was probably the first time that a young author had not only refused money but had also let him sit and stew. But sitting, waiting, and stewing was what the almighty Dr. Herz did. Result: by the time I was in shape to see him I had, in all innocence, raised the ante. (Since I play neither bridge nor poker I'll have to check this meaning.) If I remember correctly, I received five thousand marks to begin with, plus future royalties. It began to dawn on me that telling stories might be as serious a profession as playing the harp. I signed a contract that included two more books, but managed to keep open a loophole for possible dealings with other publishers.

A slight fever and bed rest always act on my brain like a good nitrogenous fertilizer, and my head was throbbing with stories that would definitely not do well on the little Ullstein carts in railway stations. As for those glorious five thousand marks, I don't know what would have happened to us without them just then. "Just then," meant that from one hour to the next the dear, uncompromising creature I was married to lost his job. Suspended, fired, black-listed to wreck and ruin. I never found out exactly what had happened because he refused to talk about it, or perhaps he did not quite know himself. Shock, trauma, amnesia, with insanity or even suicide in prospect—in the world of the theater every trouble assumes cosmic proportions, and a hitch in the career equals cataclysm. The less my man talked, the more talk there was backstage, in the papers, all over town. The different versions boiled down to the fact that there had been a Scene between Lert and the *Intendant*, a stink, a terrific row; some spoke of Lert's having slapped his superior's face. In subservient Germany this, indeed, meant the end of the world.

The superior who, by the choice of the artists' and workers' council had replaced old, tone-deaf Baron Putkamer, was a pleasant-looking, middle-aged actor, more or less a has-been, a man ridden by all the devils known to stage people—jealousy, vanity, envy, and a megalomaniac conceit. He hated opera, bitterly begrudged it the space, time, money, that he, as the *Intendant* of the theater, and thus responsible for both drama and opera, was obliged to allot it. That the audiences preferred opera, that the opera performances were better, newer, vastly more exciting and successful, must have been bitter poison to him. Still deeper seated, I believe, was the frustration of an actor no longer allowed to act and his furious envy of that young fellow Lert who just waved a baton in front of a public that couldn't applaud him enough, call him often enough before the curtain. Yet, with all his shortcomings, the *Intendant* was a likable fellow and I, for one, was quite fond of him. Perhaps I understood him better than he did himself. He was a man possessed. But so was . . . is . . . my husband. One thing is certain: whatever caused the fateful Grand Scene, it was not one of the things men usually fight about. Not a woman, not money or power. Probably no more was at stake than a stupid insult to Mozart that could only be washed in blood, or a disagreement about the number of rehearsals necessary for a new opera.

Fired on the spot, my husband changed into a caged panther. Day and night he paced up and down, not talking, but growling irrationally, making it impossible for me to reach him. Incommunicado. Sometimes I feared: finished.

Bless Ullstein's five thousand marks that gave us a foothold in the midst of the landslide.

One of the enlightening experiences of those months was to learn how people behave when you're suddenly *persona non grata*, particularly people in the theater. Audiences, too. Great Heavens, how easy it is to stir up the emotions of a crowd, the nasty and murderous, as well as the warmly enthusiastic and those Holy Roller instincts for trances of all kinds. Suddenly we were ostracized, people feared us, avoided us. It's a weird feeling to become invisible; nobody sees you, nobody greets you on the streets. Only two or three of the old patrician families dared to remain our friends; they had nothing to fear. In the end they even intervened for us, those dear oldish businessmen who didn't care a fig about opera or art but did care about justice and increasingly empty houses. At last an honorable truce was negotiated and Lert was reinstated. At his first performance hoodlums surrounded the theater, there were noisy street demonstrations against him, poisonous handbills were distributed. It was a completely incomprehensible outbreak of mob hysteria, as no one could have less to do with politics than my dear innocent. Nor had those shouting roughnecks ever seen or heard an opera. I can only suppose that such minor tumults were arranged to give the future Nazis their training. They did not need a reason; on the contrary, their brains had to be deadened before they could later be used in the earnest pursuit of cruelty and murder. Just as unreasoning, the audiences rallied around the returning hero and there was no end to the ovations, the trampling and shouting that greeted him at every performance. "I wish they'd show a bit of discrimination," he would complain, "those idiots. It was an awful performance tonight, the quintet completely loused up, but did they notice it? No! They call for me and I take my curtain calls like a trained chimpanzee. Aren't you ashamed of me?"

Life for me in those first years after the war was like entering a new and different land where I felt blissfully at home. I had found myself. I guess it was simply that I had become a grown-up person— behind my back, so to say—and high time for it. I had two little sons (and about those two I shall not permit myself to speak at length as there's nothing so boring, sentimental, and shameless as the indiscriminate display of a mother's love) and I began to look for at least a minimum of security, a thing for which I had never cared a damn; the murky residue of my bourgeois upbringing, maybe? At the same time, I was buoyed up by a feeling of freedom. I could fly, I could dance.

The latter, the dancing, is to be taken literally. What Gustav

Mahler, Wagner, Ibsen, and my first love with the Flying Dutchman had meant to my adolescence, Mary Wigman and her circle, her new dance—that, by now, sadly, has become old hat—meant to my adulthood. But in each generation there are a few great people who open the doors, show new ways into unknown promised lands, prepare the road for their successors. Today all those new vistas belong to science, technical and mechanical wonders. In my time the artist was the pacemaker.

It is amazing how much Mary Wigman and Martha Graham resemble each other; those high cheekbones, the large mouth, the high, naked forehead, the hunger of those two faces, the trances in which their dances are conceived and performed. And, above all, the down-to-earthness behind it all, professionals that they are, both of them. I never had the good luck to know Martha Graham personally, but I hung on to Mary Wigman with all my might. These were dances as I had dreamed dancing ought to be. This was what I had tried to dance in the secret *cave* below the concert podium of the old Musikverein in Vienna. Here was my rebellion against the stupid ballets, the stupid balletomanes—my father at the head of them—of the Hassreiter place in opera. What a comedian Mary was if she chose to be; the hilarious persiflages she produced at the snap of a finger; the divine disdain for money she had, all modern dancers had. I remember her, cooking huge potfuls of thick soup to fill her thin, hungry disciples. Her deep-voiced laughter when she felt her power, had won a hard fight with a hostile audience. "In Italy," she would tell me, "after the first three dances, they threw tomatoes and rotten oranges at me. At the end they stood and screamed *Bis! Bis!* and wouldn't go home."

Our new stage director, Dr. Hanns Niedecken, brought Mary and her young troupe to Hanover. Hanns became our closest friend, we were inseparable, he even moved into the same apartment house to be near us. He was a giant of a man, a mighty beer-drinker, wurst-eater, and cigar-smoker, a fighting, cursing, sweating, outgoing man's man—and homosexual. I had never met a homosexual before, but I was a female who had no erotic designs on defenseless and attractive boys, so I was not dangerous. Some of my nicest, most loyal, most generous and amusing friends are among the citizens of that sexual no man's land.

One of my very best friends was Max Terpis. Terpis, with his hard, wood-carved Swiss face, yellow hair, his rare mixture of nervous sensibility, controlled calm and coarse, stomping mountaineer's wit, was an extremely attractive person. He had meandered into the New Dance by something resembling the serpentine trails of his mountains. He had prepared himself for the priesthood, found it incompatible, had become an architect, but his ideas were too uncommercial, too far ahead of the time. Dance, with its demands of composition, with the human body as building material, was a temporary answer to Terpis' search. He was a good though not a great dancer, yet he was a great teacher, building enthusiastic and capable groups of new dancers, first in Hanover and later at the Berlin State Opera.

The last time I saw him was in 1949, in Zürich. Ours was the sort of friendship that picks up a conversation where we left off, as if the separation had lasted an hour instead of twenty years. By then, Terpis had left dancing behind and become an accredited psychologist, and once more we had a mutual interest as I was just then deep in psychological research in preparation of my next book.

Those were good years, from 1921 to 1923. Good years in spite of the runaway inflation, the return of hunger and cold, worse than ever. Niedecken and Lert made a fine avant-garde team; together they launched a mighty Handel revival, and created a new style, the first time in many years, for staging opera in general, precursor of present Bayreuth. Mary Wigman left some of her best young dancers with us—Kreutzberg, Georgi, Hanya Holm. Terpis became choreographer, and around this nucleus there was an explosion of painters, composers, singers, writers. Soon they all made a name for themselves, went on to the Metropolitan Opera, to international fame. To me it seemed that for the first time life and art were marching together, the one not just an ornament, but a direct expression of the other. Cubism, futurism, expressionism, whatever name you put on the label, this was how we were, *our* world, so shaken up that the walls wouldn't stand straight, the colors and lights we saw were born of fevers, hunger, nightmares, everything of a clarity more real than reality. Surrealism, of course. We were yearning for the sharply pointed angles, the cut-up forms, the dissonances, the gall-bitter humor of our young poets. Perhaps we were the first generation to tell the truth about war, every war, whether won or lost. We had the courage to say Bunk! to war's glories, to hero worship pounded into malleable youth in all the history classes of the globe. In our total disillusion we threw away insipid beauty and discovered the magic of ugliness.

In Hanover, Lert clamored for singers less covered with flab and blubber, whose moving and acting would put less of a strain upon the imagination of the audience. Terpis obliged by establishing dance classes for them and for any enthusiasts who would like to take part. And would I like it!

We were ordered to come in shorts and loose tunics and—there was the rub—barefoot. A few years later it was discovered that females had legs, but meanwhile a heavy load of shame, secrecy, and chaste covers were appended to those limbs, in spite of all the new freedom. In one of the dressing rooms I changed into my homemade outfit, and I felt outrageously nude. Bare feet, all right, but those chilly, goose-pimpled bare calves, bare knees, shivering stretch of bare thighs! It took me at least five minutes before I found the courage to wade out into the bottomless cold of the ballet hall. (Decent bathing suits of that vintage covered the knees, and decent girls wore stockings and sandals for swimming. Chic-est outfit you ever saw!)

After five minutes of fundamental calisthenics I was at white heat, I had forgotten my legs, I left myself behind, which is the ever-new miracle of dancing, for me, at least. And when at the end of class I was allowed to improvise, express whatever I wanted, I felt as though my life had begun only that afternoon.

Among the questionnaires one receives from various sources, I remember one from a very stern and important woman's college: "In spite of your international success as an author, is there some ambition that has remained unfulfilled?" And like a shot I fired back: "Yes. I missed becoming a dancer."

Dancing, and, next to it, interior decorating, are the professions I missed and in which I might have done good work. In any case, I kept thrashing around and blissfully expressing myself in dance classes for more than ten years, an incomparable outlet for emotions that might otherwise have turned sour. Also, I submit to occasional outbreaks of the interior-decorating rash; my sons claim that "each time Mum comes home from a trip she brings so much junk she has to add another room to the house." Recently I read somewhere that this urge to stuff the nest with bits and scraps points to a neurosis in the female stuffer. Perhaps so, but it's better than being a solitary drinker, isn't it? But there is, it is true, an incongruity between my nest-building instincts and my urge to be free, without ballast or burden, a nomad, a gipsy.

Some of the friends of those years were still in Germany when I was already an American; some had tried desperately to get out but were caught by various German consulates and sent back into the next war. Some were killed, some disappeared. And my best friend, Hanns Niedecken, I had to cast off when he continued his career under the Hitler regime. It was a painful amputation for me and it hurt him deeply, for he lacked any understanding of the what and why. He was a typical sample of that strange German amnesia, that enabled decent men of honor to put wax in their ears to avoid hearing the screams of Auschwitz and Dachau. There's a sickness in this, a guilt so strong that they can neither forget nor remember, just as we are sick with the bomb of Hiroshima and the curse of having to make more and more bombs ever since.

In Hanover, more than ever I was split in two, a schizophrenic living in two worlds. There was the new dance, the new friends, new perspectives, wide new vistas in every direction. Out of the frictions and the agreements, out of the good, rich ambiance and talks, I wrote what I think are my best books. *Ulle,* the story of a freak, a dwarf, a circus clown, is actually a book about loneliness as the fundamental human condition. In Pfitzner's difficult opera *Palestrina* I had found my motto: "The world's core is loneliness." When I said before that I had grown up, it was in writing that story. Self-pity is always immature, and so are laments about loneliness. In *Ulle*

I had reached the adult knowledge that accepts loneliness as self-evident, not something to complain about but to know and carry with the peculiar pride that is part of it.

The other book was a volume of short stories or rather novellas—a form and length for which there is a good tradition in French and German writing. I called it *Die Andern Tage,* a title taken from a poem by Maeterlinck. "Wait till the other days will come," it says, and another voice answers: *"Les autres jours sont aussi lâches, les autres jours ne viennent jamais."*

*The other days are also weary,*
*The other days will never come,*
*The other days will also die*
*And you will die with them.*

For obvious reasons, I took great care to keep these two titles hidden from Ullstein's busy little paperback book carts and from the English and American markets. They were, I ask your pardon, literature.

While I put forth these first fruits of my new inner freedom, my daily life took place on an entirely different plane. The tail end of my five thousand marks had quickly melted away in the raging inflation, and the hunting and chasing after food took up most of my days. To make up for the lack of milk, meat, vegetables (vitamins were sorely missed although not yet discovered and named), I exposed my little boys to huge portions of fresh air, despite the endless rains and snows and the winds blowing from the large flat northern heaths.

You see me, a thin, gay, enterprising ninety-five pounds, setting out in the morning, my four-year-old hanging onto my hand, my six-month-old baby grinning or sleeping in his clumsy carriage. I am dressed in a navy blue something covered by a navy blue coat. The boy, too, is in navy blue, one of those smart little sailor suits, whose fly, however, is out of whack because I never learned to master the tricky bit of asymmetry needed to sew those little pants. On my arm hangs a large sack of the same navy blue material. This sack is known as "the full udder," and when we await my husband at the stage door from which he emerges after a morning's rehearsal, he never fails to quote the old poem from the schoolbooks:

*Da kommt mit vollem Euter*
*Die alte Geis gesprungen,*
*Sie suchte Gras und Kräuter*
*Für ihre Jungen.**

A lucky day if the navy blue udder bulges a loaf of bread maybe, the extra ration of flour or barley allowed nursing mothers, or a chunk of horse meat, a rare, mouth-watering delicacy. That we are a symphony in blue is no accident. Sartorially we lived on hand-me-downs from Mother Lenzberg's wardrobe, the same friend who had introduced me to the domestic method of growing tomatoes in time of stress. Mother Lenzberg was, at a guess, in her early sixties, but dressed as if she were ninety. As dress materials had entirely disappeared from the stores, she gave me some of her clothes to do over for myself and the boys. That's where the navy blue comes in. Actually, Mother Lenzberg had quietly forsaken the correct black mourning garb of widowhood to keep me and my family suitably covered. My shoes, though, wooden soles with uppers made from patches of old carpeting, didn't add much to the harmony of the ensemble.

One time during the revolution I, my kids, baby carriage, and blue udder happened to get into the firing line of some snipers. Such a thing sounds more interesting than it is. After the shocked second it took me to understand the situation, instinct took over and I simply trotted off and ducked into the nearest open door. I was surprised to see only an astonished grin on the faces of the others who did the same; I guess I, too, grinned. I saw the same queer laughter once more when I was caught in a riot on the main plaza in Mexico City.

---

* The good old nanny goat
  Comes leaping with full udder,
  She looks for grass and herbs,
  For kiddies' fodder.

The rioting workers and students had blocked every exit from the trap of that wide, sunny, suddenly empty, plaza. All stores swiftly rolled down their shutters and the cathedral locked its portals. Suddenly there was a police force bringing up fire engines and water hoses. Just as suddenly there was a thick tumble of sneering, yelling rioters. They were laughing, they threw rocks at the police, they overturned the fire engines and set fire to them. It looked like childish fun. Then there came that clatter of shots, very thin and small in the hugeness of the plaza. The rioters screamed, stampeded for cover. We, too, together with two Mexicans, took cover behind the trunk of a small palm tree. It suddenly seemed the smallest palm tree in the world. It didn't even throw a shadow onto the noon-yellow ground. Never have I felt so large, so protruding on every side as I did crouching behind that pathetic thin trunk. It was absurd and we laughed. The whole plaza laughed, even the police with their rifles. The evening papers said that eleven people had been killed. I couldn't believe it. I was sure they had fired into the air. I have a faint idea that true drama is never as dramatic as that on the stage, the screen, or in paintings by Delacroix.

Home after the foray of the forenoon, I would feed my little boys and, man, did they eat! I feel sorry for children who lack the experience of going hungry—those spoiled, overfed American children stuffed with in-between snacks, soft drinks, hot dogs, candies, chocolate bars—sorry for their parents, too. The problems and bickerings at meals, the dynamite in the casserole, the psychology that goes into feeding an overfed child! Poor little tykes, to miss one of the greatest pleasures in life: to have something to eat when you're really, honest-to-God hungry.

My two (they're middle-aged men now) were no problem children; I don't remember a moment of trouble with them except, of course, when they were sick or in the war. Nor do I believe—and this I say with a bit of excusable pride—that I am a problem mother. I share the idea that the character of a child is formed by the time he's four; after that it has hardened in its mold and resists changes, might even break. I have great respect for children, their secrets, their privacy. I gave mine as much independence as possible as early as possible. I think I didn't ask many questions, didn't pry, or, so help me God, nag. I only hope they enjoyed their early years one-tenth as much as I enjoyed them.

I have to confess here, though, to one of the strongest, meanest streaks in me: I am hellishly jealous. I might have turned into a devil of meanness had I not been an only child. As it was, I learned to keep this jealous streak reasonably under control; married to an opera conductor, I had to.

I think our marriage has kept some of its pleasant freshness by the frequent stretches of having had to live apart. I shudder when I observe some of those Siamese-twin marriages, those clinging, clutching couples who never draw apart except when they're at last so sick and tired of each other than nothing but divorce will help. Like every girl, I had packed a good load of illusions into my hope chest, the main one being that our marriage was to be like no other, something unique, exemplary, perfect. It's a stale truism to say that no marriage ever is. Our marriage had been founded on the firm understanding that we were not to stand in each other's way, particularly in professional matters. I thoroughly respected Lert—still do—as a musician, a conductor. For several years I didn't think he really noticed that I had found myself a new profession. What I did during my evenings was of no great concern to him, and it was many more years before he ever glanced through a book of mine. That's as it should be. The fictions of women writers are not attractive to men. Musicians, especially, are locked away in their own abstract world. Men, at best, read for instruction, for philosophies, ideas, history. At the worst, they read for the little tickle that descriptions of violence and sexual intercourse so amply provide in certain paperbacks. When my older son was about ten he put his arms around my neck and announced sweetly: "Now I've read all your books, Mum." At which I swelled up a bit and asked, "Well, and how do you like them?" He stroked my cheeks and answered in a condescending tone of consolation, "Well, my poor little Mum, they're stupid and boring."

Need I say that I was delighted with this thoroughly masculine reaction?

Lert was called to Mannheim to fill the much-coveted position of General Music Director. Tradition had made this the penultimate step to a conductor's top place. Bodansky, Furtwängler, Kleiber, had received their last polish in Mannheim before advancing to international fame. Now it was Lert's time to rise. He went off to Mannheim and I embarked on another book; I remained in Hanover with the kids until he could find an apartment for us. After endless negotiations, we hopefully followed the impatient, lonesome *paterfamilias*. Ugly and alien as Hanover had been, it was quite a wrench to leave behind so many and such stimulating friends. Yet I thought of Mannheim as a homecoming, the Southland, the Rhine, where I could speak and hear once more that droll, childish dialect, live among the warm, jolly, wide-open tribes I had known and liked.

The venerable institute, the Mannheim National Theater, had a true tradition and a right to be proud of it. Schiller's stormy drama *Die Räuber* had opened there. Mozart and Weber had been active guests. A musical style had been established and handed on from teacher to pupil, frequently from a father to the entire family. The Mannheim Opera had sent, and was still sending, outstanding singers, musicians, conductors into the world, all of them taking along some of the finesse of this particular Mannheim style—*bel canto*, elegant polish, a preference for romantic sweetness, a certain reserved calm, let's call it Apollonic. But the trend of the arts at the beginning of the '20's was decidedly Dionysiac, ecstatic, excited and exciting, and we, my husband and I, were part of it.

In Hanover we had been living, breathing, swimming in Expressionism. In Mannheim, Lert, the reformer, found himself thrown back many years to opera as it had been before war and revolution, before Mahler's ideas had taken hold. (Apropos of this, it is incomprehensible to me that the New York Metropolitan Opera audiences, as well as the management, insist on similarly prehistoric productions, untouched by the new imaginative creativeness of ballet and musical comedy.)

In Mannheim, as in most theaters, the keepers of the grail were old-timers. An elderly bass buffo would be the opera's stage director, an elderly actor, well schooled in the classics, did the plays, and another oldish actor was appointed the *Intendant*. To be the *Intendant* of a German theater must be like constantly dancing on a razor's edge, combining, as it does, the necessity of balancing a never-sufficient budget, luring the public into the theater, giving them enough entertainment without ever neglecting the classics, keeping the actors and singers happy and fully occupied, and, above all, infusing the whole with the creative spirit and enthusiasm that gives a theater its face. Obviously one ought to feel pity for the poor man at the top (but do we ever feel pity for the President of the United States? And would he like it if we did?). One ought at least to treat him with patience, leniency, and respect. But the General Music Director, responsible for the whole body of opera and concerts, is on a hot seat, too close to see matters in their proper perspective. The situation was all too familiar: enthusiastic audiences, a willing following among the singers, the full respect of the orchestra, but distant lightning and the rumbling of a thunderstorm on the horizon.

Too bad that the *Kurfürst* who planned the castle, the theater, and a few other buildings in the city, was no Pericles. (Only in the U. S. Midwest did I find towns laid out on a similarly unimaginative design.) All streets crossed at right angles, block after block, so impersonal they did not even have names, just letters, running alphabetically, and numbers. Not a lane, not a tree leaning over an old wall, none of the German loveliness of the irregular. And being *Frau Generalmusikdirektor* Lert, third person formal, I met the same people again and again. On Main Street—Rheinstrasse was its name—in the theater, at concerts and exhibitions, mornings on the wet planks of the Rhine baths, and in the constant exchange of society's events. Even in the classes of the Wigman School the pretty young daughters of society were doing their cultural duty, but there was no Terpis to breathe life and zest into the puppets. In a poor district outside of the quadrangles I discovered at last one, just one, crooked street where the fall of light and shadow played its little magic on the shabby walls; that's where I went when I wished to give myself a treat and a change.

And, of course, there was Heidelberg, not as close as it is now with our cars and highways, but still close enough. An oasis whose air I drank like a thirsty camel storing away a bellyful of water for a long droughty trek through the desert. It was my only outlet, an experience that condensed itself into my novel *Stud. Chem. Helene Willfuer,* a great success in Europe, an abysmal flop in America. More cleanly than anything else, this disparity in reception showed me the deep gulf that lies between the American and the Continental ideas of education. But it would take another book to explain those unbridgeable differences.

Alas! Mannheim was not all I expected. There are towns that gave me claustrophobia, I get choked, asphyxiated. In the United States, Pasadena is such a place. This makes me feel like a louse, a veritable monster of ingratitude, because both communities have been very good to both of us, Lert and me, and gave us the friendship and affection of some fine people. But there it is, and I can't help it.

After the good sharp wind that blew so invigoratingly through stage and art life in Hanover, after that keen feeling of being at home in my own time and day, Mannheim was like a journey into a stale past. It was the old bourgeois world from which I had run away. The subscribers of the theater were well-to-do people, prim and proper, unbearably patronizing toward anything that smacked of art. There it was again, the well-fed, self-satisfied complacency of my aunts and uncles, laced with a good splash of snobbism. Most of Mannheim clung like barnacles to the sunken keel of the style and tastes of the '90's; they called it tradition and were very proud of it. Not all of them, of course, but those whose money and opinions gave the town its face—the society, and if there were ever a word and conception I loathe, this is it.

Once more I had landed in a place where I couldn't put down roots. Even the apartment into which we had moved, without a choice, irritated me. It was not only too expensive, but it was in one of those ill-designed, pompous houses that were the fashion of the gorged '90's, full of wrought-iron balconies too small to stand on, covered with a rash of false rococo curlicues inside and out, the latter in turn covered with thick ivy inhabited by scurrying packs of rats. Situated between the Rhine and Neckar rivers, the old town was besieged by the rat population of both shores. Across the Rhine Bridge was Ludwigshafen, still occupied by French troops, and the huge I. G. Farben plant there frequently wrapped Mannheim in a thick, brown chemical stench. Los Angeles' notorious smog has nothing on it.

I won't blame it on our ill-designed apartment with the dark rooms, nor on my general dissatisfaction, but my energy began to leak out of me; it felt like an internal hemorrhage, and perhaps it was. With a very bad conscience, I stayed in bed till ten or eleven, unable to drag myself up and around in the heat. Even the Wigman School dance classes didn't give me back my zest. I saw a good specialist. He put me into the hospital at once, for surgery the next morning. "What is it? Cancer?" I asked him. "Let's hope not, but I've never seen anything like it that wasn't cancer," was his cheerful diagnosis.

Part of my work in building this exemplary, unique, perfect marriage of mine consisted in keeping trouble and worry out of my man's way. Men, I have found, are generally frail creatures, musicians somewhat more so than the rest. I made my will that evening, told my General Music Director nonchalantly that I had some slight female trouble to be looked into and was going to have what I referred to as my opening the next morning. Two days later the surgeon put his head in the door, said: "No cancer, congratulations," and was gone. Friend husband had to be revived with a shot of brandy.

I loved the hospital, I gobbled it up along with the complete writings of Proust, a task for which I had never before found enough time. Hospital was a great experience, each room, each bed a story. I've never written them down, though. Later I got more hospital experience than I wished for. There are such stretches when sickness and operations pile up in a family. Luckily, they are as soon and easily forgotten as last night's unpleasant dream.

I remember, though, the day I was rushing to the hospital where my husband was undergoing some minor surgery. On the way I was stopped by a certain Dr. Pinnes, an outsider like myself; a bearded White Russian, philosopher, chess player, amusing, unkempt, too poor to get his teeth fixed. "Did you send something to the *Köln-*

*ische Zeitung?*" he called across the street. "No, why should I?" I called back.

"I did," Pinnes announced. "I could use their prize money, couldn't you?"

He crossed over, pulled a ragged, much-used copy of that highly esteemed and respected newspaper from one of his coat pockets that served him as a sort of mobile library, and pointed to an announcement. In those days prizes were not as readily handed around or earned as now and this was, by God, a most serious literary contest, rich in money and honors for the winner. Thomas Mann was one of the three judges, the great idol whose writing I venerated above all others, the man whose books had formed much of my own and my generation's thoughts and style. Manuscripts had to be submitted anonymously. First prize: five thousand marks! And down the line: three thousand, one thousand, five hundred. Dizzy amounts for just a story, an unpublished novella of no more than thirty pages. There was just one drawback. "It's too late now, too bad," Pinnes said, commiserating.

"Why didn't you show this to me sooner?" I wailed. Resigned White Russian shrugging. "I was sure you knew about it. Everybody and his grandmother have sent their stuff; all of Heidelberg, all of Frankfurt, Berlin, Hamburg, too. Well, never mind, you wouldn't have much of a chance in any case. *Auf Wiedersehen,* and speedy recovery for our director."

I grabbed the paper from him. The manuscript had to be in Cologne day after tomorrow. Could I make it? Could I? Why not, if the mails worked promptly. (Naturally, a thing like airmail was still sleeping in the womb of the future.) I plunged into a stationery shop and bought some copybooks and half a dozen pencils. My mind was always full of stories, half-baked ideas, impressions, themes, a ragbag stuffed with odds and ends. If I was lucky I might, maybe, pull out something I could use.

It was a strange evening and night. I found my husband moaning miserably; the local anesthetic was wearing off and he complained about unbearable pains. Nurses rustled in and out, shook their heads, scolded him; it couldn't be as painful as all that, now really! Don't make such a fuss, pull yourself together, don't act like a baby! he was told. Even I myself grew impatient with him; barely managed to act like a compassionate wife, a good Samaritan. (The poor fellow, only days later was it admitted that the pains must truly have been unbearable because the doctor had botched so badly that the minor surgery grew until it became major.)

Sedatives didn't help; sleeping tablets calmed my moaning patient for ten minutes during which I began writing my story. He was tossing around, groggily moaning for morphine. An intern appeared, wrote down some orders. Pantopon, the syringe. The needle plunged deep into my memory . . . Mama yelling for morphine. Now he was quiet. I went on writing, as if in a fever. Then he was moaning again, waking up, sitting up, vomiting. Oh God, no, please, not that! The night nurse, tired, angry that she has to change the silly hospital gown—monkey jacket, they call it, with the innate cuteness of all nurses' language. Another intern. Another injection. More vomiting and, after he's emptied out, more pain. Rising temperature. I am worried. Something is terribly wrong, the prescription? I concentrate, I write, I'm writing like crazy in that queer trance that the toxins of exhaustion usually bring about in my brain. I am a nurse once more, doing all of a nurse's small services, but I am more than that, for I am trying to pull my sick boy's pains out of him and into myself. It's an old trick, very exhausting, but it helps, a little at least.

Writing, worrying, nursing, overshadowed by memories of those other, childhood hours like this, the night passes. At dawn Hans falls asleep. I finish my story; Der Weg, I call it ("The Road"). The head nurse, a strict sergeant of a woman, sends me home.

My husband recovered after the botched operation was repeated and repaired. And my story, duly typewritten and sent by special delivery, might or might not have arrived on time. I didn't know because I didn't hear of it for months, long after the date of the prize-awarding was past. All right, so it wasn't good, so they threw it away, I thought, and forgot all about it, seasoned throw-awayer that I was.

One of the few real friends I had in Mannheim was the very young beautiful wife of our young conductor Breisach, later of the

Metropolitan Opera. Whenever I see her she tells me about that story; she made quite an anecdote of it, which sounds funny now but was a deeply serious matter then. I must have pinned a bit of a daydream on that story after all, at least in the beginning. Like Dorothy Parker's unforgettable girls of her "Standard of Living," we used to play a game: "If you got a prize—not one of the big prizes, naturally, but let's say a consolation prize of five hundred or three hundred marks—what would you do with it?" Suzie would ask.

Good Heavens, what *wouldn't* I do with it? Buy a complete new evening outfit for the *Generalmusikdirektor,* the old, overworked one was a disgrace. A sofa and chairs for our living room to re-place the wicker furniture. New shoes and winter coats for the chil-dren. And if there were still enough money left, a really good suit for myself, with two blouses, and not, under *any* circumstances, *not* navy blue.

After I had completely forgotten that story of which no copy existed—the pressure had been too great—there arrived a telegram from the *Kölnische Zeitung.* They had given me first prize! What did I say, they? Thomas Mann, my great patron saint, had deemed me worthy of this honor. He, in person, opened for me the doors to literature, or so I believed at that time.

"Five thousand marks! What are you going to buy now that you're rich?" Suzie asked me.

"Now? Not a thing. You can squander five hundred," I am re-ported to have said, "but five thousand have to be kept together. I'll put them into a savings account. For the future. For an emer-gency."

Funny? I don't know. I am not a worrier by nature and being cautious goes against my grain. But there was that old pull: my duty, my obligations, my responsibilities. I had two children, I couldn't forever live *sur la branche,* it was time to build a nest and feather it.

That's our trouble: when we are young our parents run our lives; when we get older, our children do.

So far there had been nothing steady, reliable, secure in our day-to-day existence. Volcanoes kept rumbling underneath and I sensed the approach of new eruptions. As usual, some of them threatened from the old fault in the ground, the theater. There was the day when my man came home, his dear bald head wrapped in a black cloud, wouldn't eat, wouldn't talk. "What's the matter, darling? Bad rehearsal? A stink? A row with the *Intendant?*"

"Stink isn't the word! But I told him off, by God! If I didn't have to take care of my wife and children I wouldn't stay in this pigsty another day! I'd cancel my contract tomorrow. No more of this eternal compromise, compromise, compromise. . . ."

When I get deeply hurt or terribly angry, not only does my blood feel like ice water, but my always deep voice drops to *basso profundo* depths, frozen calm. "You don't have to compromise with anything, certainly not on our account," I heard that deep voice say, dangerously quiet. But the *Herr Generalmusikdirektor* had left the room.

That was another time when I tumbled into one of my most important decisions without a moment's reflection.

t a certain point in our negotiations the Ullstein publishers invited me to come to Berlin for a meeting, all expenses paid. This was during the worst inflation times and I could use a little interruption to my navy blue period. A large black car with chauffeur was put at my disposal day and night. I was taken to plays, to the movie studios, through the boiling, broiling Ullstein House in the Kochstrasse and the mighty printing plant, largest on the Continent, in Tempelhof. My escort and constant adjutant during those five days was Paul Wiegler, the editor to whom I had returned the advance offered on my second novel. Paul was a fine, sensitive, soft-spoken man, quite an exception among the other sharp-tongued, witty, hard-boiled editors. His humor was gentler and mellower, and there was a streak of melancholy in his large, blue-gray eyes even when he made a joke. We became friends quickly and remained friends. I suspect that he was as harmless an animal as I, two rabbits in a lair of foxes.

Occasionally I occupy myself with the question, "What prevented the lions from tearing Daniel to pieces, eating him and licking their chops after the meal?" I've come to the conclusion that they were baffled by his innocence; Daniel simply didn't know that lions are carnivorous, therefore he wasn't afraid of them. He probably smiled at them and scratched them behind their ears.

That, at least, is how I explain in retrospect why I was never hurt, torn apart, or eaten up in any of the lions' dens I got thrown into. I simply never realized that studying at the Vienna Konservatorium or being the only female in an orchestra, rather good-looking and young at that, was not without its dangers; in my years of affiliation with the opera, first as a musician and then as a wife, I was never exposed to the gossip, intrigues, jealousies, and outright insults that thickened the air. Later, as a magazine editor or a movie writer in Hollywood I sleepwalked blissfully among crossed swords and murderous feuds without noticing a thing. And with the same harmless gratitude I made friends left and right on that first visit to Berlin, not realizing for a second that Ullstein didn't love me on account of my beautiful eyes, but that they wanted to get me away from the Deutsche Verlagsanstalt which had published my last three, more ambitious, more literary, books, and tie me down good and firmly. Among other ceremonies I was presented to Hermann Ullstein, one of the five powerful brothers. He reigned over the Third Floor, Magazines and Books. He was a dry, much-feared small man with a keen sense for sales propaganda, packaging, and slogans. Not so good at stimulating ideas in his editors and authors, he employed men with the warmth and imagination necessary for such jobs. During my visit he had suggested that I write a novel about "an efficient girl." I have an inkling that he pictured such a girl somewhat along the lines of his secretary Pfeifer *Eins,* so called to differentiate her from her younger sister, Pfeifer *Zwo.* Although I subsequently grew quite fond of Pfeifer *Eins,* a thirtyish, plump, worried, washed-out blond, and she certainly was efficiency personified, I could not see her as a novel's fascinating heroine. What I did evolve, out of my love for Heidelberg, and with some of the greatest physicians and scientists there helping me in my research, was *Stud. Chem. Helene Willfuer.*

It is an overwritten, uneven book but I think it caught the sweat and smell and work of those poor-as-church-mice German students. Innocent as ever, I learned that I had written something worse than pornography, something sensationally indecent and swinish: the honest story of a girl student who gets pregnant, tries for an abortion or a suicide, but finally rises above her problem and fights through to the top. For several years Ullstein shelved it, did not dare publish the nasty thing: when they finally did it was a huge success. I understand it still is, or again is, quite popular in Germany. It always makes me smile when white-haired ladies, every day as old as I, confess that they read "Helene" when they were schoolgirls, read the forbidden, dirty book secretly, in most cases in the W.C. My amused impression is of a whole generation of girls, and probably their mothers, too, sitting on countless toilet seats devouring my poor novel.

I had finished and delivered that book shortly before my husband informed me that he was bearing up with unbearable debasement only on my and the kids' account. I thought it pretty wonderful that he would think of our welfare even in the heat of battle. For a few days I waited for my husband to ask to be released from his contract. We had five thousand marks in the bank; meanwhile, I lost no time in brooding. I wrote a long letter to my friend Paul Wiegler in which I summed up my few assets and humbly asked if Ullstein's would possibly take me on as an apprentice.

I am sorry I have no copy of that letter for it must have been an exceedingly funny document. My vague idea was that it couldn't be too hard to become a fashion designer. Why not, indeed, after all the things I had created out of those navy blue hand-me-downs? Somewhere I had read that fashion designers earned good money, but I would have gratefully accepted any kind of job in the buzzing Ullstein beehive. Among my assets I mentioned that I could type at fair speed, though only in my own hit-and-miss-two-finger method. On the debit side I confessed "no shorthand," but added that I would gladly learn quickly if necessary. Or maybe they needed a music critic? Someone who knew the stage inside out? Perhaps a reliable secretary? I am willing and reliable, I boasted. Perhaps they could use me as an assistant in the corner for recipes, advice to housewives and mothers? If they would teach me, I was willing to do anything at all. I was in a heroic mood, ready for any sacrifice to relieve my husband from the ball and chain of supporting a family. (Still an echo of *Great Men—Noble Deeds!*)

In this sweeping noblesse of soul I did not realize that the pleasant prospect of taking myself away from Mannheim played a not inconsiderable, if subconscious, part in my decision. Nor did I notice that I was my father's daughter, after all: I wanted a job, something solid and regular, with a fixed salary in my hands the first of each month. A five-thousand-mark prize was nice but it was a once-in-a-lifetime accident, like winning the lottery, gossamer stuff, fool's gold, nothing to stand on.

I have no idea why I didn't think for a moment of counting among my assets my easy gift for fiction writing. Probably it seemed the most unreliable. For although by that time I had published six books, written two more, thrown away maybe a dozen, I could not be sure I would write another one, ever. I wanted a *job*. I had two children and a man who must not, under any circumstances, sell his integrity. Please, dear, dear Ullstein publishers, give me a job, I'll gladly be a file clerk, a charwoman, anything at all.

Of course I didn't tell my husband about this letter. Perhaps I had an inkling that he would have laughed me out of my sacrificial mood. Came a wire from Berlin: "Very interested. Expect you here for discussion at your earliest convenience. All expenses paid. Affectionately Wiegler."

Immediately I began some feverish preparations. Anxious to prove my aptitude for a fashion designer's well-paid job, I filled a large drawing pad with designs for all sorts of attire, from alluring morning negligées through street, house, and afternoon dresses to elaborate evening gowns. I added patterns for embroideries and fabrics, sofa pillows, lamp shades, and for good measure some furniture sketches I had discussed with the owner of a large furniture plant.

I remember especially drawing a tableau in which I tried to combine all my ideas. Elegant ladies in various dresses—in fashionable tea gowns or simple smartly-tailored outfits, with or without hats—were standing, sitting, or leaning amid a super-abundance of pillows, lamp shades, and other accessories, all looking something like the Tower of Pisa, as the entire drawing had the same slant as my handwriting; not one of those modish creatures stood straight. I found my handiwork most impressive, though I must admit that the slant of Bemelmans' drawings looks better, somehow.

Armed with this collection I presented myself on the Third Floor of Ullstein House. I was full of palpitations, stage fright, and dignity as I was led into the presence of five or six amiable but serious executives: Hermann Ullstein in person; Dr. Emil Herz, head of the book department; Kurt Szafranski, director of the magazine department; and Kurt Korff, the great editor in chief of the *Berliner Illustrirte.**

I don't remember who the spokesman was, but I won't forget the gist of his first few sentences. Ullstein's were quite interested in tying me to the House more closely, he said; they hoped I could find my own niche there; indeed, I might find quite some stimulation and material by working there for a while in one or the other capacity, and that would be to our mutual advantage, wouldn't it? *But,* they said, clearing their collective throat, they just hoped I had no fantastic notions about the salary they could pay me at first. True, I might easily develop into the highest paid fiction writer in Germany (Who, me? Oh, my God!), but the best authors often did not possess one grain of the intangible qualities that make an editor. (Me, an editor? In Berlin? At Ullstein's?) I had had no experience in editing, had I? Well, not much, I said (better not mention my experience in editing and running into the ground a lousy, short-lived Little Magazine). All right, Ullsteins were willing to try me out, if I did not harbor exaggerated expectations of the remuneration they could offer me.

"Well," I said, and now the throat-clearing was mine, "well, you see, if I move my family to Berlin . . . it all depends . . . I would have to discuss it with my husband first, of course. I am seeing an old friend of ours tomorrow, Kleiber. . . . I mean, if my husband would receive a call to the State Opera, he might agree to let me accept a job here in Berlin." (This, of course, was just a balloon full of hot air; a sudden revelation which hit me under the pressure and dizzy excitement of the situation.) I took a deep breath and concluded nonchalantly, "Well, how much would I get, at first?"

---

* "Illustrierte" is, of course, the correct spelling. However, in error the first issue of the magazine emerged as *Die Berliner Illustrirte,* and thus it remained.

"Sorry, but we couldn't offer you more than eight hundred a month," I am told, with more embarrassed throat-clearing.

Eight hundred a month! Well, well! Think of that! "Well . . . ," I say. This is the unforgettable moment when I lift my behind a little and very discreetly slip the portfolio with the slanting ladies under it and out of sight; I am sitting on it to the end of the conference, in tight discomfort and complete bliss. "Well . . . ," I say grandly, with calculated hesitation.

"And, naturally, you can easily make twice that much, as we hope you will, if you write some little fillers for the magazines; we'll pay you one mark per line, our highest rate," Korff adds quickly.

This was the introduction to the happiest, most interesting, and most fruitful years of my life. Berlin, 1926 to 1931, on the Third Floor of Ullstein House.

As a footnote I might mention that I did talk with Kleiber the following day and that he was as good as gold, loyal and understanding, our former baby, our old friend. A position at the State Opera was offered my husband, as a guest conductor at first, and only later as first *Kapellmeister*. Because by the time I returned home, he and the *Intendant* were on friendly terms again; in fact, Lert remained *Generalmusikdirektor* in Mannheim for two more years, with his integrity, and our marriage, intact, the latter once again refreshed by weeks of separation and the pleasures of occasional visits and long summer vacations together.

There is a secret that our quickly divorced couples don't seem to have discovered. It's the difference between a love affair and a marriage. Speaking as an impassioned gardener: Love affairs are annuals; once they have bloomed and died they are finished forever. Marriage, on the other hand, is a hardy perennial; if you will only await its time, it will bloom again and again and again. Amen.

If you talk about Berlin to people who lived there during the middle '20's, they will give a great sigh of nostalgia and tell you that there never was a town as alive, as fascinating as Berlin in those years. With all respect to Christopher Isherwood's memories—what he knew and described is only a very small segment, the beatnik fringe, seen through Anglo-Saxon eyes. Ullstein House, though, was one of the several hearts of the city. It was the focal point of liberalism, and to be a liberal by no means carried the connotations it does now, especially in the United States. I often wonder about the semantic tricks whereby the praise of yesterday becomes the insult of today. To be called a liberal and an intellectual then was a high honor, a goal worth working and fighting for. At Ullstein's this liberalism meant that the doors were wide open for a great diversity of opinions, ideas, thoughts, directions. The authors we published were a veritable rainbow from the scarlet of the far left—Brecht and Toller—through the entire scale of the Expressionist school, to young Remarque's antiwar, antimilitaristic *All Quiet on the Western Front,* and down to the dark green, old, moss-covered regional writers like, for example, Richard Skowronnek.

I remember old Skowronnek in particular as he became my first editorial task. Altogether, my first day at Ullstein's was anything but triumphant. I was ordered to start on my vague job at nine-thirty on a certain morning. If I have any claim to a neurosis, it is my exaggerated punctuality. Like all neuroses and vices it's a leftover from my early youth. In school, I always arrived twenty minutes before the others because this was the only time I could spare for my homework. At orchestra rehearsals and concerts, I was always half an hour early because it is infernally difficult to tune a harp once the fiddling and tooting of the others begin. Then there were those breathless gallops back and forth to be on time for Mama's injections. And so, naturally, I appeared in the Kochstrasse at 9:00 A.M., unaware of the class distinction by which stenographers and secretaries are nine-o'clock creatures while editors and executives retain their superiority by coming in at nine-thirty. I was coldly received by *Botenmeister* Appel, a significant personage on the Third Floor. Captain of a flock of uniformed messenger boys, Appel was superhumanly reliable, disciplined, a born militarist. Or, as Berlin called it: a bicyclist, bowing upward and kicking downward. From a slip of paper he noted that I claimed to have an appointment, I didn't quite know with whom, offered me a chair in the waiting room and informed me that nobody was there yet. This waiting room for outsiders was actually a kind of lobby, and I settled down eagerly and sniffed the scent of The House. I was greatly intrigued by the elevator, a so-called paternoster; I guess it works more or less on the principle of tanks and caterpillars. There were no doors or stops. The open cars went past, up and down, and people of various ages and sexes skipped on and off with nimble feet. I thought if an editor's post demanded that I, too, use this devilish invention, I'd better quit right away. I thumbed through some of the Ullstein magazines: the incomparably popular weekly *Die Berliner Illustrirte*; the sophisticated biweekly fashion magazine *Die Dame* (the German equivalent of *Vogue*); the *Blatt der Hausfrau*, unsurpassed as a family journal; the small-format monthly *Uhu*, something new with its mixture of fiction and information, humor and serious essays, text and photos. There was the superintellectual *Querschnitt*, a children's magazine *Der Heitere Fridolin*, a magazine *Die Koralle* for readers interested in nature and science, and probably a few more that I don't remember. So rich a menu, and so cleverly staggered that it covered the entire field, made me slightly dizzy. I put the magazines down and waited. The clock on the wall said 9:47. Now there was a steady coming and going; a few of the chiefs passed without noticing me at all, and I, timid by nature, missed the opportunity of making myself noticed. I waited. I was sorry that I had given up smoking to please the enraged antismoker I am married to. A cigarette would have made me look slightly arrogant, perhaps. At 11:30 Herr Szafranski, the master of the Third Floor, discovered me, or maybe *Botenmeister* Appel had called his attention to my yet unexplained presence. Szafranski met me with a somewhat preoccupied and slightly embarrassed air. It was obvious that he had forgotten entirely about me and my possible assignment. But being of the people Caesar wanted around (a personification of the Ullstein spirit: warm, jolly, invincibly optimistic; "Our Little Sunshine," the Third Floor called him), he greeted me profusely and took me down a corridor lined with doors of frosted glass. "Well, now . . . let's see . . . we'll have to find you a desk . . . It's only that just now . . . well, never mind . . . hurrah, I've got it," he muttered, and opened one of those doors and let me enter. "This'll do until we get you settled.

If you want anything, call *Botenmeister* Appel," he said and was gone. I sat down at the scarred desk and looked out of the window. It gave on to Charlottenstrasse; across the street stood the usual gray apartment houses. After a while it struck me that an uncommonly hectic activity of window-cleaning seemed to be taking place on the two lower floors. At each window one and sometimes two young girls, all pretty, most of them in slips or open negligées were going over their windowpanes with white rags, and in circular motions. When I opened my own window to watch them, they smiled and waved to me, and I smiled and waved back, pleased at the quick, friendly contact with the neighbors.

Later, when I had become a real editor and a steady inhabitant of my cubicle, I learned that the pretties were prostitutes, but classy, above the rank and file of streetwalkers. They were plying their trade from their rooms. Since the police did not permit them to call out invitations, beckon or whistle to prospective customers down on the street, the constantly moving, flicking white rags had to do the trick. After a while I was so used to them I did not notice them any more. We would call good morning or good night across the street, maybe a few words about the weather. I had gotten into the habit of leaning my head against the window and staring out with unseeing eyes whenever I needed to concentrate.

During the first hour on my job I felt as exposed as a canary in a cage. The room was small and narrow, with the desk between the window and the door to the corridor. This door had neither frosted glass nor a curtain; nothing to protect me from the curiosity of all the people who passed by, stopped to stare at me, went on but came back to stare some more. After stewing for a while in front of my empty desk I took the phone and called for *Botenmeister* Appel. "Yes, Frau Baum?" he said. (Look, the good man even knew me by name!) "I was just wondering," I said. "I feel like the baby chimpanzee in the zoo. Couldn't I . . . I mean, couldn't you get me some sort of little curtain for my door? You know what I mean? Like they have in offices?"

Appel seemed flabbergasted. "But . . . but, Frau Baum! That's for Herr Hermann Ullstein to decide. You could make an application, but I doubt . . . no, I really don't think it advisable. You really can't expect green curtains the first day you are with us. . . ."

I must point out here that in Germany—probably in all of Europe —editors, rewrite men, and whoever else make up the journalistic hierarchy, didn't work in those huge, crowded, clattering stables as they do in the United States. It takes the American sociability and imperviousness to crowds and their noises to be able to do some reasonable work under such circumstances. At Ullstein House each editor had his solitary cell; at the most, two compatible people were thrown together. As for myself, I am so used to writing only at night, in complete quiet and solitude, that I doubt I could function in an American editors' pool.

The following description is taken from an article my colleague Paul Schlesinger wrote for a book commemorating the fiftieth year of the Ullstein enterprises:

> There are gentlemen with five, four, three, two, or just one telephone.
> There are editors' rooms with genuine Oriental rugs; there are editors' rooms with Axminster rugs.
> There are editors with just a bath mat under their desk.
> Those who have just one telephone, no intercom and only a bath mat will strive to get at least a little green curtain for their glass door; this lends a certain prestige.
> If your request for a little green curtain is not granted you may be convinced that you are not a greatly influential personage. But be assured that even the greenest little curtain doesn't give you any influence in the House.

I definitely didn't rate anything as elevated as a little green curtain for at least three months. I remember that my throat grew tighter and tighter while I was sitting there that day, so completely useless as I had never been in my life. By and by some of the onlookers, having been informed of the identity of the strange new animal in its cage, entered for a moment, introduced themselves, made a little joke, and left. I grew hungry. Once more I phoned Appel. "Where may one get something to eat, please?" I asked.

"In the cafeteria, upstairs. Better hurry, Frau Baum, after two they don't serve anything but coffee."

"Cafeteria? But where is it? How do I get there?"

"You take the paternoster. You can't miss it."

"Thanks," I said, "thank you very much." Eating wasn't as important as all that, was it? I'd been hungry before. Plenty.

Shortly after three a new face stared at me through my door. A man, small but dangerous and wild-looking, entered. "Beg your pardon, but this is my desk!" he said with suppressed fury. "May I ask what you are doing at my desk?"

"Sorry. Herr Szafranski put me in here," I said, getting angry myself.

My opponent's eyes bulged a bit, he looked sick, his cadaverous skin had a gray tinge and his teeth grew from receding gums; he was ugly in a rather attractive way. "Oh, Szafranski did, did he? And who would you be, may I ask?"

"My name is Vicki Baum," I whispered, feeling obscure like a hidden hole in a sock.

"Vicki Baum? So? And why aren't you home writing another of your best sellers, may I ask? What are you doing in this crocodile tank? By the way, I'm Stefan Grossmann."

"No!" I called out. Grossmann was one of the most feared and most admired journalists, an unfailing critic of the stage, also of politics and politicians. A sharp observer, a witty prose writer, he would use his own magazine *Das Tagebuch* ("The Diary") to wound as well as to caress. Somewhat like Alexander Woollcott in New York, he would dip his pen in vitriol for opponents or into syrup for those he liked.

He decided to like me. I suppose he felt flattered by my being so visibly impressed. "Come, let's have a word with that scoundrel, Szafranski," he said, and linking his arm into mine, he marched me down the corridor, past the two fluttering secretaries in the anteroom, straight into the high and mighty's lair. Szafranski was, among other things, a trouble shooter of high degree and had us disentangled in no time. Another, better room and desk were assigned to Grossmann, who gallantly accompanied me back to my cell and left me there with much fine advice and his skeptical blessing.

Perhaps I would have been left forever in solitary confinement, lost and forgotten, except for Grossmann's intervention. My later fellow editor and good friend, the fiction writer George Fröschel used to tell how he went down those long, dim corridors one day and discovered a door he hadn't noticed before, just where the new wing had been joined to the old building. He knocked and entered; inside he found an old, gray-haired man standing at one of those old-fashioned high desks, working. Around the walls, shelves from floor to ceiling were filled with ledgers and filing cases. Fröschel introduced himself, they shook hands, and the old gentleman explained that he was the attorney of the company's founder, Leopold Ullstein.

"But the Old Man has been dead for I don't know how many years!" cried Fröschel, bewildered.

"Precisely. But, you see, when the new and the old house were joined together this room was created and they forgot me here, together with dear old Herr Ullstein's files. Naturally I'm not such a fool as to remind them of me. I draw my salary and enjoy my obscurity. I hope you'll do me the favor not to mention that this room exists, and me in it!"

The characteristic thing was that most people at Ullstein's willingly swallowed this well-invented anecdote as something that could easily have happened.

As for myself, I was asked to Mr. Korff's office shortly after Grossmann had left. The editor in chief of the *Berliner Illustrirte* was a short, dapper man, a true genius of journalism and a real original. (I shall tell about him later.) He got up, he never failed to get up and to bow slightly when one of us, collectively known as The Ladies, entered. He would rest his hands on the flawless top of his desk and remain standing until I, The Lady, was seated. When Korff stood he seemed a bit shorter than when he was sitting down, at least that was my impression. A small number of my future colleagues, his staff, were looking me over with ill-concealed amusement while Korff gave me my first assignment. He made it sound very serious and important but I sensed that he was a bit embarrassed.

"We have Skowronnek stewing in the waiting room," he said, "and none of us has time to talk to him. Would you do me the favor and do it? You know who Skowronnek is, of course?"

"Yes, more or less. But I've never read one of his novels."

"Well, we printed dozens of them in the 'paper.' He has millions of readers, enormously popular. We are enormously grateful to him, you understand, selling so well for so many years. Getting a bit old, though, very regrettable, that. So you never read his stuff? Good. You'll be more detached; objective; very desirable if you've got to reject an old collaborator. We have his latest novel here"—a thick manuscript was juggled into my hands—"it stinks to high Heaven. Blood and soil and Vaterland and bunk, all that's sacred to us and our magazine. Will you do me the favor and give it back to him? With all our compliments, admiration, etcetera. Flatter him all you can; I hope you'll have the right touch; if he gets furious, call *Botenmeister* Appel before he can shoot all of us. Well, I guess you, too, have received plenty of amiable rejections, you must know how it's done. . . ."

"Sure," I lied, a bit depressed that never having been rejected went on my debit side.

Even while I followed Appel down the corridor to the small waiting room reserved for the inner circle of collaborators, I dimly realized that this was an awful task, a prank designed by the staff to test my mettle. Skowronnek was as East Prussian as they come, to me an absolutely alien race.

A huge grizzly bear rose on his hind legs at my entrance. In my memory he had with him a beautiful setter and a rifle; at least that was my impression, but then, a writer's impressions are not reliable. I shall never know by what outrageous flattery, insincerity, and bare-faced lies I managed to hand back his novel to the famous old man. I hadn't known myself what an actress had been lost in me. I blackened the reputation of all the Ullsteins, Korff, his "paper," his staff of readers. Creatures of the asphalt, all of them, decadents, city people who had never sat on a horse, never put their nose into a stable, didn't have any feeling for nature, the woods, the pastures. I waxed lyrical—ah, to walk down along the stables at sunup, the warmth, the smells, the sounds! Only Skowronnek's descriptions had made me understand them. I made common cause with the old man, we two who came from the soil, against the depraved metropolitans. I, who literally couldn't kill a fly, spoke enthusiastically about the hunt, the thrill of waiting for snipe at dusk, the wild ducks—who but Skowronnek had ever written as beautifully about these things? This last novel now, it was simply much too good for the *Illustrirte,* that was all. I should feel miserable to find it in such wrong surroundings. He listened, entranced. "How come you know these things? I thought the theater was your domain—singers, dancers, the backstage flimflam?" he asked.

"I was raised in the country," I said modestly. "In Austria, such a small country, true, but aren't we all forever faithful to the landscape in which we grew up?" And noticing that I was edging close to the border between acting and the truth, I excused myself, I had to go back to my desk. I didn't think the old man was naïve enough to fall for my antics but I had tried to save his face and he accepted the rejection with the controlled attitude, the *Haltung* that is second nature to Prussian landed gentry. We parted with warm assurances of mutual admiration, and I received a bone-cracking bearhug as a bonus, plus a sly little flicker of a smile beneath Korff's well-groomed mustache. I had passed the test. I was one of eight thousand four hundred Ullstein employees.

At first my position and my duties at Ullstein's were only vaguely defined. I was reading loads of manuscripts for the literary sections of the magazines. I read and condensed and wrote careful reports, an activity that took large bites out of my Sundays. (In parenthesis I'd like to remark that the German "Economic Miracle" has its basis in the German six-day week; seven days and some nights if you want to get somewhere.) After a while the book reviews for two of our magazines were entrusted to me, a job really quite up my alley. Then there were various folders circulating through the house containing all the leading foreign magazines, some accompanied by rough translations. Reading those and recommending what we might buy took much time. It is remarkable how certain qualities come through even in poor translations. Thus, I discovered Fannie Hurst for our magazines, while Sinclair Lewis and Ernest Hemingway found their way into our more highbrow publications in really dreadful versions. Another folder held assorted letters from our readers, for me to answer. Also, after my initial success with Skowronnek much of the correspondence with our authors was handed to me. By and by I became an assistant editor, which is a full-time job in itself. But I earned my badge as a sort of girl-of-all-work. If an author let us down with a short story or an article three days before the deadline, I was told to write it, and I did. After the training I had had during my marriage to Max Prels this, to me, didn't seem a skill worth bragging about. The less so as it was a fundamental principle of Ullstein House never to praise an employee. I liked that attitude; only dilettantes have to be fed their doses of pabulum. Soon our chief typesetter saved himself the detour through higher echelons and came to me directly whenever a hitch developed in the layout. "Frau Baum, I need a filler here. Twelve and a half lines. . . . Frau Baum, we're five lines short, maybe a little aphorism? . . . Frau Baum, Herr Ullstein kicked out the photo on page six, too morbid, he wants this half-page nature study and a spring poem on the side of it; can I have it by five o'clock?" Sighing deeply I would get up, lean my forehead on the windowpane, concentrate for three minutes on the white rags of the girls across the street, and make a poem out of hot air: "April is a young woman with a new hat. . . ."

Hermann Ullstein, the power above us, was constantly condemning photos that we, the editors of the *Berliner's* small sister, the *Uhu*, tried to get in. Just as adamantly he replaced them with nature studies, meaning nude (or as nude as permissible) females; this, of course, is an understandable and excusable trend with publishers of illustrated magazines in general. What went against my grain, but also amused me, was the hypocrisy with which such illustrations were maneuvered onto our pages. Herr Ullstein would never permit himself to say frankly: "Look, we've got to give them more flesh and skin or the stuff won't sell!" Instead, he would push away our nicely laid-out dummy and shout angrily: "Too morbid! Not enough beauty! *Beauty!* I want to see Beauty! Nature! Joy! What about those travel studies Putkammer brought from China?"

Putkammer had brought countless photos from China, each show-ing a very young, very lovely Chinese girl, artfully lighted by a Chi-nese lantern. Sometimes there was also a gong, a drum, or a bamboo branch. In a word, nothing Putkammer couldn't have shot in any Chinatown night club, Shanghai brothel, or even in Kantstrasse, Berlin, for that matter. Dated as these photos are, they are still around; with nostalgic tears I encounter one or the other in some magazine over here, remembering the grim cry, "Beauty!"

*Cheerfulness* was written on the Ullstein banner, and though we did not have quite such strict taboos as Hollywood where *virgin* is a word on the forbidden list, we had our taboos just the same. Once one of our press photographers caught that ever recurring but always sensational shot of a man on a window ledge, about to take the lethal leap. "Suicide!" the caption stated. "Breathless crowd watches man about to leap to his death from ninth story." "Too morbid," Her-mann wrote on the margin. "Not in the Ullstein spirit. Replace photo with more cheerful one." Naturally, it would have broken Korff's heart to throw out that sensational shot. Resourceful as he was, he found a compromise: ". . . but he didn't do it!" was added to the caption. From then on, "but he didn't do it" became the Third Floor slogan for unfinished enterprises, broken promises, unfulfilled threats of murder, and resignations.

Editors, in general, are brighter than the paper or magazine they edit. Usually they aren't permitted to call a spade a spade; they are taught to call it a silver spoon, and hope that the touchy segment of their millions of readers will accept it as such and that the intelligent ones will know what is really meant. In a way, the demand for cheerfulness and optimism gave Ullstein House its pleasant atmos-phere; it kept everybody on his toes; all those clever, witty, lively people flitting in and out of one another's cubicles, putting tomor-row's new joke into circulation, making fun of each other and of themselves, and killing any sprouting pomposity through laughter.

Unavoidably we were a cynical lot, though probably not as cynical as editors and writers are made to be in movies or on TV. And there was one thing to be said for the German press before Hitler: in seri-ous questions, you never had to write against your convictions.

There were newspapers for every one of the many political parties, from the reddest radical left to the most hard-livered reactionary and chauvinist right; no paper would employ people of a different hue, and consequently nobody had to make a living by selling his soul to the devil of falsehood. A far cry from, let's say, MGM in Hollywood where Louis B. Mayer would call a meeting of the entire staff and, after shedding a few habitual crocodile tears, would ask that each of us—an overwhelming majority of pro-Roosevelt voters—pay one day's salary into the campaign fund of Roosevelt's opponent. Voluntarily, of course.

At Ullstein House in Berlin I felt that I was sitting right in the navel of the world. Life streamed by in thousands of photos, hundreds of people, in voices from the entire globe. The corridors echoed with the wit and laughter of the keenest spirits of the big city. The best, most advanced authors of those days were published at Ullstein's. They brought to us their bitter, postwar, postrevolution, postinflation, disillusioned humor, and their burning idealism in spite of everything.

The theaters of Berlin in the '20's were said to be by far the best in all of Europe. I believe they were, because not only those supported by state and city, but many of the others, knew nothing of the commercialism that hangs over Broadway like a bad smell. There was Reinhardt, another one of those demon-ridden, obsessed ones. He would produce some play by one of the new authors, stage it according to his vision, and wouldn't give an inch. Each evening, with the house completely sold out, he would lose more than five hundred marks on his production. But somehow his magic was so strong that there was always more money available for him.

I remember one evening that, to us, seemed to be the culmination of everything Germany had paid for so dearly. It was the première of Zuckmayer's *Captain from Köpenick* at Reinhardt's Deutsches Theater. It was one of those rare evenings when everything was right, the play, the acting, the sets, the spirit behind the production. I remember that during the intermission all of Berlin met in the pleasant upstairs foyer (another thing sadly lacking on Broadway). There was such a happy feeling of liberation in the air you could almost touch it. We were all a little drunk with it, we smiled, strangers were smiling at each other like lovers sharing a secret. At last, at last militarism was finished in Germany. Militarism had been fought in books, in newspapers, it had been stabbed and shot at and killed in many plays, and been sworn off officially by our politicians. But in Zuckmayer's play we had at last come to the point where we could smile at it, tolerantly, amused, good-naturedly as you smile at the bully you hated in school when you find him years later, beaten and finished. And the best of it was that Zuckmayer had used a real character, a true story. All of Germany had laughed about the penniless aging convict who, by the simple act of putting on an officer's uniform, could command, rob, and terrorize a whole Prussian town. Thank God, those times are past, we said, never again will there be uniforms, soldiers, officers, war, and death. Done with, we said, let's laugh about the farce that's gone for good.

And so, perhaps, Ullstein House was not the omniscient navel of the world, after all. . . .

I remember a small whiff of dire foreboding one morning when I passed the chancellery in the Wilhelmstrasse on my way to Ullstein House. A crowd had assembled in front of its high wrought-iron fence, men and women craning their necks as for a parade. "What are they waiting for?" I asked a policeman at the corner. "Hindenburg?"

"Nah. Who wants to see Hindenburg? It's that little king, Abdullah."

It set me thinking when, on returning in the evening, the crowd was still there, a much larger crowd than in the morning. If the people are that eager to get a glimpse of a king, however small and alien he may be, it's because they want a show. They want a parade and a spectacle. Hindenburg without a uniform isn't much to look at. The Republic, sober and colorless, leaves some hunger in them unstilled. They still venerate uniforms, pomp, ceremony. The Britons know much better how to handle that mob urge. "Not by bread alone"—bread the new democracy was giving us. Now they want to look at a king. Abdullah. He probably wore a uniform and decorations. Or maybe a turban. Something colorful, regal.

Ten years later, the day Hitler declared war on Poland, I remembered that morning. Hitler, bred by the mob, knew what the mob wanted; and gave it to them.

But for the time being we only laughed at this fellow Hitler. A crank, we said, a clown, a nut, we've plenty of them, a whole new crop raised in the war. Faith healers and stigmatized virgins and prophets, *putschists* and assassins, and what else? Their time is past. They'll calm down and shut up by and by.

Berlin was wonderfully gay, full of a strange electricity. Night clubs—I had never seen a night club until I came to Berlin. We are getting Americanized; too bad, our middle-aged conservatives grumbled, cocktails instead of the noble wines that had been consumed before. "Before," that always meant before the war. Now costume balls in private homes, costumes exposing skin and flesh, and wild goings-on. A little too free for our taste, our doddering elders would snort. But this freedom was precisely what we wanted and needed.

In those days the "paper," the *Berliner Illustrirte,* was by far the most widely read magazine in Europe. In any one generation there are, at the most, two or three really great editors, and Korff was one of them. In the '30's, when he left Germany on account of Hitler, he brought to New York the finished plans for founding an illustrated weekly modeled exactly after the *Berliner.* He found the men and the money to try the experiment; he laid out the first few issues of this kind of magazine, which was something new for America. Perhaps he poured his last reserves of energy and enthusiasm into this work because he fell ill, grew weaker from day to day, dwindled away, died an easy death. The weekly is alive, though. It is called *Life.*

At Ullstein's we all respected and loved Korff, and to win and retain the respect and affection of his hard-bitten, cynical, clever lot of editors was almost a miracle. He never let us down, neither collectively nor individually. He never let the readers down. He respected his readers, was always aware of all classes on all possible levels of education or literacy; of the limitations of the huge block of ignorance inherent in any mass of humanity. For instance, he gave us strict training in the ticklish art of writing captions. I remember one time I was called on the carpet because of a caption reading "The Dôme des Invalides with Napoleon's tomb."

"And who, pray, is Napoleon?" he asked me. "I assume everybody knows all about Napoleon," I said. Korff took the telephone and called *Botenmeister* Appel. "Who's your brightest boy, Appel? Adolf? All right, send Adolf over." Adolf appeared, seventeen, blond as a half-baked roll, well-drilled, eager. "Tell me, Adolf," said Korff, "who was Napoleon?" Adolf stammered something. "Napoleon? Maybe he was French? Maybe not. Maybe a French king? We had him in history but I don't remember right now. . . ."

"Thank you, Adolf, you'll find out in our next issue," Korff said. I was left with the hard work of compressing Napoleon's biography into the fifteen words allowed for a caption. I still am what my best friend, author Gina Kaus, calls "an epic writer," a rambling, long-winded storyteller. I can only say that this isn't *Direktor* Moosbauer's or Korff's fault.

Korff never ran dry, an incomparable quality for the editor of a weekly. There's a big letdown after the week's issue has gone to press; you feel that the irretrievable last drop of editorial brain power has gone into it, your last spark of energy, and, worse, the last reserves of printable material saved in the lower left desk drawer for emergencies. You slink home, convinced that this is irrevocably the end; you will be forced just as irrevocably the next morning to fill a certain number of empty white sheets of paper, to serve the reader some surprise, entertain him, interest him, keep him and the magazine going. And there is Korff at the morning conference, crisp as ever, getting us, the staff, out of the doldrums, conjuring up new material, new ideas before our amazed eyes. Once more the wheels begin to turn, cartoonists are fed some witty subjects, photographers are dispatched, photos are sorted, come to life under Korff's glance and pointing finger. We, blind mice, learn to see, learn to absorb the human, the funny, the effective or the beautiful hidden in those photos. Our regular authors are called, wheedled, nudged into work, articles are discussed and ordered.

Korff never allowed "the paper" to fall into a routine, it had to be reborn week after week. We, The Ladies, were called in, received with great formality, and begged to consider the feminine point of view, assist him, a mere ignorant male, with our opinions. With sensitive tact he kept us, me and my charming, elegant colleague Anita, apart from the coarser grained ladies of the fashion department and their garment-industry jargon. There were another two Ladies responsible for the humor page, gags, jokes, puzzles, funny little ditties. These two were real ladies, unmarried, middle-aged, lachrymose. I have seldom seen them other than crying, complaining, desperate, possibly due to the well-known fact that in all the world and through all time there exist only seven basic jokes. It takes brigades of gagmen to supply new variations for any half-hour TV show, and a Bob Hope to deliver them, and I am sure they suffer the same desperation and breakdowns we had daily in our spinsterish humor corner.

Korff's humor, though, never flagged; a quiet, dry, sly kind of humor. Once Hermann Ullstein, not a very generous or broadminded man by nature, reproached Korff for having gone to the barber shop during office hours to have his hair cut.

"I grew it during office hours, so I get it cut during office hours," said Korff with finality.

His wife was French, very mondaine, attractive, elegant; it pleased Korff to refer to her in a worker's rough argot, The Wife, never by her name, Margot. He liked to entertain us with reports about The Wife's sadism, cruelty, frigidity of heart. They had no children but it was my impression, especially during his sickness and end in New York, that this was an exceptionally good marriage. Childless, they doted on Mingo, a most beautiful and unbearably spoiled white cat. Munkacsi's portrait of Mingo, white on white, has made photographic history. "Now I'm in trouble with The Wife," he said. "It's about that first prize Mingo got at the cat show while The Wife was away in the south of France."

"Oh, did Mingo get a prize? I didn't know you had him in a show."

"Frau Baum," he said with a certain strictness, "you are a mother, you have children. Would you have your children locked into a cage and put on exhibit for a whole week? No, you wouldn't. Okay, neither would I do it to Mingo."

"But the prize?"

"I gave it to him, I myself, and nobody is going to tell me he doesn't deserve it," Korff said proudly, producing a large bronze medal. During The Wife's absence he had had an exact copy made of the real trophy. The Wife, who before had always nagged him to exhibit Mingo, was happy. Mingo was happy. Korff was happy about the successful prank. The Wife displayed the medal to all her friends; naturally some of those friends, likewise cat lovers, brought her a special little magazine called *Pets* and pointed out that Mingo wasn't mentioned among the prize winners. The Wife cried; Korff promised to have a word with the pet magazine's editor. Soon The Wife received a letter with a faked letterhead and ditto signature in which said editor humbly apologized for the oversight; the letter was larded with high praise for Mingo and the promise to correct the mistake in the next issue. Now Korff was in for it. At this point, another Ullstein character entered into the plot. Herr Büttner, our chief typesetter, a bearded, gnomelike figure, his face blackened indelibly by lead and printer's ink. To him Korff trusted a piece of work worthy of a master counterfeiter: to lay out, cut, and manufacture an exact replica of that pet magazine, complete with masthead, index, and copy. Submerging himself into the spirit and style of *Pet's* editors and readers, Korff himself composed eight pages of text; it was a labor of love, and I think he was as proud of the finished product as he had ever been of the best issue of "the paper." Triumphantly he carried it home to show The Wife the correction on page 3: Mingo's first prize, name and picture, and, of course, Frau Margot's name as the owner of the beautiful white Angora. But, as Schiller stated so poetically, "the curse of an evil deed is that it must always engender more evil." The Wife was not satisfied with just this one copy of Korff's and Büttner's handiwork. She needed a lot of them to give to her friends. "Never mind," Frau Margot said, "I'll order them directly." There ensued a slight panic as Korff, in haste and trembling lest those precious eight pages were destroyed, rushed to the print shop at dawn of day; and so the Ullstein presses went to work printing five hundred copies of the forgery.

I could fill a book with anecdotes about Korff's twisted sense of humor, his knowledge of humanity, his enormous snobbism in all

matters of fashion and attire, the snobbism of the little boy who had
started way down and arrived to see himself a man of the world. His
blind admiration for certain actors and actresses. His sixth sense for
what fitted his magazine and what didn't. The conflicts in his character. He was a great gourmet, an *arbiter elegantiarum,* and yet a
puritan. Calloused, cynical, yet unbelievably naïve. I can never say
enough about all he taught me and did for me, that funny little man
with the Napoleonic bearing. Above all, he was a man possessed, a
man in my growing collection of such people.

On his twenty-fifth anniversary, if I remember correctly, Ullstein's
presented him with a beautiful villa and garden in Dahlem, an exclusive suburb of Berlin. "A villa in Dahlem, what does Korff want
with a villa in Dahlem?" he grumbled. "A goddamned garden to take
care of, and at five o'clock in the morning those goddamned birds are
singing at my window. And The Wife . . . you have no idea how
The Wife hates it. Afraid of burglars. Lonesome. Bored. You know
what would really make me happy? A furnished room right here in
the Kochstrasse. Where I could be in my office within three minutes
whenever I'd like it. Day or night."

"In one of those houses where all the whores sit at the windows? I
doubt it," I said. Korff's eyebrows went up in reproach.

"I really don't know what you are talking about, Frau Baum," he
said primly. A few weeks later he appeared at the office, beaming.
"Last night the burglar came at last," he announced. "I told you how
afraid The Wife was of burglars out there in Dahlem, didn't I? I
swore I would protect her with my fists, my life, if necessary." "You?
Don't be ridiculous," said The Wife. "A shrimp like you." "Well, last
night I showed her, and how! Oh, I was magnifiicent! There was this
burglar creeping through the hedge, with a gun in his hand. You
ought to have seen me! I jumped him, threw him down, trampled him;
I strangled him, I almost killed him. I pulled his gun from him and
he ran away, bleeding. The Wife, oh, she was simply overcome
with admiration and love. She just didn't know how strong I was.
Fifty marks was the fee I had agreed on with the boy, not too much
for such brilliant results. Nice kid, maybe you've seen him, one of
Sabri Mahir's young hopefuls. I broke one of his teeth by mis-

take, so I gave him a ten-mark bonus and I'll have to pay the dentist. But it was worth it," Korff said. He had a kind of O. Henry technique in saving the point for the end, and then more or less dropping it.

Sabri Mahir was another original who did great things for me and for many others. A former prize fighter known for his astuteness, he was a stocky, barrel-chested man near forty. Born in Turkey, the son of a well-to-do family, he showed the indelible imprint of a good background. As a young boy, he had run away from home and worked his way to Paris: he wanted to become an artist, a painter. When I knew him he was still painting, very dramatic and very awful pictures. I think he was communicating his passion for the well-built body to all his disciples at the training gym near Tauentzienstrasse. He had one ostentatious feather in his cap—he had trained the German heavyweight champion Franz Diener. There were, of course, some lesser stars among the young professionals he put mercilessly through their paces in that invigorating atmosphere of sweat and rubbing alcohol and leather, and its incongruous mixture of sadism and affectionate loyalties. I have never been to Stillman's, but I assume that Sabri's stable was smaller, more refined, if the word can be applied to a boxing ring. That place, the office and massage rooms upstairs, the gym in the basement, was distinctly Sabri Mahir. In the street, in a restaurant, at a première with his beautiful, soft-spoken blond wife, he was a gentleman; at work, in his gym, he was a roaring tiger, a slave-driver, a Simon Legree made of stone and iron.

As is usual, a few boxing fans, sportsmen, writers, actors handed themselves over to Sabri to be kept in shape. I don't know how the feminine element sneaked into those masculine realms, but in any case, only three or four of us were tough enough to go through with it (Marlene Dietrich was one).

The funny thing about Sabri was that he was incapable of distinguishing between the training of professionals and those who only wanted a good workout. He was relentless. Stamping, cursing, shouting, screaming his commands, he made you keep up his speed, he wouldn't let you off when you felt you had no more breath, no

feet, no arms, not an ounce of strength left. A heart attack would be
the next step. Roaring in four or five languages, a sort of circus
catch-as-catch-can lingo, you were told to take your junk and get out
and never show your face again—and maybe your junk would be
thrown into your face. At that moment, miraculously, you found the
strength to do another ten knee-bends or push-ups. What Sabri gave
me, and what I could well use in those years, at the verge of turning
forty, was the feeling of my own strength. Each workout was a bout
for me, reviving my old war cry "I can take it!" He was in my corner, giving out an almost tangible stream of energy to his warrior—
me, five-foot-three, one hundred and four pounds. I had never done
any sport; my teachers, both the Professors Zamara, hadn't even permitted me to carry as much as an umbrella for fear I'd ruin my hands.
Besides, I'm the most unsportive person possible. The idea of competition, of wanting to win, has been left out of my construction. But
win against myself?—ah, that is another matter. In Sabri's basement
I lived through a few failures and some glorious victories, such as
the time I matched Franz Diener's rope-skipping routine, a champion's test of speed, wind, and endurance. Sabri put one limitation
on women—no sparring in the ring, no black eyes, no bloody noses.
Punching the ball was okay, though, to develop a pretty mean
straight left, a quick one-two; a woman never knew when she might
have to defend herself, right?

The self-assurance he carefully planted into me, as if I'd have to
fight and be sure to win any day, and the habit of not giving in
under any circumstances, did me a heap of good in those years. Even
now, in my seventies, I occasionally detect traces of Sabri-instilled
endurance, and then I go through with digging another flower bed
or writing for another hour.

I sometimes wonder at the amount of work I could stand in those
years, but I couldn't have done it without my hour at Sabri's.

I got up early (in those days I never stopped to figure out how few
hours I had slept), discussed and organized my household with the
maid, and then, since we lived near Grunewald lakes, the whole family would drive out in spring or summer, after a light breakfast, for a
quick swim. In winter I, a poor but ambitious swimmer, would go to

an indoor swimming pool alone. Afterward, we—my husband and I —would deliver the boys near their school, although, for Heaven's sake, never directly in front of it: arriving in a car came under the disgraceful heading of conspicuous consumption. Then we drove downtown, where Hans dropped me off at my office, and went on to the opera house. At Ullstein's, a few hours of work, conferences, fun, stimulation. During my lunch hour I used to take a fast walk to Sabri's for a workout, and then, sweated clean, feeling like a boned chicken, rubbed and massaged, I would share with him a strictly supervised lunch. Back to my office for another four hours' work, and often more. Home by bus or car, some fun or play with the boys. Dinner, with much boys' talk if their father had a free evening, or with considerate quiet if he had to concentrate on an opera performance. As soon as the tail-coated master of the house was gone, the three of us talked or played some more and then the youngsters went to their bedroom while I soaked out the day's fatigue in a hot bath. Then followed what I called my second breakfast and my other day. I had a quiet three-by-three nook all to myself, and that's where and when I wrote my novels (one of them was *Grand Hotel,* but that's another story). Often, thank Heavens, friends would call me at midnight. "Time for you to stop working; what you need now is to go dancing; right?"

Right.

After a thirteen to fourteen hours' workday, dancing took the kinks out of my body, brain, and nerves. Some of my sire's genes rumbling in me, I guess.

Getting old means, among other things, giving up a succession of various pleasures, one after another. Nothing was harder to resign from than dancing, a sacrifice to an old woman's precarious dignity.

t all started with Aunt Minna in Lundenburg. Aunt Minna was the prettiest of Mama's sisters, a genuine platinum blonde, a tiny Dresden figure, a little pastel vignette. She married an assistant manager at the sugar mill in Lundenburg. Lundenburg, at the Moravian border, was the prototype of a small provincial town mentioned in jokes, like Podunk. Lundenburg was all sugar; the small town had crystallized around the huge plant. Except for the Moravian peasants who came to town on Sundays in their colorful *Bartered Bride* garb, everybody belonged to the hierarchy of the sugar plant. Aunt Minna and her husband, on their annual visit to Vienna, invited me urgently to come to Lundenburg and play a concert there. It seems that Uncle was something very important, like vice president of the Lundenburger Männergesangverein, the center and apex of "Sugartown's" social life. Aunt Minna, who had lost most of her frail prettiness in that provincial mass grave but whom I liked a lot, indicated that it would mean a great deal to Uncle's career if he could import me with my harp, show off his own prodigy niece to the priests and deities of sugar manufacture. I was still a schoolgirl but I had played solo in some students' concerts. Aunt and Uncle seemed to believe in my being famous and wished to bathe in the reflection of my glory. I did not have the heart to show them my contempt for the Lundenburger Männergesangverein; I didn't want to be a damned snob or risk a scene with my parents. Thus it happened, when I was thirteen years old, I spent my Easter vacation in Lundenburg, of all places.

Only when I arrived there did I realize what an overwhelmingly grand affair that concert was for the town. The only hairdresser began to pile up pompadours at 6:00 A.M. in order to get all the ladies coiffed by evening. The gentlemen's tail coats, grown tight since the weddings for which they had been made, came out of trunks and chests, and the whole town smelled of mothballs. The ladies, one and all, were going to wear their ubiquitous Good Black Silk. White gloves were cleaned, the fumes of benzine battling with naphthalene, brilliantine. Aunt Minna who, during her exile, had lost a front tooth, came running in excitedly, "What do you think, should I wear my tooth?" By God, she had a tooth, very white and shiny, to be screwed into what was left of the lost one. All this interested me enormously. During the three days of my visit I built for myself an image of the small town and its lives. It culminated in the figure of the little man who, in the concert, stepped out of the chorus for one moment to sing a tenor solo of eight bars, and then stepped back again.

He made a lasting impression on me, a mixture of the comic and the pathetic that ever since has been the essential in the characters of my imagination, humor and compassion, conceived by me for the first time when I was a thirteen-year-old brat. My little man was too thin for the perhaps borrowed frock coat; his voice was a small, thin, trembling treble, emerging from under an enormous Nietzsche mustache. Obviously this little tenor solo was the crowning point of his small Lundenburg life. He had a large Adam's apple, I saw the hollow between the two sinews running down his neck into his stiff white collar, the neck of a hungry little boy, with owlish eyes behind his bookkeeper's spectacles. And in his inadequate and frightened singing I thought I noticed some unbookkeeperish emotions, something that had wings and dreams and desires—well, I was only thirteen.

Back in Vienna I began to write this little man's life into a copybook. Like a greedy worm I dug myself through the layers of that life. He courted and married a Fräulein Sauerkatz, daughter of the grocery store Sauerkatz. She made a dutiful but nagging wife for him. Because he was so thin and coughed a lot, the family Sauerkatz, worried about his lungs, forced him to take out a large life insurance policy. From then on, he saved and scrimped and denied himself every little joy just to meet those high premiums. His wife nags, his father-in-law is a holy terror, I imagined, and wrote down little Kringelein's entire poor, shabby life, until it isn't his lungs that give out on him, not T.B., but a stomach cancer. He is operated on, gains maybe another year on the same treadmill of life. At last he goes to Berlin to see a real specialist, and there he gets his verdict: two, maybe three, more months to live. Enjoy them while you can.

And so Kringelein cashes in his life insurance policy and goes off alone to live his last days in the gayest and best hotel in the Big City.

Through the years, I dragged around with me the copybook with the beginning of Kringelein's small existence. Someday I'll finish it, I thought, or the *id* in every writer's mind whispered to me. I would forget it for years, then suddenly it would come back to me. But the daily harvest of photos and news in the Ullstein House swept other things my way. An out-of-town businessman, in Berlin for some negotiations, wrestled with a burglar who had tried to get into the hotel room where he, that respectable provincial businessman, and his wife were sleeping. He knocked the burglar out, or injured him somehow, I don't remember the details, and delivered a long-sought criminal to the police. Shortly before this I had been to a ballet featuring the fading Pavlova and her shabby small troupe of dancers. I came away with an infinitely melancholy impression, a half-empty house, an audience that, under the influence of Mary Wigman, had grown tired of ballet, and yet there was the luminous glow of a great, a born, dancer.

All this flowed together in my mind and the wooden puppets grew flesh, arteries, veins, nerves. I pulled them together in a hotel where their ways might cross. I wanted the hotel to be a symbol of life as such. I rubbed it in, let the doctor, a war-damaged wreck, point out this symbolism close to the verge of bad taste. I'm still waiting for just one reader with ears for the symbolism and the meaning of my story.

All right, I thought, let's try a little experiment. Let's take the most hackneyed figures and situations and put a light inside of each, illuminate them, make them transparent, as it were. Let's try to make human beings of them. I threw away all of Kringelein's existence in small town Lundenburg, cut him down to just those last splurging days. In the German original, the novel had an ironic, almost untranslatable subtitle: "A dime novel with undercurrents" is as near as I can come to it.

The ironic fact is that nobody noticed the irony; the book, the play, the moving picture, owed their success entirely to just those hackneyed elements I made fun of.

The novel was first published in the *Berliner Illustrirte*. I was paid a record fee for it and it was well received. I remember a letter I found on my desk one Monday morning. "Three days have passed already since Baron Gaigern died, and we still can't believe it. [Gaigern is the happy-go-lucky burglar in my story.] We, the undersigned, can't bear the loss of the dear, beautiful young man who has brought so much glamour and adventure into our humdrum life. Dear Miss Baum, we demand that you bring him back to life again in the next issue." There followed several suggestions by the good ladies as to how this miracle might be achieved, and about thirty signatures, a whole woman's club or society or knitting circle. Poor darlings, how hungrily they must dream themselves away from their unadventurous husbands if a handsome young heel of fiction had hit them with such impact. But, as the old charwoman said, "Life is okay, if it just wasn't so *daily*."

In due course the book was published, and sold well. Perhaps I ought to say here that from my very first volume to this day the publication of my books leaves me absolutely cold. To say that I am detached, disinterested, is a gross understatement. As I never, I swear, never, expect or hope for a success, I'm not disappointed if a book falls flat on its face. Serves the damn thing right, I think, because the finished product always falls far behind the vision I glimpsed at the glorious moment of conception. *Grand Hotel* was my tenth book, and not once had I gone through the spasms, conundrums, and feverish tensions in which, I am told, most authors spend the weeks before and after publication. Running up and down the streets to see if their book (*their* book) is well displayed in the stores. Sweating at autographing parties, literary luncheons, radio and TV interviews. Calling the publishers to inquire about sales. Scanning with palpitations the reviews, the best-seller lists, and suffering the torments of the damned if the little flare of publicity quickly dies down. About all this I don't care because I know with great clarity that nobody else cares, least of all the reading public. Maybe I am jaded, and was even then, in 1928. Maybe I am simply arrogant in my own amiable way.

If I am, my arrogance consists mainly of being critical of my own writing and knowing my place. Before the program "The Author Meets the Critics" moved on from radio to TV and acquired a sponsor, I found myself on that program after each new book. We had loads of fun together, the critics and I. I liked them and I believe they liked me. In contrast to many finer strung, highly sensitive authors, I am bound in a kind of impenetrable sharkskin. The pricks of a critic's pen just tickle me and make me laugh. I know so much better, and I told them, where and how badly I failed in the opus under discussion; it took the wind out of their sails. I am too arrogant inside to be touched by outer criticism or praise. When I've written potboilers I did so deliberately, to hone my tools, prove my skill, and, naturally, because I needed money. I've also written a few good books, too good to be out of print, not as good as I'd have wanted them, but in every case, fully as good as my storyteller's talent, zest, and technique allowed. That my timing went wrong, that my problems and backgrounds—Japan, China, East India—were often ahead of the popular trend, and that I'm dated by now is beside the point. I know what I'm worth: I am a first-rate second-rate author. I have no glowworm's illusions of immortality. I never had the conceit of thinking myself a first-rate first-rate writer, or that any of my books would survive me. As for that nebula called immortality—a word so childishly batted around in America—let's wait a minimum of five hundred years and see whose books are still being read.

But to go back to *Grand Hotel*. It was not a potboiler, although countless cheap imitations and adaptations gave it a bad name; nor what I call a really good book, partly because of my deliberate use of hackneyed characters and situations, and partly because it sags badly in parts while the plot (stories still had to have plots in the '20's) is pushed forward with too much trickery. But there are human beings in it—*Menschen* is the German word badly missing in English, and the original German title was *Menschen im Hotel*. If you would take the trouble to read the novel now I think you could feel with them, be sorry for them, funny as they are. The atmosphere is right, as in most of my books. It is readable. But one must remember that its background is the beginning of the Depression years, with the widening chasm between the haves and the have-nots.

One morning a certain Dr. Erdey appeared in my office, sent to me by the well-known theatrical publisher–agent George Marton. Both Marton and Erdey were Hungarians, nice, cultured, and slick gentlemen, and both subsequently became my friends, as far as friendship in business with Hungarians will go. Marton had the idea that a play could be made from *Grand Hotel*, and Erdey, Marton's sidekick, was to help and assist innocent me with the dramatization.

Well, I had spent the last fifteen years in and around the magic circle of the stage; I lived with the theater not only in my marriage, but all over. I never missed a new play or opera, I know all the in's and out's of productions, I chewed for many nights on the problems of my closest friends: stage directors, dramatists, stage designers, *et al.* With my children, I had built a little theater and improvised plays for it; after polishing and enlarging, these children's plays became a successful yearly Christmas feature at many leading theaters. If I knew one thing, it was the technique of writing for the stage. This was the reason that I cried havoc and refused outright to commit rape on my poor *Menschen.* "Why, you and Marton must be crazy," I told Erdey. "Too many characters, too many plots running side by side. It would take three hours just to introduce them. No, no, no, it's impossible. I won't even try."

"All right; if you won't, is it okay if we try it? Sketch down the first act and show it to you?" Erdey asked.

"I don't care if you break your teeth on this nut," I said sulkily. (Herr Büttner had asked me for a filler of eighteen lines and my collection of aphorisms and anecdotes, mostly apocryphal, were spread all over the place, waiting.)

For a few weeks Erdey gave out hopeful bulletins over the phone. As I had foreseen, there were problems, but he was getting them licked one by one. He was getting warm, warmer, hot. Soon he would have the first draft of the first act ready. And, Eureka! now he had it, it was grand, I would be delighted. He would show it to me tomorrow.

Erdey was in my office when I arrived. I read his first draft. It was terrible. It was worse than anything I had feared. It was absolutely and completely hopeless. "It's impossible," I told him, "but that's not your fault. The more characters you cut out the worse it gets, don't you see? I won't have goulash made of my novel. I told you there is no way of bringing in all these people, except . . . except. . . ." I said. I got up and went to the window. "Except if I open on a row of telephone booths and in each booth one of the characters is talking, so you know the core of his or her problem," I said in a trance. I could see the scene, I heard them talking.

"Who's crazy now, me or you?" Erdey cried. "Telephone booths! Who'll produce that? It's nonsense, it's absolutely impractical, you don't know the stage!" I'm afraid Erdey, weaned and reared on Hungarian and French salon comedies, belonged to the school that opens on a chambermaid and a feather duster. It is also not impossible that George Marton had ordered him to needle me into work by confronting me with his unacceptable trash. "Thanks for the work you've put in," I said, "but it won't do. I'll have to write the stuff myself."

It was easy and it went fast. *Menschen im Hotel* opened in the Theater am Nollendorfplatz; Gründgens, then one of Max Reinhardt's young hopefuls, directed it.

If I am cool about the reception given to my books, I am positively arctic when it comes to theatrical productions. I can't understand why this is so when I remember how stage-struck I was as a kid, or the agonies of stage fright I suffered when I played the harp in a concert. Perhaps I had moved too close to the theater, grown too analytical about it. I approached the opening night with singular peace of mind. I took my seat in the proscenium box and I remember looking at the full house and saying to my husband, "Isn't it ridiculous that my play depends on the tastes and moods of all these morons? Let's hope they all had a good dinner and no fight with their wives on the way, or we'll get a flop."

Gründgens came into the box, and the house lights went down. He was a fascinating actor but did not yet have much experience as a stage director, and he seemed tense and nervous enough for both of us. Not without reason. He had become so absorbed in rehearsing the second act that the third act was, to my knowledge, still unrehearsed and would be more or less an improvisation.

The curtain went up. The phone operator's voice on the dark stage: "Grand Hotel!" "Grand Hotel!" "Go ahead number five-oh-two. . . ." "This is the Grand Hotel." And there were my phone booths where one of my people after the other hastily spoke a few lines that contained the keynote to character and problem; their leitmotives meshed, their voices formed a counterpoint, the stage began to revolve; there was a flicking of signals, ringing of bells, and the stage was dark once more. It had taken no more than two minutes. An explosion of applause shook the house. I grabbed Gründgens' arm. "Oh, for God's sake, who gave the claque the wrong cue?" I whispered. Gründgens gave me his glittering, Mephisophelean grin. "There's no claque in this theater. They're applauding. That's the audience! Just listen to the racket! We've got them! We're on top of 'em!"

I've seen the play since in many places and in various kinds of production; this spontaneous applause after the first scene never fails to explode.

If I were writing an orderly autobiography, and if I weren't so singularly uninterested in success, I suppose this is where I should end my story. Previously, of course, I should have built it up to this triumphant climax, exposing all the earlier hardships, the thousand and one refusals, the wounds my ego sustained, yet the unflagging belief in my creative power; throw in some graphic descriptions of the cold sweat, the bellyache and retching every self-respecting dramatic author seems to undergo at opening nights. Well, I'm not built that way, and probably I have missed many of the usual thrills. It didn't even occur to me to sit up all night waiting for the early morning papers, or to drop in at Ullstein House and see what our own critics thought about the play. I went home and slept the untroubled sleep of the righteous.

I wish I could still sleep like that instead of turning around and around in my bed, like an old dog arranging his aching bones on the hearth rug.

One of my nicest colleagues at Ullstein's was an elephantine man with many chins to his ripe Burgundy face. He wrote a witty gossip column that he signed Sling. He was in love with the theater or, rather, with the actors, their jokes, their affairs, their secrets, vices, tragedies, and joys. He spent his nights at the actors' club and in the two restaurants frequented by the stage folk. He would sit there, smile and listen. His was the sweetest, shyest smile ever seen on an elephant. I remember him best for one of his main axioms: "Man needs either food or sleep. To have both is wasteful." As he seldom got more than three hours' sleep at night he stuffed himself with immoderate amounts of choice food—a gourmand and a gourmet. Only yesterday I happened to read that this is how the elephant lives: little sleep, but tons and tons of food. Sling's instinct was right.

The next morning Sling's beaming face was the first to inform me of the play's success. "Well, that's fine," I said, and went on with my editorial work. As successes go it was not sensational. The notices were friendly, with slightly patronizing overtones because, after all, I was another journalist, one of those highly overpaid Ullstein authors. The play ran for a while and petered out, as plays and love affairs will. The royalties were negligible but I didn't care. I'd had lots of fun during my sessions with Gründgens, and at the last rehearsals. One little episode in particular still makes me laugh whenever I remember it.

I had my first conference with Gründgens during a matinée of Schiller's *Räuber,* where he received me in his dressing room, in the monstrous Franz Moor's redheaded hideous make-up. Every so often a fattish young man put his face in the door, a shapeless face as if made of sponge or dough, and each time Gründgens hollered, "Get out!" muttering curses at that unbearable nuisance, a bad actor pestering God and the world for a part.

As I left the theater the fellow was waiting for me in the dusk outside the stage door. He had read my novel, it had simply bowled him over because there, that figure, that Baron Gaigern, why, that was simply himself. It was *his* part, *his* role, and if he would, by some dark and infernal machinations be deprived of it, he'd . . . he'd kill himself . . . he'd cause a scandal that would shake all of Berlin, all of Germany. Taken as a type he was complete: the mincing gait; the adolescent, squeezed voice ("a dumpling voice," it's called in Viennese opera jargon) emerging from the rosebud mouth of a fat man in his late thirties; the blond hair—a flagrant case of the unemployed and unemployable actor who mistakes being stage-struck for being talented.

I told him that I did not have the slightest influence on the casting (which was God's holy truth) and shook him off by jumping into a taxi. From then on this unpleasant pest pursued me relentlessly; daily I found his letters, senseless clippings, miserable photos on my desk; daily his flabby person appeared at my office, patrolled the corridor, stood guard at my door, broke in on me at the most inappropriate moments. When I told Gründgens of it he advised me to have him kicked off the Ullstein premises, by force if necessary. *Botenmeister* Appel took care of this gladly.

I was surprised when I dropped in on a rehearsal and discovered The Pest among a cluster of young actors watching the stage, probably students of the Reinhardt school and obviously admirers and hangers-on of Gründgens. "How did he get in?" I asked. Gründgens' shrug seemed faintly embarrassed. "It's the best one can do with a psychopath; if it makes him happy to watch me rehearse we'll have peace at last," he said.

And a few days later he informed me with a little snort: "I stuck Walter in among the extras, for the gambling scene." (I don't remember his name, but Walter will do.) "Nuts like him can get quite ugly, you know." The boys' cluster in the orchestra giggled and made bitchy remarks when Walter appeared among the walk-ons. "Pure blackmail," they muttered.

Walter kept on trampling on my nerves. He now demanded that I write some lines into his part—my God, he called it a *part!* He composed some lines, had them typed on yellow sheets, pushed them into my hands, read them to me, *furioso, molto vibrato,* displaying his dumpling-voice mannerisms.

I must say here that the gambling scene of my play is sheer melodrama, supportable only if it's acted and directed tactfully, in subdued colors, understatements, nuances. This, Gründgens and the actors had achieved. There are silences, and the laconic bidding of the poker players, elegant clients of the Grand Hotel. Little man Kringelein wins and wins—beginner's luck—he expands, he orders champagne, more champagne, he drinks, it's the first champagne in his life and he gets as high as a kite. Simultaneously his new friend, handsome, athletic, elegant Baron Gaigern, in desperate need for enough money to follow the prima ballerina with whom he has fallen in love, is losing his last penny. But although a cat burglar, he is too well brought up to show his momentary despair. Quietly he puts down his cards and goes to a console table, downstage left, to pour himself another drink and light a cigarette. A similar table stood downstage right, and there, to my amused surprise, I saw Walter, gyrating and writhing and shaking his fat butt within an inch of his life. "For God's sake, what's the matter with that nut?" I asked Gründgens. "Well, I had to give him some silent business to get me peace; it's much better than if we had given him a line. Stuck him tight, downstage, with his back to the audience, see? Couldn't risk showing his idiotic mug. Now the fool is acting out Gaigern's despair, I guess. Don't worry, we'll keep it so dark on his side he'll be practically invisible."

Well, well, I said to myself, what a forgotten little friendship and a little blackmail won't do. . . .

Came the opening, came the poker game, came the Big Scene of little Kringelein, the climax before the all-important second act curtain. Kringelein, more than half-drunk, euphoric, totters to his feet and, champagne glass in hand, he, the hopelessly moribund, toasts life. Melodramatic but made bearable by the groping, awkward words of his speech—and quite effective. Well acted, beautifully staged.

And what happened, just at the highest dramatic point, just before Kringelein is felled by a sudden attack of his cancer pains?

Walter had written for himself the line I had refused to give him. As lines go, it was a masterpiece. Suddenly, he precipitated himself to the footlights, pushing Kringelein out of his way, and there he stood, the center of it all, two hundred pounds of blubber, raising his glass toward the audience with a gesture learned in a third-rate drama school. And with his squashed, inadequate dumpling-voice he shouted his line: "Yah!!!"

Curtain.

And you ask me why I feel cool toward the theater? Gründgens was in a white heat of fury about the ruined second act while I laughed until the tears came. Lucky me; where would I have been if I had taken the stage seriously?

In one of the Ullstein cubicles there hovered a little man with the face, clothes, and behavior of the born stamp-licker and string saver. Herr Gronle represented, rather inappropriately, the foreign department of the mighty Verlag Ullstein. I was not surprised to learn that he was one of the first to join the Nazis.

Herr Gronle, then, sold the foreign rights of such Ullstein authors as were in demand outside of Germany. I happened to be one of them, that is to say, my novels appeared regularly in the Scandinavian countries, Holland, and all over the Continent. But *Grand Hotel* was the first of my books to be translated into English. Herr Gronle, who had no concept of the prices paid for novels outside bankrupt Germany and got dizzy at the sight of a British pound sign, made a rather miserable contract for my book, of which Ullstein's received one-third. The procedure of such sales was very simple: Herr Gronle would come into my office, shove a paper under my preoccupied nose, put a short finger on a dotted line, and say: "Sign here, please."

I never read contracts and it wouldn't help if I did because I don't understand a word in them. My impression was always that lawyers invented legalese for the particular purpose of confounding their clients and/or opponents. Moreover, I learned by experience that with decent people you don't need a contract, and that others will always find a way to do you in. I'm stating this without rancor; I accept it as a part of nature like rain, wind, and heat waves.

The novel was a great success in England, for which I have to thank mainly the masterly translation by Basil Creighton. Whenever I happened to visit England though, Creighton went underground. Incommunicado. It took me years to find out why: he could not speak a word of German, only read and translate it. I understood this only too well as I suffer the same handicap in French. I read it with the greatest possible enjoyment and catch every nuance, but I am paralyzed when I have to tell my Paris taxi driver where to take me. Only years later, after I had learned English, did I succeed in meeting Creighton and thanking him in person for what he had done for me. My English publisher sold *Grand Hotel* to my American publisher, Nelson Doubleday, who pushed it hard and made it a best seller in the United States. These things happened more or less without my knowing or caring. In the meantime, George Marton had seen the play and introduced his New York representative to me, an unobtrusive, chunky, very short, blue-eyed, sandy-haired, and deadly serious chap, the absolute opposite of the typical Hungarian. Dr. Edmond Pauker was multilingual which means he spoke a number of languages, making all of them sound Hungarian. He thought he could place my play on Broadway, and promptly another contract was shoved under my nose. Once more I sold my life away, or so, to my chagrin, I found out later. At the time, the entire matter seemed so nebulous that I forgot it completely.

I was on a trip in Russia and was tramping up and down in the thin snow of a small, lost station platform to shake the stiffness out of my legs, when my name was called out and a cable handed to me. It had come from New York to Berlin, and my husband had relayed it to me. "Grand Hotel greatest Broadway success in thirty years. Congratulations." It was signed with the name of the dearest friend of my early years of whom I had lost sight when she emigrated to America. Steffi Goldner, who later married the conductor Eugene Ormandy and eventually divorced him, had been my pupil when she was a little girl and I still a teen-ager. Her wise, warm, humorous, and altogether wonderful mother had a most felicitous influence on me during the toughest years of my youth and, I'm happy to say, Steffi is still one of my dearest friends. Their home, full of fun and laughter, was a lifesaving oasis for me. In fact, I was so pleased to hear from the Goldners, in the middle of Russia of all places, that the contents of the cable made no dent at all. Broadway, to me, as to most Europeans, was a street where gangsters shot at each other. Okay, I said to myself, success on Broadway, so what? crumpled the cable, threw it away into the snow, and crept back into my car. It simply didn't occur to me to think of the matter in terms of money.

This indifference must seem quite stupid to today's security-hunting young people. But I had gone through periods of almost unimaginable poverty and need and discovered that it could touch no more than your epidermis; it did not hit me, the essence of myself, it had not even greatly changed our way of living. Our table was always nicely set even if there was nothing to eat, and I always had flowers around even if they were only a few dandelions or an evergreen branch swiped in the park. I painted our walls in colors that pleased me, lemon yellow or lobster red for stimulation, a soft dark blue for restfulness. And if you had a long shelf full of books and scores, any old cave would be a fine home.

Of course, since I had children I, too, wished for security; that's an innate biological urge in every mother animal. Only I didn't believe that such a thing as security, outside of oneself, really existed, least of all a security based on money and possessions. Yet, just as a doubter and unbeliever is advised to go to church often and pray assiduously and faith will come to him, so was I, compulsively, superstitiously setting aside every penny I had earned in book royalties. As if a bank account could bring us security; as if I didn't know better. Already the ground was trembling under our feet once more. After war, blockade, famine, revolution, flu epidemic, inflation, and a second famine, the next thunderheads were coming up over the horizon. A worldwide depression, worse in impoverished Germany than elsewhere. Unemployment. Hunger parades, street fights, riots, bitter demonstrations, the old German ghosts of fratricidal hatred.

We had become fatalistic; there was nothing the individual—I—could do about it but preach peace and common sense, hope for the best and, in the meantime, enjoy the good years. We never had better ones. We were content in our jobs, both of us, and our joint salaries afforded us all the comforts we might have wanted. We had a car that, by the way, declared itself my enemy from the first drive; we had a maid, and temporarily even two. The boys went to our very good public schools and did exceptionally well. Most of my friends from Hanover had been transferred to Berlin, and with them and my stimulating new Ullstein-bred friends, my cup was running over. After the meager years, my husband and I were at last well-dressed. We could afford nice family vacations and I was given time off for some traveling besides. Indeed, at forty, I had my second bloom, sort of. Berlin made me a smart, sophisticated woman of the world. You may say, under such pleasant conditions it's easy not to worry about money, which is true, except that, as a rule, the more money people have the more they want and the more they worry about it. Amassing property, what moneyed people call a fortune, demands a peculiar talent and obsequious concentration. In this the money-makers are like actors, artists—they overrate its importance; and they overrate the importance of losing some of it to such a ridiculous extent that they become victims of a millionaire's depression complex, an epidemic of suicidal jumps from the men's rooms of clubs and banks.

Poor blind beggars, didn't they trust themselves to be strong enough to face the world with maybe just some measly $300,000 left in the safe? Was a crash on the stock exchange really "The greatest catastrophe in all the world's history," as I read not so long ago in an article by a very learned sociologist in a very select magazine? Don't they ever learn that booms are followed by crashes and depressions in an ever-repeated cycle?

As for myself, I was not afraid of whatever might be in store for us—stupid perhaps in view of what happened a few years later—but I adhered to my self-imposed taboo of never touching my savings. We used up and fully enjoyed what we earned in our daily jobs, and faithfully salted away what they paid me for the pleasure of telling my stories on paper. We had a neat four-digit savings account, and when we emigrated to America we were magnanimously allowed to take along fifty German marks of it. The rest went into Hitler's till. That's why I smirk a bit when I hear our youngsters clamoring for "security."

After the friendly reception given *Grand Hotel* I wrote a slight little comedy poking a bit of fun at the new fad of cosmetics imported from the United States via Elizabeth Arden. Gründgens was the director, and there was very good acting in it, Darvas, Wohlbrück, among others. It was mildly successful, but just mildly. Dr. Pauker popped up once more, fresh off the boat, and couldn't tell me enough about the difficulty he had encountered in trying to find a producer for *Grand Hotel,* and what a proud triumph it was for him to have given Broadway such a hit.

"I wish you would come to New York and see the production. You really must not miss such a thrill. The whole town will be at your feet. Please, say the word, and I'll try to arrange something," he wheedled.

"Yes, I probably will," I said. I had got into the habit of taking one journey each year, and I had vaguely considered that after last year's visit to Russia it would be a good idea to see something of America this year. Dr. Pauker seemed overjoyed. "You would? Really? If you mean it, I'll arrange something. How would you like to write the movie script? What? You never worked for the movies? Never mind, it doesn't matter. Now that the talkies are coming in, nobody knows how to write for them. I'll fix up something. I'll write you. You'll hear from me."

With me, things of this sort go in one ear and out the other. Unfamiliar as I was with the power of the American woman and with the mechanics of the absolute commercialism of the American stage, meaning Broadway stage, I was amused by the strange ballad of little Dr. Pauker's jumping all hurdles and winning on a dark horse, but could neither imagine nor believe the things he had told me.

He had submitted, offered, peddled *Grand Hotel* to every one of the Broadway producers; every one of them rejected it. I could well understand their reasons. The kaleidoscopic construction was unfamiliar, the small, shallow Broadway stages were geared to the primitive demands of sedate little variations on the love triangle, my name was an unknown quantity in spite of my best-selling novel, and no backer wanted to lose money on such a hare-brained experiment.

But at last Dr. Pauker found an angel in the somewhat unprepossessing person of a frumpy middle-aged Chicago clubwoman. Mrs. Moses, bless her memory, was a short, stocky lady, not pretty, but bright and ambitious. Her husband, Mr. Moses, was a well-to-do manufacturer of men's underwear. Like a majority of American husbands, he was proud of his wife's superiority in matters of education, taste, and what is loosely called culture. She had acted in amateur performances of some drama clubs; she had tasted blood and was thirsty for more. She had read my novel and, through some channels, acquired a rough translation of my play. When the happily married Moseses' silver wedding anniversary drew near and Mr. Moses got ready to surprise his lady with several more large-carat diamonds or emeralds to add to the many she already had, she stopped him from spending money on such impersonal baubles. "If you really love me," she told him, "you'll fulfil the only wish I have: back a production of *Grand Hotel,* with me in the role of the prima ballerina. It fits me like my own skin, it's written for me and no one else. It's what I've been waiting for all my life."

On such whims and accidents depends success in the theater. I suppose the good lady had been hypnotized by the word "aging" in the novel and had never observed her face and figure in profile; never considered that a ballerina's aging, like a prize fighter's, begins when she is still in her twenties. Anyway, a truly outstanding director was found in Hermann Shumlin; he assembled a cast of almost unknown actors and the rehearsals got under way.

And here I take my hat off to Mrs. Moses' integrity and, indeed, superior intelligence. When she saw what the play needed, what Shumlin wanted, what amazing performances he hammered out of that young ensemble, she stepped back and gave way to an actress

really and truly born for the part of Grusinskaya. Eugenie Leontovich was Russian (White Russian they were still called in 1930,
and New York City, like any other metropolis, was full of them).
She had been a ballerina and to move like one was second nature to
her; she had been a well-known actress in Russia, she looked,
laughed, cried, felt like the Grusinskaya of my vision. When I
came to New York and saw Leontovich as Grusinskaya it took my
breath away, it almost frightened me, so much did she resemble the
image I had carried inside of me.

I never found an actor to look or act like my idea of the cat
burglar and lover, Baron Gaigern, which convinced me that it was
an ill-conceived, badly written figure, *Kitsch,* as the Germans say. It
never does any good if an author falls in love with one of his characters. . . .

Whatever its merits, *Grand Hotel* was next made into a moving
picture, a monumental birthday cake with twenty-five eggs instead of ten, with a gaggle of great stars fighting tooth and nail for
every line. I mean, with two Barrymores in it, you had to count
the words so that John wouldn't get one more line than Lionel. I
don't know how the balance between young Joan Crawford's dynamic ambition and Garbo's queenly reign was achieved. Anyway,
it was such a success that it completely overshadowed my novel so
that ever after I was known primarily as the writer of that nice old
movie. Not an honor I ardently pursued or enjoyed.

Of the triumphant first night of that picture I remember distinctly only the mighty rumps of two horses in front of and high
above me. The horses belonged to the mounted police that kept the
curious crowd in Times Square behind ropes and made a lane
for me and my escort, Noel Coward. Once in a while one or the
other horse dropped a steaming little cascade of dung onto the
pavement; with my silver shoes and long silver lamé gown and my silver lamé train I tried my best to step across the slippery hills of
horse manure. "Nice symbolism," I muttered to Noel Coward and
both of us, successful authors, grinned understandingly at each
other.

And suddenly, in the middle of Times Square and the hollering crowds and the shrill glare of the searchlights and the entire hurly-burly of a big opening and the horses' generous rumps, I was back in my childhood, in my village, I was sitting on the box of the ca-lash, next to Binder Franzl. Because horse manure has the same rustic, strong, pleasant smell the world over.

And so my *Grand Hotel* brought me to the United States in 1931, long before the great exodus, the wholesale torturing and dying had begun in Germany; for this I'm infinitely grateful. Otherwise, by and by I grew unspeakably tired of the successful opus, but like the sorcerer's apprentice, I couldn't stop the thing from propagating and reproducing itself. What I had conceived as a symbol of the brief stopover we call life—the innate loneliness behind all those doors, the ephemeral encounters, the brushing past each other, the inescapable meeting and parting—all quickly became a mechanical toy, a formula to be bought and sold on the market. Still, thirty years later, I'm branded, I'm made responsible for this unwanted and uninvited progeny. It makes me feel like the innocent and rather nice grandmother of dozens of misfits, delinquents, heels, bums, and tramps whenever I read in a contemptuous review of some rather contemptible piece of writing that it is "another *Grand Hotel*."

No wonder my blood pressure rises every time I am supposed to answer, by now for the thousandth time, the ever-recurring inane questions: "Miss Baum, how would I go about writing? Something like *Grand Hotel*, you know what I mean? A best seller?" And: "Which hotel did you have in mind when you wrote it? . . . But you *must* have, how could you describe a hotel if you hadn't known it?" And: "How long did it take you to write it?" (with a tactfully unspoken but clearly visible appendix: "And how many millions did you make from it?")

Well, my darlings, if I had a recipe for writing best sellers I definitely shouldn't use it, especially not if I were young and ambi-tious. I shouldn't dream of studying a hotel, let alone a certain hotel. When I visited London for the first time, as the guest of the P.E.N. Club, I found myself embroiled in one of the hottest cases of bitching between various literary coteries, as they seem to flourish there. Arnold Bennett had done some exceedingly arduous and detailed research about every department of the Savoy and written the novel *Hotel Imperial*. It so happened that his book and mine were published almost simultaneously and that *Grand Hotel,* with its impressionistic unstudied background and expressionistic technique, sloppily and quickly written as it was, took the feeble wind out of Bennett's sails. It seems he took it rather hard that the book of an unknown whippersnapper, and of a German to boot, was preferred by a good part of the critics and readers. I felt sincerely sorry about this because I had great respect for Bennett's *The Old Wives' Tale*. But it's inevitable that the most painstaking research can't replace the pleasurable free play of fantasy, and that old writers are overtaken by younger ones. Be it so, no reason to feel hurt: what I may have to tell yet is also an old wives' tale and nothing else. . . .

I am a slow thinker but a fast writer. The time of gestation for *Grand Hotel* was about twenty-five years; I wrote it within six chock-full weeks. I spent years of my life, though, to live it down. I was, and remained, "the girl who wrote *Grand Hotel.*" It made me feel like a cat with a tin can tied to its tail.

A few years ago I made a desperate effort to get rid of this clattering, empty tin can, to get away from myself or, as Madison Avenue would have it, my public image. I wrote a book considerably different from most of my others; I dug myself deep into certain problems of the American Way of Life: the prevalent neuroses and neurotics it seems to breed in the homosexual, the drug addict; alcoholism, incest, hysterical epilepsy, and simple, pampered, self-centered phobias and compulsions. It was long-drawn-out and rather heartbreaking work, but I still think it is one of my best books. I went so far as to leave my good and faithful publisher, Doubleday, because some of my friends, their editors, might have still recognized me behind the psychological mask. I asked my agent at that time, a fairly circuitous person, if he would play ball with me if I wished to perpetrate a little hoax, and I saw a responsive and amused gleam in his eyes. I went to Europe that spring of 1949 and wrote him that I had met a young writer, a Scotsman living in a remote village in the Alps, a passionate mountaineer, a recluse, and, to my mind, not without talent. Could I send him this Thomas Laird's manuscript? And would he agree to carry on any subsequent correspondence via myself as said Laird was constantly on the go? This my agent did faithfully; there was never another word between us to indicate what I was up to. As frequently happens, I was a bit ahead of the then current fashion in fiction; it was the time for war novels and four-letter words; the study of mental sickness and various aberrations arrived a little later and only now has incest become a salable commodity. But my agent succeeded in placing my book with a fine publisher, Dial Press.

I had beaten the game. I had flung out a challenge at myself and come out on top. I had thrown away all the advantages of having a name, of being somebody (at a sneak preview of a friend's movie I was surrounded by kids clamoring for my autograph. "Okay, but who am I?" I had asked laughingly. "I don't know," answered one of the boys, "but you sure are Somebody."), of having loyal publishers who would print and sell anything I wrote; in short, once more I had thrown security to the wind, taken a chance and started from scratch. I had gotten rid of the old tattoo, "The girl who wrote *Grand Hotel*"; I had put myself through rebirth and transformation.

There was a polite long-distance call: would I permit my agent, now that everything was settled, to tell my new publisher in all confidence who Thomas Laird was? It would be such a thrill for him and his editors to find their judgment confirmed.

"Well, if you think so, why not?" I stuttered. I still consider the telephone my personal enemy and a monstrous contraption and, naturally, I'm not at my best in long-distance conversations.

I had called my novel *A Little Lower Than the Angels* (that's how the Bible says the Lord created mankind), but when it was published it had been renamed a colorless *The Mustard Seed*.

Guess what the front of the jacket said? "A New Novel by VICKI BAUM, Author of GRAND HOTEL."

n 1931 I was invited to come to America for two weeks. Thirty years have gone by and I'm still here.

I arrived in New York at six o'clock in the morning, an impossible hour for everyone, and in a thick fog filled with the howling of foghorns. The moment I set foot ashore I stepped into a muddle. There were three different parties awaiting me. My husband's brother, Dr. Ernst Lert, one of the Met's stage directors, and his wife. I had deliberately not informed them of my arrival, not wishing to inconvenience them; indeed, I saw Ernst gnashing his teeth and tensing the muscles in his cheeks when I was first greeted by deputy No. 2, Dr. Edmond Pauker and his sidekick, Shumlin. But the real difficulties started when a gentleman approached me, hat in hand, and introduced himself as my publisher, Nelson Doubleday.

I find it easy to remember, over the years, how his appearance astonished me. He seemed the almost too glorified replica of the Americans I had seen, but not believed, in the illustrations and advertisements of the American women's magazines that it was my job to scan at Ullstein's. A tan, smiling, well-proportioned face the color of Indian peaches; shiny, smooth dark hair with just the right amount of silvering at the temples. Slender, with the loose movements of the trained sportsman and the equally loose, carefree elegance Bond Street clothes assume on American gentlemen. I don't know if he was actually six feet eight inches tall as he claimed, but, although he had a polite habit of leaning forward and down when he spoke, there was still a formidable distance between my level and his. I stood and gaped. All the English I had hurriedly acquired in six weeks of Berlitz School lessons vanished. Three of these weeks had been spent in the Berlitz Method's ironbound efforts to teach the beginner the difference between "on" and "at." "The teacher sits *at* the table. The teacher puts the pencil *on* the table. Where does the teacher sit? *At!* Miss Baum, *at* the table, not *on*, never *on!*" Hard work for me; even in German the Viennese can't understand the difference between *am* and *auf dem*. And, even if I could have remembered, what good would it do me to inform Mr. Doubleday where the teacher puts the pencil?

At this painful moment another person stepped forward, not a beautiful American from the ads, just a person. Although he, too, was tall and slender, he looked rather unremarkable compared with this publisher of mine. "I brought my interpreter along; he speaks German," said Mr. Doubleday.

"Oh, good! *Sie sprechen deutsch?*"

"*Mittelmässig,*" said the interpreter, which convinced me that he spoke it very well indeed. He had unkempt red hair, a bad skin, and bloodshot eyes, but there was such a remarkable brightness and friendliness in his expression that I followed him trustingly to the customs shed. "Please, will you explain to them that the large bottle contains only my eau de cologne—I'm so used to this one, you know, I hope they'll let it pass, it's eau de cologne, not alcohol," I prattled. In Germany we had heard so much about Prohibition that this bottle had worried me during the entire crossing. It was a large bottle, designed to last the two weeks I was to spend in New York.

My interpreter slid me through the customs inspection like oiled lightning. I didn't even have to open my luggage. Aha, I said to myself, he bribed them. American corruption. This, too, I had from hearsay.

Emerging from the customs shed I was confronted with somber and angry faces and one of the sudden feuds that easily flare up between Europeans. My husband's relatives (I hardly knew them) took it for granted that I was to stay with them, sleep on the living-room sofa, no trouble at all, really. Dr. Pauker had taken a little suite for me at the St. Moritz, where all visiting Hungarians stopped;

he had even successfully haggled with the manager for special rates. Mr. Doubleday had made reservations for me, as his guest of course, at the more expensive and exclusive Pierre. At last my interpreter smoothed things over with great wisdom; I felt like Solomon's baby, with the exception that I would be cut not in two but into three parts.

I was to stay at the St. Moritz—after all, it was Dr. Pauker who had arranged a five-thousand-dollar sale to Paramount just to bring me to New York for two weeks. I was to have lunch with my in-laws at Rumpelmayers. And Mr. Doubleday would take me there in his car. To my great relief the interpreter came along and the two men had a friendly conversation of which I understood only two words: My Bootlegger. An unfamiliar strong, almost tangible odor hung in that car, an American odor that was soon to become quite familiar to me. American gasoline? I wondered. No, whisky.

As we drove uptown the fog thinned away and suddenly a fantastic shaft shot up high in the sky, peeled off its ragged white swaddling and towered above the roofs and skyscrapers of New York, about which I had read and which I had seen in countless photos without believing them to be true. My interpreter grabbed my arm and shook me. "Look, Vicki, look! The Empire State Building! Say you like it, please say you do!" he called out in English. Suddenly something opened up in my benumbed skull. I understood English, suddenly I could even speak it.

"I like it, oh, I love it!" I stammered. "It is not credible, *wunderbar!*" At which the redheaded person took me into his long arms, enfolded me in his whisky breath, and covered me with kisses.

When he let go, I was baffled, but laughing. Look here, I told myself, this is America. Here you get kissed by the hired help, an interpreter. That's democracy, see? It's nice, I like it. Nelson Doubleday was shaking with laughter: "Vicki, may I introduce my friend Red to you? You may have heard of him: Sinclair Lewis."

"I wanted to be the first to greet you and show you New York," Sinclair Lewis said. "And a more miserable night no two men ever had," Doubleday added. Afraid they would miss the *Statendam*— those cursed Dutch boats arrived at such ghastly hours—they waited out the night in Hoboken, drinking.

This explained the alcoholic fumes, but it would be years before

I learned to recognize when men who handled their drinks like gentlemen were high as kites; stinking, as slang has it. The ladies, I found out, were not so good at it. They grew visibly foolish, aggressive, and amorous, and as they were a pretty shrill kind of bird to begin with I felt sorry and embarrassed for them. I had never seen a drunken woman until I came to America.

I was deeply touched by this kindly gesture of Red Lewis'. It was my first sample of the easy, inexhaustible generosity and friendliness that is at the core of the American character; so unused are foreigners to this at first that it stuns them, like a blow over the head. I believe that much of the anti-American feeling at large in the world derives from the inability of other nations to understand and accept with ease what is offered so naturally and easily. Instead of gratitude—which isn't expected and would only embarrass the friendly giver—he reaps distrust, malice, at worst, hatred. Of course, how could people without close acquaintance with America synchronize the innate goodness of the average American with the simultaneous rampant ugliness that is gleefully served up in daily doses by the press?

As for me, I plunged into the warmth of this first welcome, with Sinclair Lewis' arm around my shoulder and Nelson Doubleday on the other side holding my hand, both chatting away, laughing about me, my misfiring English, and the success of their little joke. I, in the meantime, gulped up the astonishing spectacle of New York with greedy eyes, nostrils, pores of my skin, and drumming heart. I have known cities with much more beauty and less ugliness, but none whose uniqueness overwhelms the newcomer with such force. Of course, New York has changed enormously in those thirty years since my first arrival, but its character remains the same: it grows out of its narrow island between two rivers like a druse of needle-sharp crystals. An organism not planned, not laid out, but hardened into the shapes of its own hidden laws. That first day was sunny and cold, early April; since then, I have seen the town steaming in tropical summer heat, or buried in deep white snow, white for a few hours only. I have spent many early mornings on my balcony, loath to miss the colors as the sun burned off the fog—gray, green, heather, buttercup yellow. And again, in late afternoon, I would watch those slablike walls become transparent and the windows burn in orange and coral fires in the glow of the sun sinking beyond the cobalt blue of the Palisades. I have eaten up, swallowed, and made it my own, this New York, and there has never been a day when I didn't love it.

And so we arrived in front of the St. Moritz Hotel on Central Park South. Having taken my first scent of Nelson Doubleday, I saw him faintly shrink, hesitate, escort me to the revolving door but not enter. To him, the patrician, the Mediterranean clientele milling around the small lobby of this somewhat European hotel was not quite up to snuff. You find these unconscious traces, and frequently more than just traces, in most Americans of Anglo-Saxon descent. I remember how bewildered I was when I, reared on the European worship of classic Greece, learned that Greeks in this country were considered an inferior race.

With the help of a nice, hand-kissing Viennese manager and a motley many-lingual flock of what in Europe would have been young pages but here were middle-aged Italian, Hungarian, German, Polish, and Levantine bellhops, I was installed in my two rooms, overlooking the park, as the advertisements promised. Such an end-less expanse of green was the last thing I had expected in the midst of New York. There is a cliché, especially in European books, that labels the New York streets as "canyons," *Dunkle Schluchten*, the German writers called them, with a depressing mouthful of black *U*'s and thick consonants. I guess they thought that Wall Street was New York. Uptown the streets were wider than any I knew, filled to the bottom with air and sunlight. Only on my last visit to New York did I notice that the skyscrapers growing higher and higher leave one side of the avenues in the shade all day long. But down there on my arrival I saw the sharp first green of spring, the first forsythia stretching its yellow twigs across some narrow trails; there was a lake, and varicolored boats, shaped like swans, swayed directly below my windows.

My first impression when I entered Rumpelmayers downstairs was of being caught in the parrots' aviary at the Schönbrunn Zoo. For this was the exclusive roosting place of women, or rather, ladies (if to have money and time to squander it makes women into ladies). Shrill, loud parrot voices and parrot colors all around me. Still, after thirty years, I am amazed at the decibels a roomful of American girls can produce. My first encounter with this noise was shattering. I don't know why the American in general can't conceive of having fun without being loud, except when fishing or hunting, I suppose. Why do the girls think that shrieks, giggles, and peals of laughter stand for being as young and gay as they were during recess in their school's play yard? Do they have to drown out so much trouble, anger, and disillusion? When Maxim Gorky visited Coney Island he asked: "Are the people so unhappy that they need so much fun?"

I felt like a most bewildered blackbird among all these wildly made-up ladies in their silk prints and costume jewelry. I myself wore the well-dressed European woman's uniform. A black suit, designed by the best Berlin tailor. A blouse of the finest white silk, hand-sewn, and a bit of old lace at the collar. A little Parisian hat the fashion editor would have called saucy. White kid gloves. Large, real pearl earrings. Black patent oxfords with two-inch heels. In Europe only strumpets wore high heels on the street. (In Berlin, on the Tauentzienstrasse, some also displayed a certain kind of Cossack's boots, for the fancy trade.)

In the afternoon, with Dr. Pauker's help, I stumbled through a press reception. Later, in the catty society columns of the evening papers, I read that I was the typical German housewife, drab, with big feet in clumsy oxfords.

To write about a country, you have to know it either one week or many years. The first impression of an immensely rich, incomparably friendly, very naïve, not to say provincial, town, boiling with vitality and the intangible quality they call freedom, etched itself so sharply into my memory that the slow unveiling of the following thirty years seems pale in comparison. I fell in love with New York at first sight, a euphoric condition inviting all kinds of foolishness. Not acquainted with the taboos and the ironbound conventionality that pervade American life, not knowing the language, my first week was an uninterrupted chain of *faux pas*. I just seemed to have my big feet in my mouth all the time.

Everyone took it for granted that I was panting with impatience to see my play the very first evening. But, like a moron, I had accepted a cabled invitation to be the P.E.N. Club's guest of honor and make a speech that night. Now the European P.E.N. Clubs are not the pleasant cocktail-soaked social gatherings they are here. They take their position and obligation—ethical, literary, and political— very seriously; to be their guest of honor, as I had been in a few cities over there, was a solemn distinction not much below receiving the Nobel Prize. Consequently, I had proudly accepted and, in fact, spoiled any fun I might have had during the crossing by laboriously working on my speech. I wrote it in German and an amiable Dutchman, being at home in four or five languages, put it into fine English for me; the finished product I painfully learned by heart.

By six o'clock that first afternoon I had succeeded in making a poor impression on the reporters, in hurting my in-laws' feelings, getting Shumlin and Paramount very irritated, and Dr. Pauker plain mad. Soaking out the first day's piled-up tensions in a hot bath, I went over my speech once more and then put on my dignified lecturer's garb. Black, of course. Real Chantilly lace, long sleeves, high neck, and the inevitable good pearls and virginal white kid gloves.

The theme of my speech was: "Compassion and humor—the moving forces in literature." It took fifty minutes to deliver it.

Beyond question, Americans are the most good-natured and polite audiences in the whole world. They let me pour forth my ponderous interminable theories in my murderous pronunciation, suffered through it with saintly smiles, and if they fell asleep they did it discreetly. As a matter of good taste, I carefully refrained from saying a word about myself; I had no idea that the personal touch, the anecdote, the wisecrack is almost the only thing that counts. As a rule, I'm not a bad speaker, I never had trouble getting through to an audience before, but here I felt with every nerve that things went wrong. I praised the American writers I had read in German translations and greatly admired—Dreiser, Sinclair Lewis, Dos Passos, Hemingway—but I sensed that this went against the grain of the elderly ladies who formed the main contingent. No wonder they applauded when the ordeal came to an end. The chairman got up and thanked me in a few words for the message I had given them. I didn't know that this is a standard receipt handed to authors. I didn't know what was meant by message; I looked it up in my dictionary and still didn't get it. I thought it was a Biblical word that belonged to the pulpit. Used elsewhere, I still dislike the sonority of it. I don't care for books that set out deliberately to give a "message" and I don't like readers who search for a "message" in every run-of-the-mill popular novel.

There were two more guests of honor at that dismal party. Red Lewis, who popped up and gave his famous parody of a Southern candidate for the Senate; and Marc Connelly who told Negro jokes that I, naturally, didn't understand. So that's how it's done over here, I told myself, and kept blundering on through my first week. At a big formal luncheon given in my honor I refused to say a single word, not even "Thank you." I wasn't going to make speeches, oh, no, not me! I addressed Edna Ferber as Miss Hurst; I'm not sure she has forgiven me to this day. Invited by a women's club and asked how one writes a successful play, I threw quotations from Goethe at them—"Real theater is what you can play with puppets for an audience of children"—I don't think they recognized the name in the German pronunciation. There appeared a garbled report in the papers that "Miss Baum, avoiding a straight answer, told about some famous German author who was playing with dolls." I received a handwritten letter from *the* Mrs. Vanderbilt, the then reigning dowager queen of society, inviting me to be her guest at some huge charity affair. Incapable of piecing together an English letter of thanks, and ignorant of Mrs. Vanderbilt's royal status, I told my secretary to call up the lady and accept for me. In the meantime, another lady called me up and asked me whether I was interested in social activities. Social, to me, meant taking care of neglected children, paroled convicts, and the hungry families of the unemployed. My answer was, of course, an eager, "Oh, yes indeed!" Thereafter an overdressed lady of killing gentility appeared and offered to get me invitations to some of the leading lionesses of New York society, in exchange for a small fee, fifty to a hundred dollars per invitation. I thanked her in mild panic.

By that time, however, I had spent my first weekend among the Upper Four Hundred and had not quite recovered from it.

Somehow I had imagined that my weekend at Nelson Doubleday's place in Oyster Bay would be patterned after the English country house weekend. Perhaps because the Long Island air, landscape, the large estates along the restricted roads out there, reminded me so much of what I knew of England. Nelson was a gay, most amiable host and I was delighted with the air of informality, the almost Bohemian mixture of his guests. Sinclair Lewis was there, in those days married to Dorothy Thompson. Marc Connelly of *Green Pastures*, Dan Longwell, then a Doubleday editor, later managing editor of *Life*, some exceedingly pretty girls or wives; all of whom understood enough German to help me out with my madly sprouting English. Of course, most of the time I didn't know what or of whom they talked about, it was too witty, too fast, and too locally limited. But merry as they all were, I felt some depression hovering over the house and the park—gardens, I should say. A sadness, a feeling of emptiness as if someone, something, had died. If I possess any sixth sense, it is a dog's nose for atmosphere.

I remember, for instance, entering a house Kay Boyle had rented in Nyack. It was an old, somewhat unkempt house, but there was a fire cozily burning in the fireplace, Kay's numerous lively brood making happy children's noises, and Kay, newly married and pregnant, was as beautiful and vibrant as ever. Yet something made me stop at the threshold and ask, "Where did the murder take place?"

"Oh, never mind, it was in one of the upstairs bedrooms, and anyway, it's more than sixty years ago. Come, let me have your coat," Kay said, unconcerned. She took it for granted that I must have heard about the sensational crime committed there in the Victorian past.

In the house in Oyster Bay nobody had been killed, but a marriage had died: and later, after I knew enough English to become a friend of Nelson's, I learned how deeply the divorce proceedings had hurt him. But for the time being, my finer sensibilities and my

Ullstein-sharpened wits did not come into play. I was sitting there openmouthed, a deaf mute, an imbecile, an extremely hungry imbecile as the hours went by and no tea, not the smallest cucumber sandwich, was forthcoming. Just trays and more trays of mint juleps, artfully constructed by Dan Longwell and served by a most correct Swedish butler whom I shall call Palmquist.

It's one of my grave shortcomings that I don't forget names as much as I muddle them up. If I meet, let's say, a Mrs. Barkley who doesn't look Barkley to me, I shall ever after address her as Mrs. Potter, Mrs. Pritchett, or Mrs. Grumbly. And so, this butler remains Palmquist in my memory, whatever his real name might have been. There was also a nice, comfortably broad-hipped Swedish upstairs maid who could speak a few words in near-German. Influenced by British belles lettres, I expected to find my clothes neatly laid out and, if necessary, even pressed. In fact, intimidated as I was by my ideas of those flawless, perfect, and arrogant servants on a millionaire's estate, I had gone and bought myself some dazzling, much too expensive nightgowns, just to prove to the maid that I was a real lady with a real lady's lingerie. Because all the thick, scratchy garments in which I was commanded to sleep as a child have inflicted on me the proletarian habit of sleeping in the raw, I had owned nothing to wear in bed. But my suitcase sat there, unopened, and when I unpacked, Elsa, the maid, looked with disdain at the seductive cream satin and black lace creation I displayed. (How could I know that the Broadway store where I bought it catered mostly to the girls at Minsky's and the other 42nd Street burlesque shows?) I had also brought along a low-cut evening dress; it was a bit crushed, but I put in on for dinner anyhow. None of the other girls had changed.

Such are the mistakes of the stranger in town, particularly a town as set in the ways and conventions of its highly stratified classes as New York.

I don't know why we, in Europe, were, and perhaps still are, so fascinated by the thought of American Negroes. Probably it is the influence of bad, and long since obsolete, literature that built up such a lopsided, cross-eyed image of the Negro as a romantic, picturesque, woolly-headed slave. It stands to reason that among Negroes there are just as many differences as among people in general. To consider the Negro as something quite apart, as Europeans do, means to deny him the basis of equality. But I don't wish to write an essay on the Negro question here, I only want to say that I came to America filled with the same full-blown spirit, the curiosity and fascination I find again and again in all newcomers. And so, when Nelson during dinner mentioned his old plantation in South Carolina, his darkies riding and hunting with him and singing at night around the bonfires in front of the mansion, I shot out such fireworks of enthusiasm and wonder that Nelson said: "Would you like to come down to my place for a few days?"

Would I!

"Okay. We'll go tomorrow, then; all that want to come along say Aye."

Loud "Ayes" around the dinner table. Overcome, I muttered that I had an appointment with Mr. Lasky, the president of Paramount who was paying me those five thousand dollars for two weeks, but Nelson waved this aside. "It's okay, I'll take care of that. Maybe Lasky can come down South, too. Palmquist!"

"Yes, Mr. Doubleday?"

"Listen, Palmquist, you make reservations for five? . . . six? . . . nine? . . . on the morning train. When does it leave? Eight-twenty? All right, you take care of everything—luggage, two cases of whisky, two cases of champagne, that should hold us for the first three days, shouldn't it? You get on the train with us and tell Wallace I won't bring my horses down there until Tuesday—there are plenty of ponies for the guests—and, listen, Palmquist, send a wire to François, or no, wait, you better phone him right now to have everything ready—dinner, guest rooms, the blue corner for Miss Baum. . . ."

"Yes, Mr. Doubleday."

"We'll meet for breakfast at seven-thirty; it's a gruesome hour for the girls, I know, but if we want to catch the train . . . perhaps we ought to say good night soon. Get your beauty sleep. Breakfast at seven-thirty; did you hear, Palmquist?"

"Yes, Mr. Doubleday. . . ."

Old Massa Doubleday! This was fairy-tale land, millionaireland, exactly as we, in impoverished Europe, pictured it. I went upstairs in a daze and washed my stockings and handkerchiefs. I was equipped for a weekend in Long Island, not for a week in South Carolina. God only knew how women dressed down South. In crinolines, as far as I knew. I didn't sleep much that night, I was too excited, too happy. I had not been so happy since the morning my first baby was born.

At seven in the morning I was packed, dressed; I felt like a little red balloon that had broken the string that held it down to earth up to now. I tiptoed out into the quiet hallway and downstairs. As usual, I was too early. The sun was just coming out behind the morning fog on the Sound, the house was quiet. I groped my way through the silent house. Not a stir anywhere, no breakfast preparations. In the dining room the curtains were still drawn and the table not quite cleared of last night's glasses. I looked at the prints in the hall. I crept into the library, there was a fragrance of last afternoon's wood fire. I took out a volume of Conrad, struggled through the difficult English and wondered if I could ever learn to write in that language as he had. But why should I? A two weeks' passing guest.

Shortly before eight o'clock I heard the clatter of china and silverware somewhere in the recesses of the house. I followed the sound and found Palmquist, dressed not at all like the butlers in books, but embarrassedly pulling a bathrobe closed over his underpants.

"Good morning," I said. "Won't we miss the train?"

"The train? Oh, Madam means the train! I see. No, Madam. We are not going South." I must have looked so startled that he added, "Mr. Doubleday was only joking."

I scrambled around in my rudimentary English. Joking? Jockey? Shocking? Joe King? "Joking . . . ?"

"Yes, Madam. Mr. Doubleday likes to have a little fun with practical jokes. When he is, well . . . stimulated. High, you know. . . ."

What does this remind me of? I wondered numbly, and then I had it: *City Lights*. Charlie Chaplin and that huge rich man who was so magnificent in the evening when he was drunk, "stimulated," and didn't remember a thing in the sober morning.

"Anything Madam wishes?" asked Palmquist.

"No, thank you. I think I shall take a walk."

Taking a good stiff walk has always been my most effective medicine when I am sad, worried, disappointed with myself or the world. From the window I had admired the slope of the wide lawns toward the waters of the Sound which were leaping with small white-caps, the wooded slopes of those parklike gardens where some entirely unknown flowering shrubs asked to be investigated. All right, all right, I told myself, so no trip to that fabulous Southern plantation, no singing darkies, no new food for my ever-hungry eyes, no picturesque experience to carry home with me. Mr. Doubleday had been high and had made fun of me, to the delectation of his other guests. Okay, I said aloud, okay, okay. I was disappointed, angry, and miserable as a seven-year-old.

It was my first collision with a phenomenon so thoroughly American that it took me years before I learned to cope with it. Inevitable as the tides, the constant seesaw of high and low, depending not on the moon but on the drinks. With a few drinks in him—or her—the American is witty, sparkling, enthusiastic, lovable, rich in plans and creative ideas, some of them foolish but still tempting. Sober, he is like a high-powered car out of gas. To discover this in the midst of Prohibition, on my first weekend, was an experience quite different from any I might have expected.

Trying to retrieve my inner bearings I reached the end of the garden where another disappointment waited for me. I had thought the garden would run directly into the sandy beach. Instead, I was faced by a fence or a wall, I don't remember which, only that it was rather high. I pulled up my skirt, climbed across it, jumped a ditch, and found myself on a highway alive with Sunday morning traffic. And every single car, truck, or jalopy stopped to offer me a ride. There, then, was another basic truth to ingest: nobody walks in America. Everybody and his grandmother had his own car, a rather startling discovery if you came from Europe in that Depression year of '31. And one more: everybody in this fortunate country is of an inborn, deep-rooted generosity that wishes to help, give, share.

Europe may "Americanize" till the older generation gets blue in the face and the youngsters behave like the stars they see in pictures (who, of course, do not for a moment behave like real live Americans), but without this one distinctive national quality—generosity—they'll only acquire all the shortcomings of a still raw population of immigrants.

After tramping along the highway for a while, I was tired of causing so many traffic jams; I wanted to take off my much too sensible shoes and give in to my old vice of going barefoot, feel the cool, wet sand between my toes. It's strange how sometimes the smallest detail will stick in the memory. There were a few ramshackle huts along the beach, and from one of them a few wooden steps led down to the water's edge. As I was sitting there, pulling off my stockings, a woman came out of one of the shacks and smiled at me. She looked as a poor fisherman's wife looks all over the world—freckled, broad-hipped, of uncertain age, with work-knotted arms and hands. She had one baby on her arm, a toddler hanging on to her skirt, and she was pregnant, which perhaps explained the worn, bleached-out wide skirt with the uneven hem and a wet stripe across her belly, as though she had just been leaning over a wash tub. She was the first really poor and shabby-looking woman I encountered in that rich country where everybody, including the Upper Four Hundred—indeed, the Upper Four Hundred in particular—complained incessantly about taxes, losses, and the tragedy of the Depression. I supposed she had come out to see who I was and what I was doing on their grounds, their steps, their piece of beach, but before I could assemble the words of an excuse, this simple woman said, "Oh, please, don't bother. Sorry if I disturbed you," and went past me down around the shack. It was so unexpectedly polite, tactful, sweet-mannered—I have no better word for it—that it remained with me like a warm little candle flame all through that rather dismal day, and through all the years since, as the first example of the *politesse de coeur* (Goethe) these roughneck Americans are born with.

By the time I returned, unshaven men with tousled hair and sloppy bathrobes over rumpled pajamas were scattered all over. Some of them carried drinks with them while searching for cigarettes. The ladies were still invisible. Nobody had missed me; they thought I had had my breakfast in bed like everybody else (breakfast in bed is my personal idea of crumby discomfort), and when I reported that I'd been out for two hours, hiking, I could see that they thought me not only odd, but plain nuts, as the slang of the early '30's had it. In the face of this I didn't dare ask for a delayed breakfast out of bed. With a sudden pang of homesickness I thought of the friendly pause in Europe for *petit déjeuner,* the ten o'clock snack at Ullstein House, with the daily suspense of what the various wives might have put into their men's sandwiches.

In the meantime, High Life took its relentless course. Red Lewis remained invisible, Dan Longwell went riding, a set of doubles was arranged on the tennis court (Heavens, millionaires had their own private courts!), and Nelson showed me around the kennels and gardens. Dogs, horses, and gardening were his hobbies; they, plus everybody's bootleggers and their methods and prices, were the main topics of conversation. My English advanced by leaps and bounds, but I had nothing to contribute to these themes. My walk and the fresh breeze along the Sound had made me hungry, but no food appeared to appease my stomach used to its regular five meals a day. To be hungry made me feel very plebeian. I added dogwood blossoms to my botanical wisdom, admired Nelson's azaleas, shuddered secretly at a corner that served as a dog cemetery, with dreadfully bad statues of his deceased dogs standing over their little graves. I began to feel hollow and a bit dizzy and headachy. A few neighbors dropped in on horseback, handsome couples informally dressed in sweaters and jodhpurs; they were served a stirrup cup, and by noon Dan Longwell was back to fixing mint juleps. Also by noon, everybody, with perhaps the exception of Dorothy Thompson, was slightly and pleasantly high again. On the terrace, Palmquist placed a plate of tiny tidbits, very salty and hot, on an improvised bar; they were well designed to keep up the guests' thirst but burned a searing hole into my empty stomach.

Nelson, the attentive host, must have noticed my discomfort but, saturated with alcohol and never having known hunger in his life, naturally he didn't dream that all I wanted was food. Instead he came up with the nicest thing he could think of; he excused himself for a moment and arranged for a phone connection with my family. A conversation across the Atlantic was still very costly and rather on the sensational side. I was paralyzed when I heard the operator's "Go ahead, there's your party."

"This is me!" I yelled into the receiver.

I heard my husband muttering in Berlin, nudging the boys to say something. "Hallo!" said the one. "Hallo!" said the other. "Hallo!" said my husband.

"Hallo!" said I. "Can you hear me?"

"What?" the trio asked.

"Whether you can hear me!"

"Yes, it's so clear it's unbelievable. Where are you?" my husband hollered.

"I'm in New York, that is, outside of New York. Long Island. Mr. Doubleday's place."

Pause.

"How are you, Mum?" the older boy asked.

"I'm fine. And you boys?"

"We're also fine. What time is it in America?"

"I don't know exactly, what time is it in Berlin?"

In Berlin it was six hours later than in New York, and then we were running out of topics. "You have thirty seconds left," said the operator.

"How's the weather in America?" Berlin asked.

"Fine," said I. My heart was drumming hard. "Say how do you do to Mr. Doubleday," I said and handed Nelson the receiver. "How do you do?" they both said in their neat school English, and Nelson grinned and said, "How are you, kids?" then we all yelled *Auf Wiedersehen* and the momentous conversation was over. I was beginning to forgive Nelson last night's joke, which he had obviously and completely forgotten.

I was tired and, after the emotional strain of hearing my boys' voices, hungrier than before. I took the volume of Conrad and went to my room for a rest. I waded into his complex English with my small pocket dictionary beside me, not knowing that I was going to continue reading like this, as a strict discipline, for the next two or three years. In a disturbing counterpoint I was reflecting on the possibility of asking Palmquist for a sandwich with the five o'clock tea I hoped for. But there was neither rest nor tea. I was swept from my room into a car with specially built-in leg room for Mr. Doubleday's length, and put down at the Piping Rock Club. I did not know how exclusive these realms were, nor did I understand the first thing about golf. An idiot once more, I was marched off by a small cluster of spectators to watch Mr. Doubleday play, and beat, a gentleman he picked up on the club terrace. Numb with hunger and fatigue, I dragged along, feeling so out of place I could have cried, if I had belonged to those fortunates who can cry easily.

I am sure that a club terrace is a lovely place to sit and sip a drink after your eighteen holes, but the vermouth I asked for, instead of cheering me up, made me still hungrier and quite melancholy. So this is how the other half lives, I told myself. Well, Heaven save me from ever becoming rich, is all I can say.

This small prayer Heaven granted me.

Not that I disdain the middle-of-the-road comforts that one's middle-of-the-road earnings buy. But property and great wealth seem an awful burden if you do not have an inborn affinity with money. At least, I've never seen people in modest financial circumstances worry and lament over money as much as real wealth does.

Without mercy the hours crept on; I shivered, I took a long hot bath, I was homesick. In all my life and travels, before and after, this is the only time I ever felt homesick. I had hunger visions, I saw, smelled, tasted, an abundance of food as in the times of our starvation. I was homesick for my kids, my home, for Sabri Mahir to massage me, scold me, repair my damaged self-assurance; for my office in Ullstein House, for my colleagues and our bright sharp conversations in a language I could speak and understand. I lay down on the elegant four-poster and felt sorry for myself.

Dinner time arrived, but no dinner gong sounded. Avoiding my mistake of the night before, I left the champagne-colored chiffon in the closet and went downstairs in my gray jersey dress. In the library I found Dorothy Thompson in full regalia, talking with Nelson and Dan Longwell, both terribly impressive in a kind of garment I had never seen: what on the Continent was known as a smoking jacket but here was called a tuxedo, only these were not black. Nelson was splendid in bottle green, Dan's shade I have forgotten. All the other guests had left for the city. Only then it struck me that I hadn't seen Sinclair Lewis all day long. "He didn't feel up to snuff," I was told (and, pray, what did that mean?), he had done some proofreading but he would come with us. He was just getting dressed.

"Maybe I ought to dress, too?" I suggested. "No, no, don't," Nelson assured me, "it's very informal. We're just dropping in on some neighbors for dinner."

The neighbors, where we arrived after a long wait for Red Lewis and a still longer drive, turned out to be the Andrew Mellons, his was a name famous in finance and industry. All I noticed was that Mr. Doubleday was a poor man compared to Mr. Mellon. Here I saw for the first time Thorstein Veblen's conspicuous consumption at work. Everybody was dressed up to the gills, and when we went to dinner, after an endless stretch of aperitifs, each setting rested upon a solid gold plate. As for the aperitifs, I had chosen champagne, a comparatively harmless beverage to which I was more or less inured, and I fell to the canapés with a vengeance. (And why did they called them canapés? In Europe a canapé was a kind of sofa, something to sit on; here it was an anchovy or a morsel of pâté de foie gras on a little sofa of cottonlike bread.) I had not known that there was Pernod mixed into the champagne, and it was amazing in what a rush my self-assurance returned. The hell with my mouse-gray knitted sportsdress and Nelson's ignorant advice about not changing. No wonder his wife had left him! And the hell, most of all, with the smart Vanity Fair crowd to whom I was thrown like a bloody hunk of meat to the lions. They sniffed me out with professional curiosity because, after all, I was news, I was "Good copy." Perhaps they took the mouse-gray as a demonstrative piece of impertinence, arrogance amid all the nouveau riche splendor.

Thanks to the Pernod-champagne, I was high myself, and the only thing that kept me from haughtily talking shop with my editor was the lack of sufficient English.

Filled up with good food, replenished in body and spirit, I trooped out with the other ladies after dinner, a ritual I had learned in England and even there it had struck me as barbarian, all the men remaining by themselves to drink and tell putrid stories, all the ladies marching to the bathroom in solemn procession.

As early as my first lunch at Rumpelmayers the strict segregation of the sexes had stumped me. The men downtown, the women uptown. Two separate ways of life. No wonder the American woman pushes herself more and more into business. In countries that still hold a vestige of charm in daily life, in France, Austria, Italy, the man spends his bits of leisure with the woman of his choice, be it wife, girl friend, or mistress. He takes his noonday meal with his family, his children; he enjoys, maybe, his *heure bleu* flirting or seeking love. He may show his peacock's tail feathers in after-dinner conversations shared by both sexes, while the common American businessman is panting along all day long in the rat race.

But that's only by the way.

Upstairs, to my surprise, I found in the exclusive realm of the ladies a young Negro at the piano. After all the things I had read and heard about rabid racial discrimination, lynchings, and exploitation, it amazed me to see the apparent intimacy between these golden girls and the dark young man in his flawless tuxedo. "Honey," they called him, and "Sweetheart," he called them. They leaned on his shoulders, they offered him generous glimpses into their low-cut dinner frocks, they wheedled and flirted with him in a way that showed no discrimination at all. But perhaps his presence in the women's realm was the most debasing thing to this single, male Negro. As though he were a eunuch. As if he did not count at all. There are a few occupations that can be similarly emasculating, such as that of the masseur, the swimming teacher, the actor. I remember a biting cartoon in an early *New Yorker*: an actor being put into an ornately seductive bed with a superlatively seductive star, and the director in-

troducing the two with great formality: "Miss Brent, meet Mr. Tal-
bot!"

While the young Negro softly played the season's hit songs, two
beautiful young women took me to a sofa and, sitting down left and
right of me, they took my hands. "Now you must tell us about
Europe," they said. It sounded urgent.

"About Europe? What do you want me to tell?"

"About the girls over there. What they feel. Do they cry? Please
tell us the truth."

"Cry? About what?"

"Oh, you know. Afterward. Do they cry afterward?"

"Afterward . . . ?" I asked, baffled. Then I saw the light. "Well,"
I answered judiciously, "I guess some cry and some don't. It depends, you see."

"We cry, all of us; each time, afterward," the young woman at my
right declared violently. She was the most beautifully built, dressed,
and jewel-hung decorative creature I had ever seen. It is true, in
my elegant, snob-oriented fashion magazine *Die Dame* we did show
our Parisian artist's sketches of such long-stemmed, slender ladies
wearing such *dernier cri* creations, but we never believed that such
figures, faces, gowns, jewels, really existed; they were an abstract,
a platonic ideal of the Woman Beautiful. They never looked like
this in Germany, but here the room was spilling over with this
exquisite beauty, grooming, posture, the glow of hair, teeth, skin,
slimness of ankles and wrists, smallness of hands and feet and
waist. I enjoyed looking at them, wondering at the same time if
"crying afterward" was part of a traditional pretense thought to be
charming, a frigid convention, or some lack in their men. Also,
their perfection had dealt a hard blow to my feminine self-assurance
in spite of having no reason for "tears afterward."

The next day I handed myself over to Elizabeth Arden who
promptly turned me into an eyebrowless platinum blonde, severely
commanded me to have what she called five eliminations daily—
that's a mere matter of will power, she said—and in simply no time
starved me down to a nervous shadow of myself. At the end of the
treatments I still did not look at all like those incomparable Oyster

Bay wives and daughters, but I had gained enough self-assurance to swindle six years off my age in *Who's Who,* and only put them back on my seventieth birthday.

Certainly, on my first weekend in America I collected a basketful of new impressions, observations, and experiences; not the last of them that still endures is the remarkable wealth of smarty-smart small talk and the great lack of real conversation. When we trooped downstairs to join the gentlemen, they were back at the same three topics: the Depression, the taxes, the bootleggers; add to this the seasonal topics of football and baseball and the angry exchanges every four years before a presidential election. Since the emergence of *Homo suburbius,* couples bore each other interminably about their children, their PTA, their do-it-yourself equipment, the doings of their Supermen.

The Americans, I then concluded, and these conclusions still hold, care for drink more than for food; for the looks of their food more than for its taste. The fruits look gorgeous, but, picked long before they are ripe, they have no aroma at all. For the European palate the white bread is no more fit for human consumption than a piece of soggy cardboard; their sponge cake is precisely what it says: sponge. All sweets are too sweet to our palate, and here I catch myself still saying "our" in contrast to "their," even though I have lived here longer than anywhere else. But I found out that the seat of the greatest patriotic loyalties is in the stomach. Long after giving up all attachment to the land of his birth, the naturalized American citizen holds fast to the food of his parents. That's lucky, because with a bit of scurrying around you can find anything you want, if not for yourself then for your guests, be they from Finland, Japan, Greece, or Indonesia, not to mention such run-of-the-mill Americans as Mexicans, Italians, Swedes, or Hungarians.

I myself was fed sauerkraut wherever luncheons and gala banquets were given in my honor during my first weeks in New York. Because sauerkraut, as everybody knows, is the German national dish. They served it to me—and I still shudder at the memory—with scrambled eggs and champagne, with breaded *Schnitzel* and with fish, with a complete misconception of dumplings. I *loathe* sauerkraut.

Even that first High Life weekend terminated in a hideous product launched at that time by some enterprising canning company: sauerkraut juice. Very healthy. Chock-full of vitamins. It topped our most unpleasant drive back to the Doubleday place when everybody was glum and mad.

I didn't quite gather why, but as it turned out the why was the fact that Sinclair Lewis, probably as bored as myself with the doings of the Upper Four Hundred, had gone upstairs, undressed, and passed out on a bed that, unfortunately, happened to be the dainty and fragrant bed of our hostess. There, after a long search, Nelson routed him out, pushed him into his clothes, and more or less carried him to the car. I deduced that he had got the great writer out of his stupor by rather indelicate methods that Lewis resented.

We marched in through the servants' entrance and indulged in another American ritual: raiding the icebox for milk and crackers, said to counteract the too much alcohol consumed in the course of the evening. I couldn't look a glass of milk in the eye but conquered my timidity enough to ask for some fruit; an apple, please, maybe? But there was, in that enormous kitchen with its supercolossal refrigerator, not a smallest trace of fruit to be found. Slightly depressed, I said good night and retired.

It was then that Nelson Doubleday, in one of his sweetest moods —and he could be as lovable as any publisher I've ever known— appeared personally at my door with that confounded sauerkraut juice. It stood on my night stand and stank up the room. After a while I got up and flushed it down the toilet.

Thus my weekend among the Upper Four Hundred ended.

What came next was the charity affair to which Mrs. Vanderbilt had invited me. As I was still in a newcomer's daze I don't remember where it took place or what it was for. I remember, though, that I was seated at a round table at Mrs. Vanderbilt's left, and though the old dowager queen was my hostess she showed me not only a cold but a deep-frozen shoulder, because of my innocently committed gaffe of having had my secretary phone her instead of the handwritten letter I owed her according to Emily Post. But I had gained some basic English during my weekend and when I was called upon to make a speech, I marched boldly up to the platform, perhaps a bit needled by Mrs. Vanderbilt's arrogance, and said: "I've been in New York only a few days and I have learned only two words of your language: one is Swell, and the other is Lousy." (Those were the current slang expressions of that year.) "It's swell to be with you and excuse, please, my lousy English!"

That did it. That was my breakthrough to popularity. No more quoting of Goethe, no more lectures about humor and compassion in literature. The next day I made lots of headlines. The papers called me simply Vicki, and to be called by your first name in the American press means that you're popular, whether you are a queen, a movie star, a murderess.

Or even an author.

I don't think the publicity agents of thirty years ago worked as hard in those primeval days of public relations to impose their products' or clients' image upon the public as Madison Avenue does today. Still, Doubleday was pushing my novel for all its bestselling worth. *Grand Hotel* was advertised in the Fifth Avenue buses (those lovely buses with the open upper decks that now are only objects of fond nostalgia), and no sooner had I undergone my first Elizabeth Arden treatments, a blown-up photo of beautified me was added. It was important, Nelson explained, to stamp a successful author's face upon the consciousness of the readers, past, present, and potential. Maybe so. In any case, it made me feel less of a stranger. Also, it amused me to observe how the play was benefiting from the book's publicity; Metro-Goldwyn-Mayer, getting ready to make a movie of the book, in turn profited from the publicity for the play, and vice versa all around. What I couldn't quite understand, though, were the motives that had impelled Paramount Pictures to invite me to New York and pay me five thousand dollars for nothing. It seemed quite obvious that not even a genius among experienced movie writers could produce anything usable within two weeks, and I was anything but a genius nor did I have the haziest idea how movies were written. However, Lubitsch, who had instigated this invitation, assured me that Paramount wasn't losing anything in the deal. "For their paltry five thousand they're getting two hundred thousand worth of publicity," he explained. "And who knows, you might give them another million's worth of an idea." The movie industry, breaking away from mute to talking pictures, was frantically searching for new material, for authors who could make with words, depict characters, write dialogue.

Lubitsch, the wittiest director of his time, the most loyal of friends, formerly an actor at Max Reinhardt's theaters, had been one of the first Germans to be called to Hollywood. A small, dark man cut on Mephisto-Napoleonic lines, he had black, glowing eyes. If you threw out a little line that gave him an idea for one of his famous "touches," an amusing bit of business, a pointed repartee, you could actually see a tiny red flame kindle behind the black of the pupils. He spoke a fluent, vernacular English with an atrocious Berlin pronunciation and was one of the best-loved people in the Hollywood swamps—and justly so. Being a hard worker himself, he understood my urge to go to work at once, to meet the challenge of the new medium. "Don't worry," he told me, "you write a short novel, in German, of course. I'll do the rest. Of course you understand what's expected of you: another *Grand Hotel*. Lots of characters woven into one plot, one pattern, one piece of fabric. Nothing simpler for a writer like you."

Nothing simpler. Oh, my God!—it had taken me almost thirty years to give birth to one single little Kringelein!

I had a few sessions with Lubitsch, and we agreed to put the action into a department store instead of a hotel; the plot and characters would develop automatically. I went downtown to Wanamaker's, New York's oldest large department store, and with the help of an elderly sales lady, who spoke a queer sort of Pennsylvania Dutch, I took the scent of the atmosphere. At night I sat up in my hotel room like a fatigued spider, squeezing thin threads from my innards and sort of weaving them into a net. I must say it was the hardest work I ever did for five thousand dollars. Lubitsch seemed pleased with the product. So were the bigwigs at the Paramount office. I suppose they had not expected me to do any work at all. To my surprise, they offered to extend my contract for another six weeks, at the same incredible two thousand five hundred dollars weekly.

Ullstein's, after a hectic exchange of wires, generously prolonged my leave, and my husband reluctantly consented. Being a worker in New York City instead of a mere loafing tourist was a marvelous experience. Not only did I study the inner organization of Wanamaker's, but I tried to approach as closely as I could a salesgirl's way of life. What a wealth of impressions I received from each subway ride at the rush hour, the bad food I shared, the cold-water flats overrun by cockroaches, the cheap, smart little dresses, the beloved jerks they had for boy friends or husbands. I daresay that all I could absorb within those short weeks was only the most superficial, but then, that's all the movies wanted.

I think I saw more of New York City in those first weeks than many a born New Yorker sees in a lifetime. For this, I had to thank a happy accident. In the anteroom of the Paramount offices I met the greatest cameraman of his time, Karl Freund. A jovial man drowning in his own fat and speaking a jabberwocky mixture of steadily deteriorating German and not-quite-English, he honored me with his friendship, at that juncture a priceless gift. In Berlin, Freund had made a film on his own, which is still being shown at the Museum of Modern Art, I believe. I think he called it: *Berlin, Portrait of a Big City*. It was something completely different; a picture consisting entirely of impressions, brief flashes, atmosphere, yet enormously exciting in its complete absence of plot, story, action. Hollywood had grabbed this man, and now he planned to do a similar collage about New York City. And so he took me along on many nightly excursions: through the lowest haunts of Harlem and to Holy Roller services and revivals at Negro Baptist churches; to the missions and Salvation Army stations, where prayers and charity soups were ladled out in equal portions; down to the Battery, to the waterfront, the fish market; to the lower Bowery, where just then the worst slums were being cleared, where the bums and drunks were sleeping in the huge gas pipes piled up on the cleared lots. We went to flophouses where the lowest dregs of the town were still separated into two classes: the higher paying guests being furnished with pallets, the poorest ones resting their arms on a rope and their heads on their arms and, thus suspended, sleeping off their drunken stupor. We found still more class distinctions in the early mornings when missions and flophouses shook their guests out onto the streets, to follow the signs to the barber schools where the future Figaros learned their trade on those poor bleary faces, free of charge. However, for five or ten cents, those who could afford it, could buy a rub with a steaming hot towel and emerge refreshed into the dawn.

Except for some minor regional differences, it is almost impossible for a newcomer to classify people by their clothes, their manners, their way of speaking. Yet, I found this so-called classless society more strictly stratified than any other, aristocratic Old Vienna, for instance, or Grand Ducal Darmstadt. Here, where everybody calls everybody by his first name and "Thou shalt conform" is the first commandment, you are separated by the amount of money you earn or possess (and which is duly, if not always correctly, reported by the press), by your adherence to one of the two almost indistinguishable political parties, and by your address.

Punctual as Old Faithful, I finished and delivered my treatment (it was called a treatment by then) of the department store story, was amply congratulated on it, after which it was shelved. I might have had a foreboding that this would happen, if the shelving had not coincided with Paramount's offering me a six months' contract. Six months, twenty-five weeks, at two thousand five hundred dollars each. Six months in this new world for me to discover.

There were frantic wires to and from Ullstein's, which finally agreed to grant me this long leave of absence. More wires and letters to my husband who let himself be wheedled into spending his vacation with me in Hollywood, the boys first to be dispatched to summer camp.

The reason for all this excitement was contained in the magic name of Maurice Chevalier.

Chevalier, almost as young and charming thirty years ago as he is now, was to play the lead in Oscar Straus's *Ein Walzertraum,* which Hollywood had renamed *Smiling Lieutenant.* I was chosen to dream up a second vehicle for Chevalier, also to be directed by Lubitsch and composed by Straus. As there exists only one Maurice Chevalier, Hollywood had no occasion to be confused about him. But as to the three Strausses: Johann, Richard, and Oscar! Only by sheer good luck, or probably through Lubitsch's intervention, Front Office had managed to reach the actual composer of *Ein Walzertraum,* but undoubtedly had expected, if not the late Johann Strauss, at least Richard Strauss of *Rosenkavalier,* and I doubt that it ever got things entirely disentangled. Anyway, Oscar Straus and his wife, Clara, stopped in New York before going on to the Coast. If there is such a thing as love at first sight, the same may happen with friendship. With us, perhaps it was because we had come from the same Viennese background, had studied music with the same teachers, remembered the same premières, concerts, scandals and fights, first performances. Strangers in New York City, we had our own little island to retire to, swap jokes, musical memories and anecdotes, and exquisite Viennese recipes—entirely without sauerkraut.

I remember a few pleasant nights our little troupe spent together, much fun, some thinking, some hatching of ideas, a fine optimism pervading our miniature Tower of Babel conversations. Oscar spoke French, English, and German with an agreeable though pronounced Austrian accent. Clara had only a smattering of French and English but used it with admirable self-assurance. Chevalier hated to hear us talk German and was careful not to damage his superb Parisian accent by learning English too well. I was losing my French conversation as fast as I was learning to make myself understood in English. And Lubitsch, with no French at all, nursing his tough Berlin idiom and equally fast Berlin-ish English, gave off fireworks of wit, inspiration, and theatrical wisdom.

When they went on ahead to Hollywood to work on *Smiling Lieutenant,* I waited in New York City for my husband, and then we followed them.

The most remarkable thing about Hollywood is that it does not exist.

Hollywood is just one of the numerous small communities that together form the giant city of Los Angeles, and not a very different or characteristic one at that. How many of them are there today? About two hundred, I read somewhere; maybe five hundred tomorrow. Only two of the movie studios are situated in Hollywood —proper, unobtrusive, outmoded buildings on rather obscure sidestreets. During the thirty years I've been here I never saw a star so much as cross a Hollywood street. Altogether, it is an older, therefore somewhat run-down part of Los Angeles, and the sporadic efforts at sprucing it up show meager results. Here you find none of the elegant stores, none of the first-class restaurants, the smart new hotels, not even one of the new shopping centers. When I first saw Hollywood, it still had a certain sleepy small-townish charm, but this has given way to more and louder trashiness, a gaudy aspect dominating the streets and many of the people thronging them.

Hollywood, in a word, has no center, never had one, no city hall, courthouse, church, square; on second thought, however, it probably has some of these elements, but they're so aimlessly thrown in with the general jumble of shacks and small apartment houses, gasoline stations, markets, and hot-dog stands, skyscrapers-in-the-making, and cozy little bungalows beneath the county-fair atmosphere on the main drag, The Boulevard, that I, for one, never found them.

Like most Europeans, and, perhaps even some Midwesterners or Easterners, I had pictured Hollywood as something compact, a community built around its moving picture studios, from the center of which a few residential streets would radiate. There, the great stars would live in princely splendor and you would meet them all the time, Garbo and Dietrich and Chaplin and the Barrymores. Nothing could have been farther from the real Hollywood. I often wonder what tourists think about this place, if they're as disappointed as I was at first or if it really satisfies them to crowd into the front yard of that monstrous Grauman's Chinese movie theater and stare at the prints in concrete of stars' and starlets' hands and feet and take snapshots of them. Somehow it must be a throwback to atavistic magic, like the printing of hands you see in the Lascaux caves, still older than the prehistoric paintings there. It also sets me to thinking of how drab and empty and poor the lives of those must be who find their wish-fulfillment in the treacly illusions of movies and TV. And I feel sorry, too, for all those who come to Hollywood in pursuit of that magic: the cheerful, slightly overdressed tourists with their hunger for the shoddy thrills they expect from us; the hopeful youngsters, the little beauty queens and high-school heroes in search of a short easy street to fame, glamour, and riches—who end up haughtily yawning at you from behind dime-store counters or sweating in the basement as shipping clerks. But this has been told so often I would be ashamed to mention it, except that it still goes on and one can't shout a warning often enough.

I wonder who first invented the pleasurable legend of the Hollywood writer who draws a huge salary by hanging around, undiscovered for months, doing absolutely nothing. According to all that I witnessed, and personally experienced, Hollywood writers work very hard and all the time, thinking up plots, brooding over angles and twists and gimmicks; shaping roles to the stars' measurements and limited abilities; catering to producers' tastes and depending on the judgment of brigades of people. It's extremely hard work, and frequently you can't see the pie for all the fingers in it. Writers go around with haggard faces, they worry incessantly, they can't sleep, lose their appetites, live on a diet of benzedrine and tranquilizers; they grow stomach ulcers, suffer migraines, drink heavily to ease the strain. I suppose it's worse in the other occupations bunched together under the heading of communications: radio, television, and all the branches of public relations. Considering the mountains of creative brain power, ideas, wit, and labor pains, the mice born to these mountains are rather small.

Of course, in the early '30's, the arts of communications were still in their diapers, but even then I had the impression that everybody, including the Front Office and the top stars, was constantly haunted and quite unhappy. Nobody seems to feel secure in either the game or their position in it, even less in themselves. I think the reason is that nobody really knows his craft, if it is possible to learn a craft that has no laws, rules, or traditions, that devours enormous amounts of money and aims to attract and entertain a mob of millions. Because an audience comprising all ages from three to ninety, all classes, all stages of intelligence, from the pious to the agnostic, the almost imbecile to the egghead in his ivory tower—such an audience can only be called a mob. And so, the big chief in the Front Office is afraid of his backers, or of losing his own money. In general, he has neither the time nor the inclination to read a manuscript, and if he would or could read, he would lack the judgment or imagination to envision it as a screenplay. Actually these top men in the industry have an acute sense for the qualities that make a star, the sexual attraction in a woman, the strength or sparkle in a man. Acting ability, as we know, plays a very minor part in the selection. True, with enough publicity pressure—meaning money—a star may be created out of a void of either talent or personality. But that's the exception. Some producers, such as Sam Spiegel, for instance, are seasoned, plucky gamblers; they take failures without blinking, stake everything on one card, and once in a while come up with a first-class picture like *The Bridge on the River Kwai*. Sam Goldwyn, to my mind, thinks like a great chef. If you take a well-proved recipe, use the most expensive ingredients, and don't rush the kitchen help too much, you'll serve a fine dish in the end. This formula succeeds most of the time, but even the greatest chef's soufflé falls once in a while.

Of course, there are always outsiders, those producers experimenting with new approaches and occasionally getting a prize in Cannes or Venice. And if any experiment should succeed with the audience that is antiexperimental by nature, then it will create a trend and be imitated *ad nauseam*.

Anyway, this is how major movies were created at the time I entered that three-ring circus: the play or book or, in rare cases, original story, will be condensed into a twelve-page synopsis; if Front Office decides to read the stuff it gets compressed a second time into a scant three pages. (At the time, I thought this an utterly barbarous procedure, but found out since that the old rule, "if you can't tell it in three minutes it's no good for the movies," is quite correct.) I can't say how it was handled in other studios, but at Metro-Goldwyn-Mayer, where I worked for several years, we had two storytellers, Scheherazades, upon whose way of presenting your story to the Great Pasha, Louis B., your fate depended. If they liked you and your story, they told it in a way to make the Pasha smile or, more easily and frequently, wipe a tear from his sentimental crocodile's eyes. Next, the twelve-page synopsis went to the supervisor of a small group of producers; one of them was assigned to it and together they discussed it as a possible vehicle for a certain star. If the star had the right to choose his next vehicle, as most top stars had, perhaps the original manuscript was handed to him or, more often, to her. This was, and is, one of the chasms in which manuscript and author most frequently disappear. It is an unfortunate fact that stars very rarely know what's good for them. That's where *their* feeling of insecurity sets in. They want to be fascinating, interesting, exciting; at the same time, they don't want to be shown in any situation that may cost them their audiences' naïve sympathies. Foremost, they want their part to be bigger than anyone else's. They want to play the whole gamut, be chaste yet seductive, dynamic yet sentimental, they want to do heroic deeds, sacrifice themselves for their man, tenderly love babies, and ruthlessly kill the villain. They want to be saved after an airplane crash with not a hair out of place, and from a deadly fight with a rapist with their lipstick and mascara in good order. The same, transposed into more masculine endeavors, holds for the male stars.

Many of these initial difficulties are bypassed if the script derives from a successful play on Broadway that Front Office, supervisor, director, and stars have seen with their own eyes. If Miss X was brilliant in it on the stage, Miss Y is certain to be even more brilliant on the screen. If the play had run two or three seasons, the picture can count on reaping millions.

Although this procedure doesn't always pan out this way, the industry continues to hold its childlike trust in it, pays fantastic sums for successful plays or best-selling novels that are obviously poor screen material. As a rule, the public has heard or read enough of these successes to fill the movie theater. Sometimes, though, the industry falls flat on its face, when, to the detriment of the craft of movie-making, the production ignores all the mobility, imagination, and unreality that is possible on the screen and limits itself to a static reproduction of the stage. That, to my mind, is a great loss. Of course, meditations like these make me blatantly unsuited to be a movie writer. But in the beginning it was a challenge, and learning a new skill has always had an irresistible attraction for me.

I can talk about my vain efforts at movie writing with the same detachment one might feel about a marriage that ended in divorce twenty-five years ago. I don't blame the moving picture industry as some of my illustrious fellow authors do. If we sell ourselves or our product—and most of us do it gladly and for a very good price— we have no right to complain. Speaking for myself, once I realized that I had no talent for movie writing, I withdrew from it. To have nothing to do with the studios is my one great luxury. If my agents, and it happens rarely enough, succeed in selling a story of mine to the industry, I am pleased but by no means elated; it's not my property any longer, I don't care what happens to it, and I avoid seeing the picture. That's part of my simple method of needing neither drinks, nor dope, nor tranquilizers.

Sometimes I get a trifle sentimental when I remember what this insatiable octopus of a town was thirty years ago. Now that we live in an ill-smelling, khaki-colored tent of smog, it's hard to believe that there ever was a gentian-blue sky above us, filled with glittering stars and the perfume of jasmine in the cold nights; hillsides and gardens sparkling with dew each morning, with all the colors of a wild Van Gogh palette as the sun rose, the air so clear you didn't want to breathe but drink it. I think I stayed drunk for weeks with this sun and air and the beauty of the hills. Drunk also with my new work. I pulled out ever fresh ideas to see the little red flame kindle in Lubitsch's shrewd eyes, to stick more and more raisins into the dough we were kneading into shape for Chevalier.

Everybody was delighted with the manuscript while it was in process, and showered me with praise when I, punctual as ever, finished and delivered it. Then there were two days of ominous silence, followed by my first collision with the brutal methods that are also a part of Hollywood.

I was called before a tribunal of unfriendly-looking gentlemen whom I had never seen before: The Legal Department, worlds apart from the bright, talented, tortured fools who create pictures.

"Miss Baum," one of them said, staring straight and menacingly into my face, "we've read your manuscript, and we don't like it. We think you'd better pack up and go back where you came from."

(How many things we, the naturalized Americans, leave unsaid, swallow in silence, to avoid getting clubbed by this ubiquitous, if rarely loudly expressed, xenophobic sentiment.)

I was stunned. Like the knocked-out fighters in the comics I saw stars, crazily turning wheels, an avalanche rolling over me. "But . . . but . . . ," I stammered, "but I have another five months to go . . . my contract . . . Ullstein. . . . I'm on a leave of absence . . . I rented a house here. . . . What will my husband say? . . . What about my contract?" (What did Napoleon tell Josephine after Waterloo?)

"Your contract is canceled. And, Miss Baum, let me say that you would be ill-advised to go to court about it," pronounced The Legal Department.

"Excuse me, I'll have to . . . have to think, talk it over . . . ," I muttered and stumbled out.

I don't remember who the good Samaritan was that found me leaning dizzily against the corridor wall. One of the gag men, I think. "Something the matter, kid?" he asked kindly.

"It's nothing. A little trouble. I can't understand it. They canceled my contract. Can they do that?"

He whistled. "Depends on the small print. Sons of bitches," he said. "Hit you in the solar plexus, did they? Aw, forget it. Go home and get drunk, kid. That always helps."

It was well-meant but to me, fresh from Europe, it seemed an absurd piece of advice. I have since learned, though, that all of America muddles through its troubles, collectively and individually, in a befogged alcoholic state of euphoria instead of facing the difficulty straight on. In my experience, serious difficulties don't vanish by themselves, they are standing around your bed when you open your eyes the next morning. But evasion of individual problems is more and more becoming a national problem, and I had better let the sociologists worry about it. Except, if it worries them too much they, too, are told to forget it, go home and get drunk.

My own troubles, in any case, were straightened out after some hectic activity. To this day I don't know what caused Paramount to drop me, or to try to scare me out of my contract. Under Lubitsch's angry but quiet pressure they paid it out, after all, shelved my Chevalier manuscript, asked me to write a story for Marlene Dietrich; this one they also seemed to like a lot and also shelved. The ways of the moving picture lords are inscrutable, and I just have no talent for the medium. I can't think in the mosaic of shots, nor am I able to visualize my characters' faces in close-ups fading out on a kiss 18×24 feet square.

I would have run away from movie-making right then and there had I not at that point stepped into a most pleasant and satisfying six months' assignment—I was taken over by MGM to work on the treatment of *Grand Hotel*.

I think it is my great good luck that I am congenitally blind and deaf when it comes to gossip, intrigues, antipathies, jealousies, and related crocodile tank matters. Indifference to most of the things that worry, trouble, and poison most people is a wonderful lubricant for life; I didn't invent it nor learn it through hard knocks; I was, happily, born with it.

I didn't know that my tussle with Paramount had given me a black eye in Hollywood, nor that MGM had grabbed me on the bargain counter. Least of all did I realize that a weekly salary of two thousand dollars instead of one of two thousand five hundred meant a dire loss of status. In Hollywood, society is perhaps still more severely striated by income than anywhere else, and a cut in salary drops you automatically onto a different social level. Neither did I have the faintest idea of the grim infighting that was going on between the two feuding camps at MGM: The Front Office in the person of Louis B. Mayer on one side; Thalberg and his partisans on the other. As Irving Thalberg was head of the production unit that prepared *Grand Hotel,* I belonged automatically to his party. I didn't know it, but if I had had a choice I should still have taken his side.

At that time the MGM lot was a small-townish conglomeration of hastily nailed-together structures. The writers were housed in the worst slums of that little community, a fair enough arrangement as long as the silent movies were written "off the cuff" during the shooting and incredibly high salaries were shoveled out to such geniuses as were able to think up and put into written words the subtitles that substituted for dialogue. I liked those poor clapboard structures of the so-called writers' buildings with their crisscross of creaky wooden outside stairs, and the tiny cubicles with the small windows where you fried in the California heat waves or froze during the rainstorms and frequent floods of the cold months. True, there was a little gas stove in each of our cells, but there was always something the matter with them; besides, they leaked and smelled, gave you terrific headaches, and numbed your brains into impotence. Still, there was a feeling of *bohème* about these rickety hovels, an air of devil-may-care shabbiness in which we, the writers, felt at home. I never learned to feel at home in the imposing new writers' building with its endless echoing prisonlike corridors, impersonal super-de-luxe office furniture, and cold lights; and for some reason the new air conditioning, together with the sealed windows, caused us worse headaches, head colds, and pink eyes than the leaky gas pipes had done.

But this building was erected years later, as a memorial to Irving Thalberg. During those happy first six weeks at MGM, most of my time was spent in the sumptuous residential district of the lot, a kind of glorified Hollywood where the studio had built a home away from home for each of the great money-making stars. Most of those villas were built in the pseudo-Spanish style that was just going out of fashion; their small walled gardens planted with palm and banana trees and thick curtains of Bougainvillaea were a trifle too photogenic, dazzling, picturesque, like the stars who used them during the hectic shooting of the picture. And, also like their tenants, those houses were frequently in movies.

The director of *Grand Hotel,* Eddie Goulding, had been installed in one of the nicest of those villas; it had been vacated by that era's great screen lover, John Gilbert. Next door Buster Keaton had his bungalow, an unprepossessing replica of an old Western mining camp's bar and the gayest, most hospitable spot on the entire lot.

In spite of my rudimentary English and Eddie's nonexistent German, there was an immediate warmth between us that leaped all language barriers. Eddie was a stocky fellow in his middle forties, I should think; he had the broken nose and damaged profile of a former professional fighter, he had come up from the lowest depth of the London slums, and where, en route, he had acquired his sensitivity for the finest nuances in taste, speech, dress, behavior, I wouldn't know, unless it was by sheer talent. Eddie was one of the few truly original and interesting people I met in my brief film career. I've never seen such a bag of contrasts in a single man's chest, guts, mind, whatever you want to call it. He was amusing, charming, gentle, tender; sensitive to a fault to other people's feelings. Naturally, he was also chock-full of every man's coarseness, reinforced by the rough swamp where he grew up. He had been an orphan of charity, maybe a little pickpocket. As a twelve-year-old butcher boy he had been seduced by a rich old homosexual. Later he had lived, or been tolerated to live, in a brothel—petted by the girls, used for their little errands, and, presumably, seduced and initiated in their own more or less normal sexual habits. Or so, at least, he told me: he might have invented it all on the spur of the moment, just to amuse me.

But Goulding—and those six months—would not have been complete without his butler, Ransom. Ransom was as British, as reserved, correct, and impenetrable as they come. Ransom served us lunch, a very good, simple British lunch. He saw to it that his master either rested or played tennis after lunch. He appeared at four-thirty on the dot with the tea, the cucumber sandwiches, the paper-thin slices of bread and butter. Later he served us a very British dinner, with boiled rather than roast mutton, overcooked vegetable, savories, and port. And about eleven o'clock at night he had a way of tactfully indicating that it was time for us to withdraw—myself and my two German-speaking collaborators—and leave the field to Eddie's night guests who might be girls or boys and usually came not singly but in clusters.

Moreover, Ransom kept an hour-by-hour chart on his master's moods and actions. It was in code—once Eddie showed it to me—crosses for accomplished sexual feats, circles for business appointments. A hilarious map, on which a strip-teaser might get two crosses at 3:00 P.M. and a tennis game with the then still Prince of Wales be marked for 3:15. "Master in good form. Beat him 6:4, 7:5, 6:3," Ransom would jot down.

The work progressed pleasantly, although I had envisaged something quite different from the star-studded wedding cake we had in the making. Then I realized what had made my *Grand Hotel*, the novel and the play, a world success: it was probably the first of its kind to be written in a sort of moving picture technique. By now that's the oldest of old hats, but in those days the kaleidoscopic effects, brief ever-changing scenes, flashes, staccato dialogue, were new, surprising, and exciting . . . on the stage. On the screen, I felt, this technique was the usual old stale shopworn thing. In my innocence I had great ideas for creating something equally different and new for the film—an expressionistic, almost abstract hotel, a constantly moving maelstrom of faces, bodies, backgrounds, phones, bells, beds, objects.

I daresay this, too, has meanwhile found its way into moviemaking. But when I brought my conception to Thalberg he crouched down as if in pain, buried his head in his arms and his arms between his knees, and said No and No and No.

Whenever you mention the name of Thalberg, it's like setting off a record that announces: He was a genius. Well, a genius by Hollywood standards isn't quite what the word means to the rest of the world. He was slim, dark, young, alert, ambitious, nervous, sensitive, tortured. An overheated dynamo, working too hard on too many projects. It was almost impossible, at least for underlings of my kind, to have a conference, a discussion, or just a ten-minute concentrated conversation with him. What set him apart was a simple fact: Thalberg was the voice of No in a land of Yes men. And he didn't talk down to the audience, didn't treat them as twelve-year-old morons, but as his equals. His aim was to make good pictures, and he often made them. He knew what he was doing when he swept my arty ideas under the table and stuck every available star into *Grand Hotel*.

It made millions for the company and would have been a dismal flop if done my way.

When the shooting script for the movie was finished and had received a priceless Okay from the powers above, I returned to Berlin where my desk and my work at Ullstein's awaited me. I liked it there as much as ever, yet in my own sleepwalking way I arrived at the most important decision of my life.

I was going to leave Germany. Emigrate. Become an American citizen.

As in a love affair, distance and separation had taught me perspective. Have you seen a painter step back from his canvas to see it better as a whole? After my seven months in the U.S.A., I had a much clearer picture of what was happening in Germany than had the clever, well-informed, experienced political minds at Ullstein's, the citadel of Germany's liberal ideas. To them it seemed impossible that Germany would ever go back to militarism and autocracy. Hitler was still a clown, spouting nonsense, a ridiculous chowderhead with a fanatic following of other harebrained chowderheads. You laughed about him, maybe not as heartily as in years past, but, now really, you couldn't take that guy seriously, could you?

In America they did. In America they thought Hitler a grave menace, and the leading American and English foreign correspondents in Berlin had gathered to cover the impending general election. To tell the truth, I don't know any more, and didn't quite know then, what issues were at stake. In a way, I think, the young German Republic was unschooled in political thinking, and the importance and possibilities of a free election had not deeply penetrated the consciousness of the people; except, of course, the Communist organization on the farthest Left and, on the other end, the equally radical and organized Nazis, bloated with nationalistic slogans. For the time being, their cohorts slugged it out among themselves in meetings, riots, street demonstrations, and every conceivable kind of mischief.

I remember one night when some homosexual friends, great idealists filled with pacifist brotherhood-of-man ideas, invited some stalwart warriors of both camps for an earnest debate, a civilized exchange of ideas and, so they hoped, better understanding and rapprochement. I was honored to function as their hostess, the only female admitted to the conclave. My friends' pad consisted of two rooms; we were sitting on the floor in the first; in the second they had crowded a jumble of couches, pillows, cots, and mattresses. The men of the feuding parties arrived in small tight clusters, they were very young, rather shy, their honorable wounds from the last slugging feast picturesquely bandaged. (Nothing soothes a small child's injuries as quickly as a fascinating, boastful, much too large bandage.) There was plenty of beer, embarrassed fretting, some small talk, shy smiles, furtive glances; the exchange of ideas never got off the ground, but the rapprochement worked out splendidly. Soon friend and foe, amiably mixed, quietly retired two by two to the dark padded mattress cave to indulge in their own version of brotherhood of man. I rinsed the beer glasses, took my coat, and went home, reflecting that homosexuality in diplomatic circles might have its uses toward international understanding after all.

I spent the election night with my new pals, the foreign correspondents, trying to share and understand their excitement. They swept me with them, here, there, everywhere. Unfortunately, or maybe fortunately, I'm completely lacking in political sense. I have to look at things from all sides which, of course, makes me useless for partisanship. I can't comprehend all the finagling, the underhanded deals; the gas-filled oratory makes me slightly sick, and the tedium of all those manipulations puts me to sleep. And I only have to read the back numbers of magazines to see again and again how ephemeral, how passing, changing, and meaningless any political situation is. There, as in so many matters of world-shaking importance, my small ant's brain is unteachable. I'm too primitive to understand the complications. I can only absorb the simplest, most obvious facts and let my instinct draw the conclusions.

As for that election, which my foreign correspondent friends celebrated with such great elation, I couldn't help thinking: if the victory of a tired, doddering, not very bright old soldier like Hindenburg over an ugly, hysterical upstart is the best we can do, then, Germany, good night indeed!

The next day I cabled Pauker in New York that I was willing to sign up with any of the studios that had offered me contracts before I left. I also went into immediate action about emigration papers for me and my family, at that time still a very simple little formality. At Ullstein House they asked me if I'd lost my mind. Leave Germany, just now, just when *we'd* won the election?

Well, salmon must make their hard journey upstream to deposit their spawn at the right place, and sea lions return to their own cliff for mating and giving birth to their pups. I was blindly driven by a similar urge to bring up my children in a safer country than in this desperate and desperado-filled Germany. I looked at the faces of the demonstrating mobs on the streets; the haggard sharp-jawed faces and sagging old trench coats of the disenchanted veterans and the unemployed; I saw hatred and fanaticism everywhere in this world, so well painted by George Grosz and expressed by Bert Brecht, and I thought: I have two nice boys; what will Germany make of them? Will one become a Nazi and the other a Communist? Will they fight each other as Germans do all over the place?

And although Pauker, my best friend, had no contract for me, Eddie Goulding didn't answer my letters, and I knew how fickle and tricky Hollywood could be, I left behind my safe and pleasant job, my friends, and my life's savings and sailed to America to build once more a home for my husband and sons.

I've been informed that, according to the present findings of science, the thing we oldsters called instinct doesn't exist. If so, I don't know by what I've lived, certainly not by rational thinking and deep cerebration. By electromagnetic impulses of the brain, I'm told. Well, that's only another word for the intangible forces that make us act, think, feel, and function the way we do, isn't it?

I'd left Germany by instinct. Now it certainly was a lucky instinct that prevented me from selling myself completely to MGM when they offered me a contract at last. I agreed to work six months of each year for the movies, six months for myself. I needed to keep at least some of my independence. I had to be free to write my books, travel, get away from the squirrel cage of movie-making, live among normal people, meet, see, and absorb my new country. This caused much head-shaking all around. It cut my income in half, and to run a year-round Hollywood household on a half year's income presented a problem. I had been taken down another notch and now belonged to the seventeen-hundred-fifty-a-week crowd. In Hollywood you had to swim with your crowd or sink. That was one of the many new difficulties I had to face: spending those huge earnings on the all-pervading conspicuous consumption, on show, prestige, status. Me, who only yesterday, it seemed, had gone hungry, covered rather than dressed in that cursed hand-me-down blue! Me, with my Viennese mandarin disdain for money and the bandarlog doings of Society!

Invitations were an eye-for-an-eye, tooth-for-a-tooth affair, and I was constantly invited. This meant a large open house, servants, gardeners, auxiliary butlers and waitresses and bartenders for the frequent parties I was more or less forced to give. In Hollywood, if you invited sixty guests they would bring another forty uninvited ones. Being my pixilated Grandma's true offspring, naturally I'd prepare food for a hundred and fifty. Neither I nor my husband drink or smoke, but rivers of alcohol were poured incessantly into my guests' dry gullets—and bootlegged drinks of good quality were ridiculously expensive. Like anybody else in the higher bracket, I had my share of hangers-on, spongers, barnacles weighing down my fragile little craft. How to organize life on an income that was too high for my simple tastes—although low by Hollywood standards—was way over my head. So you take a manager, and he absconds with a few thousand dollars. You invest, like everybody else, in timid little enterprises; having no affinity for money you lose it, or, being such a blatant greenhorn, are swindled out of it. I can truly say that I never earned one dollar by any method without giving two dollars' work for it.

I don't know how the social life of Hollywood is handled today; movie people earn fantastic sums, pay fantastic taxes, but write off their inevitable entertaining under public relations expenses. Entertaining is an elastic concept and I remember with a grin a little scene I watched in the lingerie department at one of the carriage-trade stores. A huge motherly Negro woman, loaded with the merry bounce of about 180 pounds of fat, wanted to buy herself a nightgown. The salesgirl was spreading before her some nice size 46 garments, thin flowered flannel, I think, with tiny rosebuds and forget-me-nots. "No, honey," the customer said, "you don't understand what I'm after. I wants them nighties for *entertaining*, see?"

Well, luckily, I don't have to entertain any longer. I've become a self-sufficient old hermit living peacefully removed from the hurly-burly of the movies.

n all the countless interviews I've given, I've never been asked the questions I would like to answer and, naturally, no interviewer sees me as I see myself or asks the things I would like to tell.

My house, for instance; that's a part of me. It stands in the hills north of Hollywood, shielded against the noise and ugliness of the town. You may stand in front of it and still not see it because my house is like a good shoe: small outside, yet large and comfortable on the inside. You go down a few rough steps, the little path curves toward the door according to the Japanese precept that the guest faces the entrance by surprise. Which reminds me how depressed I was by the perfect symmetry and formality of the great Chinese architecture of Peking. Perfection bores me, in art, in music; most of all, in people. Luckily, perfection is rare.

A bit of the tropics grows in front of my house; a few royal palms, fern trees, a thick stand of proud shell ginger fourteen feet high, a jacaranda tree, a blue cloud when in bloom, and through it all twists the gray and silver snake of a sycamore trunk. A little heap of junk guards the low black door, the sort of things children would collect: a large Mexican water jug, a rotting African drum, bleached fan corals, broken abalone shells, along with some grotesque Balinese carvings, weathered Aztec stone pieces, and large pebbles I picked up on the beaches of the seven seas. Next to the doorknob squats a very small carved beggarman from Bali. In his beggar's bowl there are always a few coins. It amuses me to watch people's behavior with my little beggar. The friendly ones pat him and smile; the kind ones, too weak to resist, throw him a few cents; and the superstitious or worried ones take out a penny, for good luck! And the children, sound realists that they are, rob his little bowl to buy ice cream from the cart that tinkles its ever-repeated nursery song along the hilly lanes, slow on the up-grades, *molto allegro* on the down. I often think that this will be the melody I shall faintly hear through the numbed weakness of my final hour.

There is another gay *memento mori* in the small entrance hall whose rococo and baroque furniture I've painted and wiped off and painted over in washed-out greens and Mexican pinks and magentas, the sort of colors you find in the churches and on the doors of eighteenth-century Mexico where people happily covered each peel-ing, rain-washed layer with a coat of whatever paint or color was on hand. On a full-bosomed Dutch chest you will find what is known as "my funeral."

Which has a little history. Some years ago a conversation with my physician made it seem advisable for me to put a few matters in order and let my last wishes be known. In a letter to my older son, I stated in no uncertain terms that I wanted my remains to be simply carted off and burned, without bothering friends and family with the tear-jerking nuisance of a funeral. My boy accepted this as casually as it was offered. But when I was still around and kicking, long after my exit was due, he sent me a hilarious funeral procession, all gold and lemon yellow and shocking pink (penis pink, an artist friend of mine calls it), the primitive clay work of some Mexican village. There are plump women carrying flowers and candles and babies, and a priest twice as large as the laity bearing crosses and censers, and four tall pallbearers with skull masks; but in the magnificently painted, boat-shaped casket the body of the dear deceased is sitting up, straight as a ramrod, enjoying the festive occasion. "So there," my boy wrote me, "is your funeral. And you won't get another one."

Here the interviewer, with an embarrassed gulp, inevitably asks: "How old is the boy?"

"Forty-three, the younger one is thirty-nine. I have four grand-children—two boys, two girls, the oldest is twelve, the youngest five,"

I quickly report to get this out of the way. "Now look at the masks over there, don't they make you laugh?"

There are masks scattered all through the house. Masks have fascinated me since my earliest childhood, and at one time I had quite a collection. But there came a spell when such an uncommon accumulation of worries, troubles, sickness, and hard luck piled up in my house that I began to wonder if some black magic, some evil forces might not indeed emanate from those masks of demons and deities of death, just as the native priests had warned me. "Get rid of them," another collector of masks told me, a skeptical, quite sophisticated author. "But listen, don't sell them, don't simply throw them away. You must burn them and let the ashes be swept out to sea." This I did, and matters cleared up. Probably they would have done so in any case. Now I have only friendly, harmless, smiling or comical masks around. Those in the entrance hall I got in Guatemala, took them off the dark, sweaty faces of some Highland Indians right after a ceremonial dance. One is what they call *El Tigre*, the sleepiest, most good-natured, freckle-faced, and stupid tiger imaginable. The other is a funny, impertinent, black, gray, and pink honey bear.

After the playful, small, not very bright entrance hall the space and light and plainness of the front rooms—running the entire length of the house—are a surprise. The reason is that only the small windows of bathrooms and closets look out toward the street, while the back of the house, with its glass walls west and south, stands high above the garden. The rooms are large, uncluttered, and during the day flooded with sunlight.

Let me add that our books and opera scores have spilled over into a cramped little cubicle, the anteroom of the guest toilet, on whose walls are hung all the diplomas and honor rolls and what-have-you's given to my husband and me in our more or less limelit lives. By the time you enter the living room you ought to have a fair idea of the sort of person I am.

The downstairs, though, is more or less my dignified husband's domain, what with an almost life-sized St. Cecilia, from a seventeenth-century Bavarian church, watching over the workworn Blüthner concert grand, the indispensable gadgetry, the tape recorder, the research papers and books—scores of books, a remarkable library filling the paneled room from floor to ceiling. No television set, though. If you come upstairs with me, there, too, are books everywhere and masks and Balinese wood carvings and Kawa bowls filled with my own infantile treasures: shells and pebbles and driftwood and fossils and other such unidentifiable, fascinating objects as you might find in a small boy's pocket. No paintings, I can't live with them for any length of time; to me, paintings are obtrusive, distracting. But many flowers, because arranging flowers is one of the few joys that has remained with me, unchanged since I was a very little girl, while getting older has made me fold up and pack away, one by one, most other joys—dancing, adventuring, making music, making love.

The adjoining room was formerly a chaotic lair reserved for the toys and uninhibited games of my grandchildren. Since they have outgrown this, I recently changed it into a den of Japanese simplicity where, at present, I am writing these rambling memoirs. I also use it for all sorts of useless dabblings—bookbinding, mosaic-making, designing things, sewing, daubing paints on canvas, all with happy enthusiasm and truly fearsome results. In a word, my kindergarten. On the door outside I pinned a sign I stole from an airplane; it indicates that I am working in earnest: BLOCKED, FOR PROPER WEIGHT DISTRIBUTION. And my grandson completed this with a small tag reading: DANGER! FEROCIOUS PROTON WITHIN! ENTER AT YOUR OWN RISK. This refers to an interview I gave recently to a voracious young journalist who introduced me to the readers as a "ferocious proton," whatever she may have meant by that. At the same time, another interviewer reported that I have "tired eyes and give a listless impression." I think she was one of those girls who brings along a notebook in which she has put down beforehand the stereotyped questions learned in high school, and to which you can only give stereotyped answers while trying not to fall asleep from boredom.

How do I look when I interview myself? What is my own image of myself, to use Madison Avenue jargon? Tired? Yes, occasionally, and for good physical reasons . . . not giving in to it, though, I hope. Ferocious? . . . not a bit. I can't shout, I can't cry or scream, let alone throw or smash things. I abhor scenes. In all my life, I have made only three scenes—one with my parents when I was sixteen, and two during the forty-five years of my marriage to an equally peaceable, mild, absent-minded gentleman.

Making a scene is terrible and ugly but, oh, what a relief! I sincerely envy people who have the talent and temper for it. As for me, I get headaches and backaches and a stiff neck and a pulse rate of 104, along with the self-command to keep smiling.

Now let's step out on my lanai and look out, across terraces shaded by *copa de oro* vines, and down on an expanse of lawn and flowers and a blue swimming pool with its own little waterfall; over the tops of eucalyptus and gravelia, down the slope where the garden runs out into other gardens and they in turn into the native vegetation of our hills—manzanita, coyote shrub, wild oats, sage, and black-eyed Susans. Far below, usually swimming in fog and smog, is our village, then the immense city, and, way out, the Pacific with its spectacular sunsets. This garden is my joy, my toy, my heaviest work, my constant worry and responsibility. Perhaps a garden is just an old woman's surrogate when there are no lovers, no children left to be taken care of. Compared with master gardeners like Rebecca West, I'm a poor, much too arthritic, much too quickly tired dilettante. Still, the pride, the elation, when something exciting happens to my plants. When a rare black iris unfolds its petals for the first time, when a rose shoots up into a garland of white fragrant blossoms; the simple little miracles of spring—the carpets of violets, narcissus, high-stemmed tulips—how we women come together, compare, discuss, advise, jealous yet admiring and generous in swapping slips and cuttings and wisdom.

The size of my garden is my last, almost my only luxury. Perhaps I am still conditioned by the boundless freedom in the vast forests of my childhood summers. I need elbow space; the worst deprivation I know is to have neighbors breathe down my neck, look into my windows, have their radios and TV's blare into my ears and tear my concentration to shreds. I have to plant trees and lawns around me to keep the asphalt world from encroaching. Even as a little child I worried deeply about the good, living earth being choked

to death beneath the paved city streets. One of my first poems—
a terribly bad one—was addressed to a hardy, obstinate blade of
grass that had worked its way through a crack in the asphalt toward
sun and air.

The large room upstairs suits me to perfection with its plain
furniture, large worktable, a twenty-foot wall of books, masks, carvings, and more books around the broad couch on which I sleep; it
looks more like the abode of an assistant professor of anthropology
than a woman's room. It's cozy, lived-in, plain yet friendly in its
faintly South Sea way. Hidden below my bedside shelves are a few
ridiculous little friends to put me to sleep when I land on my couch
around 3:00 A.M., keyed up from work—various puzzles, games,
brain teasers, scrabble boards, and the blessed aspirin bottle. On a
separate small stand, easy to reach, are a few of the books I'd want
with me if shipwrecked on that island: the Bible, in Luther's earthy
German; the King James version, a bit too learned and Latinized
in comparison; and the gospels in Spanish which, to me, seem the
most unadorned and natural. The confessions of St. Augustine
which are such good literature until he repents and becomes pious
and maudlin. Marcus Aurelius, needed from time to time to give
my slackening moral fiber a brisk massage. John Donne, for the
laughter in some of his poems. Angelus Silesius, for the simplicity
of his mysticism. One or another volume of Goethe, the most human
of beings but, alas, untranslatable. And a few books I read over and
over: fairy tales, Proust—of whom I can take only a teaspoon at a
time and only in French—Tolstoy, Dostoevsky, Thomas Mann, with
undiminished joy. Joyce, but rarely, and with murmurs of protest.
Kafka? No.

And that, maybe, takes care of the unavoidable question of
whose writings have influenced me the most. That my own writing
remains so far below is regrettable, but perhaps there is some small
virtue in recognizing the limits of one's talent and not trying to puff
it up and pad it immodestly. Not that I ever lacked the sensitivity
(or else the courage) to soar to the pinnacle of joy and plunge into
the deepest abyss of suffering; I was never cautious in my emotions
—much too curious, much too hungry to experience everything
"whole." I always liked Möricke's prayer:

*Do not heap upon me*
*Either too much joy*
*Or too much sorrow.*
*For only between the two extremes*
*Lies sweet resignation.*

During the months I lived on Bali, a charming little boy appointed himself to be my child, guide, servant, and faithful shadow. Nine-year-old Lambon, a poor widow's son, had all the princely grace, the wit and dignity of his race. Yet he was still a child, full of childish whims and desires, and the object he craved most in all the world was a cowboy belt worn by one of our tourist guests. It was a garish atrocity, its leather studded with glass beads of every color. Poor little Lambon, blinded and drunk with all the sparkle and glitter, thought these were royal jewels like the rubies, sapphires, and emeralds encrusting the scabbard of a rajah's priceless kris. Touched by the boy's obsessive admiration, our tourist friend, on leaving, gave him this belt instead of a tip. Lambon bowed; he smiled like a sleepwalker, his lips turning so white in his bronze face I was afraid he might faint. He carried the belt away on outstretched palms, in the immemorial donor's gesture of presenting an offering to the gods. Indeed, I think he put it down at the foot of one of the many house altars for the deity to accept and enjoy the essence of it, as is—or was—the Balinese custom. In any case, he did not wear the belt. "I save it to wear with my new *kain* (the Balinese word for sarong) for Galungan." (Galungan, the feast of the new year, is their highest holiday.)

On the first day of Galungan my Lambon appeared, beaming, the belt proudly encircling his narrow waist. But not a single bead was left, only the small, round holes where they had sat in the leather.

"Where are the jewels, Lambon?" I asked, disappointed.

"I removed them, *Nonja.*"

"Oh, and what did you do with them? Sold them in the market? Swapped them? Lost them, gambling?" I asked, angrily guessing at the most usual weaknesses of the local men and boys. "Or did somebody steal them?"

"My jewels? *Nonja!* Let anyone try to get them away from me, just let them try!" cried Lambon, strangling the air between his small hands. He pulled a small silk pouch from inside the belt and showed me what it held: the glass beads, those incomparable, precious, those coveted-above-everything glittering beads.

"But tell me, little friend, why did you pull them off?" I asked in my white-skinned, thickheaded incomprehension.

"Because, *Nonja*, because I am just a poor, filthy boy; it does not befit me to wear a rajah's jewels on my belt," Lambon answered.

Something similar has been my attitude ever since I began to write. It does not befit me to use big words, to stud my writing with either genuine jewels or the sparkle of glass beads, even though I can well discriminate between them. A sense of modesty has prevented me—thank Heavens!—from thinking that I am writing *the* great prewar novel, or *the* great postwar novel, or any other damn representative novel of any kind. While writing, I am thoroughly aware of the ephemeral character of what I write. Authors, even great authors, who consider themselves immortal or keep writing with an eye to posthumous fame, make me smile, with respect but also with regret. The more definitively they are representative of their own period the more unreadable they will be the day after. Automobiles and refrigerators are not the only things to become obsolete; excuse me, obsolescent is the word this season.

As for myself, I may occasionally have a thought, an idea, a maxim for living, but the same befitting modesty prevents me from serving it up as philosophy or poetry or literature. I live, love, and write according to Hofmanssthal's line from *Rosenkavalier*—"*mit leichten Händen*"—and I leave it to the very few great writers to wear the rajah's belt.

Now, let's sit down for the usual interview.

*Tell me, Miss Baum, at what age did you begin writing?*

On the day I could handle a pencil. I had to get rid of the things that were buzzing in my head, by putting them down on paper. By the time I was eight I went around asking people: "Do you like to get letters?" Most answered "yes," and the next thing they knew they had a letter from me. Strange, but I never felt like writing a diary.

I suppose I had a born storyteller's urge to communicate my ideas and impressions.

Not what Madison Avenue means by communication, you understand. . . .

*How old were you when you were first published?*

Fourteen. In a magazine. It was the outcome of a bet. I used to know a boy of about seventeen, a conceited guy whom I detested. Once he bragged that a poem of his would be published in some newspaper because his father was one of the editors. This got my hackles up and I said, "I bet you I can write something and get it published although my father is anything *but* an editor!" So I wrote a little story with a sort of Maupassant *pointe*, slightly more risqué (as it was then called) than I understood myself. I sent it under some fantastic nom de plume to *Die Muskete,* a sharp, witty magazine more or less an equivalent of the *New Yorker,* and won my bet, a bar of Swiss chocolate. Plus fifty kronen and an invitation to send more.

*And did you?*

You bet! This was money my parents knew nothing about since I carried on my literary correspondence through the Konservatorium. Letters to students were displayed in a glass box to which only an old janitor had the key. He shook his finger at me. "Say, girlie, aren't you a bit young for getting love letters on the sly?" he warned.

I'm afraid my approach to writing was purely commercial in the beginning. Suddenly I was rich. I could buy myself all the fruit I had been craving, for fruit was one of the items on Father's incomprehensible prohibition list. Like candy, or chocolate, like ice cream or sweet rolls, sweet anything. "Ruins your stomach and spoils your character. Don't you know people get cholera from eating fruit?" Cholera was still a serious menace. In Hamburg they had had an epidemic of it, and every small bellyache was severely suspicious. Well, now I indulged myself in all the forbidden, perilous pleasures; bought myself hair ribbons—also forbidden—opera tickets for me and my friends, presents for my mother. Twice I hired a fiacre and rode in the Prater all by myself where, each afternoon, the elegant world and the demimonde paraded their horses and carriages up and down the Hauptallee. "Languorously leaning back in the silken upholstery of her fiacre, the young countess smiled with half-closed eyes . . ." was what I felt. The stories I sent to the *Muskete,* though, were brisk and full of cold irony.

*Tell me, Miss Baum, you've written so many books. How many, actually?*

Too many, I suppose. When I can't sleep I sometimes try to count them. Instead of sheep, you know. But I always get mixed up, forget some, count others twice. Must be something like thirty, I guess. I know I had written ten by the time I sailed to the U.S.A., in the wake of *Grand Hotel,* in 1931. I had thrown away at least twice as many before then, and many more have gone into the trash can since. To me, writing is not a profession. You might as well call living a profession, or having children. Anything you can't help doing. It's always difficult, at times painful, but on the whole great fun. And something you can't help, in any case.

I believe that training to become a professional musician is the best preparation a future writer can have. It teaches you patience and precision. No clinkers permitted when you play in a concert, no misplaced words or surprise expressions. You watch your every comma as carefully as you used to watch every little staccato dot to give each note its full rhythmical weight and accent. (What the printers do to it afterward, that's another story!) And it teaches you form, dynamics, phrasing—form in freedom. It imbues you with that intangible instinct that demands a percussion, a repetition here, a brief lyrical interlude there, a sense for light and shadow, for the necessity of a crescendo, an allegro, a rest, a dramatic racing and shortening as in a *stretta.* Even today I think in musical terms; I might report to my conductor husband: "This evening I goofed. I wrote this chapter as a rondo when it really calls for a variation form."

Above all, music stimulates your nerves, your sensibilities, your imagination. And not having thought of myself as a writer, but as being firmly anchored in music, I was spared all the sufferings of boomeranging manuscripts, rejections of precious brain children, of poems sent out with such immense hopes and returning like homing pigeons.

These musical memories have swept me far off our imaginary interview, but that's as it should be for I was, first and last, a musician; not until many years after I had been published did I think of myself as a writer. To tell the full truth, I still don't. Not quite.

Speaking about those too many books of mine, I wish I had hit upon the idea of calling some of them novels and some entertainments, as the eminently readable Graham Greene does; Simenon, too, I believe. Women, I think, don't have the same conception of ethics, morality, and conceits as men. Nothing easier for a woman than to compromise in artistic matters if a compromise helps the family, the home, the children, the friends. We women, thanks to nature and biology, are adjustable and realistic. Whenever it was necessary for me to earn money I wrote books that did not attempt to be more than readable and entertaining, escape literature that would bring home the bacon. I never wrote down, though; I did those lightweight stories as conscientiously and well as I could and, by the way, writing to please a large number of readers is harder than writing what and how you like for yourself. Writing readable stories is a question of craftsmanship, what the French call *le métier*. Hemingway says somewhere that commercial writing is like losing your virginity—once you've done it you're never the same. Maybe so. In my experience, once you're publicly stamped as having lost that literary virginity because some of your books happened to become best sellers, you'll never be able to clear your name. Only, please don't come to me with the girlish question: "How does one write a best seller, Miss Baum? How do I go about becoming a successful author?"

I don't know. I swear I don't know. I have a total lack of some organs, no inner barometer reacting to success or failure. I couldn't care less for either. In these matters I'm tone deaf or blind or carapaced like a giant turtle. I guess this saved me much grief and hurt and disappointment, but it also robbed me of the joys and triumphs of which I can only read in other writers' confessions.

The old wisdom of the anthill: Not so important, I and it, not so important at all.

If you were to ask me what I cherish as the most necessary thing in my life, I would answer without a moment's hesitation, my independence. I know this sounds pompous, but I can't change it. My idea of being independent is somewhat on the Spartan side, though, having a lot to do with self-discipline. Obviously—and this I learned quite early—you can't depend on your parents, family, friends; and, heaven forbid, not under any circumstances on your children. In this rapidly changing world, this universe, you can't depend on anything to remain as you are used to it. Not your country or her politics, the place you've made for yourself, your relations with other people, not even on mathematics.

You can only, only, depend upon yourself. That's where the rub is. You have to peel off one need after another, throw out the ballast. Each habit, each possession, each urge and want creates another fear in us—and I don't like to be afraid. Sure, a reasonable amount of comfort, such as money, is pleasant, if we don't become cowardly dependent on it, if we never forget that we can do with a minimum of it. The exaggerated fear of Communism belongs in the same category. They talk of their freedom—"They'd rather be dead than slaves." That's hogwash. What they mean is they'd rather be dead than lose the unrestrained enjoyment of spending huge amounts of money.

Now then, I never cared a damn about other people's opinions of me. I was born that way and did not have to learn or train for it. Not to let oneself become dependent upon alcohol, coffee, nicotine, tranquilizers or anything else seems so fundamental and, by the way, so easy, it's not worth talking about. To keep independent of cliques, political movements and parties, of current fashions in causes, art, and literature, in other words, of the "trend," is also a fortunate part of my nature. I realize that many people receive a lift, a kind of self-magnifying satisfaction in "belonging." Bless 'em; where would the Pied Piper be if the children wouldn't follow him?

To my mind, I'm sorry to say, the most debasing dependence is dependence on, or transference to, any of the psychologists of the various denominations. I belong to those hard-nosed oldsters who believe that most sprouting neuroses can be weeded out or, at least, kept in trim, if we gave our children more character training and less indulgent pseudopsychological abracadabra before they grew out of their early environment.

When my younger son, a nonsmoker like myself and his father, went overseas in the war I said: "Look, isn't it time you learned to smoke? I understand a cigarette can be some help out there when you are in a tight spot."

"Yeah," said the youngster, "but if you are used to cigarettes and don't have any just when you get into a tight spot, that makes it really hell. So why should I start to make myself dependent on something I am not?"

I liked that. And he worked out of some tight spots, without smoking.

I have trained myself to be fairly independent of illness, fatigue, and pains, but only fairly so. I am what my grandson calls "maybe a delicate stoic?" The hardest thing to shake off is the dependence on love and sex, but if you have to, you learn that too, as millions have done before. When you grow old the fires bank down, they warm but don't burn.

There are two things on which I'm still dependent and I wouldn't want it to be different: I need what is probably an only child's privilege: privacy, solitude, quiet—lots of it, a great luxury today.

And I hope I won't lose my need to love—someone, something. The more and the deeper, the better. To be in love, to love and be loved is my need. Fortunately, I never lacked this to this day, and that's a funny thing to be confessed by a woman past seventy. André Gide called the book he wrote in his last years, 1950-51, *"Ainsi soit-il"* ("So Be It"), and in it he said:

> *C'est encore un conseil que je donne aux jeunes, avec d'autant plus d'assurance que je ne l'ai pas toujours suivi: sachez tenir pour préférable ce qui vous coûte le plus d'efforts.**

Well, as I said, I'm a square and old and I have to strain hard to feel much sympathy for the kids of today. But then I tell myself:

* Here is some advice I give to the young although I have not always followed it myself: Hold on to those things that have cost you the greatest effort to achieve.

it's not so important, our little anthill, and, as the wise man said, it all passes. Instead of tranquilizers I recommend reading the year-old magazines you find in your dentist's waiting room. As you will see, the excitements of those days, the panics, the prophecies, bright or dark, the fears and menaces, the threatened doom, are past, buried and forgotten. It's not so long ago that scientists and statisticians lamented the low and still falling birth rate. Lord, what's going to happen to the nation, to the whole world, if married couples refuse to have more than two children, or none at all? Now, the same statisticians have coined the slogan "population explosion" and bat it all over the place, full of bleak forebodings and catastrophes.

As if they had never heard that nature still takes care of such fundamental problems. That animals bear large litters for two reasons only: if there's abundant food and times are favorable, as is true of the present; or that the species instinctively prepares for some immense disaster, a drought, a flood, an earthquake.

A hydrogen bombing? Poisoning by fall-out?

In my village, in Peigarten, one summer, the field mice were overrunning the castle. They were everywhere; in the kitchen, in the closets, behind the stove, in the very loaves of bread they made nests for their litters. "We'll have a flood," the old peasants said, "perhaps a hurricane, like the one in eighty-seven." And sure enough, we had both; the castle being the only dry place on its hill, we had to take in not only the mice but all the villagers. After the flood was over, mice and men went back to normal.

I believe there are two fortunate conditions for a writer: to be in total revolt against, or ahead of, the times or to be intensely at home in them. I was certainly not at home in the overstuffed times of my childhood and adolescence. Not at home in the times of war, fiery patriotism and swindle, or in the times of Spartakists or the opposite fanatics, the ultrareactionary and militaristic free corps. In Berlin, in those brief years, I was at home for the first time in my own times. I thought, lived, talked, felt the same as most people did; I had the cadence of their speech in my ear and their problems on my mind. I had shared their experiences, so their memories were mine, too.

That's why it was easy for me to write about them, and as easy for them to read my tales. They found in my books what even the most choosy reader likes best, whether he knows it or not, self-identification. I lost this advantage in my later wanderings, and I think it is a fallacy to speak of "our times." There ain't such a thing. The world lives simultaneously in different ages; there is still the stone age of the last Australian aborigines; the dark and feudal Middle Ages in many parts of Asia; while Russia is just entering the period of virtuous, complacent citizenship, bad taste in art and style, with the privileged classes of party and bureaucracy running the show. And America? With all her fetish worship of progress, in most matters my chosen country is usually lagging fifty years behind, except in gadgetry. But even this, I found, is not achieved so much through a specific American talent for technical invention as it is by being rich enough in money, space, and manpower to support and perfect what others have discovered and invented.

I felt fairly well at home in the United States during the Depression, and as long as Franklin D. Roosevelt and his brain trusters set the tone. And being somewhat primitive myself, I was told I understood rather well the primitive people whom I met in my foreign travels.

No one who has lived in the United States for any length of time can cope with life anywhere else; we are so spoiled, so demanding in material things and daily comforts. Still there remains in us some unstilled hunger for the Old World; for the hilltops, crowned by a castle, a convent, a church, or a ruin that sits up there like a rakish old hat; for the unhygienic, merry bustle of the markets, the cherished loveliness of waterfront and riverside, the unshakable old stone bridges with their saints protecting them. For the sound of church bells. For the taste and snap of a carelessly grown apple.

But maybe what I remember is not there any more, and Austria is just a little rag of countryside, living off the largesse of American tourists, not understood by them and, in turn, snickering behind their backs with Austrian malice and double-faced amiability.

I love America, not only as a home where I have spent more years of my life than anywhere else, a country that was and is kind and generous to me; but as you might love your very own child, not blindly but wishing him to be or become perfect; and you hurt when you see where he falls short.

I stopped being at home anywhere since Pearl Harbor. And not only am I not at home in these times, but I find myself constantly irritated by, and fiercely opposed to, the present. For a writer, that's a small tragedy because it paralyzes the *nervus sympaticus* whence all feeling, thinking, creating is set in motion. To get old is not an undiluted pleasure in any case, but to have been young on one planet, to have been exploded across immeasurable time spaces and to get old on an alien, hostile planet—well, it's tough.

I'm writing this in Easter Week, 1960. I was just reading the evening paper. On the front page a seventeen-year-old girl who, with the encouragement of her whoring mother, became a prostitute at the age of twelve, has now shot one of her boy friends. In smaller headlines, the usual crop of people are killed through reckless driving or jet plane crashes. More riots and deaths in Algeria, South Africa, Cuba. At home, the jockeying for inside places and the outrageous lies and promises of an election year. And, to celebrate Easter, our darling teen-agers have taken over the beach resorts for their Rites of Spring, breaking down the peaceful natives' houses, raping, fighting, stabbing, and, occasionally, killing each other. Hospitals and jails are crowded with our youthful heroes.

Will the human race ever be normal again? Sometimes I wonder. I ask myself if *Homo sapiens* is not, perhaps, one of the species destined for extinction, one of the not quite successful experiments of nature, biology, call it God if you wish. The dinosaurus with his peanut-sized brain in his enormous mass of body was such a failure. Sometimes I think we are only a transition, an overdeveloped brain at the expense of instinct and physical ability. Perhaps mutation is precisely what's needed. If it is, never mind, we'll get it. As we are constituted at present there's nothing to be proud of.

I don't like to analyze myself and I loathe to preach; writing about myself makes my swollen ego feel uncomfortable, like a bad case of the mumps. But here I am, a living contradiction of any alibi your psychoanalyst may hand you. I am that most abnormal phenomenon —a fairly normal person. Peaceful, merry, as unneurotic as they come, well-adjusted, easily amused; so help me God, a square. In my own life, I found every bit of grief and hardship balanced by a counterweight of good luck. And so I say my loud and clear YES to life, while all around me a chorus shouts NO in jittery, plaintive, neurotic fortissimo.

But then, I was and am a lucky girl. As lives go, mine was, and is, a good life; hard enough to develop muscles of spirit and will power, not so hard as to break me.

That's the point where my inborn optimism is indistinguishable from pessimism. A few steps further and I shall deny reality altogether. I beg to differ from the modish existentialists whose blackest philosophy can state only that we exist.

I am not sure. It is just possible that we do not exist outside of our illusions. Since I can remember, I have disbelieved in the existence of time and space except as a convention, something to keep us from going over the edge. I believe that what we please to call time is not a chain, where some things happened before and some things will happen later. I think it is an altogether; that there is no before and after, just as there is no above or below in the universe; and so anything that will happen has happened already. Outside of our puny human reality.

I can't deny it: the *Weltschmerz,* the hysteria, the noise, the generation of crybabies, make me quite impatient. I am but an old woman, and a simple storyteller. I have no loud voice, never could shout, either privately or in print. But in all my books I tried, or the *it* that writes my books tried, to express one innermost belief, call it *Lebensmut*—in the untranslatable German word—the courage to live and get the most from it, come what may.

And so, I won't apologize. I'm putting my life down on paper because there's the familiar itch, the urge to do it. I've always written what I pleased, and if some of it was bad, it was still the best I could do.

Here you have the innermost confession of a woman, which

means: a born realist, a good cook, housewife, mother, one who worries about the threadbare rug, the shrinking savings account, and the grandchildren's measles.

*May the vulgar trade of letters that I have plied in this life, all the folly of wild words, idle chatter, and fine phrases be transformed into a hymn of praise to cause the great wheel of law to turn.*

—Po Chu-I, Chinese poet
—772-846 A.D.

# INDEX